Epistemology

Epistemology

New Essays

EDITED BY

Quentin Smith

OXFORD
UNIVERSITY PRESS

Great Clarendon Street, Oxford ox2 6DP

Oxford University Press is a department of the University of Oxford.
It furthers the University's objective of excellence in research, scholarship,
and education by publishing worldwide in

Oxford New York

Auckland Cape Town Dar es Salaam Hong Kong Karachi
Kuala Lumpur Madrid Melbourne Mexico City Nairobi
New Delhi Shanghai Taipei Toronto

With offices in

Argentina Austria Brazil Chile Czech Republic France Greece
Guatemala Hungary Italy Japan Poland Portugal Singapore
South Korea Switzerland Thailand Turkey Ukraine Vietnam

Oxford is a registered trade mark of Oxford University Press
in the UK and in certain other countries

Published in the United States
by Oxford University Press Inc., New York

© the several contributors 2008

British Library Cataloguing in Publication Data

Data available

Library of Congress Cataloging in Publication Data

Epistemology: new essays / edited by Quentin Smith.
p. cm.
Includes index.
ISBN-13: 978−0−19−926493−3 (alk. paper) 1. Knowledge, Theory of.
I. Smith, Quentin, 1952−
BD161.E627 2008

121 — dc22   2008016742

Typeset by Laserwords Private Limited, Chennai, India
Printed in Great Britain
on acid-free paper by
CPI Antony Rowe, Chippenham, Wiltshire

ISBN 978−0−19−926493−3
978−0−19−926494−0 (Pbk.)

1 3 5 7 9 10 8 6 4 2

CONTENTS

Introduction

Quentin Smith

This volume presents new essays by some of the philosophers who have influenced the course of epistemology over the past few years or decades. In some cases, the authors' first epistemological writings were written in the 1960s as responses to Gettier's 1963 article. These authors include Alvin Goldman, John Pollock, and Ernest Sosa. Other contributors first published on epistemology in the 1970s (Robert Audi, Panayot Butchvarov, Richard Feldman, and Peter Klein), the 1980s (George Bealer, Anthony Brueckner, Earl Conee, Hilary Kornblith, and Timothy Williamson) or the 1990s (Marian David and Ted Warfield).

The chapters are, for the most part, developments of theories or groups of ideas with which the authors' names are associated. Strictly speaking, their successive publications present different theories, but the convention is to refer to their evolving lines of thought by a single name, even though its earliest version may differ significantly from later versions.

A clear example of a name of a "theory" in this broad sense is Alvin Goldman's *process reliabilism*, a theory that appeared in its earliest version in 1979. Goldman's extension of process reliabilism to the issue of immediate justification is the topic of his chapter in this volume. In Kornblith's chapter, he notes that the externalism/internalism debate began in 1979 with the publication of Goldman's first version of process reliabilism.

A second example is Conee's and Feldman's *evidentialism*, which began to be developed in the 1980s and whose latest version is explained in their chapter in this volume. This is a type of internalism; Conee and Feldman are known in part for their defenses of internalism and their criticisms of externalism, especially their criticisms of process reliabilism.

Virtue epistemology is commonly traced back to Ernest Sosa's work in 1980 and (with different terminology) his 1974 article "How Do You Know?" He continues the development of this theory in his discussion of "dream-skepticism", which is the main topic in his chapter for this volume.

John Pollock's *theory of rationality*, which is related to his earlier writings on *procedural epistemology* and principles of defeasible reasoning, is developed in his chapter on the origin of errors in reasoning.

The argument known as *the anti-luminosity argument* is associated with Timothy Williamson, which he develops in a probabilistic version in his chapter. This argument is a part of a broader theory developed in earlier writings, especially his 2000 book *Knowledge and its Limits*, where he argues that knowledge should be taken as fundamental and evidence defined in terms of knowledge.

The other authors are often associated with certain theses, or names of fields of epistemology, rather than a name of a particular theory. These associations are often manifold.

For example, Hilary Kornblith is associated with the thesis that *justification is not a necessary component of knowledge*, which he defends in his chapter against various theories, such as contextualism, virtue epistemology, and Goldman's process reliabilism. He is also known as a principal defender of *naturalized epistemology*; he emphasizes its non-normative nature, in contrast to normative epistemology, which understands knowledge in terms of the normative concept of justification.

Peter Klein has developed several theories and is known as a proponent of a *strong defeasibility* theory of knowledge and, since 1999, a theory he calls *infinitism*, which differs from foundationalism and coherentism. In his present chapter, he does not wish to presuppose or assume these theories, but to present a thesis about knowledge that appeals to both reliability theorists and defeasibility theorists. Klein presents a detailed argument that false beliefs are a part of knowledge or the production of knowledge, which is a strong challenge to traditional and contemporary theories of knowledge.

Robert Audi is known as one of the principal proponents of *moderate foundationalism*, but his influential role in developing the new field of *moral epistemology* in the late 1980s and 1990s is pertinent to his chapter, which is on the nature of self-evidence, rational disagreement about moral principles, and other issues that belong to moral epistemology (which should be distinguished from both normative ethics and meta-ethics).

Anthony Brueckner has written on a variety of topics, including justification and skepticism. His essay in this volume is a criticism of a number of different theories of the justification of perceptual experience, ranging from various versions of internalism and externalism (such as contextualism, virtue epistemology, and process reliability) to different versions of coherentism and foundationalism.

George Bealer's prominent role in developing *modal epistemology* is the relevant association with his essay, which is on errors in modal beliefs or intuitions. The basic ideas about (intuition-based) modal epistemology come from Kripke's 1971 and 1972 works on naming and necessity, and identity, and were gradually developed by Nathan Salmon and others. By the 1990s Bealer (and DeRose, van Inwagen, and others) had fashioned a new field of epistemology, which was soon called "modal epistemology".

David and Warfield's chapter is a detailed criticism of several versions of the *closure principle*, which has been a central premise in many arguments for skepticism. It is also an indispensable premise in Gettier's criticism of the theory that knowledge is justified true belief.

Panayot Butchvarov has been writing on epistemology since at least 1970. In his 1970 book *The Concept of Knowledge*, he developed a strong version of classical foundationalism. His book on *Skepticism in Ethics* in the late 1980s is one of the early books on moral epistemology. In his chapter in the present volume, he argues that both naturalized epistemology and subjective epistemology are unsatisfactory because they are human-centered epistemologies. He outlines a dehumanized epistemology, which is an *epistemic logic of non-formal inferences*.

1

Knowledge Needs No Justification

Hilary Kornblith

The Standard View in epistemology is that knowledge is justified, true belief plus something else. There is a very large volume of literature on the question of what that something else might be. And there is a very large volume of literature on the question of what justification might be, subject to the assumption that justification is one of the necessary conditions for knowledge. That knowledge requires justified, true belief, however, remains a fixed point around which much[1] of the literature in epistemology revolves. In this chapter

A version of this chapter was read at Tufts University and the Free University of Amsterdam. I am grateful to the audiences there, and especially Kate Elgin and Jonathan Vogel, for useful discussion. Additional comments on a written version of the chapter from David Christensen and two anonymous referees were particularly helpful.

[1] Most, but not all. Some (e.g. William Alston and Stewart Cohen) have argued that the notion of justification should simply be dispensed with. (See Alston, "Epistemic Desiderata", *Philosophy and Phenomenological Research*, 54 (1993), 527–50, and Cohen, "Is There an Issue about Justified Belief?", *Philosophical Topics*, 23 (1995), 113–27.) And some have tried to get around the Gettier problem, arguing that justified, true belief is not only necessary, but also sufficient for knowledge. Timothy Williamson (*Knowledge and its Limits* (Oxford: Oxford University Press, 2000)) holds instead that justification should be explained in terms of knowledge. Richard Foley has recently proposed exactly the view I defend here. He defends this view in "What Must Be Added to True Belief to Get Knowledge? Just More True Belief", *Philosophy and Phenomenological Research*, forthcoming, where it is presented as a consequence of a very controversial account of knowledge (which I would reject), and also, independent of that account of knowledge, in his review of Williamson's *Knowledge and its Limits*, in *Mind*, 111 (2002), 718–26. I am very much indebted to Foley here.

I argue that the Standard View should be rejected: knowledge does not require justification. We may better understand the nature of knowledge, and we may better understand the nature of justification, if we stop viewing justification as one of the necessary conditions for knowledge.

1

For more than twenty years, epistemologists have been arguing over whether a proper account of justified belief should involve a commitment to internalism or externalism.[2] Internalists have argued that the features of a belief in virtue of which it is justified must, in some sense, be internal to the agent who holds it. Thus, on certain versions of internalism, an agent must be able to tell, by way of introspection alone, whether a belief is justified; on other versions, the features of a belief that make it justified are internal to the agent in that they are restricted to features of the agent's mental states. Externalists, however, deny that the determinants of justification are restricted in any such way. Thus, for example, reliabilists hold that a belief is justified just in case it was produced or sustained by a reliable process; but the reliability of a belief producing (or sustaining) process is not a fact about features wholly internal to an agent.

Now it is interesting to trace the early history of this debate. When Alvin Goldman first presented his causal account of knowledge, he broke with the Standard View that knowledge requires justification. In "A Causal Theory of Knowledge",[3] Goldman argued that knowledge that p is nothing more than true belief caused by the fact that p. And when this account was modified (in "Discrimination and Perceptual Knowledge"[4]) to deal with a number of difficulties, Goldman again presented an account of knowledge that required no justification: knowledge was seen as true belief that is produced by the exercise of certain discriminatory capacities. Roughly contemporaneous accounts of knowledge by Armstrong[5] and Dretske[6] also left justification out of

---

[2] Some of the central papers in this debate are collected in H. Kornblith (ed.), *Epistemology: Internalism and Externalism* (Oxford: Blackwell, 2001).

[3] First published in 1967. Reprinted in Goldman, *Liaisons: Philosophy Meets the Cognitive and Social Sciences* (Cambridge, MA: MIT Press, 1992), 69–83.

[4] First published in 1976. Reprinted in Goldman, *Liaisons*, 85–103.

[5] D. M. Armstrong, *Belief, Truth and Knowledge* (Cambridge: Cambridge University Press, 1973).

[6] Fred I. Dretske, *Knowledge and the Flow of Information* (Cambridge, MA: MIT Press, 1981).

the picture. But, in "What is Justified Belief?",[7] Goldman returned to the fold. The reliability account of knowledge was now presented, not as an alternative to the Standard View, but rather as a consequence of that View when conjoined with a reliability account of justification. And it was this move on Goldman's part—reading the reliability requirement on knowledge back into the theory of justified belief so as to conform to the Standard View—which gave rise to the debate between internalists and externalists about justification.

For those who are sympathetic with a reliability account of knowledge, what reason is there to follow Goldman here and, by way of the Standard View, opt for a reliability account of justification, rather than follow Armstrong and Dretske in rejecting the Standard View, thereby leaving justification out of the picture entirely? Surprisingly, Goldman has said relatively little in print about this issue. Thus, in "What is Justified Belief?", Goldman remarks, "In previous papers on knowledge, I have denied that justification is necessary for knowing, but there I had in mind 'Cartesian' accounts of justification. On the account of justified belief suggested here, it *is* necessary for knowing, and closely related to it."[8] But this, of course, does not explain why we should follow Goldman rather than Armstrong and Dretske. Problems with Cartesian accounts of justification can be dealt with either by reliabilizing justification (with Goldman) or by simply doing without it altogether (with Armstrong and Dretske).

Goldman's distinctive move is, I believe, motivated by two ideas. The first of these is that justification is a legitimate and important epistemic category in its own right. The second has to do with considerations of theoretical simplicity, considerations that are deemed sufficient to motivate viewing justification as a necessary condition for knowledge rather than as a separate, though import-ant, epistemic category. Justification is seen as important because knowledge is important, and justification is a necessary condition for knowledge.

I am entirely sympathetic with the first of these two motivations. Justification is, I will argue, an important epistemic category, and we should not simply do without it. But the second motivation, the argument from theoretical simplicity, is one I do not endorse, and I will argue against it here.

A position of the sort I favor may seem to open up the possibility of a rapprochement between internalism and externalism. If justification is not

---

[7] First published in 1979. Reprinted in Goldman, *Liaisons*, 105–26.
[8] Goldman, "What is Justified Belief", in *Liaisons*, 105.

a necessary condition for knowledge, then one might hold that externalists were right about knowledge, but wrong about justification, while internalists were right about justification, but wrong about knowledge. And this might be thought to be a happy result: each side was right about something, but wrong about something else; the debate between the two sides was merely a matter of each talking past the other. This would, perhaps, be a happy result, but it is one I will not endorse. While rejecting the view that knowledge entails justification makes logical room for this sort of view, I do not believe that it is correct. In particular, I do not believe that internalism will prove to be right about justification, even once we divorce our account of justification from our account of knowledge. So I will not be arguing for a simple and equitable resolution of the internalism/externalism debate. The payoff for divorcing justification from knowledge will need to be found elsewhere.

2

What then is justification, and why have epistemologists been interested in it? Let us look at the way in which the topic of justified belief is introduced by a number of epistemologists.

Roderick Chisholm introduces the topic of justified belief by way of the idea of Socratic questioning.

> We consider certain things that we know to be true, or think we know to be true, or certain things which, upon reflection, we would be willing to call *evident*. With respect to each of these, we then try to formulate a reasonable answer to the question, "What justification do you think you have for counting this thing as something that is evident?" In beginning with what we think we know to be true, or with what, after reflection, we would be willing to count as being evident, we are assuming that the truth we are seeking is "already implicit in the mind which seeks it, and needs only to be elicited and brought to clear reflection".[9]

Chisholm is quite frank that, in conceiving of justification in this way, he is stacking the deck in favor of internalism, but there is no denying that this idea of linking justification to Socratic questioning is extremely natural. Richard Foley

---

[9] Roderick M. Chisholm, *Theory of Knowledge* (2nd edn.; Englewood Cliffs, NJ: Prentice-Hall, 1977), 17. The phrase that appears in quotation marks at the end of the passage is from C. I. Lewis, *Mind and the World Order* (New York: Scribner's, 1929), 19.

makes a similar suggestion, linking justification to belief in a proposition that is the conclusion of an argument "such that were the individual in question to be carefully reflective, he would think that it is sufficiently likely to be truth preserving".[10] While Foley's account of justification, unlike Chisholm's, is highly subjective—since reflective individuals must merely *think* that the arguments supporting their beliefs are likely to be truth preserving—in both cases the notion of justification is linked to arguments that individuals might provide to themselves in support of their beliefs.

Laurence BonJour is of a similar turn of mind: "Perhaps the most pervasive conviction within the Western epistemological tradition is that in order for a person's belief to constitute *knowledge* it is necessary (though not sufficient) that it be justified or warranted or rationally grounded, that the person have an adequate *reason* for accepting it."[11]

BonJour makes clear that reasons, on his view, are cognitively accessible to those who have them; he is an internalist about justification. While noting that reliabilists have rejected such a conception of justification, BonJour comments: "My conviction is that views of this kind are merely wrong-headed and ultimately uninteresting evasions of the central epistemological issues."[12]

It is not hard to see why BonJour has this attitude toward reliabilism. If reliably produced belief is all that is necessary for justification, then believers may be justified when they have no conception whatever as to why they should think their beliefs to be true; worse still, they may be justified even when they possess excellent reason to think their beliefs to be false.[13] The very idea of justification, if it is to make contact with important epistemological issues, it seems, must be tied to the having of reasons, and this means that an agent who is justified is in possession of an argument in favor of the belief in question. It is for this reason that I have referred to this conception of justification as the *arguments-on-paper view*.[14]

While Chisholm, Foley and BonJour develop the arguments-on-paper conception of justification as a form of internalism, it is important to see that

[10] Richard Foley, *The Theory of Epistemic Rationality* (Cambridge, MA: Harvard University Press, 1987), 15.

[11] Laurence BonJour, *In Defense of Pure Reason* (Cambridge: Cambridge University Press, 1998), 1.

[12] Ibid. 1, n. 1.

[13] These two points are made by way of a justly famous series of detailed examples in Laurence BonJour, *The Structure of Empirical Knowledge* (Cambridge, MA: Harvard University Press, 1985), ch. 3.

[14] Hilary Kornblith, "Beyond Foundationalism and the Coherence Theory", *Journal of Philosophy*, 77 (1980), 597–612.

the connection between justification and available argument does not require internalism at all. Robert Brandom and Michael Williams, for example, who insist on what they call the "default and challenge structure of justification", tie justification to the ability to respond to challenges, not from oneself, but from members of one's community.[15] Since an agent may be ignorant of challenges that the community might present, as well as the defaults that the community might permit, this conception of justification is a form of externalism. Nevertheless, unlike reliabilism, it ties justification to the ability to present an argument. Chisholm, Foley, and BonJour are concerned about being able to present arguments to oneself; Brandom and Williams are concerned about being able to present arguments to one's community. Either way, justification is seen as a matter of the ability to present arguments in support of one's beliefs.

This dialectical conception of justification is, to be sure, an important one. We are, at times, reflective creatures, and when we reflect on our beliefs, we sometimes wonder about what reason there is, if any, for holding the beliefs we do. In many cases, it seems, we are able to provide reasons in favor of our beliefs; in others, however, we cannot. And this seems to be a noteworthy difference: that some of our beliefs are ones that we can support by way of argument, while others are not. Similarly, there are challenges to our beliefs that stem not from self-examination or unaided reflection, but from outside us, from our communities. Here, too, there is a noteworthy distinction between those beliefs that we are in a position to defend against challenge and those that we cannot. Philosophers whose conception of epistemology derives from Descartes are more likely to see the first sort of challenge as primary, while those who are influenced by Hegel, the later Wittgenstein, or, on one conception, Wilfrid Sellars, are likely to see social challenges as more basic. But there is a common idea here, and it is the ability to respond to challenges.

Important as this is, justification *in this sense* seems to me a very poor candidate as a necessary condition on knowledge. Consider, first, the social version of this requirement, the ability to respond to challenges that one's epistemic community might provide. In the case of scientific theories, for example, the

---

[15] Brandom, *Making It Explicit* (Cambridge, MA: Harvard University Press, 1994), and *Articulating Reasons*, (Cambridge, MA: Harvard University Press, 2000); Williams, *Unnatural Doubts* (Princeton: Princeton University Press, 1996) and *Problems of Knowledge* (Oxford: Oxford University Press, 2001).

public defense of theories against available challenge is surely a central feature of their justification. Proponents of a theory endeavor to show that their preferred view is superior to alternatives available within the community of scientists. The public airing of such argumentation is a crucial part of justifying one's views. Theories that cannot respond to available challenge are rightly taken to be, in important respects, epistemically deficient. More than this, the social character of justification does not seem limited, by any means, to scientific claims. In mundane matters of all sorts, from views about the fastest way to get from Boston to New York to views about moral and political matters, the dialectic of challenge and response plays an important role in our epistemic practice. But while these examples do illustrate the importance of the epistemic practice of giving and asking for reasons, they do not, I believe, make a case for any sort of necessary connection between knowledge and the ability to defend one's belief in this sort of way.

Note, in particular, that the social airing of scientific theories takes place against the background of a highly idiosyncratic epistemic community. Members of this community are very highly trained; they are extremely well informed; and they are extremely adept, among other things, at the public presentation of reasons. Not all epistemic communities are like this. Consider the case of a community that regularly conducts its affairs by consulting astrological charts; where the reading of tea leaves is seen as a reliable indicator of future events; and crystals are seen as possessing magic powers which assure their owners of lasting health and startling insight. In this community, the public practice of giving and asking for reasons, or what passes for reason in this community, serves not only to spread false belief, but to misdirect the community's epistemic efforts so as further to entrench their misguided epistemic practices. While one might reasonably think that scientists who cannot answer the challenges of their peers should, perhaps, withhold claims to knowledge, one might also think that the challenges that issue from deeply deviant epistemic communities, such as my community of astrologers, do not deserve the same amount of deference. Social practices of giving and asking for reasons—patterns of challenge and default—are not all, epistemically, on a par. There are certain communities in which it is no epistemic defect to be unable to respond, in terms the community would find compelling, or even relevant, to the socially available challenges to a body of beliefs. In such circumstances, opting out entirely of the social practice of giving and asking for reasons would be far superior, epistemically, from lowering oneself to the challenge with which the available social practice presents one. But opting out of this deviant social practice surely does not rob one of knowledge. And, if this is so, being in a position to respond to socially available challenges to belief cannot be a necessary condition on knowledge. If justification is identified with the ability to respond to socially available challenges, then justification is not a necessary condition for knowledge.

Similar considerations apply to contextualist accounts of knowledge.[16] Contextualists have urged that the standards for knowledge vary widely from context to context. If my wife asks me whether I know where her car keys are, the standards that are in play dictate that, if I am looking directly at them, my claim "I know they are on the kitchen table" is true. But, contextualists say, if a skeptic should ask me the very same question, or, rather, ask a question using the very same words, immediately after having raised the possibility of deception by an evil demon, then if I should utter, "I know the keys are on the table", I am saying something false. What the standards are for knowledge, according to contextualists, depends on contextually salient standards, and the skeptic has raised the standards so high that nothing could possibly pass them. My wife, on the other hand, who is far more forgiving, has standards for knowledge that make knowledge possible. When I am looking at her car keys, I do know where they are, relative to her standards, and it would thus be false for me to state, under those conditions, "I don't know where your keys are".

Contextualists do not merely claim that there is some small amount of vagueness inherent in the notion of knowledge and that contextually salient standards serve to locate the standards we have in mind within some already narrowly defined range. Rather, contextualists have been eager to use their contextualism to address, as they see it, the skeptical problematic, arguing, as my example above indicates, that the range of contextually available standards may vary at least from the everyday standards my wife uses when she wants to know where her keys are to the ultra-high standards that the skeptic brings to bear when he wishes to insist that no one has any knowledge at all. Contextualists want to insist that the knowledge claims each of these

---

[16] I have in mind here especially the work of Stewart Cohen, Keith DeRose, and David Lewis. See Stewart, Cohen, "Knowledge, Context and Social Standards", *Synthese*, 73 (1987), 3–26; Keith DeRose, "Solving the Skeptical Problem", *Philosophical Review*, 104 (1995), 1–52; and David Lewis, "Elusive Knowledge", *Australasian Journal of Philosophy*, 74 (1996), 549–67.

speakers make are just plain true: my wife truly states "You did know where my keys were", while the skeptic truly states "You didn't know where the keys were". Since contextually indicated standards serve to determine what proposition is being expressed, we can consistently insist that, in this case, both parties are correct. And this result, contextualists insist, allows us better to appreciate the skeptical problematic, for we may give the skeptic his due (in skeptically heightened contexts) while going on exactly as before in everyday situations.

It is not at all clear that this kind of approach to the semantics of the term 'knowledge' is as charitable a reconstruction of what the different parties mean as the contextualist suggests. In particular, it is worth noting that the contextualist reconciliation of the debate between the skeptic and the common-sense philosopher (who insists that we do know a great many things, after all) has the defect, common to many forms of relativism, that it ends up denying that these two really disagreed in the first place. Although the common-sense philosopher uttered the words "I do know many things about the external world", and the skeptic replied, "You're mistaken; you don't know anything", the contextualist must insist that, because the standards for knowledge attribution have shifted from the first comment to the second, both the knowledge claim and the denial of the knowledge claim are true. But this then makes no sense of the fact that both parties believe that they disagree; indeed, this is why the skeptic insists that the common-sense philosopher is mistaken. If everybody is right, relative to their own standards, then no one is mistaken. Nevertheless, both parties in this dialogue believe that they have denied what the other has asserted.

The contextualist attempts to resolve the debate between the skeptic and the common-sense philosopher by making everyone happy: "Stop," the contextualist says, "you're both right." But this attempt charitably to reconstruct what each party means is not, in the end, very charitable, for it undermines one extremely important point on which skeptics and common-sense philosophers agree—namely, that they do disagree after all. While both parties do agree that, when I am looking straight at my wife's keys on the kitchen table, I meet certain standards and fail to meet others: one party to the debate believes that I actually meet the standards which knowledge requires; the other wishes to deny that very claim. Contextualism is forced to deny this. As an account of the semantics for the term 'knowledge', this seems terribly implausible.

But, while I think it important to reject what contextualists have to say about knowledge, much[17] of what contextualists have to say about justification is, I believe, both true and important. Contextualism offers a deep understanding of the conversational dynamics of challenge and response, the ways in which demands for reasons depend on a shared background of beliefs about what may be taken for granted and how it is that justifications are to be structured. But when justification is viewed in this way, important as it is, it is not a necessary condition on knowledge.

The challenges that issue from a community of inquirers, or from a single interlocutor, may not reasonably be seen as setting the standards for knowledge, even if, as seems more plausible, they are intimately tied to our notion of justification. But what about the Cartesian-inspired idea that the standards for justification are set by private reflection on our reasons for belief? This dialectical, but individualist, notion of justification may seem a more plausible candidate for an account of justification that is itself a necessary condition on knowledge. While meeting the standards of the epistemic community in which I am situated, however deviant it may be, does not seem necessary for knowledge, nor does meeting the standards of whatever interlocutor I happen to encounter, private reflection on my reasons for belief seems to offer an epistemic standard that is both less idiosyncratic and more demanding of my attention than the various socialized versions of the dialectical conception of justification. As such, it may seem more plausible that this conception of justification provides a necessary condition on knowledge.

There are, I believe, two importantly different motivations for this Cartesian conception of justification. Philosophers who are inclined toward some sort of rationalism will see the standards that are set by private reflection as ones that enjoy a certain sort of objectivity; the exercise of reason, on this view, puts us in touch with the one true standard for justification, and, in virtue of its objectivity, this standard may properly be viewed as setting a necessary condition for knowledge. Quite a different motivation, however, comes from noting that, when I reflect on my beliefs, I am able to discover whether they meet *my* standards, rather than someone else's. I might dismiss out of hand the standards of my community, or some individual interlocutor, if

---

[17] Although certainly not all. For further discussion of the shortcomings of contextualism, see my "The Contextualist Evasion of Epistemology", *Philosophical Issues*, 10 (2000), 24–32.

they are different enough from my own, even if I cannot explain to my challenger, in terms that will be found persuasive, why it is that I regard the challenge as unworthy; but I cannot, it seems, responsibly take the same attitude toward my own standards. The epistemic standards that I hold on reflection are, after all, mine, and that fact alone gives them a certain authority over me.

Descartes, of course, was motivated by both these considerations, as are many contemporary philosophers, but it is, nevertheless, important to recognize the very different sort of motivations that these two considerations provide. One might, in particular, be moved by the second consideration—that my standards, are, after all, *mine*—even if one is not convinced by the first—that the standards so revealed are automatically objectively correct. But any philosopher who endorses only the second of these two motivations, thereby allowing that the standards that private reflection sets may be no more reasonable, in any objective sense, than those of the deviant epistemic communities or random interlocutors we have already discussed, thereby acknowledges that such a conception of justification cannot plausibly be seen as a necessary condition for knowledge. Indeed, this is precisely why Richard Foley, who endorses a highly subjective conception of justification of this very sort, has argued that justification should not be seen as a necessary condition on knowledge. If private reflection does not set objective standards, and justification is determined by the standards it sets, than knowledge does not require justification.

The case for a standard for justification which is both tied to private reflection and, at the same time, required as a necessary condition for knowledge thus depends on the first of the two motivations described; ultimately, it is founded in a commitment to a robust rationalism. While the most common version of such a rationalist epistemology is wholly internalist, even some philosophers who favor versions of externalism show a real sympathy for rationalist epistemology. Thus, Ernest Sosa defends a distinction between what he calls "animal knowledge" and "reflective knowledge".

One has *animal knowledge* about one's environment, one's past, and one's own experience if one's judgments and beliefs about these are direct responses to their impact—e.g., through perception or memory—with little or no benefit of reflection or understanding.

One has *reflective knowledge* if one's judgment or belief manifests not only such direct response to the fact known but also understanding of its place in a wider whole that includes one's belief and knowledge of it and how these come about.[18]

Sosa defends the view that reflective knowledge is "better knowledge"; it is the kind to which human beings should aspire.

But what is it about reflective knowledge, according to Sosa, that makes it better, a fit object of human aspiration? This is where Sosa's rationalism comes in: "Since a direct response supplemented by such understanding would in general have a better chance of being right, reflective knowledge is better justified than corresponding animal knowledge."[19] Reflecting on our beliefs, rather than merely allowing our native cognitive processes to go to work on whatever input the environment may happen to provide them with, increases the likelihood, Sosa claims, that the beliefs thereby produced are correct. This is, of course, an empirical claim about the effects of reflection. In order to see whether it is true, we need to look at some of the psychological literature about what actually happens when people reflect on their beliefs.

What Sosa refers to as reflection is not, from a psychological point of view, a single type of process. Instead, there are many different processes that go to work when people reflect on their beliefs, and it would be a mistake to try to provide a one-dimensional evaluation of these diverse processes. In particular, they are not all reliability enhancing. Consider, for example, the phenomenon of belief perseverance. Once a belief is formed, individuals have a tendency to continue in their belief, and the way in which they deal with evidence manifests this tendency. Evidence in favor of pre-existing beliefs is largely taken at face value; contrary evidence is subjected to great scrutiny, and typically found wanting. In addition, evidence acquired that supports existing beliefs is well remembered, while evidence against existing beliefs is more easily forgotten. This kind of biased recall has the effect that, when an agent surveys his evidence in quiet moments of reflection, the evidence surveyed, more often than not, tends to support the belief being evaluated, largely independent of the support it enjoys from evidence the agent has considered. Far from making us more reliable, these mechanisms of reflection merely serve further to entrench whatever beliefs we already have. Reflection, in these cases, does

---

[18] Ernest Sosa, "Knowledge and Intellectual Virtue", *Monist*, 68 (1985), 226–45; repr. in Sosa, *Knowledge in Perspective: Selected Essays in Epistemology* (Cambridge: Cambridge University Press, 1991), 225–44. The quoted passage appears on p. 240 of the reprinted version.

[19] Ibid. 240.

not act as a check on our first-order processes of belief acquisition, raising the reliability of the resulting total package of cognitive mechanisms. Instead, it acts as a kind of cognitive yes-man, offering up its approval of whatever the first-order processes happen to produce. In the process, reflection tends to produce a more confident agent, one who is better able to articulate, both to himself and to others, a wide range of reasons in support of his beliefs. But increased reliability is not a product of the mechanism of belief perseverance.

I do not mean to suggest that reflection never serves to increase the reliability of agents who make use of it; clearly this is not true. More than that, my point is that any such unitary evaluation of reflection is insufficiently attentive to epistemically relevant details of the many mechanisms of reflection. Reflection can, at times, serve as a useful check on first-order processes of belief acquisition, as Sosa suggests; but it can also serve merely to entrench pre-existing beliefs, of whatever merit; and, in other cases, it may act as a monkey wrench in the otherwise smooth working of first-order mechanisms, thereby lowering the reliability of the overall process. It will not serve any useful epistemic purpose to try to lump all these disparate processes together and ask for a single evaluation of the package as epistemically beneficial or epistemically harmful. But, if this is the case, we should not simply endorse the entire package of mechanisms of reflection as one. And we cannot reasonably insist that knowledge, or the kind of knowledge to which humans should aspire, must involve reflection, whatever its effects. Reflection, in Sosa's sense, cannot reasonably be viewed as a necessary condition on knowledge.[20]

Reflection on one's beliefs thus seems like a good idea when one assumes, with Sosa, that it will inevitably increase the reliability of one's first-order processes of belief acquisition, or, at a minimum, fail to make one's epistemic situation worse. But, once we recognize that this is not generally true of reflection, the case for singling out reflection as an epistemic good in itself is severely compromised. The rationalist view on which reflection is endowed with special powers that allow it to tap into truth conducive methods of belief modification turns out not to be true. But when we reject this rationalist

---

[20] I have pursued this point at greater length in *Knowledge and its Place in Nature* (Oxford: Oxford University Press, 2004), ch. 4, and especially as regards Sosa's view, in "Sosa on Human and Animal Knowledge", in J. Greco (ed.), *Sosa and his Critics* (Oxford: Blackwell, forthcoming).

view of reflection, we thereby undermine the case for viewing reflection as a necessary condition on knowledge.

The dialectical conception of justification, whether in its social form—which requires an ability to justify one's beliefs to one's community—or in its more individualist form—which requires that one be in a position to justify one's beliefs to oneself, does not present us with a plausible necessary condition on knowledge.

3

Dialectical accounts of justification fail to provide us with a necessary condition on knowledge because they fail to be sufficiently objective. But this then just motivates a conception of justification that requires that certain more objective standards be met: certain logical constraints on inference; standards of probabilistic consistency; or de facto reliability and the like. Precisely because these standards are objective, they do not suffer from the problems to which the dialectical conception gave rise, and, for that very reason, they seem far more plausible as necessary conditions on knowledge, although obviously any particular account of this sort would need to be examined in detail. What I want to argue, however, is that, the more objective we set our standards, the less plausible it is that these standards are standards of *justification*.

Consider, for example, requirements of probabilistic consistency. Idealizing somewhat, we may assign subjective probabilities to each of an agent's beliefs. Thus, for example, although I believe that the sun will rise tomorrow and I also believe that I have more than $100 in my checking account right now, I do not assign equal probabilities to these two claims, even though I reviewed my account balance only yesterday. I have made too many mistakes in my checking account over the years to attach anything like the same probability to these two claims. But the various beliefs I have are not probabilistically independent of one another, and there are consistency constraints that the probability calculus lays down so that, once I have assigned probability assessments to some of my beliefs, probability assessments of others are thereby determined. The probability calculus may, therefore, be seen as laying down certain objective requirements on my distribution of probabilities.

May we therefore view the probability calculus as laying down certain objective constraints on justification? It seems to me that we may not.

Probabilistic relations of consistency are objectively difficult to determine. Suppose I believe even as few as one thousand probabilistically independent propositions. In addition to these propositions, I believe logically complex conjunctions, disjunctions, and conditionals in which they are embedded. The probabilities of these complex propositions is entirely determined by the probabilities of their atomic constituents (together with the probability calculus), but figuring out those probabilities may be far beyond anything of which I am remotely capable. This is not merely a result about mathematically dim-witted agents, for the problems of computational complexity which arise here make calculations of this sort ones that are beyond the calculational capabilities of any physically embodied agent.[21]

Why should this count against viewing the constraints of the probability calculus as constraints on what I am justified in believing? There is something odd, to be sure, about a conception of justification that makes assessments of justification hopelessly beyond the reach of any possible human agent. If a particular belief of mine is probabilistically inconsistent with others I hold, but determining that would take from now until the end of the next millennium, the suggestion that I am, nevertheless, unjustified in this belief sets a standard for justification that can play no possible role in governing my beliefs. To the extent that a theory of justification is designed to provide us with epistemic advice—guidance as to what we ought to believe—the unusability of the probability calculus automatically takes it out of the running as an account of the conditions required for justification.

The same is true, of course, for various logical requirements among my beliefs, now viewed in a binary, all-or-nothing fashion, rather than subject to differences of degree, as the probabilistic account would have us view it. Tracing out the logical implications of my beliefs will, like the probabilistic consistency requirement, run into problems of computational complexity.[22] If I cannot even tell whether my beliefs satisfy the logical requirements, and no physically embodied agent could possibly tell before the end of the next millennium, then the standard set by the logical requirements does not propose a meaningful requirement for justification.

---

[21] This was first pointed out, I believe, by Gilbert Harman in *Change in View: Principles of Reasoning* (Cambridge, MA: MIT Press, 1986), 25–7.

[22] See Christopher Cherniak, "Computational Complexity and the Universal Acceptance of Logic", *Journal of Philosophy*, 81 (1984), 739–58.

The standard of de facto reliability is, in this regard, importantly different. While it is always unreasonable to believe that one's total body of beliefs satisfies standards of probabilistic consistency (it would surely be a miracle if they did), and the same is true of logical consistency, it is not unreasonable to think that we have beliefs that are formed by reliable processes.[23] We do sometimes check to see whether our beliefs are reliably produced, and this sort of checking can have useful consequences for the accuracy of our beliefs. The standard of reliability is one that is intimately involved in our justificational practices. What this shows, however, has little to do with reliability accounts of justification. According to reliability views of justification, it is the actual reliability of our processes of belief acquisition that determine whether a belief is justified, not their perceived reliability, nor even their perceived reliability after careful and responsible examination. There will, in principle and in practice, always be gaps between the actual reliability of processes of belief acquisition and their perceived reliability, no matter how carefully that may be investigated. But this is just to say that our justificational practice, while it attempts to realize a standard of genuine reliability, does not always meet it. Or to put the point only slightly differently, we may be justified without having succeeded in achieving the goal of reliable belief acquisition. Actual reliability is more plausibly viewed as the standard we set as our goal—a requirement for knowledge—than it is a requirement for justified belief.[24]

---

[23] One might think that the standard of reliability genuinely is on a par with logical and probabilistic standards for, although it is certainly reasonable to believe that many of one's beliefs are reliably produced, it would be completely unreasonable to think that all one's beliefs are reliably produced. By the same token, although it is completely unreasonable to think that one's total body of beliefs satisfy demands of logical or probabilistic consistency, one might reasonably think that some small subset of one's beliefs satisfy such standards. While the parallel does indeed extend this far, this is of little help to those who would offer accounts of justification requiring logical or probabilistic consistency. On such accounts, given the total evidence requirement, it is logical or probabilistic consistency over one's entire body of beliefs that is required for justification. Reliability accounts of justification, on the other hand, make no requirement that all of one's beliefs be reliably produced.

[24] Would it help to distinguish here between the practice of justifying beliefs and the property which beliefs sometimes have of being justified? The suggestion would then be that my argument shows only that the practice of justifying beliefs does not require reliability. This is perfectly compatible, however, with the view that a belief has the property of being justified only if it is reliably produced. While I am fully convinced that the property of being reliably produced is a necessary condition for knowledge, the question at issue here is whether this property is usefully identified with the property of being justified. For the very reasons given in the text, it now seems to me that any such identification proves more misleading than illuminating.

4

Let me briefly review. When we provide a subjective requirement on justification, as the various dialectical accounts do, we make it implausible that justification, so understood, is a necessary condition on knowledge. But the more objective we make our requirement for justification, thereby making room for a real connection with knowledge, the more implausible it is that the actual phenomenon of justification is captured by it. Knowledge requires that some sort of objective standard be met; justification requires the meeting of some more subjective standard; but knowledge does not require justification.

How did this state of affairs come to pass? In Descartes's view, of course, meeting the subjective standard guaranteed that the objective standard was simultaneously met; on such a view, justification is reasonably thought of as a necessary condition on knowledge. But once we allow, as everyone now must, that the standards for justification, whatever they may be, may at times be met even by beliefs that are formed in ways that are, by any objective standard, very bad, the motivation for seeing justification as a necessary condition for knowledge is thereby undermined. We are right to see the justification of belief as an important epistemic practice, one that when properly carried out, may be conducive to knowledge. But, once we abandon Descartes's rationalist optimism about the fit between justification and knowledge, we should no longer believe that justification is required for knowledge.

But, if this is right, why then is the intuition that knowledge requires justification so extraordinarily robust? Why has it seemed for so long, and why does it continue to seem to so many, that justification is a necessary condition for knowledge? There are, I believe, a number of reasons for this. First, it is important to note that, when people find out that a belief of theirs is not justified, they typically withdraw any claim to knowledge. If I reflect on my beliefs and find that a certain belief fails to meet my standards for reasonable belief, I stop claiming to know that it is true. And, if I am challenged by my community, and I cannot meet their objections, I will also typically withdraw my claim to knowledge. We may explain why this should be so, however, without supposing that justification is necessary for knowledge. When I discover, on reflection, that a belief fails to meet my standards, I typically give up the belief. Because I believe that my standards at least roughly track the truth, failure to meet them is reason for thinking that

I lack the objective connection with the facts that is required for knowledge. And, if I believe that the standards that prevail in my community are roughly truth-tracking as well, then my inability to meet them will also be taken by me as reason for thinking that I lack the connection with the truth that is required for knowledge. None of this requires that justification be seen as a necessary condition for knowledge. Failure to meet the standards of justification is, however, evidence that one does not know.

What about third-person cases? Suppose that Jack fails to be justified in a belief of his. Do we not ordinarily take this as sufficient reason to believe that Jack does not have knowledge, and does not this show that we regard justified belief as a necessary condition for knowledge? It is certainly true that, if Jack has a true belief that is merely a product of wishful thinking or the like, we deny that Jack genuinely knows. But this need have nothing to do with justification. Jack fails, in this kind of case, to meet the objective conditions on knowledge—for example, conditions such as those captured by de facto reliability requirements—that are not plausibly thought of as conditions on justification. What should we say about cases in which Jack does meet whatever objective conditions are required for knowledge—perhaps de facto reliability—but fails to meet the subjective requirements on justification? If Jack cannot, for example, meet the standards of his community, he will sometimes give up his belief for this very reason, and, since belief is, in everyone's view, a requirement for knowledge, he no longer knows. In cases where Jack rejects the standards of his community, and goes on believing in the face of their objections, and where Jack's belief genuinely is reliably produced, it is not at all clear that Jack does not know. Note in particular that this sort of case arises every time that a reasonable person fails to be bowed by the standards of a deviant epistemic community. Similar considerations apply to private reflection. In the most typical case, if Jack fails to meet his own standards, this will cause him to give up his belief, and the fact that belief is a necessary condition for knowledge explains why he no longer knows. In those cases where Jack notes that a belief of his fails to meet his standards but he maintains his belief nonetheless, it is not at all clear that he thereby fails to know even if his belief meets all the objective requirements on knowledge. So we may certainly explain why it is that, at least typically, failure to meet the standards for justification deprives one of knowledge even if justification is not a necessary condition for knowledge.

I have tried, throughout this chapter, to avoid taking a stand on just what the correct account of justification is and, similarly, to avoid taking a stand on what the correct account of knowledge is. Whatever one's preferred account of justification, and whatever one's preferred account of knowledge, one should not view justification as a necessary condition for knowledge.

2

Useful False Beliefs

Peter D. Klein

The purpose of this chapter is to examine the role of false beliefs in the production of knowledge. False beliefs are generally thought to play no role, and certainly no "essential" role, in the production of knowledge, which some philosophers have defined as true belief that does not rely in an essential way on a falsehood.[1] To the contrary, I will present some cases in which false

I dedicate this essay to Jerome Balmuth, a former colleague and valued friend, in celebration of his fiftieth anniversary of teaching at Colgate University.

I wish to thank Anne Ashbaugh, Alice Koller, Claudio de Almeida, Trent Dougherty, Mylan Engel, Brian Kierland, Jonathan Kvanvig, Kenneth Lucy, Matthew McGrath, Brian Mclaughlin, Andrew Melnyk, Ted Posten, Bruce Russell, Quentin Smith, Robert Shope and Ernest Sosa for their comments on this chapter and their helpful discussions about some of the claims in it.

A distant ancestor of this chapter was presented at a conference at the Pontifical Catholic University in Porto Alegre, Brazil, in 1999; the discussion there was very helpful. Not so distant ancestors were presented at the University of Miami, February 2004, the University of Missouri, October 2004, the University of Nevada, November 2004, and Wayne State University, March 2005. The chapter was revised after each of the discussions at those universities. In addition, I would like to thank the anonymous referee who provided a useful criticism (see n. 35). For another approach to the problem, see Ted A. Warfield, 'Knowledge from Falsehood', *Nous-supplement*, 19 (2005), 405–16.

[1] See, e.g., Michael Clark, "Knowledge and Grounds: A Comment on Mr Gettier's Paper", *Analysis*, 24 (1963), 46–8; Gilbert Harman, *Thought* (Princeton: Princeton University Press, 1973), esp. 118–25, Keith Lehrer, *Knowledge* (Oxford: Oxford University Press, 1974), esp. 219–20, and, more recently, Richard Feldman, *Epistemology* (Upper Saddle River, NJ: Prentice Hall, 2003), esp. 33–7. Feldman succinctly states the received view in the following: "The moral [of the cases

beliefs play an essential role in both the justification and causal production of cognition, and then I will propose a general account of the conditions in which such false beliefs—what I will call "useful false beliefs"—can make essential contributions to the acquisition of knowledge.[2]

1. Some key notions employed in this chapter

I want first to explain some of the key notions employed in this chapter, although I will not defend them in any great detail. I have discussed many of them in other papers, and some of them are not contentious, so I state them merely to ensure that the reader and I share a common vocabulary. In addition, they will help to clarify some aspects of the otherwise puzzling phenomenon of useful falsehoods.

1.1. Propositional justification and doxastic justification

The two notions of propositional justification and doxastic justification can be explained in turn.[3] I take propositions to be the contents of beliefs or

discussed] is that knowledge requires justified true belief and something else as well—there is a fourth condition of knowledge. Saying just what that condition is turns out to be remarkably difficult . . . What seems to be crucial is that the justification not *essentially depend* upon anything false" (p. 37; emphasis in original).

[2] Of course, there is a non-controversial way in which a false belief can play an essential role in producing knowledge, if that means merely that had I not had the false belief, I would not have acquired the knowledge. For example, believing falsely that today is the day on which trash is collected, I could come to know that there is a rabbit in the yard as I carry the garbage can to the sidewalk. If I had not had the false belief, I would not have discovered the rabbit. But, in such a case, my knowledge that there is a rabbit is neither justified nor caused by my false belief. The claim I will be making is that in some cases the false belief is essential both to the justification and to causal production of knowledge.

[3] As far as I know, this distinction was first introduced by Roderick Firth in "Are Epistemic Concepts Reducible to Ethical Concepts?", in Alvin Goldman and Jaegwon Kim (eds.), *Values and Morals* (Dordrecht: D. Reidel, 1978: 215–29). Later, Alvin Goldman distinguished *ex ante* justification from *ex post* justification, a distinction that, in many ways, parallels that between propositional and doxastic justification, respectively. See Alvin Goldman, "What is Justified Belief?", especially sect. III. It was originally published in G. S. Pappas, (ed.), *Justification and Knowledge* (Dordrecht: D. Reidel, 1976), 1–23. It has been reprinted in many places that are more accessible, for example, in Quentin Smith (ed.), *Epistemology* (Oxford: Blackwell, 2000), 340–53, esp. p. 351. The terms "propositional" and "doxastic" justification are better suited to this chapter, since they make clear that the former concerns the evidential basis for a *proposition*, and the latter refers, in part, to the causal conditions that produce a *belief*.

other mental states such as perceptions or memories.[4] A proposition may be justified for S although S does not believe it. We can say that a proposition, *h*, is *propositionally justified* for S, just in case S has an *epistemically adequate basis* for *h*. My primary concern is with cases in which that epistemically adequate basis is either another proposition that S believes (occurrently or dispositionally) or a proposition that is merely *available* to S. If foundationalism is correct, that basis could be something other than the propositional content of a belief. For example, the content of a perceptual state or even an event or state of affairs in the "external world" could provide an adequate epistemic basis for a proposition. I will explicitly attempt to accommodate these foundationalist views at relevant points in this chapter.[5]

For a proposition to be *available* to S, it must either (i) be the propositional content of S's actual mental states, or (ii) be appropriately "hooked up" to S's actual mental states. For example, if S believes that *p*, and *p* (relevantly) entails *q*, then *q* is available whether or not S recognizes that consequence of her beliefs.[6] A difference between Holmes and Watson is that Holmes recognized what was available, whereas Watson did not put two and two together. Whether Holmes's ability to draw the available conclusions is best understood as (i) having a

---

[4] Some might prefer to limit the scope of propositions to the contents of beliefs because, they claim, the contents of perceptions and memories are neither true nor false. Those contents might be deemed accurate or inaccurate, rather than true or false. While understanding that reluctance to take my rather permissive view of the scope of "proposition", I will use "proposition" to designate the full class of mental contents, for the sake of ease of presentation. Nothing in the argument depends upon that choice. Wherever appropriate, the reader may use, e.g., "proposition-like" when referring to the contents of all mental states, and, e.g., terms like "accurate" and "inaccurate", rather than "true" or "false."

[5] I have my own view about what is required in order for a proposition to be justified, but I will not be urging that view here, since I want the account of useful false beliefs to be sufficiently general to be applicable to foundationalism, coherentism, and infinitism. The latter is my favored view. For a defense of infinitism, see: "Human Knowledge and the Infinite Regress of Reasons", in J. Tomberlin (ed.), *Philosophical Perspectives*, 13 (1999), 297–325; "Why Not Infinitism?", in Richard Cobb-Stevens (ed.), *Epistemology: Proceedings of the Twentieth World Congress in Philosophy* (2000), v. 199–208; "When Infinite Regresses Are *Not* Vicious", *Philosophy and Phenomenological Research*, 66/3 (2003), 718–29; "What *IS* Wrong with Foundationalism is that it Cannot Solve the Epistemic Regress Problem", *Philosophy and Phenomenological Research*, 68/1 (2004), 166–71; "Infinitism Is the Only Solution to the Epistemic Regress Problem" and "Response to Ginet", in Matthias Steup and Ernest Sosa (eds.), *Contemporary Debates in Philosophy* (Oxford: Blackwell, 2005), 139–40, 149–52; "Human Knowledge and the Infinite Progress of Reasoning" and "How to be an Infinitist about Doxastic Justification", *Philosophical Studies*, 134/1 (2006), 1–17, 25–9.

[6] I will discuss later whether availability requires that the connection between the contents of S's mental states and other propositions must be as strong as entailment.

disposition to believe that q, or (ii) having a second-order disposition to form a disposition to believe that q, is a matter of detail that can be set aside.[7]

My primary concern in this chapter is with the conditions in which a proposition is justified by another proposition.[8] Determining the conditions under which one proposition justifies another proposition is a central and difficult task for epistemology as a list of only a few of the suggestions currently on issue makes apparent. A proposition, say p, is held to be an *epistemically adequate basis* for q **iff**:

(a) p is probable, and if p is probable, then q is probable; or

(b)   in the long run, p would be accepted as a reason for q by the appropriate epistemic community; or

(c) p would be offered as a reason for q by an epistemically virtuous individual; or

(d)   believing that q on the basis of p is in accord with one's most basic epistemic commitments.

Luckily, we do not have to settle this matter here. We can just help ourselves to whatever turns out to be the best account and plug it in whenever we use the expression "x propositionally justifies y".

Beliefs—that is, belief states—are the bearers of doxastic justification. I will take a belief that h to be *doxastically justified* for S when and only when the belief that h has an *appropriate causal pedigree*.[9] Doxastic justification, and not mere propositional justification, is what is referred to by the "J" in a JTB account of knowledge—that is, S's belief that h must be doxastically justified in order for S to know h. For, even if S holds a true belief that h, and h is propositionally justified, and there is no genuine defeater of the propositional justification, it does not follow that S has knowledge. S must also believe h for the "right" reasons. It is widely assumed that those "right" reasons must be true. This chapter challenges that assumption.

---

[7] For a discussion of those issues, see Robert Audi, "Dispositional Beliefs and Dispositions to Believe", *Nous*, 28/4 (1994), 419–34.

[8] Although, to allow for foundationalism, we must also consider cases in which something other than a proposition can provide an adequate epistemic basis for a proposition.

[9] There are other accounts of doxastic justification—for example, an explicitly normative account in which a belief that h is doxastically justified for S just in case S believes h in an epistemically responsible way. I choose to employ the explicitly causal account because, as it will soon be apparent during my discussion of evidential and causal overdetermination, doing so helps to make clear the particular issues under discussion here.

Propositional justification and doxastic justification (where the cause of the belief is another belief) are related in at least these ways:

I (a proposition, e, propositionally justifies another proposition, h) ≡ (for any S, if S were doxastically justified in believing that e, then S would be doxastically justified in believing that h if S were to believe that h and S's belief that h were to be caused by S's belief that e);

II (S's belief that h is doxastically justified by another belief that e) → (S's belief that h is caused by the belief that e, and e propositionally justifies h).[10]

Both concepts of justification are conceptually opaque if we cannot specify one of them without appealing to the other. Which, if either, is basic might be a good way to characterize the fundamental disagreement between normative epistemology and naturalistic epistemology, but I will not discuss that in this chapter.

What is crucial here is that, although the two notions are closely related, they should not be confused with one another. One has to do with the epistemic status of a *proposition*, the other with the epistemic status of a *belief* (that is, a belief state). The reason for keeping them distinct will become clear immediately below.

1.2. Causal and evidential overdetermination

We can say that an event or state is *causally overdetermined* **iff** it has at least two actual causes each of which, in the actual circumstances, acted as a sufficient cause to produce that state or event.[11] For example, it *might* be thought that two forces, each sufficient to move an object, can overdetermine that it moves, or it *might* be thought that turning on both the hot and cold water

---

[10] There are at least two reasons that this is not an equivalence. First, the belief that e must have some epistemic status in order for it to be able to render the belief that h doxastically justified. Second, since propositional justification is defeasible, we would have to add a clause requiring that S's beliefs contain no overriding propositions of the justification of h by e. There might be other necessary additions to the consequent in order to make it strong enough to entail the antecedent. Exactly what those additions are and how to address the impending possible regress are issues that I will discuss briefly at points in the chapter, but, for our primary purpose—namely, determining the role that useful falsehoods play in the production of knowledge—it will suffice to note the entailment. That there is such an entailment, I think is not contentious.

[11] It is important to distinguish causal overdetermination from causal pre-emption. The proposed definition is designed to do that.

valves overdetermines that water flows from the faucet.[12] On the other hand, propositions cannot be causally overdetermined, because they are not the kind of thing to be caused at all. Beliefs, however, are caused, and, hence, they are the kind of thing that might be causally overdetermined.

Whether there are any genuine cases of causal overdetermination is a contentious matter.[13] For the sake of my argument, I will grant that there can be such cases. Permitting beliefs to be causally overdetermined makes my task much harder. For, as we will soon see, if beliefs cannot be causally overdetermined, then previous attempts to characterize the role that false beliefs play in producing knowledge are *obviously* mistaken. I will argue that those previous characterizations, which implicitly presuppose that beliefs can be causally overdetermined, are mistaken about the role false beliefs can play in the acquisition of knowledge even if there are instances in which beliefs are causally overdetermined.

We can say that a proposition, *p*, is *evidentially overdetermined* for S **iff** there exist at least two independent evidence bases available to S each of which is sufficient propositionally to justify *p*.

That there are cases of evidential overdetermination is uncontroversial. The proposition that someone is at the party can be justified by two truth-functionally independent propositions—for example, *Anne is at the party* and *Peter is at the party*. This is a case in which the evidential base consists of two propositions each of which *entails* the propositionally justified proposition. But it is also easy to construct cases in which there are two independent evidential bases each of which contains sufficient, but not entailing, evidence to justify a proposition.

Suppose I want to know whether the Yankees won the baseball game today. I ask someone who attended the game, and she says that they won. Later I read in the sports pages that the Yankees won. In such a case, although having two pieces of evidence might increase the degree of propositional justification, each piece of evidence is sufficient propositionally to justify (to the degree required

[12] Thanks to Ernest Sosa for the water-flowing example.

[13] See Martin Bunzl, "Causal Overdetermination", *Journal of Philosophy*, 76 (1979), 134–50. Bunzl argues that there are no genuine instances of causal overdetermination and that all supposed instances are actually instances of something else—for example, evidential overdetermination or causal pre-emption. But see Douglas Ehring, "Bunzl on Causal Overdetermination", *Philosophical Studies*, 39 (1981), 209–10, for a response to Bunzl including a supposed example of overdetermination.

by knowledge) the claim that the Yankees won. If one were to hold that only the combination of the two pieces of evidence provides an adequate evidential base propositionally to justify that the Yankees won, just change the example so that two people who attended the game tell me that the Yankees won and two newspapers independently report that the Yankees won.

1.3. Knowledge

Although this is not the place to present a full discussion of the analysis of knowledge, some brief comments are necessary if we are to determine how false beliefs can play an essential role in its production. I do not expect these comments to convince anyone that my account of knowledge as true, genuinely undefeated, justified belief is correct in all aspects. I have developed and defended it in other places.[14, 15] For the purposes of this chapter, it is sufficient to take that account as a working hypothesis in order to see how it should be amended in the light of the existence of useful falsehoods.

The basic intuition that informs the defeasibility account of knowledge is that S's doxastically justified, true belief falls short of being knowledge if S felicitously acquired the true belief on the basis of part of the relevant evidence when some other part of the evidence, if combined with the evidence S did acquire, defeats the justification. S is lucky to have acquired the evidence that led her to the truth, for she could have acquired that very evidence along with further evidence that together would not have led her to the truth.

Since our concern is with the role that false beliefs can play in the production of knowledge, we can confine our discussion primarily to inferential knowledge.[16] Although an important revision of this definition will be required after

[14] See my "A Proposed Definition of Propositional Knowledge", *Journal of Philosophy*, 67/16 (1971), 471–82; *Certainty* (Minneapolis: University of Minnesota Press, 1981), esp. 137–66; "Knowledge, Causality and Defeasibility", *Journal of Philosophy*, 73/20 (1976), 792–812; "Warrant, Proper Function, Reliabilism and Defeasibility", in Jonathan Kvanvig (ed.), *Warrant and Contemporary Epistemology* (New York: Rowman & Littlefield, 1996), 97–130; and more recently "Knowledge is True, Non-defeated Justified Belief", in Steven Luper (ed.), *Essential Knowledge* (New York: Longman, 2004), 124–35. For a very similar view to my earlier proposals, please see Risto Hilpinen, "Knowledge and Justification", *Ajatus*, 33 (1971), 7–39.

[15] For a discussion of genuine and misleading defeaters, see the items listed in n. 14 and "Misleading 'Misleading Defeaters'", *Journal of Philosophy*, 76/7 (1979), 382–6; "Misleading Evidence and the Restoration of Justification", *Philosophical Studies*, 37 (1980), 81–9.

[16] Since I believe that all knowledge is inferential and that there is no such thing as basic knowledge (see n. 5), this definition would cover all instances of knowledge. But nothing in

we discuss useful falsehoods, here is the standard way to define inferential knowledge within the defeasibility theory of knowledge:

S *inferentially* knows that *h* **iff**:

(i) *h* is true.

(ii) S believes that *h*.

(iii) S's belief that *h* is inferred (directly or indirectly) from and doxastically justified (directly or indirectly) by another belief, say the belief that *e*, which is doxastically justified.[17]

(iv) There is no genuine defeater of the propositional justification of any of the propositions in the evidential path up to and including *e*, and there is no genuine defeater of the propositional justification of any proposition between *e* and *h*.

I should note that condition (iii) does not itself lead to an infinite regress of doxastically justified beliefs. It is consistent with foundationalism because some beliefs could be doxastically justified but not caused by other beliefs. For example, beliefs that arose as a result of a perception or a memory could be doxastically justified. Condition (iii) is also consistent with coherentism of various sorts, since nothing in condition (iii) prevents mutual causation (as teepee poles are mutually causally responsible for each other's remaining

---

this chapter depends on that controversial claim. Further, throughout the chapter I employ, at least implicitly, a foundationalist picture of propositional and doxastic justification in which the propositions inherit their justificatory status from other propositions or proposition-like entities, and the beliefs inherit their justificatory status from other beliefs or belief-like mental states. My own view is that the inheritance view of justification is mistaken, and that (i) propositional justification exists only when there is an infinite chain of non-repeating propositions that are reasons for the given proposition, and (ii) S's belief reaches the required degree of doxastic justification when S has traced those reasons back far enough. (See the papers mentioned in n. 5, especially "Response to Ginet" and "How to be an Infinitist about Doxastic Justification".) But the inheritance view of justification is so familiar and so widely accepted that, for the purposes of this chapter, it seemed best to explicate both propositional and doxastic justification employing it.

[17] Some might think that the belief that *e* need not rise to the level of doxastic justification. On this view, a set of beliefs with some positive degree of doxastic plausibility (but not as high as the level required for justification) can, coupled with the fact that the set is coherent, gain additional positive degrees of epistemic warrant. A kind of bootstrapping might occur. (See, e.g. Roderick Chisholm, *Theory of Knowledge* (Englewood Cliffs, NJ: Prentice-Hall, 1966), especially 53–4.) If so, they could rewrite condition (iii) as follows: S's belief that *h* is inferred from and doxastically justified by another belief, say the belief that *e*, which has the appropriate degree of doxastic warrant. In the interests of full disclosure, I should point out that I think that even this revised condition is too strong for the reasons mentioned in n. 16.

erect). Finally, condition (iii) is consistent with infinitism, since it does not rule out an infinite, non-repeating series of beliefs, each such that it is justified only if some other belief is doxastically justified.

Further, if someone were to hold that a doxastically justified belief could causally depend upon another belief that was not itself doxastically justified, as some coherentists, foundationalists, and infinitists might, condition (iii) could be modified appropriately. I think it will be granted that the belief having *e* as its content must have some positive justificatory status if it is to provide the inferential basis for and doxastically justify the belief that *h*.[18] For example, we could replace "doxastically justified" with "doxastically plausible" in condition (iii) if someone were to hold that in order for the belief that *h* to be doxastically justified by the belief that *e* we need require only that the belief that *e* rise to the level of doxastic plausibility (that is, some positive level of epistemic entitlement lower than justification). For the purposes of this

[18] Ernest Sosa has suggested a possible exception to this claim. Suppose that S is not at all doxastically justified in believing that *p* (B*p*), but is doxastically justified in believing that he or she believes that *p* (BB*p*). Is not this a case where B*p* is not doxastically justified but it is a belief that doxastically justifies BB*p*? The answer is that although B*p* is not doxastically justified and BB*p* is doxastically justified (if one takes introspection to be a reliable indicator of one's beliefs), what doxastically justifies BB*p* is not B*p* but rather S's introspection of his or her beliefs. So, this is not a case in which a doxastically justified belief is *inferred* from another belief that is not doxastically justified. The doxastically justified belief (BB*p*) is produced or caused by the introspection. I take it that introspections, like memories and perceptions, are not themselves beliefs—although they typically give rise to beliefs and they do have propositional, or what I have called "propositional-like", content (see n. 4). I think they are not themselves beliefs because it strikes me as logically possible for S to introspect *x* and not believe that *x*—if, for example, S has no confidence whatsoever in his or her powers of introspection. Of course, non-doxastic mental states like introspections, memories, and perceptions as opposed to, say, wishful thinkings, can confer some positive doxastic status on beliefs that they cause, and for which they provide the inferential basis. If S believes that *x* because S infers that *x* from his or her memory that *x*, then, *ceteris paribus*, S's belief that *x* has some positive doxastic justificatory status because memories have a positive, but defeasible, epistemic status. Whereas, if S believes that *y* on the basis of an inference from his or her wish that *y*, then, *ceteris paribus*, S's belief that *y* has no positive doxastic justificatory status.

Nevertheless, since "belief" is so elastic, I could imagine someone insisting that introspection is enough like a typical belief so that it should be counted as a belief. But the general claim would still remain true because BB*p* is inferred from and is doxastically justified by the introspection that B*p* (which is now considered to be a belief). The introspection that B*p* now being taken to itself be a belief does not provide an exception to the general claim since introspection is not a form of inference. Even if the introspection that *p* were a doxastically justified belief, S does not infer it from the totally unjustified B*p*.

chapter we can stipulate that the appropriate degree of entitlement is doxastic justification in both this definition of inferential knowledge and the account of useful falsehoods I present later. Nothing crucial depends upon the level of entitlement that is required.

A word or two about defeaters. Suppose that there is a chain of justifiers from e to h : e justifies e_1, e_1 justifies e_2, e_2 justifies e_3, . . . e_n justifies h.[19] A defeater, d, of the propositional justification of h by e is a true proposition that is such that either (1) the conjunction of d with any proposition that precedes h in the chain fails to justify its immediately succeeding link in the chain to h or (2) d renders plausible some other proposition, d_1, and d_1 renders plausible d_2, and d_2 renders plausible d_3, . . . and d_{n-1} renders plausible d_n, and the conjunction of d_n with any proposition that precedes h in the chain fails to justify its immediately succeeding link in the chain to h. That is, a defeater can defeat directly or it can do so indirectly through a series of propositions each of which is rendered plausible by a previous member in the series. All defeaters are true, but some of them defeat only by initiating a series of rendered-plausible propositions that contains at least one false proposition. Defeaters that depend on false propositions in order to defeat are "misleading defeaters". Genuine defeaters employ only the truth to defeat. For example, in the so-called misleading Grabit Case, S has good evidence that Tom Grabit stole a book. In fact, Tom stole it. But Mrs Grabit (Tom's mother) says, apparently sincerely, that not Tom, but his identical twin, John, stole the book. The proposition *Mrs Grabit said, apparently sincerely, that John was the thief* is a defeater. However, if what she said is false and there is no twin, that proposition is a misleading defeater, because it defeats only by rendering plausible the false proposition that John stole the book. On the other hand, if there really is a twin who stole the book, then *Mrs Grabit said, apparently sincerely, that John was the thief* is a genuine defeater.[20] The distinction between misleading and genuine defeaters will be

---

[19] In other places I have defended the view that the chain of justifiers is infinite. The account here would have to be modified slightly to account for the chain being infinitely long. (See n. 5.)

[20] Of course, there can be more than one genuine defeater. In the non-misleading Grabit Case, *Tom did not steal the book* is the most obvious genuine defeater of whatever propositionally justifies *Tom stole the book*. Thus, the defeasibility account can insure the tight connection between warrant and truth, if "warrant" is taken to be whatever must be added to true belief to raise it to the level of knowledge. To generalize, if the propositional justification of h has no genuine defeaters, h must be true (because $\sim h$ is a genuine defeater). Thus, there is an answer available to Linda Zagzebski's worry about the ubiquity of the Gettier problem presented in her "The Inescapability of the Gettier Problem", *Philosophical Quarterly*, 44 (1994), 65–73.

important when we "test" my account of the role that useful falsehoods play in producing knowledge.

2. Setting the stage: A brief review of the Gettier Problem

There are two ways of viewing the Gettier Problem. The first focuses on the two principles upon which it depends; and the second focuses on some specific cases that illustrate a consequence of accepting the principles. Both perspectives can help us understand the issues surrounding useful falsehoods.

Gettier's principles are these:

III	Fallibilism	A person, S, can be doxastically justified in believing a proposition, p, and p can be false.
IV	Closure	If a person, S, is doxastically justified in believing a proposition, p, and p entails q, and S comes to believe that q on the basis of deducing it from p, then S is doxastically justified in believing that q.

Since a false proposition can entail a true proposition, the combination of the two principles leads to a recipe for constructing any number of counterexamples to knowledge construed as mere doxastically justified, true belief. Just locate a true, doxastically justified belief that S has inferred from a false, doxastically justified belief. In every such case, it might seem appropriate to claim that S will have a doxastically justified, true belief that will not be knowledge. S cannot gain knowledge on the basis of a false belief. Or so it might seem.

A typical Gettier Case might help to reinforce that unfounded intuition: the Havit/Nogot Case.[21]

Nogot, Havit and I are classmates. I see Nogot driving a Ford, I watch him park it in his garage, and I hear him tell me that he owns the Ford. So, I come to believe that Nogot owns a Ford, and I deduce that someone in the class owns a Ford. Suppose that someone in the class does own a Ford, but

---

[21] I think Keith Lehrer was the first to use this example in "Knowledge, Truth and Evidence", *Analysis*, 25 (1965), 168–75.

that it is not Nogot. The owner of the Ford is Havit, about whom I have no beliefs whatsoever concerning what automobiles, if any, he owns.

Even though the belief that someone in the class owns a Ford is doxastically justified and true, it is not knowledge. In such a case, I do not have knowledge; I arrived at the truth only by a lucky break. I was lucky to arrive at the truth because there is a genuine defeater of my justification—namely, *Nogot does not own a Ford.*

It might seem, then, that any belief that is doxastically justified by a false belief cannot be knowledge. But that would be a hasty generalization. Even though the Havit/Nogot Case is a clear case of the felicitous coincidence of a doxastically justified belief and a true belief (and hence is not a case of knowledge), the conjunction of the Fallibilism Principle and the Closure Principle does not entail that *all* true, doxastically justified beliefs deduced from a doxastically justified, false belief fall short of knowledge. There still could be cases in which a false belief provides an adequate basis for knowledge.

3. Examples and preliminary discussion of useful falsehoods

Although Gettier showed only that *some* doxastically justified, true beliefs fall short of knowledge, are there really any cases in which S arrives at knowledge that *p*, as a result of inferring *p* from a false belief? Here are four such cases.[22]

A   The Appointment Case. On the basis of my apparent memory, I believe that my secretary told me on Friday that I have an appointment on Monday with a student. From that belief, I infer that I do have an appointment on Monday. Suppose, further, that I do have an appointment on Monday, and that my secretary told me so. But she told me that on Thursday, not on Friday. I know that I have such an appointment even though I inferred my belief from the false proposition that my secretary told me on Friday that I have an appointment on Monday.

---

[22] Risto Hilpinen has given several other examples of what I call useful falsehoods; see "Knowledge and Conditionals", in J. E. Tomberlin (ed.), *Philosophical Perspectives*, 2 (1988), 157–82, esp. 163–4.

B   The Santa Claus Case. Mom and Dad tell young Virginia that Santa will put some presents under the tree on Christmas Eve. Believing what her parents told her, she infers that there will be presents under the tree on Christmas morning. She knows that.

C   The Average Rainfall Case. Weatherman believes that the average annual precipitation in Northwest Montana is about 13 inches because he believes that accurate records have been kept for over eighty years and the rainfall depicted in the number of years that records were kept averages to 13 inches. The average rainfall is about 13 inches, but accurate records were kept for only seventy-nine years. Weatherman knows that the average rainfall is about 13 inches.[23]

D   The Ptolemaic Astronomer Case. The date is 2 September 1203; the place is Oxford University. An astronomy class is in session and the instructor, one of the most noted Ptolemaic astronomers of the thirteenth century, is showing students how to calculate the relative positions of the sun and planets both backward and forward in time using the deferent and epicycle orbits of those bodies and their (then) current positions. After carefully explaining the method, he asks the students to determine whether Mars will be visible from the earth 800 years later, supposing, of course, that it is not cloudy that night, that both the Earth and Mars still exist, and so on. The students enter the (then) current relative positions of the Sun, Mars, and Earth as they believe them to be according to Ptolemaic astronomy and then they extrapolate using the method they have just learned. They conclude that, *ceteris paribus*, Mars will be visible on 2 September 2003. On the assumption that the assigned orbits and then-current relative positions of the three bodies allow for sufficiently accurate extrapolations, the students know that Mars will be visible on 2 September 2003, even though their beliefs are based on false beliefs about the fixed position of the Earth and the orbits of the Sun and Mars.

Some of these four cases might more obviously be instances of useful falsehoods leading to knowledge than others. But each of them is such that

---

[23] This case is similar to one presented by Risto Hilpinen in "Knowledge and Conditionals", 163–4, and it is similar to the one presented by John Turk Saunders and Narayan Champawat in "Mr Clark's Definition of 'Knowledge' ", in *Analysis*, 25/1 (1964), 8–9. I think the Saunders and Champawat article is the first contemporary mention of the role of false beliefs in the production of knowledge. However, they do not discuss the case or its significance in any detail.

it is plausible to believe that at least some people will take it to be a case of a false belief producing knowledge. Near the end of this chapter, I will suggest that a test of the correct account of useful falsehoods is that it can explain varying intuitions that might arise when considering whether to classify these and other cases as knowledge.

All these cases have three relatively obvious features in common:

1. The two extant "rival" theories of knowledge—that is, the defeasibility theory and reliabilism, do not have straightforward ways of accounting for these cases.[24] *First*, the defeasibility theory takes inferential knowledge that *h* based on *e* to obtain only if there are no genuine defeaters of the propositional justification of *h* by *e*. But that account runs afoul of the problem of useful falsehoods because there is a genuine defeater of the justification in each of the four cases—namely, the denial of the useful falsehood. For, if some false belief that *e* doxastically justifies S in believing that *h*, then, since $\sim e$ is true, there is a genuine defeater ($\sim e$) of the propositional justification of *h* by *e* because the conjunction (*e* and $\sim e$) fails to justify *h* (since it cannot justify anything).[25]

---

[24] I do not take these to be genuine rivals because *(the belief that h arose in some fashion F in context C) & F is not a reliable process in C* is, if true, a genuine defeater of the justification of *h*. Thus, reliabilist intuitions can be captured by the defeasibility theory *without incurring the generality problem* because no general account of reliable processes is required by the defeasibility theory. All that is required is to fill in a particular description of *F* to specify the defeater.

[25] Claudio de Almeida, in a paper entitled "Benign Falsehoods: A Lesson about Inferential Knowledge", given at the Central States Philosophical Association, Chicago, October 2003, presented an account of useful falsehoods that employs the assets of defeasibility theory. Here is his suggestion using the terminology developed in this chapter:

b is a useful falsehood in producing S's knowledge that *h* iff :

1 *b* is false, and the belief that *b* doxastically justifies the belief that *h*.
2 There is a true proposition, b_1, such that *b* renders b_1 somewhat plausible—even if very weakly so.
3 S believes (at least dispositionally) that b_1.
4 No proposition that is incompatble with *b* is a genuine defeater of the justification of b_1.

If I've understood the suggestion correctly and correctly stated it in the terminology employed in this chapter, I think the proposal excludes too many useful falsehoods—indeed, I think it excludes them all. First, though, two general comments about his proposal: (1) This proposal is similar in many ways to the structure of the proposal in this chapter, in part, because de Almeida's proposal was designed to correct my account of useful falsehoods presented at a conference at the Pontifical Catholic University in Porto Alegre, Brazil, in 1999; (2) I wish that his account were correct because it is a much more elegant solution than the one I am present-ing here.

Hence, the defeasibility theory is too strong. It will rule out all cases in which a false belief doxastically justifies another belief.[26]

Second, the four cases of useful falsehoods point to a particularly virulent instance of the generality problem for reliabilism.[27] In these cases, a false belief plays an essential causal role in producing the cognition, so the problem for reliabilists is to specify in some *general* way the conditions in which false beliefs can reliably bring about knowledge. Reliabilists can employ subjunctive

But, for the reason just cited in the text, I do not think this proposal will succeed because $\sim b$ is a genuine defeater of the justification of h, and it is a genuine defeater of the justification (however weak) of b_1. If that is correct, it makes this suggestion too strong because it rules out all cases of useful falsehoods. To see that, consider the Santa Claus Case:

b Santa will put a present under the tree on Christmas Eve.
b_1 Either Santa or someone will put a present under the tree on Christmas Eve.
h There will be a present under the tree on Christmas morning.

Now, $\sim b$ is a proposition incompatible with b and it is a genuine defeater of the justification of b_1, since, according to his account, the proposition that justifies b_1 is nothing other than b, and, as we have seen, since $\sim b$ is true and such that the conjunction (b & $\sim b$) fails to justify (or even render weakly plausible) b_1.

I think the only possible response here would be to claim that $\sim b$ is not a genuine defeater of the justification of b_1. But the result of accepting that response is that we would, then, have to say that S has knowledge based upon a useful falsehood in some standard Gettier Cases. Consider the following values:

b Nogot owns a Ford
b_1 Either Nogot owns a Ford or Havit owns a Ford
h Someone in the class owns a Ford

If $\sim b$ were not a genuine defeater of S's justification for b_1, then S could arrive at knowledge that someone in the class owns a Ford on the basis of the false belief that Nogot owns a Ford.

[26] This is not just a problem for my particular way of stating the defeasibility theory. Consider Keith Lehrer's version. Lehrer asks us to consider the "verific alternative" to S's actual doxastic system. Over the years, Lehrer has modified the way in which that alternative system is characterized, but one constant is that all the false beliefs in that system are first removed, and then one determines what S is still justified in believing. But, since the useful falsehoods will be removed, there will remain no justification for believing what was based upon the falsehood—*unless there is another belief that provides such a basis*. I will argue shortly that there is no guarantee that there is a true belief that provides such a basis. Hence, whenever there is no such true belief, S would fail to know. See Lehrer, *Knowledge*, 224 ff., and Chisholm, *Theory of Knowledge* (2nd edn.; Boulder and San Francisco: Westview Press, 2000), 169–75. Robert Shope makes this point regarding Lehrer's defeasibility analysis in his "Conditions and Analyses of Knowing", in Paul Moser (ed.), *The Oxford Handbook of Epistemology* (Oxford and New York: Oxford University Press, 2002), 46.

[27] For a discussion of the generality problem, see Earl Conee and Richard Feldman, "Internalism Defended", *American Philosophical Quarterly*, 38 (2001), 1–18.

conditionals of the form: If S were to have used a true belief, *t*, that can be characterized in some way, *W*, in order to reach the belief that *h*, then the process would have been an instance of a reliable one. For example, as I will soon argue, in each of the four cases, there is a true proposition, *t*, entailed by the useful falsehood that is such that, had S employed the belief that *t* to reach the belief that *h*, then S would have employed a reliable process. But the force of the generality problem in this instance is that the useful falsehood entails many true propositions—an infinite number in fact—and only some of them are such that, had S used them, S would have gained knowledge. For example, in the Appointment Case, the false proposition *my secretary told me on Friday that I have an appointment on Monday* entails both of the following true propositions: *my secretary told me that I have an appointment on Monday*, and *either my secretary told me on Friday that I have an appointment on Monday or 1 is a number*. Only the former true proposition justifies the proposition *I have an appointment on Monday*. Thus, the problem for reliabilism is to develop some characterization, *W*, of the true propositions entailed by the useful falsehood such that S's doxastic justification of the cognition depends on just those true propositions that satisfy *W*. To anticipate a bit: I will offer such a characterization below and, even though the characterization I will offer makes use of the normative notion of propositional justification, I will show how a reliabilist can adopt that characterization. In other words, my proposal should be acceptable to both defeasibility theorists and reliabilists. I take that to be a point in favor of it.

2. General skeptical worries aside, in all of the cases of useful falsehoods, knowledge is obtained even though some of the beliefs on which the cognition was *causally* based contain false propositions.[28] The false propositions in the cases are:

Case A   My secretary told me on Friday that I have an appointment on Monday.

Case B   Santa Claus will put presents under the tree on Christmas Eve.

Case C   Accurate rainfall records were kept for over eighty years and the rainfall depicted in the number of years that records were kept averages to 13 inches.

Case D   The Sun and Mars orbit the Earth as depicted in Ptolemaic Astronomy.

---

[28] From now on, I will speak of "false beliefs" when I mean to be referring to beliefs whose content is false.

The qualification that we are here ignoring general skeptical worries is important. Those worries are serious.[29] But I can set them aside here because they would apply to cases in which *all* the beliefs employed in acquiring the further beliefs are true (the skeptical worry is whether the further beliefs rise to the level of knowledge). Hence, those worries are not directly relevant to the issue at hand—namely: how can false beliefs produce knowledge?

3. A false belief plays an essential causal role in producing knowledge in each of the cases. That is, if the false belief were simply removed from the actual causal chain that resulted in knowledge, no causal chain resulting in the cognition would remain. This fact is crucial to understanding what I take to be the central issue because, although some epistemologists have noted that false beliefs could play a role in the production of knowledge, they take those false beliefs to be inessential. Keith Lehrer considers a variation on the Havit/Nogot Case (call it *the harmless falsehood Havit/Nogot Case*) that we can put as follows:

> Suppose that I am doxastically justified in believing that Havit owns a Ford (which is true) and also justified in believing that Nogot owns a Ford (which is false). On the basis of those two beliefs, I infer, and thereby come to know, that someone in the class owns a Ford.

In this case, Lehrer says, "though *part* [emphasis added] of what justifies me in accepting that at least one person owns a Ford is my false belief that Mr Nogot owns a Ford, I have a justification that does not depend upon my false belief".[30] After presenting a similar case, Alvin Goldman writes that this is "a sort of case in which one of S's grounds for p may be false without preventing him from knowing that p . . . [because] the false proposition is a dispensable background assumption".[31] Gilbert Harman puts the point succinctly when he writes that

---

[29] I have tried to take skepticism seriously in the following: "Skepticism and Closure: Why the Evil Genius Argument Fails"; "Skepticism", in Moser (ed.), *The Oxford Handbook of Epistemology*, 336–61; "How a Pyrrhonian Skeptic Might Respond to Academic Skepticism", in Steven Luper (ed.), *The Skeptics: Contemporary Essays* (Aldershot: Ashgate Press, 2003), 75–94; "There is No Good Reason to be an Academic Skeptic", in Steven Luper (ed.), *Essential Knowledge* (New York: Longman, 2004), 299–309; "Skepticism: Ascent and Assent?" in John Greco (ed.), *Ernest Sosa and his Critics* (Oxford: Blackwell, 2004), 112–25.

[30] Lehrer, *Theory Of Knowledge*, 157. I changed the make of the automobile from what Lehrer used—a Ferrari—to a Ford in order to make the case more intuitively accessible to us poor philosophers!

[31] Goldman, "A Causal Theory of Knowing", *Journal of Philosophy*, 64/12 (1967), 368.

"reasoning that essentially involves false conclusions, intermediate or final, cannot give one knowledge".[32]

Indeed, the generally received opinion among epistemologists is that a false belief can play a causal role in producing knowledge only when those false beliefs are benign or "harmless" (to use Lehrer's term).[33] Put another way, the claim is that, so long as "enough" true beliefs are contained in the causal ancestry of the known proposition, the false beliefs can be considered as inessential or harmless because the known proposition is both *propositionally* justified by enough true propositions (of the proper sort) and the belief is *doxastically* justified because it is appropriately caused by enough true beliefs (of the proper sort).

To use our terminology, in the harmless falsehood Havit/Nogot Case the cognition is held to be both evidentially and causally overdetermined. The true proposition (*Havit owns a Ford*) and the false proposition (*Nogot owns a Ford*) each separately fully justifies the known proposition that someone in the class owns a Ford, and, further, both the true and the false belief are sufficient causes in the actual causal chain that results in the cognition.

I am willing to grant for the sake of the argument in this chapter that there are cases of harmless falsehoods even though I am far from certain that there are any such cases. Although there are clear cases of evidential overdetermination, it is not clear that these cases are also cases of causally overdetermined beliefs. In the case just considered, S's belief, o, that someone in the class owns a Ford, would be causally overdetermined by the belief, n, that Nogot owns a Ford and by the belief that h, that Havit owns a Ford only if (1) both the belief that n and the belief that h actually contributed to the causal production of S's belief that o, and (2) both the belief that n and the belief that h actually acted as independently sufficient causes to bring about S's belief that o.

I can imagine how to fulfill condition 1. Just consider some S such that both the belief that n and the belief that h actually contribute causally to the belief that o. Such an S would be an *extremely* cautious epistemic agent, perhaps bordering on epistemic cowardice, who, in general, is so afraid of coming to believe something that, in order to believe that o, he or she must have two beliefs such that the propositional content of each entails o. S would be so

---

[32] Harman, *Thought*, 120.
[33] Lehrer refers to them as "harmless" errors in *Knowledge*, 219.

constituted that in this case were he or she to lack the belief that Nogot owns a Ford, he or she would not believe that someone in the class owns a Ford. But, then, this would not be a case of causal overdetermination since condition 2 is not fulfilled. For if the false belief that Nogot owns a Ford were simply dropped from the set of S's beliefs, our overly cautious S would no longer believe that someone in the class owns a Ford.

Perhaps there is a way to construct a completely clear case involving harmless false beliefs that bring about knowledge, but I do not see how to do it. Nevertheless, even if there were such cases, those false beliefs would not be at all useful in producing knowledge precisely because they could be eliminated from among the causes of the cognition, and S's knowledge would remain intact (because a true belief is still acting as a sufficient cause of the cognition). *Our* target here is false beliefs that are essential to the production of knowledge. Harmless falsehoods, if there were any, would be epistemic danglers precisely because, if they were simply removed from the cause of the cognition, the cognition would remain (because, supposedly, the cognition is causally overdetermined). But, if we simply drop the false belief in the four cases of useful falsehoods, there might not be a true belief that S already has (either occurrently or dispositionally) that is capable of causing and justifying S's cognition.

Someone might object that the false proposition in each of the four cases is equivalent to a conjunction one of whose conjuncts is the false proposition itself and the other conjunct is both true and sufficient propositionally to justify the known proposition. Those equivalences are:

Case A *My secretary told me on Friday that I have an appointment on Monday* ≡ [(*My secretary told me on Friday that I have an appointment on Monday*) & (*My secretary told me that I have an appointment on Monday*)]

Case B *Santa will put a present under the tree on Christmas Eve* ≡ [(*Santa will put a present under the tree on Christmas Eve*) & (*Someone will put a present under the tree on Christmas Eve*)]

Case C *Accurate annual rainfall records were kept for over eighty years and the rainfall depicted in the number of years that records were kept averages 13 inches* ≡ [(*Accurate annual rainfall records were kept for over eighty years and the rainfall depicted in the number of years that records were kept averages 13 inches*) & (*Accurate annual rainfall records were kept for seventy-nine years and the rainfall so depicted averages to 13 inches*)]

Case D   *The Sun and Mars orbit the Earth as depicted in Ptolemaic astronomy* ≡ [(*The Sun and Mars orbit the Earth as depicted in Ptolemaic astronomy*) & (*The relative positions of the Sun, Mars, and Earth are such that they repeat in a manner predictable just as if Ptolemaic astronomy were correct*)]

The false propositions are equivalent to these conjunctions simply because each equivalence is an instance of the general principle that if A → B, then A ≡ (A & B). That the instantiations of A and B are such that A entails B should be obvious. Further, in these cases the true conjunct, B, does propositionally justify the known proposition.[34]

Case A   *My secretary told me that I have an appointment on Monday* propositionally justifies *I have an appointment on Monday*.

Case B   *Someone will put a present under the tree on Christmas Eve* propositionally justifies *there will be a present under the tree on Christmas morning*.

Case C   *Accurate annual rainfall records were kept for seventy-nine years and the rainfall depicted in the number of years that records were kept averages 13 inches* propositionally justifies *the average annual rainfall is 13 inches*.

Case D   *The relative positions of the Sun, Mars, and Earth are such that they repeat in a predictable manner just as if Ptolemaic astronomy were correct* propositionally justifies *Mars will be visible on 2 September 2003*.

It could then be claimed that, since S believes the useful falsehood in each case, S would also believe the conjunction, and, hence, each conjunct. If so, then perhaps there is no crucial difference between a merely harmless falsehood and a useful falsehood. For, as we saw in the harmless falsehood Havit/Nogot Case, it could be claimed that **if** S believes two propositions and (i) one proposition (*Havit owns a Ford*) is true and sufficient propositionally to justify *someone in the class owns a Ford*, and (ii) the belief that someone in the class owns a Ford is doxastically justified by the belief that Havit owns a Ford, **then** the belief that Nogot owns a Ford is a harmless falsehood. There are two possible replies to this objection.

First, although it is true that the false proposition is equivalent to the conjunction in each of the four cases of useful falsehoods, there are well-known problems of substituting truth functionally equivalent propositions

[34] All these are defeasible justifications, and, strictly speaking, require a clause that refers to additional background beliefs. But listing all the background beliefs would needlessly complicate the exposition.

into belief contexts—for example, the Hesperus/Phosphorus Case. Hence, we cannot automatically assume that, if S believes a proposition that is equivalent to a conjunction, then S believes the conjunction. In addition, even in the most simple of cases, it seems to me that S could believe p but not believe that (p & p), because S either lacks the concept of conjunction or fails to deploy it. Finally, in some of the four cases, even though S has the false belief, S might either lack a concept required to reach the true belief or fail to deploy it. For example, Virginia could have the appropriate belief about Santa but lack the existentially generalized concept of "someone", or she might fail to deploy it; and the Ptolemaic astronomers could possibly lack the rather sophisticated concept of "as if", or they might fail to deploy it.

Nevertheless, I am willing to grant that, with some ingenious chisholming, the four conjuncts might be stated in a way such that one could plausibly claim that, necessarily, for any S, if S believed the false proposition, S would also believe the conjunction, and, hence, each of the conjuncts, while at the same time satisfying the constraint that the true conjunct be sufficient propositionally to justify the known proposition. Therefore, this reply to the objection is not absolutely compelling.

However, a *second* reply to the objection is irresistible. Recall that the objection seeks to show that the supposed cases of useful falsehoods are nothing but implicit cases of harmless falsehoods. In cases of harmless falsehoods, if one were to remove the false belief, a true belief would remain that in fact was actually acting as a sufficient cause of the cognition. But in the four cases of useful falsehoods, if the false belief were removed from S's belief set, there is no guarantee that the true belief would remain. Indeed, if believing the false proposition really is identical to believing each of the two conjuncts, then removing the false belief would result in removing the conjunction from S's belief set.

Further, there is an important evidential relationship between the false proposition and the true conjunct. To see that, consider the Appointment Case, and suppose that I no longer believe that my secretary told me *on Friday* that I have an appointment on Monday. There is no reason to suppose that I would still believe that she told me *on any day* that I had an appointment on Monday! I *might* still believe that. But I need not. It could very well be that I believe that she told me that I had an appointment on Monday *because* I believe that she told me that on Friday. Hence, if the false belief were simply removed, there is no reason to suppose that my belief set would still contain the belief that she told me that I have an appointment on Monday. In other words, even if one did believe each of the two conjuncts whenever one believed the conjunction, there is no guarantee that the true conjunct would remain if one removed the false conjunct. By way of contrast, in the harmless falsehood Havit/Nogot Case, the true belief does remain if one simply removes the false belief, because they are, so to speak, from the beginning residing independently of each other both evidentially and causally in S's belief set.

In the other three cases, it is even more clear that the evidential and causal relationships are such that, if the false belief were simply removed, the true conjunct might not remain. For example, in the Santa Claus Case, Virginia's belief that someone will put a present under the tree (if indeed she has that belief) seems causally dependent upon her belief that Santa will put a present under the tree. Thus, these are cases in which the causal process leading to knowledge involves the false belief essentially. Remove the false belief, and the causal basis on which the cognition actually depends is eliminated.[35]

---

[35] An anonymous referee has objected to my reply to this objection in the following way: "[The cases that Klein considers] concern the counterfactual situations in which the relevant false beliefs are removed. I agree that in those situations, the conjunctions that are (alleged to be) equivalent to the false beliefs might also be removed, in which case *ceteris paribus* the agent would have no chance of acquiring the knowledge that she does in fact acquire. But the objection does not concern any counterfactual situation; it makes no claims about what would or would not happen if the relevant false beliefs were to be removed. The objection maintains that, given that the agent holds the false belief in question, the agent will (therefore) believe a particular conjunction, one conjunct of which is false (and hence accounts for the falsity of the conjunction), and the other conjunct of which is true and sufficient to justify the known proposition. The objection has it, then, that the false conjunct—i.e., the conjunct that accounts for the falsity of the belief in question—plays no essential role in the acquisition of knowledge; there is in fact nothing false that plays an essential role in the acquisition of knowledge. To show that this objection fails, one must show that there is in fact something false that plays an essential role in the acquisition of knowledge (and I'm not at all sure that this can be shown; it seems to me that the objection is sound). Talk of counterfactual situations does nothing to show that the objection fails."

I agree that the issue concerns what is actually acting as a cause in these cases. I do not agree that "talk of counterfactual situations does nothing to show that the objection fails". It is certainly not in general true that "counterfactual situations" give us no basis for claiming what is a cause in the actual world. We often look to counterfactual situations in order to provide a basis for showing that something, c, is essential to the acquisition (causal production) of something else, say knowledge, k. For example, if one could show that in every near world in which c is removed, k does not occur, then there would be fairly good (but not conclusive) evidence that c was essential to the causal production of k. It is not conclusive evidence because, for example, c could be

We can conclude that, although there might be cases of harmless falsehoods, they cannot provide a basis for understanding cases of useful falsehoods. In cases of useful falsehoods, were the false belief simply removed from the causal chain that produced knowledge, there might not be another actually present causal chain that independently resulted in the cognition. Harmless falsehoods, if there are any, do no epistemic harm, but they do no any epistemic good either. Useful falsehoods do good.

Nevertheless, there are two important lessons to be learned from the unsuccessful attempt to reduce useful falsehoods to harmless falsehoods. First, in each of these cases of useful falsehoods, the false proposition entails a true proposition that is sufficient propositionally to justify the known proposition. Second, there are important evidential relationships among the relevant propositions that must be kept in mind.

4. The proposed characterization of useful falsehoods

In the four cases of useful falsehoods, S arrives at knowledge because, although the false belief produces the cognition (that is, the false belief doxastically justifies the cognition), there is a true proposition that is *closely related*, to the false one, which is such that it propositionally justifies the known proposition, and, were S to have believed it, S could have employed that belief doxastically to justify the cognition. Hilpinen puts the point as follows: "a person can know things not only on the basis of (valid) inference from what he or she knows, but in some cases even on the basis of inference from what is not known (or even

---

an epiphenomenon accompanying the actual cause. But, in the cases we are considering, *c*, the false belief, cannot be an epiphenomenon precisely because it is alleged by the objection to be *identical* to the real cause—namely, the conjunctive belief. So, if the false belief were removed, the conjunctive belief could not remain and *k* would not arise because the "real" cause is not present.

The objection depends upon it being the case that the false belief is identical to the conjunctive belief. I suggested a reason for denying that, namely that S might have the false belief but lack a concept required to form the conjunctive belief or fail to deploy it. But, putting that aside, the point of the chapter is that the correct understanding of knowledge includes recognizing that knowledge can arise on the basis of false beliefs. Whether it actually ever happens is an empirical matter. I can only (and need only) claim that the four cases are easily imaginable—for, if so, they reveal something interesting about the role false beliefs can play in the production of knowledge.

true) provided that the latter (evidential) propositions are *sufficiently close to the truth*, (emphasis added)."[36] Here is my suggestion for capturing that intuition:

> The belief that *uf* is a useful falsehood to S (for acquiring knowledge that *h*) by producing a doxastically justified belief that *h* **iff**:[37]

1. *uf* is false.
2. The belief that *uf* is doxastically justified for S.
3. The belief that *uf* is essential in the causal production of the belief that *h*.
4. *uf* propositionally justifies *h*.[38]
5. *uf* entails a true proposition, *t*.[39]
6. *t* propositionally justifies *h*.
7. Whatever doxastically justifies the belief that *uf* for S also propositionally justifies *t* for S.[40]

---

[36] Risto Hilpinen, "Knowledge and Conditionals", 164. Hilpinen's work on this topic was called to my attention by Robert Shope in a portion of a manuscript of his that he emailed to me in June 2001. In that manuscript, commenting on the cases that Hilpinen discusses, Shope says the following: "I am not presently in a position to clarify this way of being reasonably close. But neither has Hilpinen done so. I presume that I shall some day avail myself of whatever progress epistemologists make on that issue . . . Of course, this must await a clarification of being 'reasonably close'." I hope this chapter is a first step in accomplishing what Shope called for.

[37] The reason for the parenthetical qualification is to underscore that I am interested in falsehoods that are useful for acquiring knowledge by producing a doxastically justified belief. They could be useful for other purposes. For example, suppose that I were paid $25 for each doxastically justified, false belief I acquired. Such doxastically justified, false beliefs might be useful for the purpose of acquiring money rather than being useful for the sake of acquiring knowledge.

[38] I am using "justify" here to mean "justifies overall" so that, if *e* justifies *h* for S, then there is no other proposition contained or represented in S's belief set that overrides the justification of *h* by *e* for S. I could have defined a weaker notion, e.g., "*uf* contributes to the justification of *h*" but doing so would needlessly complicate the account. It should be kept in mind, however, that *uf* could be a conjunction, each conjunct of which contributes to the justification. If one of those conjuncts is false, *uf* is false, but *uf* would imply a true conjunction (simply remove the false conjunct) and, if the resulting conjunction, *t*, satisfies the other constraints in the definition of a useful falsehood, *uf* would be a useful falsehood. It is not a harmless falsehood if the belief that *uf*, rather than the belief that *t*, actually caused the belief that *h*. If one removed the belief that *uf* from S's belief set, there is no guarantee that *t* would remain.

[39] The entailment must be a form of relevant entailment, otherwise *t* could be a necessary truth that could be known on the basis of a false proposition.

[40] It should be understood that the propositional justifications referred to in conditions 4, 6, and 7 might all have intermediate steps. That is represented by the dotted lines in the diagram depicting the branching justificational paths.

This definition does not yet fully explicate the role of false beliefs in the production of *knowledge* since I am concerned at this point only with the so-called third condition in the analysis of knowledge: the doxastic justification condition. The definition is intended to explicate only the conditions under which a false belief can produce a belief that is "held for the right reasons"—reasons that, *in some cases*, are sufficient to bring about knowledge. A central notion is that, even though *uf* is false, it is "close enough to the truth", so that, if believing *uf* causes S to believe that *h*, then, *ceteris paribus*, S knows that *h*. Although I argued earlier that ∼*uf* is a genuine defeater of the propositional justification of *h* by *uf*, the primary goal of my account of useful falsehoods is to specify a closely related path of propositions that has the potential of not being defeated. That useful path branches just before *uf*, and it continues to *h*. Where *x* is whatever doxastically justifies *uf*, that path looks like this:

$$x \begin{cases} t \ldots h \\ uf \ldots h \end{cases}$$

As just mentioned, there will be a genuine defeater of the path *x*−*uf*−*h* at the *uf*-step, but there might not be a genuine defeater at *any* step on the path *x*−*t*−*h*. The path *x*−*t*−*h* is the path not taken, but in this case its mere existence makes it possible for S to acquire knowledge by having taken the other, defeated path. Indeed, as we will see, all that is required to complete the task of explicating the role that false beliefs play in the producing *knowledge* is to flesh out the *ceteris paribus* clause by requiring that there be no genuine defeater of the evidence path from *x* to *h* that goes through *t*.

The standard defeasibility analysis of knowledge does not allow for the possibility of useful falsehoods in producing knowledge because the standard fourth condition in the analysis is:

(iv) There is no genuine defeater of the propositional justification of any of the propositions in the evidential path up to and including *e*, and there is no genuine defeater of the propositional justification of any proposition between *e* and *h*.

But, since *e* could be false, we have to amend condition (iv) as follows:

(iv) revised   If *e* is true, then there is no genuine defeater of the propositional justification of any of the propositions in the evidential path up to and including *e* and there is no genuine defeater of the propositional justification of any proposition between *e* and *h*; if *e* is false, then there is no genuine defeater of the propositional justification of any of the propositions in the evidential path up to and including *t* and there is no genuine defeater of the propositional justification of any proposition between *t* and *h*, where *t* is defined by Conditions 1–7.

Why are Conditions 1–7 necessary conditions of *uf* being a useful falsehood in producing a doxastically justified belief that is a candidate for knowledge? Conditions 1–4 are non-controversial and require only very brief comments. Conditions 5–7 require more extended discussion.

Condition 1 is analytically required because *uf* must be false.

Condition 2 is an instance of the general requirement that doxastic justification which depends on another belief requires that that belief be doxastically justified.[41]

Condition 3 is analytically contained in the notion of a *useful* falsehood that doxastically justifies *h*, since such falsehoods, unlike the so-called harmless ones, are essential in producing doxastically justified beliefs.

Condition 4 follows from the general account of doxastic justification given earlier. One consequence of that account is that, if the belief that *uf* doxastically justifies the belief that *h*, then *uf* propositionally justifies *h*.

Condition 5 is designed to capture the intuition that lies behind Hilpinen's suggestion that the useful falsehood has to be "close enough" to the truth. Since *h* is known, *h* must be true, and, if *h* is true, there will always be some other true proposition that propositionally justifies *h*. To see that, consider any false proposition, *f*. The proposition, *h*, is propositionally justified by the true proposition: $[(f \vee h) \& \sim f]$. Condition 5 coupled with Conditions 6 and 7 jointly indicate *which* true propositions are "close enough" to the false proposition so as to make it the case that S's belief that *h* is a candidate for knowledge, even though the belief that *h* is doxastically justified by a false belief.

I have made Hilpinen's "sufficiently close" *very* close by requiring that the useful falsehood entail *t*. We have seen that there is an appropriate true

---

[41] Recall that I had said earlier that "doxastic justification" could be replaced in the account of inferential knowledge with some lower degree of epistemic entitlement—for example, epistemic plausibility (see n. 17.) Whatever degree is the correct one in the account of inferential knowledge would be applicable here.

proposition entail by the useful falsehood in each of the four cases presented earlier, but *perhaps* some weaker form of "closeness", perhaps subjunctive implication, would suffice. Consider this case:

> Suppose I believe that I am witnessing Mr Butterfingers at the top of the Empire State Building apparently dropping a glass toward the empty sidewalk below. On the basis of the belief that he is doing that, I come to believe, and thereby know, that a glass will soon break on the sidewalk below. Suppose, further, that he did not *drop* the glass, but, rather, it *slipped out* of his fingers.

This is a case of a useful falsehood producing knowledge. In this case, a true proposition, *the glass in Mr Butterfingers' hand will drop rapidly to the ground*, is subjunctively implied (and not entailed) by the false proposition that he dropped the glass from the top of the Empire State Building, *and* that true proposition also satisfies Conditions 6 and 7. Thus, this case might suggest that we need not make the relation as close as entailment.

But, in this case, there is another true proposition that is entailed by the false one that also satisfies Conditions 6–7—namely, *either the glass was dropped or the glass slipped from Mr Butterfingers' hand*. In fact, Condition 5 obtains in every case I have been able to think of. In addition, what counts in favor of entailment is that too much leniency here will not honor the intuition, which extends back to Plato, that knowledge is "prized higher" than mere true belief.[42] Knowledge should not be so easy to obtain, and, since we have already allowed for false beliefs to be part of the essential cause of cognitions, loosening the connection between the false proposition and the truth might allow for too much epistemic luck. Nevertheless, because there might be some cases in which only a weaker relationship between the false proposition and the truth obtains, I will continue to employ entailment, with the caveat that some weaker relationship might suffice.

Condition 6 might look redundant. For it might seem that **if** *uf* propositionally justifies *h*, and *uf* entails *t*, **then** *t* propositionally justifies *h* because that conditional is an instance of this general principle: if *x* propositionally justifies *y*, and *x* entails *z*, then *z* propositionally justifies *y*. But that general principle is not true. The proposition, *x*, could contain a conjunction with three conjuncts: one proposition, say *e*, that propositionally justifies *y*; one proposition, *o*, that overrides the justification of *y* by *e*; and one proposition, *r*, that overrides the

---

[42] *Meno*, 97d–98b.

effect of *o* either by providing additional evidence for *y* or by neutralizing the effect of *o*. In addition, *z* could merely be the conjunction (*e* & *o*) that, by stipulation, does not propositionally justify *y*. So, Condition 6 is not redundant.

Condition 6 needs to be included simply because, if *t* were not propositionally to justify *h*, then one would wonder why it matters that *uf* is close to the truth. The truth must contribute something to the acquisition of knowledge that *h*. We have seen that, even were S to believe that *t*, the belief that *t* cannot be the actual cause of the belief that *h*, because we would then have a case of a harmless rather than a useful falsehood. If the belief that *t* does not contribute causally to the production of the belief that *h*, there appears to be nothing that *t* can contribute toward knowledge that *h* other than to the propositional justification of *h*.

Condition 7 is important because it ensures that there is some good evidence path available to *t* for S (in the sense of "available" discussed at the outset of this chapter). If such a path were not available to S, then one would wonder how a truth that is not propositionally justified could contribute to making *h* known. So I think it is safe to assume that there *must be* some evidence path that renders *t* propositionally justified for S. The question, then, becomes this: what would guarantee that there is such an evidence path to *t*?

There are only three types of evidence paths that would guarantee that, if *uf* is propositionally justified, then *t* is propositionally justified: (1) whatever propositionally justifies *uf* also propositionally justifies *t*; (2) *uf* propositionally justifies *t*; (3) *t* appears before *uf* on the evidence path that propositionally justifies *uf*. Option 1 is the only one that can help us account for the role that falsehoods play in the production of knowledge.[43]

Option 1   Whatever propositionally justifies *uf* also propositionally justifies *t*.

Recall the entailment we noted earlier:

(S's belief that *h* is doxastically justified by another belief that *e*) → (S's belief that *h* is caused by the belief that *e*, and *e* propositionally justifies *h*)

Up to this point, that entailment sufficed because we have been interested in cases in which the propositional content of the doxastically justified belief was potentially a case of inferential knowledge. But foundationalists would hold

---

[43] For more on evidence paths see my "Skepticism", 342–6, and "How a Pyrrhonian Skeptic Might Respond to Academic Skepticism", 78–90.

that in some cases—that is, cases of so-called basic beliefs—what doxastically justifies a belief is not another belief, and that it is possible that a useful falsehood could be the content of a basic belief. In order to accommodate foundationalism and allow for the possibility that something other than beliefs can doxastically justify a belief, we must generalize the entailment to this (where "x" stands for whatever doxastically justifies a belief):

(S's belief that h is doxastically justified by x) → (S's belief that h is caused by x, and x propositionally justifies h)

We can guarantee that there is an evidence path to t by requiring that whatever propositionally justifies uf must also propositionally justify t. In each of the four cases of useful falsehoods, the content of whatever doxastically justifies the false belief does propositionally justify the true proposition. For example, whatever propositionally justifies the Ptolemaic astronomers in believing that Ptolemaic Theory correctly predicts the location of Mars, the Earth, and the Sun also justifies the proposition that their locations are predictable *just as if* the Ptolemaic Theory were correct. That is so even if the thirteenth-century astronomers failed to believe the "as if" proposition. For the issue here is what *proposition* is propositionally justified; the issue is not what belief is doxastically justified.

Indeed, as we have seen, uf is equivalent to (uf & t). Thus, if the following principle is exceptionless, there appears to be an easy argument to show that Condition 7 must be true.[44] That seemingly "exceptionless principle" is this: if x propositionally justifies (y & z), then x propositionally justifies y, and x propositionally justifies z. And the easy argument is as follows:

1. Assume that x is whatever doxastically justifies the belief that uf for S.
2. If x doxastically justifies the belief that uf for S, then x propositionally justifies uf [from the generalized entailment concerning doxastic justification given above].
3. x propositionally justifies uf [MP, from 1, 2].
4. uf is equivalent to (uf & t) [because uf entails t].

---

[44] I say that there *appears* to be an easy argument, because it might be that substitution of equivalent propositions in step 5 should not be permitted. It certainly is not permitted in belief contexts, but the reason for the prohibition in belief contexts does not seem to transfer here. That reason is that S, the believer, might not know that the propositions are equivalent. But here the issue is just about propositional justification—not doxastic justification. Nevertheless, since I am not wedded to this argument for Condition 7, even if this argument failed, Option 1 is the only one that will help in the account of useful falsehoods.

5. x propositionally justifies $(uf \,\&\, t)$ [from 3 and substitution of equivalents].
6. x propositionally justifies t [from 5 and the exceptionless principle given above].
7. Whatever doxastically justifies the belief that uf for S also propositionally justifies t for S [conditional proof, from 1–6].

So, if the "exceptionless principle" is correct, we need not list Condition 7. But I have not argued for that principle here and, thus, it seems best to include that condition explicitly.

Option 2   The proposition, t, is propositionally justified by uf.

Since uf entails t, and uf is propositionally justified, we could ensure that there is an evidence path to t by requiring that the evidence path to t include uf prior to t. The evidence path, then, would look like this:

$x - uf - t$.

In addition, I have already argued that, if S believes that t, then it might only be on the basis of believing that uf. Further, the following principle seems as "exceptionless" as the one mentioned above: if x entails y, then x propositionally justifies y.[45] Since uf entails t, it might seem that Option 2 is at least as good as Option 1 for inclusion in the necessary conditions.

But, if Option 2 replaced Condition 7 in my account of useful falsehoods, that account could not assist us in arriving at our overall goal of explicating the role of useful falsehoods in the acquisition of knowledge, since any path that contains uf would be genuinely defeated (by $\sim uf$). In other words, although there is an evidence path $x - uf - t$ that continues to h, it is genuinely defeated. Thus, although uf does propositionally justify t, Option 2 is not the appropriate way to guarantee that there is a good evidence path to t.

Option 3   The proposition, t, occurs prior to uf on the evidence path to h.

That requirement does not square with the four cases of useful falsehoods, because the propositions that justify uf for S do not include t. In general, there is no guarantee that conjuncts are in the evidence paths leading to a conjunction.[46]

---

[45] Given the restriction that x and y range over contingent propositions. Otherwise, for example $(p \,\&\, \sim p)$ would justify any proposition and $(p \lor \sim p)$ would be justified by any proposition.

[46] Here is an evidence path such that the conjunction appears *before* an individual conjunct:

$\{[r \rightarrow (p \,\&\, q)] \,\&\, r\} - (p \,\&\, q) - p$

Only Option 1 will (i) guarantee that there is a good evidence path to *t* whenever there is one to *uf*, and (ii) help us to achieve the final goal of explicating the role that useful falsehoods play in producing knowledge. Option 1 is nothing other than Condition 7.

Thus, Conditions 1–7 appear to be necessary conditions for *uf* being a useful falsehood for S's acquisition of knowledge. However, I want briefly to address three objections to these conditions before moving to consider whether these conditions are sufficient.

Objection 1	It appears that the belief that *uf* cannot be epistemically basic belief since *uf* has to be propositionally justified.
Answer	To say that a proposition is propositionally justified for S does not imply that the proposition is justified by another proposition. It is merely to say that S has an epistemically adequate basis for *h*. So, *uf* could be a basic.
Objection 2	Since S might not have the belief that *t*, how can *t* propositionally justify *h*?
Answer	The definition of "a proposition, *e*, propositionally justifies another, *h*" does not require either that S believe that *e* or that S believe that *h*. It specifies an epistemic relationship between propositions, not a causal relationship between beliefs.
Objection 3	How can *t* make the belief that *h* doxastically justified?
Answer	It does not. The false belief, *uf*, makes the belief that *h* doxastically justified.

I now turn to consider whether Conditions 1–7 capture what is sufficient for *uf* to be a useful falsehood. Although there is no definitive argument to show that they are sufficient, there are three considerations that tend to confirm that they are. First, as we examined the proposed conditions, the only qualifications that seemed at all appropriate were ones that weakened them somewhat. We considered reducing entailment to some weaker form of implication in Condition 5. We considered reducing doxastic justification to doxastic plausibility in Condition 2. That only weakening the conditions seemed worth considering does count in favor of their sufficiency. Even those weakened conditions remain within the spirit of the account—namely, that among the necessary and jointly sufficient conditions there are two that together require both that (i) there is a true proposition implied (in some form) by the useful falsehood, and (ii) the true proposition has some relatively high degree of epistemic entitlement conferred on it by whatever confers that same degree of entitlement on the false proposition. Second, I will argue below that this analysis is able to account for differing intuitions about the scope of our knowledge that arises from believing falsehoods. Third, the class of cases we have examined is diverse. Nevertheless, it remains possible that there is another class of cases that I have overlooked. So, I present this account as only the first step in understanding the important and initially surprising fact that a false belief can play an essential role in producing knowledge.

However, there is one misunderstanding of the account that might prompt a question concerning the sufficiency of Conditions 1–7 that would be useful to address—namely, this: are there not standard Gettier cases in which Conditions 1–7 are met, but yet S would fail to know that *h*? In the standard Havit/Nogot Case, Nogot and Havit are S's classmates, S acquires good evidence for the false proposition *Nogot owns a Ford*, but S has no evidence for the true proposition, *Havit owns a Ford*. It appears that Conditions 1–7 are fulfilled if *h* is taken to be *someone in S's class owns a Ford*, and *uf* is taken to be *Nogot owns a Ford*, and *t* is taken to be *Nogot or Havit owns a Ford*. But surely S does not *know* that someone in the class owns a Ford on the basis of believing that Nogot owns a Ford. The false belief in this case does not produce knowledge; yet, Conditions 1–7 are satisfied.

This objection underscores both (a) the significance of the Gettier Problem—the problem of producing a necessary and jointly sufficient set of conditions for *knowledge*, and (b) the fact that Conditions 1–7 were designed only to portray those circumstances in which a false belief yields a doxastically justified, true belief that is a *candidate* for knowledge. The conditions were not designed to specify those cases of useful false beliefs that actually produced knowledge. In other words, useful falsehoods produce doxastically justified true beliefs, some of which are knowledge and some of which are not. The revised defeasibility theory of knowledge would come into play here. If the path that contains only truths—that is, the path *x*–*t*–*h*—is genuinely defeated, then S lacks knowledge.

In the standard Havit/Nogot Case, there is a genuine defeater of the justification of *someone in S's class owns a Ford*; that defeater is: *Nogot does not own a Ford*. To see that, suppose that the evidence that S has for *Nogot owns a Ford* is that Nogot drives a Ford, garages one, says he owns one, and has a valid looking title. The conjunction of the propositions expressing those facts with *Nogot doesn't own a Ford* would fail propositionally to justify the proposition *Nogot owns a Ford*. It is crucial here to note that the same defeater defeats the propositional justification for *either Nogot owns a Ford or Havit owns a Ford*, because the only evidence for the disjunction is the false disjunct. In other words, although *either Nogot owns a Ford or Havit owns a Ford* propositionally justifies *someone in S's class owns a Ford*, there is a genuine defeater of that justificational path prior to the disjunction, and hence S does not know that someone in the class owns a Ford.

This is not the place to offer a general defense of the defeasibility theory. My current task is to show that employing that account can help to explain how useful falsehoods *can* produce knowledge. The relevant point is that useful falsehoods can produce knowledge in cases where there is no genuine defeater along the path of propositions involving *t*. Recall the diagram of the two evidential paths to *h*:

If the path from *x* to *t* to *h* is not defeated by a genuine defeater, then S would have knowledge that *h* even though there is always a genuine defeater of the path from *x* to *uf* to *h* (i.e., ∼*uf*).

To make that clear, consider the Santa Claus Case and let:

m   Mom and Dad said that Santa would put presents under the tree.
r   Mom and Dad are reliable truth tellers.
s   Santa will put presents under the tree.
p   There will be presents under the tree.
n   There is no Santa Claus.
t   Someone will put presents under the tree.

The evidence path that S actually employed looks like this: (*m* & *r*)−*s*−*p*. The defeater, *n*, breaks the path between (*m* & *r*) and *s*. That is, (*m* & *r* & *n*) fails to justify *s*.

Contrast that path with the one not taken but specified by Conditions 1−7: (*m* & *r*)−*t*−*p*. It is obvious that *n* does not break the path between (*m* & *r*) and *t* (or at any other point).

Generalizing, we can say that a belief, *h*, causally based upon a false belief that *uf*, is knowledge just in case there is some *t* for which Conditions 1−7 are satisfied, and there is no genuine defeater of the propositional justification of any of the propositions in the evidential path to *h* that includes *t*.

That is my account of the role that useful falsehoods play in the production of knowledge.

5. A test of the account

Conditions 1–7 are designed to capture the salient features of clear cases of useful falsehoods, but we should not test the account by using clear cases alone; we must also examine how it handles some not-so-clear cases, in which intuitions about the scope of knowledge will vary. A good account should be useful in explaining divergent intuitions.

Revamping the Average Rainfall Case provides one such example. Suppose that instead of there being seventy-nine years of accurately recorded rainfall measurements, there are only two. In such a case, the false belief *there are over eighty years of accurate records and the rainfall depicted in the number of years that records were kept averages 13 inches* cannot yield knowledge. Thus, somewhere in the range between two and seventy-nine years there will be some borderline cases in which intuitions will vary concerning whether S knows on the basis of falsely believing that records were kept for over eighty years. Let fourteen years be in the borderline range. In other words, let it be the case that, if there were exactly fourteen years of accurately recorded annual rainfall, some people will intuit that *there are over eighty years of records, etc.* is a useful falsehood in producing knowledge and others will intuit that it cannot be used to produce knowledge.

The point in favor of the analysis is that people with differing intuitions in the borderline cases can employ the account to explain their intuitions. Mr Lax who thinks that Weatherman does gain knowledge on the basis of the false belief can explain his own intuition by arguing that the proposition that accurate records were kept for fourteen years and the records depicted an average rainfall of 13 inches propositionally justifies *the average rainfall is 13 inches*; whereas Ms Stringent, who denies that Weatherman has knowledge, can explain her intuition by claiming that the proposition is not sufficient to justify *the average rainfall is 13 inches*. Mr Undecided can withhold judgement because he neither believes that the proposition justifies the generalization nor believes that it does not. The fact that Lax, Stringent, and Undecided can employ my analysis to explain their differing intuitions about the scope of S's knowledge is evidence that the account is correct.

Similar considerations apply to the Santa Claus Case. Someone might think Virginia does not know that there will be presents under the tree, because there is a genuine defeater of the evidential path of propositions employing the "close" truth that someone will put presents under the tree. They would point to *Mom and Dad fib all the time about Xmas matters* as a genuine defeater, because it breaks the step between (m & r) and t. Other people, however, might think that Virginia does know that there will be presents under the tree, even though they will grant that the step is defeated at that point. They will think that *Mom and Dad fib all the time about Xmas matters* is a misleading defeater, because it defeats only by rendering plausible the false proposition that no one will put presents under the tree. Once again, the account of useful falsehoods is vindicated because it can account for varying intuitions.

One final "vague" case illustrates how the defeater condition works. Consider this variation of the Grabit Case:

> I have worked with Tom Grabit for years and have come to know him quite well, but I have no information or beliefs about whether he has any siblings. I see someone I take to be Tom stealing a book from the library, and I come to believe on that basis that Tom stole the book. I infer and come to believe that one of Mrs Grabit's children has stolen a book. Suppose, further, that it was Tom's identical twin, John, who stole the book.

People will have varying intuitions about whether I know that one of Mrs Grabit's children stole a book from the library. Some will think I do know, some will think I do not know, and some will be undecided.[47] An advantage of the proposed account of knowledge based upon useful falsehoods is that all three intuitive responses can easily be explained by employing it. To see that, let be:

s   There is a Tom Grabit-like looking person apparently stealing a library book.

f   Tom Grabit stole a book.

c   One of Mrs Grabit's children stole a book.

The evidence path I actually followed to my doxastically justified belief is this: $s-f-c$. There clearly is a genuine defeater of that justification path—namely, $\sim f$—since (f & $\sim f$) fails to justify c. But those who think I do have knowledge could point to the following (very short) evidence path to c that just employs only true propositions: $s-c$.[48] They could, then, claim either

---

[47] I have given this case to many people, and the intuitions did vary. But the sample was rather unrepresentative consisting of friends, colleagues and philosophy undergraduate and graduate students!

[48] In this case, f entails a true proposition, t, and an obvious candidate for such a proposition is c. Thus, in order to capture this case in a completely parallel fashion to other cases of useful

that $\sim f$ does not defeat that justificational path, or, that, if it does, it is a misleading defeater because it defeats only by rendering plausible the false proposition that $\sim c$.[49] Thus, from the perspective of someone who believes that I have knowledge, f is a useful falsehood not only making my belief that c doxastically justified because Conditions 1–7 are satisfied, but, in addition, since there is no genuine defeater of that path, I know that c. On the other hand, although those who think that I do not know that c must grant that Conditions 1–7 are satisfied, they will think that $\sim f$ is a genuine defeater of the justification of c by s. Those who cannot decide whether $\sim f$ is a misleading defeater or a genuine one will be undecided about whether I know that c.

Therefore, in these vague cases, when we combine the definition of useful falsehoods with the defeasibility theory, we can account for varying intuitions about the scope of knowledge. The combination enables persons with differing views about the extent of S's knowledge to pinpoint exactly what leads to their differing intuitions about the scope of S's knowledge. That is exactly what a good account of useful falsehoods should do.

6. Reliabilism reconsidered

I mentioned earlier that the existence of useful falsehoods presented a particularly difficult challenge to reliabilism, but that reliabilists could accept my proposal. I would like to cash in that promissory note. Recall that the problem presented by useful falsehoods to reliabilists is that such falsehoods require them to develop an account that picks out all and only those false beliefs that reliably produce knowledge.

Because of the relationship between doxastic and propositional justification noted at the outset, if the proposed account is correct, the reliabilist can simply appropriate the set of conditions listed here and replace all uses of

---

falsehoods, we would have to say that c propositionally justifies c, and, hence, the undefeated evidence path would be: s–c–c. But some may think the correct account of propositional justification, and more particularly the correct account of an epistemically adequate basis, should preclude any proposition from propositionally justifying itself. In order to accommodate that view, we could say that f entails, o, where o is (*f or another one of Mrs Grabit's children stole a book*). That avoids the problem—if, indeed, it is one.

49 This is the view that I think Claudio de Almeida holds in such cases. See n. 25.

"propositional justification" in my account in favor of "doxastic justification".
For example, Condition 6 could be replaced with this condition:

6*   If S were doxastically justified in believing that t, then S would be
     doxastically justified in believing that h if S were to believe that h and
     S's belief that h were to be caused by S's belief that e.

Thus, even though I have used the normative/evidentialist concept of
propositional justification in formulating the account, reliabilists could help
themselves to the account. Of course, whether reliabilism is otherwise acceptable is another issue—and not one appropriate for this chapter. The point here
is that my account of useful falsehoods ought to be acceptable to reliabilists as
well as to defeasibility theorists. I take that to be a significant point in its favor.

7. Conclusion

Contrary to the received opinion, there are cases in which false beliefs play an
essential role in producing knowledge. When S acquires inferential knowledge
that h based only on truths, the causal chain to the belief that h mirrors
the evidential path to the true proposition, h. In cases of falsehoods that are
useful in the production of knowledge, the causal chain and the evidential
path diverge. The causal chain contains false beliefs that are such that their
propositional contents instantiate an evidential path that is genuinely defeated;
but the evidential path contains only true propositions and that path is not
genuinely defeated. The causal chain and the evidential path are related as
specified in Conditions 1–7.

The moral is that, in some cases, not taking a good path is just as good as
having taken it.[50]

---

[50] There is corollary of the primary conclusion. Foundationalists typically take inferential
knowledge to arise only from what is known. But as the quotation from Hilpinen indicates
(see p. 47 above), knowledge can arise from what is not known because what is known can be
inferred from what is false. Once that is noticed, then alternative accounts of doxastic justification
immediately become more plausible. (See nn. 5 and 16.)

3

Immediate Justification and Process Reliabilism

Alvin I. Goldman

1. Introduction

A central issue in contemporary epistemology is whether there is a species of (prima facie) justification that is immediate, direct, basic, or foundational. It is puzzling whether and how immediate justification could arise. This is perhaps the core issue that divides foundationalists from coherentists. An older conception of immediate justification is that some beliefs are capable of *self*-justification; they do not need anything *else* to justify them.[1] This conception of immediate justification is no longer very prevalent. Current defenders of immediate justification usually assume that a directly justified belief is rendered justified by some state of affairs distinct from it. What is special to the direct mode of justification conferral is that it does not involve *other* justified beliefs (or states or propositions) as justifiers. Deniers of immediate justification doubt that this occurs, or even makes sense.

Thanks to Rich Feldman, Jim Pryor, and two anonymous referees for helpful comments on previous versions of this chapter.

[1] For example, Roderick Chisholm (1977: 25) proposed to think of the "directly evident" as that which "constitutes its own evidence", and characterized it in terms of states that are "apprehended through themselves".

In general, questions about justification can be given either a *doxastic* or a *propositional* formulation. A doxastic formulation presupposes that the epistemic subject has a belief of interest, and the question is whether this belief is justified. A propositional formulation does not presuppose that the subject believes the target proposition. It asks whether she is in a "position" such that it *would* be epistemically appropriate for her to believe it, whether or not she does so. We shall address both types of formulation.

The issue of immediate justification can be resolved into three questions:

Q1　Is there a species of justification that is immediate, direct, or basic? In other words, are some beliefs or propositions made (prima facie) justified in virtue of states of affairs, processes, etc., that confer justification without themselves being justified?

If question Q1 is answered in the affirmative, the next question is:

Q2　How is immediate justification conferral possible? There are well-known arguments, initially plausible-looking arguments, against the very possibility of unjustified justifiers. What is wrong with those arguments?

Assuming that challenges to the very possibility of unjustified justifiers can be met, the final question is:

Q3　What types of states or process can serve as immediate justifiers, and what relations do they bear to appropriate beliefs or propositions by virtue of which justification is conferred on those beliefs or propositions and not others?

Here is a sample dilemma that appears to challenge the possibility of basic justification. Initially it seems that anything that makes a proposition or belief justified must itself be justified. This pattern is instantiated in the paradigm case of inferential justification. An inferred proposition is justified (for the subject) only if the premises or beliefs from which it is inferred are themselves justified (for that subject). But, if the justifiedness of a proposition or belief depends on the justifiedness of another belief (or belief-like state), then the justifiedness of the target belief or proposition is not basic or immediate after all. Immediate justification can arise only from states, facts, conditions, processes, or the like that are not themselves justified—that is, from unjustified justifiers. At a minimum, immediate justification arises only from states, facts, and so forth without *depending* on their justificational status (though they might *have* such status). But how can unjustified states or conditions confer justifiedness on a proposition or belief?

Another challenge to the possibility of immediate justification is prompted by a second feature of inferential justification. In inferential justification, the source of justification is prior *contentful* (that is, representational) states of the subject. The contents of these states are what fix the further propositions that are inferentially justifiable for the subject. What shall we say with respect to content for putative cases of direct, non-inferential justification? Must the unjustified justifiers themselves be contentful, representational states? If so, are the only propositions on which they confer justification the contents of the conferring states? If unjustified justifiers can be contentless, non-representational states, how do specific propositions or beliefs get selected as ones made justified by these contentless justification-conferrers?

There seem to be three possible answers to this conundrum:

A1   Immediate justifiers are contentful states of affairs (presumably, states of the epistemic agent, S).

A2   Immediate justifiers are non-contentful states of affairs.

A3   Immediate justifiers can be either contentful states or non-contentful states (or perhaps a combination of the two).

In the last few years several epistemologists have focused their attention on this nest of problems. I shall consider treatments of the topic by four epistemologists: Richard Feldman (2003), Michael Huemer (2001), Peter Markie (2005), and James Pryor (2005). Each offers helpful explorations of the territory, but none of them, in my view, offers a satisfactory positive solution. Markie, for example, treats the problem as an unsolved "mystery". I shall suggest that process reliabilism offers the most promising solution to the problem, or nest of problems. Feldman and Markie will be unhappy with this proposal, because they are on record as finding serious or fatal problems with reliabilism. I will not, however, attempt to address any of the familiar problems for reliabilism, such as the generality problem.[2] This article is limited to a defense of the thesis that

---

[2] I have proposed various reformulations of process reliabilism in a number of works that followed my initial formulation of the theory in Goldman (1979). See especially Goldman (1986, 1988, 1992, 1999a, 2001). These reformulations were intended to answer or resolve several problems, including the generality problem. Many other writers have also proposed reformulations or solutions, including Sosa (1991, 2001), Alston (1995), Heller (1995), Greco (2000), and Beebe (2004). Further efforts at improving the formulation of reliabilism are underway, but won't be explored here.

process reliabilism offers the best available solution to the puzzle of immediate justification. If this thesis can be made good, it will be a feather in reliabilism's cap, even if it does not solve other outstanding problems for the theory.

2. Feldman's proposal: A proper response to experience

Feldman, in his book *Epistemology* (2003), discusses the problem of justified basic beliefs with special attention to modest foundationalism. On Feldman's construal, modest foundationalism includes the thesis that immediate justification in the perceptual arena pertains to (selected) perceptual beliefs whose contents are external world propositions, such as "There is a tree on the hill". Feldman introduces the notion of a spontaneously formed belief, a belief that is not formed by conscious inference from other beliefs. He then considers principle P1 as a possible principle for basic beliefs:[3]

> P1   Being spontaneously formed makes a belief (immediately) justified. (Feldman 2003: 73)

This principle is quickly rejected, on grounds of excessive simplicity. To improve on P1, Feldman introduces the notion of a "proper response to experience". Only beliefs that are proper responses to experience provide (non-inferential) justifiedness, Feldman implies. Here is how he explains the notion:

When you walk into a room, see a table, and form a belief that there is a table there . . . [w]hat seems central is that your belief is a proper response to the perceptual stimulus you have. It is a suitable thing to believe given that experience. To believe something that does not fit that experience at all, such as that there is an elephant in the room, would not be a proper response to that experience. To believe something that goes beyond what is revealed in the experience, such as that there is a table that is exactly 12 years old, would not be a proper response to that experience. (Feldman 2003: 74)

Feldman then proceeds to use this notion in a revised principle for immediate justification:

> P2   A spontaneously formed belief is justified provided it is a proper response to experiences and is not defeated by other evidence the believer has. (Feldman 2003: 74)

---

[3] All the numbered principles are relabeled from their original locus of publication.

The adequacy of Feldman's solution to the problem of immediate justification obviously depends on what account is given of the newly coined phrase "proper response to experience". What makes a belief a proper or improper response to experience? Feldman gives further illustrations of positive and negative instances of this notion:

> Other examples clarify the idea. Compare a novice bird-watcher and an expert walking together in the woods, seeking out the rare pink-spotted flycatcher. A bird flies by and each person spontaneously forms the belief that there is a pink-spotted flycatcher there. The expert knows this to be true but the novice is jumping to a conclusion out of excitement. The expert has a well-founded belief but the novice does not. In the same situation, both the novice and the expert may have well-founded beliefs about the color, shape and size of the bird they see. This suggests that there is some relevant difference between such properties as being gray with pink spots and about 4 inches long and properties such as being a pink-spotted flycatcher. One might say that the former are "closer to experience" than the latter. Anyone with proper vision can discern the former in experience. This is not true of the latter. (Feldman 2003: 75)

These are instructive examples, but what general principles should be extracted from them? Feldman proposes two factors that seem relevant to being a proper response to experience.

> First, when the contents of the belief are closer to the direct contents of experience, they are more apt to be properly based on experience. Second, modest foundationalism can say that training and experience affect what counts as a proper response to experience. The expert's training makes her response proper. For beliefs that are more distant from experience, such training is necessary for the belief to be properly based on experience. (Feldman 2003: 75)

Consider Feldman's first factor for proper responsiveness—namely, closeness of the belief content to the content of experience. Feldman is obviously assuming that experience (for example, visual experience) has propositional content. He assumes, in other words, that at least some immediate justifiers are contentful states. Some epistemologists would dispute this claim, of course, at least with respect to experiential justifiers. Even if the assumption is accepted, however, there are those who will argue that, if a contentful state is to confer justification, *it itself* must be justified. If that were right, the justification it confers would no longer be *immediate*.

Setting this concern aside, Feldman's appeal to the closeness-of-content factor presupposes that proper responsiveness is always a matter of a close match between the content of the experience and the content of the belief that responds to it. Is this right? Pryor (2005) does not discuss Feldman directly, but his discussion brings out the problem of heavy appeal to content closeness. Assume *arguendo* that some mental states do not have propositional content—for example, pain states in general and headaches in particular. Suppose I am currently feeling pain, or having a headache, and I proceed to believe "I am now in pain" or "I have a headache". Each of these beliefs is an excellent candidate for a justified basic belief. Or, formulating the matter in terms of propositional justification, I am justified in believing either of these propositions. Now it appears that the justification-conferring state is the state of being in pain or the state of having a headache, respectively. By hypothesis, however, neither of these justification-conferring states has content. So neither has any content that is *close* to the content of the proposition or belief in question. Content closeness is of no help here.

This problem is readily generalized to contentful mental states, such as desires. Ralph has an (occurrent) desire that the year 2008 be free of natural disasters. In an act of self-reflection (or introspection), Ralph forms the belief that he is currently experiencing *a desire*. This is a clear, traditional candidate for an immediately justified belief. But, again, the content-closeness factor does not help rationalize its status as a basic belief. The belief's content—*I currently experience a desire*—has very little proximity to the desire's content to which the belief is properly responsive—namely, *the year 2008 should be free of natural disasters*. Although the desire is contentful, the belief in question does not address its content. The believed proposition simply says that a specified *type* of mental state is currently instantiated in him.[4]

---

[4] An anonymous referee suggests that Ralph's belief is not a response to *his desire* that the year 2008 be free of natural disasters. Rather, it is a response to *his being aware of* his desire that the year 2008 be free of natural disasters. And the content of this awareness is very close indeed to the content of the belief. One reply to this suggestion is that it is not clear what content is possessed by a *de re* awareness (an awareness *of* another state). Setting this point aside, why should we posit the existence of such an awareness? Why should we suppose that, in addition to having a desire that the year 2008 be free of natural disasters and a belief concerning that desire, Ralph also has a separate and distinct awareness of this desire? When Feldman discusses a belief that properly responds to a perceptual experience, he does not posit an extra mental state—an awareness of the perceptual experience—that is layered *in between* the target mental state and the belief. Why make such a posit here? To be sure, in the perceptual-experience case the belief is properly responsive to the content of the experience. But why should not a belief be equally capable of being properly responsive to a mental state's *type* as well as to its content? Intuitively, proper responsiveness to a state's type seems

Does Feldman's second factor for proper responsiveness—that is, suitable training—offer much help? The problem here is under-explanation. Feldman simply does not tell us (A) what constitutes suitable training with respect to a given belief, or (B) why suitable training should help confer immediate justifiedness. Presumably, suitable training does not consist in acquiring justified beliefs about the subject matter in question from which the target belief can be inferred, because this would threaten to make the target belief indirectly rather than directly justified. What, then, does suitable training consist in? The most obvious answer is that suitable training makes beliefs of the appropriate category come out *true*. But this seems like a thinly disguised way of saying that suitable training breeds *reliability*; yet reliability is precisely what an internalist like Feldman is emphatically unwilling to accept as a ground or basis of justifiedness. If reliability is rejected, however, what is Feldman's story of why suitable training confers justifiedness?[5]

3. Pryor on immediate justification

Pryor (2005) has a very instructive discussion of immediate justification. But his discussion is directed squarely at the topic announced in his title, "There Is Immediate Justification". He is concerned with supporting the thesis *that there is* immediate justification, as contrasted with explaining *wherein* immediate justification consists. In other words, Pryor's discussion focuses on questions Q1 and Q2 rather than on question Q3. He focuses on principles and arguments for the negative thesis that there is no immediate justification, and pokes holes in these arguments. He does an excellent job of expounding and exposing lacunae in such principles and arguments, but this does not provide a positive story of immediate justification. It does not help answer question Q3. Elsewhere Pryor does sketch a positive account of immediate justification (Pryor 2000). That account, however, closely resembles the more fully developed theory of Huemer, which will be discussed in Section 4. The criticisms to be lodged against Huemer's view apply equally to Pryor's earlier proposal.

as good a candidate for grounding immediate justification as proper responsiveness to its content. But, of course, this does not fit with Feldman's characterization of proper responsiveness.

[5] Feldman himself concedes that he has not adequately explained the notion of a proper response to experience. He remarks that "a more fully developed account of the conditions under which a belief is properly based on experience is desirable" (Feldman 2003: p 78).

Let us examine a few of the principles and arguments against immediate justification examined and exposed in Pryor (2005). The central principle he examines is called "The Premise Principle":

The only things that can justify a belief that P are other states that assertively represent propositions, and those propositions have to be ones that *could be used as premises* in an argument for P. They have to stand in some kind of inferential relation to P; they have to imply it or inductively support it or something like that. (Pryor 2005: 189)

Pryor diagnoses the chief argument behind the Premise Principle as follows. Consider a state without propositional content, like a headache. Since it has no propositional content, it cannot stand in logical relations to the content of any beliefs. So why should it justify any one belief as opposed to others? For example, why should it justify the belief *I have a headache* as opposed to *I don't have a headache*, or any other belief? What can the defender of immediate justification (the foundationalist) say to make the justifying relations he postulates non-arbitrary? Pryor concedes that epistemologists must give principled, non-arbitrary rationales for the justifying relations they postulate. But he says, quite rightly, that it is not obvious that they have to appeal to (states with) propositional contents to do it.

The second argument Pryor considers runs as follows:

We ordinarily understand "justifications" for a belief to be *arguments* that support the belief. If you have *reasons* for your belief, they should be considerations you could in principle *cite*, or *give*, to someone who doubted or challenged the belief. You can't give someone else a non-propositional state like a headache (at least, not in the relevant sense); you can only give them *premises* and *arguments* that support your belief. This seems to show that justification and reasons *are* limited to things permitted by the Premise Principle. (Pryor 2005: 193—4)

Pryor responds, quite appropriately, that this argument appeals to the *dialectical* notion of a reason. This notion is different from the notion of a justification-maker, which is crucial for our inquiry. Pryor next distinguishes between two construals of the verb "justify". On the first construal, "justifying" a belief in P is a matter of proving or showing the belief to be just (or reasonable or credible). On the second construal, to "justify" something is akin to beautifying or electrifying it. When something beautifies a room, it does not *prove* that the room is beautiful; rather, it *makes* the room beautiful. Similarly, on the second construal, to justify a belief is a matter of *making* the belief just or reasonable, not a matter of *showing* the belief to be just (Pryor 2005: 194). I think this is exactly right. However, it does not tell us what does make beliefs justified, especially in the case of directly or immediately justified beliefs.

Pryor provides one hint, however. He begins by distinguishing between there *being* reasons to believe P and one's *having* reasons to believe P. If *there are* reasons to believe P but you are unaware of them, they are not reasons you have. And for anyone with internalist sympathies, such reasons cannot justify you in believing P. Thus, if something justifies you, it must be in some sense *available* to you. Although the availability constraint is attractive to internalists, externalists have offered reasons for doubting it (see Goldman 1999*b*). Moreover, even if the availability constraint is accepted, such a constraint is only a necessary condition for justifiedness. And it gives us no inkling of *which* available states, facts, or conditions make *which* propositions or beliefs immediately justified. I am assuming here that we have been told—which we have not—what exactly it means to be "available". Even knowing the appropriate meaning of this term, however, would not thereby give us an answer to question Q3—namely, which available states make which beliefs or propositions justified.

4. Huemer on direct perceptual justifiedness

Huemer (2001) offers a general account of immediate justification, an account that is stated quite compactly:

P3 If it seems to S as if P, then S thereby has at least prima facie justification for believing that P. (Huemer 2001: 99)

Huemer calls this the rule of "phenomenal conservatism". The kinds of seemings (or appearances) he has in mind are of at least three sorts: perceptual seemings, memory-related seemings, and intellectual seemings (intuitions). Each gives rise, according to Huemer, to a species of justificational foundations. Three points of clarification should be noted. First, the principle of phenomenal conservatism concerns only prima facie, not ultima facie, justification. This is no different from the other approaches to immediate justification we have discussed, which are equally aimed at prima facie justification. Second, principle P3, as written, does not explicitly say anything about immediate justification. But, since the sufficient condition it offers makes no requirement concerning prior beliefs (whether justified or not), it is implicitly a principle of immediate justification. Third, Huemer specifically claims that immediate, or foundational, justification of *all* kinds is conferred by seeming-as-if states:

> I intend phenomenal conservatism to be a general principle of foundational justification. It explains not only why perceptual beliefs are noninferentially justified, but also why any other belief that is noninferentially justified is such. . . . I propose to account for perceptual knowledge by the same general principle I apply to all other kinds of knowledge. (Huemer 2001: 102)

How shall we assess this theory? Markie (2005) lodges several criticisms of it. He begins by critiquing some arguments Huemer offers in defense of principle P3. I shall not review these arguments or Markie's criticisms of them, because, even if Huemer's arguments for principle P3 are inadequate (and I definitely lean in this direction), the principle might still be correct. So let me turn to Markie's counterexamples against P3.

Markie says that mental processes that are incapable of producing prima facie justification can nonetheless determine how things seem to us. He gives an example to illustrate his point that is very similar to Feldman's bird-watchers' example:

> Suppose that we are prospecting for gold. You have learned to identify a gold nugget on sight but I have no such knowledge. As the water washes out of my pan, we both look at a pebble, which is in fact a gold nugget. My desire to discover gold makes it seem to me as if the pebble is gold; your learned identification skills make it seem that way to you. According to (PC) [our principle (3)], the belief that it is gold has *prima facie* justification for both of us. Yet, certainly, my wishful thinking should not gain my perceptual belief the same positive epistemic status of defeasible justification as your learned identification skills. (Huemer 2005: 356–7)

Next Markie offers an example very similar to Feldman's contrast between believing there's a table present and believing there's a table exactly 12 years old present (both on the basis of the table's mere appearance). Markie's example and discussion run as follows:

> Suppose that I perceive the walnut tree in my yard, and, having learned to identify walnut trees visually, it seems to me that it is a walnut tree. The same phenomenological experience that makes it seem to me that the tree is a walnut also makes it seem to me that it was planted on April 24, 1914. Nothing in the phenomenological experience or my identification skills supports things seeming this way to me. There is no

date-of-planting sign on the tree, for example. . . . It is plausible that my experience directly justifies my belief that the tree is a walnut. The phenomenological character of the experience and my identification skills combine to support that belief. However, the phenomenological character of my experience does not combine with anything I have learned, or could learn, to support my belief that the tree was planted April 24, 1914. . . . My perception cannot directly justify my belief about the planting date. Nonetheless, according to (PC) [our principle P3], both my belief that it is a walnut tree and my belief that it was planted on April 24, 1914 are *prima facie*, and so defeasibly, justified for me. (Huemer 2005: 357)

I agree with Markie that these cases are difficulties for Huemer's account. But the difficulties do not end there. Another problem with the account is that it does not cover all cases of immediate, or foundational, justification, as Huemer claims it does. In fact, the most classical type of direct justification is not covered by phenomenal conservatism.

Suppose someone both experiences pain and thinks about Vienna, and suppose he is aware of each experience and therefore forms a belief that he is in pain and a belief that he is thinking about Vienna. These are classical cases of immediately justified beliefs. How does phenomenal conservatism handle them? To sustain phenomenal conservatism, there would have to be introspective seemings or appearances analogous to perceptual seemings and memory-related seemings. In addition to feeling pain and believing one is in pain, there would have to be a "seeming as if" one is in pain; and, in addition to thinking about Vienna and believing that one is thinking about Vienna, there would have to be a "seeming as if" one is thinking about Vienna. But there are not any such introspective seemings or appearances, distinct from the feelings and thought episodes themselves and the beliefs about them. So, introspective foundational beliefs constitute counterexamples to Huemer's phenomenal conservatism. Huemer does not mention such cases, despite the fact that they are core examples of basic beliefs according to epistemological tradition.

Huemer might reply to this objection as follows. In the special case of introspective beliefs, the mental state itself is the relevant appearance or seeming. A *distinct* seeming, however, is not needed because the conscious state itself plays that role. This reply is unsatisfactory. The seemings Huemer posits for perception, memory, and a priori intellection are all mental states (or events) that resemble beliefs in two respects. First, they have propositional content: they are of the form "it seems as if P". Second, seemings are descriptive or depictive attitudes; they have a mind-to-world direction of fit rather than a world-to-mind direction of fit. Not all mental states or episodes, however, have these properties. States like being in pain (arguably) have no propositional content at all. And states like desires, wishes, and intentions are not descriptive or depictive attitudes; they have a world-to-mind direction of fit rather than a mind-to-world direction of fit. Nonetheless, all these kinds of mental states are just as capable of conferring, or helping to confer, immediate justification as states like thinking that P. One can be immediately justified in believing that one is in pain, and one can be immediately justified in believing one has a desire, or desires that Q. However strenuously Huemer may work to make introspection cases fit the "seeming" mold, it won't work for all cases. In fact, it is plausible *at most* for a small subset of cases. For the rest, a different story is needed. This casts doubt on the approach in general.

5. Process reliabilism and perceptual foundations

Let me turn now to some positive proposals of my own. As indicated in the introduction, these proposals will have a process-reliabilist theme. There is wide consensus that, if foundationalism is correct, there are probably multiple domains of basic beliefs or propositions. This is clearly illustrated by Huemer, who presents three categories of basic beliefs: perceptual, memory related, and intellectual (intuitive). This section deals with the first of these categories: perceptual basic beliefs.

Parenthetically, we should say a word or two about the relationship between reliabilism and foundationalism. My original formulation of process reliabilism (Goldman 1979) proposed a recursive format for justified beliefs. In this format, base clauses state sufficient conditions for justifiedness without invoking the justificational status of other beliefs. Recursive clauses state sufficient conditions for justifiedness that do invoke the justificational status of other beliefs. Obviously, base clauses would permit immediately, directly, or foundationally justified beliefs. Sosa (1980) calls this "formal foundationalism". Formal foundationalism does not entail process reliabilism, however. It is not committed to any role for causal processes in the conditions for justifiedness, or to reliability as a crucial determinant of justificational status. Thus, formal foundationalism is compatible with process reliabilism, but process reliabilism is only one species of formal foundationalism. Traditional foundationalism, which spurned causal factors as irrelevant to justificational status, would be another variety of formal foundationalism.

I turn now to the topic of perceptual foundational beliefs. This is a class of perceptual beliefs about the external world that allegedly qualify as immediately (prima facie) justified. Not all foundationalists, of course, countenance perceptual foundational beliefs. Cartesian foundationalism restricts foundational beliefs to beliefs about one's own current mental states (and elementary propositions of reason). But modest foundationalists typically admit the existence of basic beliefs about the external world. The present question is: what conditions, exactly, must these beliefs fulfill to be directly justified?

Let us pursue the clues provided by Feldman's examples. Although his proper-response-to-experience theory is vague and inadequate, his examples are helpful. Markie's examples are cast in the same mold and are equally instructive, but I shall stick with Feldman's.

Consider the difference between Feldman's expert and novice bird-watchers. Assume for the sake of discussion that the two have identical visual experiences. How do they differ so that the expert's belief in the species-identifying proposition ("It's a pink-spotted flycatcher") is immediately justified and the novice's belief in the same proposition is not so justified? The difference might well lie in differences in the cognitive processes by which they respectively proceed from visual experience to belief.[6] The expert presumably connects selected features of his visual experience to things he has stored in memory about pink-spotted flycatchers, perhaps securing an appropriate "match" between features in the experience and features in the memory store. The novice does no such thing; he just guesses (according to Feldman's story). Presumably, the token process used by the expert is an instance of a *generally reliable* (truth-conducive) kind of cognitive process. It involves classifying an instance of a category type by matching observed features of the instance to information about the category. This is a much more truth-conducive classification process—as befits an expert—than mere guessing. Thus, Feldman's vague notion of a *proper* response to experience might be spelled out as a doxastic response to experience that is the output of a reliable belief-forming process applied to that

---

[6] Interestingly, Markie explicitly adverts to cognitive processes in describing his versions of this kind of case. I think he is right to do so, because it makes the cases understandable. However, although he has latched onto this component of what I regard as the right solution to the problem, his dismissal of reliabilism at the beginning of his paper keeps him from seeing the full (reliabilist) solution. So his article's theme is that the problem remains a "mystery".

experience (as input). Since all the information processing that occurs in the expert's cognitive system is assumed here to be unconscious, we do not violate the requirement that the belief be formed spontaneously or non-inferentially; so it remains a candidate for being immediately justified.

Feldman's 12-year-old table example can be handled similarly. If a person sees a table for the first time, there will not be any clues in his visual experience of the table to which a *reliable* belief-forming process could be applied that would generate the output that the table is 12 years old. Any process that might be used to generate this belief from his visual experience (without any relevant background information about the table) would not be reliably formed. By contrast, it would be easy to have a reliable belief-forming process that could be applied to the same visual experience and generate the output that a table is present. Where Feldman speaks of the two beliefs as being, respectively, an "improper" and a "proper" response to the visual experience, the difference might be captured more precisely by saying that one belief stems from applying an unreliable process to the visual experience (or by applying the process without engaging the visual experience at all), whereas the other stems from an application of a reliable process to the visual experience.

I do not attempt here to give a tight formulation of "reliable". For example, I do not try to specify the domain (modal or otherwise) in which the truth ratio for a process is to be determined, or to say how processes are to be typed (the generality problem). These are questions for the general theory of reliabilism, which I intend to skirt here.[7] My aim is only to display the promise of process reliabilism as a general approach to the core foundationalist idea of immediate justification. The aim is to show, or at least to illustrate, why it is more promising than competing approaches. I am not trying to provide all the details.

In characterizing the causal process relevant to the justifiedness of a perceptual belief, I have thus far followed Feldman in considering the

---

[7] I do not doubt, however, that answering these questions could help assuage some worries about the reliabilist approach. Consider, for example, the worry that merely "accidental" reliability is not sufficient for immediate justification. (Rich Feldman expressed this worry in a personal communication.) This problem might be partly resolved by selecting an appropriate domain for fixing the truth ratio of a process. Requiring a process to have a high truth ratio in nearby possible worlds, as well as in the actual one, might help exclude processes that are only accidentally reliable. An additional constraint might be added concerning the source, or origin, of a process's reliability. I discuss this kind of constraint in *Epistemology and Cognition* (Goldman 1986: 51–3, 94–5).

process *from experience to belief*. This accords with his suggestion that perceptual justification (primarily) consists of making a proper doxastic response *to experience*. An alternative treatment, however, is available to process reliabilism. The relevant process might be a more extended one, not *from experience to belief* but *from receptor stimulation (to experience) to belief*. This more extended process has potential advantages because of what might transpire between receptor stimulation and experience. It might include events or operations influenced by prior training, and these types of events might contribute to reliability. Thus, we should leave the door open to either type of process—the more extended or the less extended process—as the optimal choice from the perspective of process reliabilism. However, I will not attempt to make a firm resolution of the issue.[8]

How would process reliabilism deal with *propositional* (as opposed to *doxastic*) justification for perceptual propositions? Suppose that, in Feldman's bird-watcher example, neither the expert nor the novice actually believes that the bird is a pink-spotted flycatcher, although they both have a visual experience that results from seeing it. We want to distinguish between them by saying that the expert, but not the novice, is propositionally justified in having this belief. How would reliabilism explain the difference? Where direct justification is in question, process reliabilism can say the following. A proposition P is propositionally justified for an epistemic agent S (at time *t*) just in case S's total mental state (at *t*) is such that, *if* S were to "target" proposition P and were to apply suitable reliable processes in her repertoire to that total state, then a belief that P would be generated in S (see Goldman 1979: 21, or, in the reprinted version, Goldman 1992: 124). In the bird-watcher example, the expert's total state and the reliable processes in her repertoire are such that, if she targeted the pink-spotted flycatcher proposition and applied (a suitable subset of) her reliable processes to her total state at the time, then a belief would be generated that the sighted bird is a pink-spotted flycatcher. By contrast, the novice does

---

[8] I am grateful to Jim Pryor for emphasizing the fact that there is a choice to be made about process extent. He personally recommends the choice of an even more extended process than either of the two considered in the text—namely, a process that reaches from *external stimuli* to experience. (At least he recommends this for the analysis of *propositional* justification, which is addressed in the next paragraph of the text.) However, process reliabilism was formulated from the start as a theory that highlights *cognitive* processes, and cognitive processes are best interpreted as operations *internal* to the organism. See Goldman (1979: 12–13; or, in the reprinted version, Goldman 1992: 116).

not satisfy these conditions. There are no reliable processes in her repertoire such that, if they were applied to her total state, they would generate the pink-spotted flycatcher belief. Of course, the combination of her total state and *unreliable* processes in her repertoire are capable of generating this belief (that is how matters transpire in Feldman's original version of the case); but that does not meet the specified condition. So process reliabilism can account for the difference between the expert and the novice in both the doxastic and the propositional senses of justification.

6. Process reliabilism and introspective foundations

Although contemporary foundationalists often allow basic beliefs to include perceptual beliefs with external-world contents, they also typically allow the set of basic beliefs to include beliefs with first-person mental-state contents—for example, *I am in pain*. We used this point in critiquing Huemer's account. In this section we ask how process reliabilism hopes to handle this subclass of basic beliefs. One question is: what cognitive process would reliabilism invoke? A second question to be addressed is how process reliabilism would handle both the propositional and the doxastic interpretations of justification in this domain.

Starting with the first question, the obvious process of interest is the process of introspection, or inner sense—assuming there is such a process. Elsewhere I endorse the existence of such a process as the best explanation of people's first-person mental-classification activity (Goldman 2006: ch. 9). Alternative philosophical and psychological accounts of mental self-classification are surveyed and found wanting. The introspective process must be rather complex, however. I suggest that it involves two stages: first, a stage of *attending* to selected portions of the mental field, and second, a stage of *classifying* what is found there. A classificational act is a judgment or belief; so, in its second stage, introspection is a species of belief-forming process.

Suppose introspective classification is a generally reliable process (not to say infallible). Then any belief formed by introspection, according to process reliabilism, will be justified. Will it be immediately, or directly, justified? If it is spontaneous—that is, not consciously inferential—then it should be considered immediately justified. And this seems overwhelmingly plausible. When we introspectively classify our mental states, there is not any conscious inference from other beliefs. True, we may unconsciously draw on information about what it is like (from an internal perspective) to have a pain, a desire, or a belief. From a psychological point of view, however, this need be no different from cases of vision-based classification, where we draw unconsciously on information about what trees or tables look like. If visual object classification is allowed to yield immediately justified beliefs, the case for introspective mental-state classification is at least as good. However, as noted in Section 3, immediate justification based on introspection does not depend on any introspective "seeming" or "appearance" on which the belief is based.

The foregoing discussion addresses the doxastic interpretation of justification. What about the propositional interpretation? Can we make sense in process-reliabilist terms of being potentially justified—of being in a position to be justified—in believing a proposition about a current mental state, even when one does not believe it? Yes, process reliabilism has a fairly straightforward story to tell. If one feels pain at a given moment, one can apply the first stage of an introspection operation to that feeling—that is, one can *attend* to it, and then proceed to the second stage of classification. If one performed both of these operations, then the belief that one feels pain would be generated, and this would be the product of a reliable classificational operation. So this is the sense in which one is in a "position" to be justified, or is potentially justified, in believing one is in pain even when one does not actually hold that belief.

7. Immediate justification and the internalism/externalism dispute

The usual ways of describing foundationalism and its key notion of immediate justification are neutral vis-à-vis the internalism/externalism controversy. In advancing process reliabilism as the best detailed account of immediate justification, however, I am promoting the cause of externalism. How might internalists respond? As a staunch internalist, Feldman obviously tries to provide an internalist account of direct perceptual justification. His key notion of "proper response to experience" is evidently crafted so as to omit all unpalatable externalist ingredients. By contrast, I argue that the only satisfactory way to flesh out the notion of "proper response" is to utilize the notion of reliability, a paradigmatically externalist concept.

Elsewhere Conee and Feldman (2001) specify the general kind of internalism about justification they mean to defend. They do not address immediate justification in particular, but their general approach to justification is clearly intended to apply to this variety of justification. They first distinguish two different conceptions of internalism—namely, accessibilism and mentalism. Accessibilism holds that the justification of a person's beliefs is determined by things to which the person has special access—for example, "direct" access, or access through "introspection or reflection". Mentalism holds that the justificational status of beliefs is fixed only by things internal to the cognizer's mental life.

Conee and Feldman favor the mentalistic brand of internalism. They say that internalism, so construed, is committed to two theses. The first thesis, (S), asserts the strong supervenience of epistemic justification on the mental:

S   The justificatory status of a person's doxastic attitudes strongly super-venes on the person's occurrent and dispositional mental states, events and conditions. (Conee and Feldman 2001: 234)

The second thesis spells out a principal implication of (S):

M   If any two possible individuals are exactly alike mentally, then they are alike justificationally, e.g., the same beliefs are justified for them to the same extent. (Conee and Feldman 2001: 234)

Suppose we accept these two theses. Do they provide the resources for resolving the justificational status of beliefs in the kinds of cases of interest here, for example, Feldman's own cases in *Epistemology*? No. Principle (M) provides a single sufficient condition for the *sameness* of justificational status, but it does not provide conditions, either necessary or sufficient, for fixing *positive* or *negative* justificational status. Hence, it does not meet the challenge of question Q3.

To illustrate, consider the two bird-watchers, who both form a spontaneous belief that the sighted bird is a pink-spotted flycatcher. In Feldman's description, the novice and expert are not exactly alike mentally (even with respect to this belief). So their two beliefs are allowed to differ in justificational status. Does either (M) or (S) provide materials for determining that the expert's belief *is* justified and that the novice's belief *is not* justified? No. The theoretical resources of the approach, as specified by (M) and (S), simply are not adequate to draw any such conclusion, even when we add the psychological details Feldman supplies (namely, that the expert has lots of relevant training, that the novice jumps to a conclusion out of excitement, and so on). Of course, Feldman tries to provide an additional theoretical principle when he talks about "proper responses to experience", and tries to explain this in terms of beliefs having varying degrees of "closeness to experience". Greater closeness is supposed to generate greater justifiedness; and the closeness motif is arguably a matter of mentality, and hence (arguably) a legitimate factor for internalism to appeal to.[9] As discussed earlier, however, the "closeness" idea does not really work. What else might internalism have on offer? I know of no other promising internalist idea.

On the other hand, appeal to process reliability generates answers that precisely match our intuitions about cases. So this externalist ingredient performs exactly the job we want performed. Reliabilist externalism has an exemplary solution to our problem, whereas mentalistic internalism (thus far) has no satisfactory solution at all. To be sure, the proposed reliabilist solution to the problem of immediate justifiedness does not address any of the outstanding problems for reliabilism. But, in so far as reliabilism seems to have a far better solution to the problem of immediate justifiedness than any of its rivals, it receives an extra infusion of support.

References

Alston, W. (1995). "How to Think about Reliability", *Philosophical Topics*, 23: 1–29.

Beebe, J. (2004). "The Generality Problem, Statistical Relevance, and the Tri-Level Hypothesis", *Nous*, 38: 177–94.

Chisholm, R. (1977). *Theory of Knowledge*. 2nd edn.; Englewood-Cliffs, NJ: Prentice-Hall.

Comesana, J. (2005). "We are (Almost) All Externalists Now", in J. Hawthorne (ed.), *Philosophical Perspectives*, 19, *Epistemology*. Malden, MA: Blackwell.

Conee, E. and Feldman, R. (2001). "Internalism Defended", in H. Kornblith (ed.), *Epistemology: Internalism and Externalism*. Malden, MA: Blackwell.

Feldman, R. (2003). *Epistemology*. Upper Saddle River, NJ: Prentice Hall.

Goldman, A. (1979). "What is justified belief?", in G. Pappas (ed.), *Justification and Knowledge*. Dordrecht: Reidel; repr. in A. Goldman, *Liaisons: Philosophy Meets the Cognitive and Social Sciences*. Cambridge, MA: MIT Press, 1992.

---

[9] Even this assumption is dubious, however. Content closeness seems to be either a species of evidential support or in the same family as the support relation. But the support relation is not rightly considered a mental state of affairs, or relation, as argued in Goldman (1999*b*) and Comesana (2005). If this is correct, then any notion like closeness is not really congenial to mentalistic internalism.

Goldman, A. (1986). *Epistemology and Cognition*. Cambridge, MA: Harvard University Press.

———(1988). "Strong and Weak Justification", in J. Tomberlin (ed.), *Philosophical Perspectives*, 2, *Epistemology*. Atascadero, CA: Ridgeview; repr. in A. Goldman, *Liaisons: Philosophy Meets the Cognitive and Social Sciences*. Cambridge, MA: MIT Press, 1992.

———(1992). "Epistemic Folkways and Scientific Epistemology", in *Liaisons: Philosophy Meets the Cognitive and Social Sciences*. Cambridge, MA: MIT Press.

———(1999a). "A Priori Warrant and Naturalistic Epistemology", in J. Tomberlin (ed.), *Philosophical Perspectives*, 13, *Epistemology*. Malden, MA: Blackwell; repr. in A. Goldman, *Pathways to Knowledge, Private and Public*. New York: Oxford University Press, 2002.

———(1999b). 'Internalism Exposed', *Journal of Philosophy*, 96: 271–93; repr. in A. Goldman, *Pathways to Knowledge: Private and Public*. New York: Oxford University Press, 2002.

———(2001). 'Replies to the Contributors', *Philosophical Topics*, 29: 461–511.

———(2006). *Simulating Minds: The Philosophy, Psychology, and Neuroscience of Mindreading*. New York: Oxford University Press.

Greco, J. (2000). *Putting Skeptics in their Place*. Cambridge: Cambridge University Press.

Heller, M. (1995). "The Simple Solution to the Generality Problem", *Nous*, 29: 501–15.

Huemer, M. (2001). *Skepticism and the Veil of Perception*. Lanham, MD: Rowman and Littlefield.

Markie, P. (2005). "The Mystery of Direct Perceptual Justification", *Philosophical Studies*, 126: 347–373.

Pryor, J. (2000). "The Skeptic and the Dogmatist", *Nous*, 34: 517–49.

———(2005). "There is Immediate Justification", in M. Steup and E. Sosa (eds.), *Contemporary Debates in Epistemology*. Malden, MA: Blackwell.

Sosa, E. (1980). "The Raft and the Pyramid: Coherence versus Foundations in the Theory of Knowledge", *Midwest Studies in Philosophy*, 5, *Studies in Epistemology*. Minneapolis: University of Minnesota Press.

———(1991). *Knowledge in Perspective*. Cambridge: Cambridge University Press.

———(2001). "Goldman's Reliabilism and Virtue Epistemology", *Philosophical Topics*, 29: 383–400.

4

Evidence

Earl Conee and Richard Feldman

We advocate evidentialism. Evidentialism is the view that epistemic justification is a product of evidence. More precisely, it holds that

E   S is justified in believing p at t iff S's evidence at t on balance supports p.

Evidentialism holds that the justification of attitudes other than belief is also determined by evidence. When one's evidence supports the negation of a proposition, disbelief is the justified attitude. When one's evidence is counterbalanced, suspension of judgment is the justified attitude.[1]

We favor a strong version of evidentialism: E is necessarily true. That is, evidence is what justifies belief under every possible circumstance. Furthermore, evidence justifies necessarily. That is, the justificatory status of a proposition for a person strongly supervenes on the body of evidence that the person has. Thus, we affirm the following strengthening of E.

SE   Necessarily, if S1 is justified in believing P, and E is the evidence that S1 has, then necessarily, (1) on balance E supports P, and (2) if E is the evidence that S2 has, then S2 is justified in believing P.

---

[1] A second epistemic evaluation is important. A person can have evidence that on balance supports a proposition, yet the person might believe the proposition not on the basis of supporting evidence but rather for some epistemically defective reason. In that case, the belief itself deserves an unfavorable epistemic evaluation, even though believing is the justified attitude. Such believing is "ill founded". Beliefs based on justifying evidence are "well founded". Knowledge requires well-founded belief.

We regard the preceding statement of evidentialism as the bare sketch of a full theory of epistemic justification. Among the things needed to develop the theory more fully are accounts of what evidence is, what it is for a person to have something as evidence, when a body of evidence supports a proposition, and what the basing relation is. In this chapter we take some steps toward clarifying the nature of evidence and evidential support. For the most part, we will simply identify our view, offering few supporting arguments. In later sections we will respond to some objections and assess some rival views.

1. Fundamental concepts

1.1. Scientific evidence and justifying evidence

According to one way in which the word "evidence" is often used, some reliable indicators of states in the world are evidence of those states.[2] Fingerprints of a particular sort on a weapon are evidence that a particular person handled that weapon, smoke rising from a chimney is evidence of a fire in the fireplace below, and the presence of certain spots on a child's body is evidence that the child has measles. Evidence of this sort is publicly available. It can serve as a theoretically neutral adjudicator of disputes about the presence or absence of the state for which it is evidence. The existence of this sort of evidential relationship is something that is discovered by finding connections between a state in the world and the factors or symptoms that reliably indicate its presence. Call evidence of this sort "scientific evidence". E is scientific evidence for P provided that E is publicly available and E reliably indicates the truth of P.[3]

Suppose that some factor, S, is scientific evidence, for some condition, C. One's knowing that S exists does not guarantee that one is to the slightest degree justified in believing that C obtains. One reason for this, but not our central concern here, is that one might have, in addition to S, decisive evidence against C. What is more important for present purposes is that one can have

---

[2] For an excellent discussion of the issues taken up in this section, see T. Kelly, "Evidence", Edward N. Zalta (ed.), *The Stanford Encyclopedia of Philosophy* (Autumn 2006 edn.), <http://plato.stanford.edu/archives/fall2006/entries/evidence/>.

[3] "Publicly available" is vague in a way that we take to match "evidence" used in this way. Availing oneself of this evidence need not be easy. Some scientific evidence can be observed only by using exotic technology. In contrast, an individual's sensory states are not sufficiently available to the public to count.

scientific evidence without having any reason at all to believe what that scientific evidence supports. A criminal investigator can know the proposition, F, that the fingerprints at the scene of a crime have precise characteristics X, Y, and Z. This can be strong, even decisive, scientific evidence for the proposition, L, that Lefty was at the scene of the crime. But if the investigator does not know, or at least have reason to believe, that F indicates Lefty's presence, then the investigator has no reason at all to believe L and is not (on this basis, at least) at all justified in believing L. To be justified in this case he must in some way grasp the connection between F and L. The investigator need not formulate the thought that F is scientific evidence for L, for F to justify his believing L. But the investigator must be informed of some indicator connection between this evidence and the conclusion for the evidence to have any epistemic impact for him.

As we use the word "evidence" in our statement of evidentialism, the investigator who is unaware of any such connection does not have evidence that Lefty was at the scene of the crime. Intuitively, the investigator who is unaware of the connection lacks any reason to believe L. As we use "evidence" in stating and defending evidentialism, one who has no reason to believe something has no evidence for it. If the investigator did have evidence, and that evidence were not defeated by some other evidence, then he would be at least to some degree justified in believing that Lefty was there. Evidence, as we use the term, is *justifying evidence*. Thus, even though F is scientific evidence for L, F is not by itself justifying evidence for L. The conjunction of F and with information about F's connection to L is justifying evidence for L. More generally, something can be scientific evidence for a proposition without being justifying evidence for that proposition. Justifying evidence is by itself a reason for belief, something one could in principle cite as a justifying basis for belief.

One could restrict use of "evidence" to scientific evidence and say that the detective does have evidence—F—that supports L. But then one would have to say that merely having evidence supporting a proposition is not enough to make one at all justified in believing that proposition. It is clearer and simpler to preserve the connection between having supporting evidence and justification, and thus to say that merely knowing the characteristics of the fingerprints but not having the connecting information is not having evidence for the conclusion. But this is not to say that in all cases one has justifying evidence for a proposition only if one knows (or justifiably believes) that one has scientific evidence for that proposition. Such a requirement would overintellectualize justification, incorrectly making all justification involve beliefs about evidence and evidential support. We reject such a general requirement. We will return to this topic in a later section.

The two types of evidence are connected in a way that makes sense of the use of "evidence" for both and gives instrumental epistemic value to scientific evidence. Gaining scientific evidence, E, for a proposition, P, is often the most practical way for one who knows the association of E with P to gain justifying evidence for P. This is a main way in which scientific evidence fosters knowledge.

1.2. Evidence for settled truths

In a well-known passage in *Sense and Sensibilia* J. L. Austin writes:

The situation in which I would properly be said to have *evidence* for the statement that some animal is a pig is that, for example, in which the beast itself is not actually on view, but I can see plenty of pig-like marks on the ground outside its retreat. If I find a few buckets of pig-food, that's a bit more evidence, and the noises and the smell may provide better evidence still. But if the animal then emerges and stands there plainly in view, there is no longer any question of collecting evidence; its coming into view doesn't provide me with more *evidence* that it's a pig, I can now just *see* that it is, the question is settled.[4]

We endorse the view that Austin denies here. We think that seeing the pig does provide additional evidence. Indeed, it is this additional evidence that settles the question. Moreover, the visual evidence one has in a case like this is a paradigmatic kind of evidence. We believe that all ultimate evidence is experiential evidence. We return to this topic below.

It is true that if two people are standing together looking at a pig, it would be peculiar for one to ask the other what evidence he has that there is a pig there. This is because it is typical for one person, A, to ask another, B, for evidence when A has some doubt about the proposition in question and believes that B has some relevant information that A lacks. But that is not the case when A and B are looking at the same pig. However, if A and B are talking on the telephone and B asserts that there is a pig nearby, A might ask for evidence for this claim, and B could with perfect propriety respond that his evidence is that

---

[4] J. L. Austin, *Sense and Sensibilia* (Oxford: Oxford University Press, 1962), 115.

he sees it. Thus, seeing the pig is evidence that there is a pig present, but it is not the sort of evidence worth mentioning to someone who sees it as well.[5]

Furthermore, when one has evidence that settles a question, it is unusual or misleading to make the weaker claim that one has evidence for that claim rather than simply to make the claim itself. Thus, if A sees that a pig is present and wants to tell B, who is not present, about the situation, it would be odd for A to say that he has evidence that there is a pig present rather than simply to assert that there is one there. But this is because asserting that one has evidence is to assert something weaker than one can properly assert, and therefore it misleads. But one does have the visual evidence in such a case. In general, we do have evidence for settled truths. Our evidence is what settles their truth for us.

1.3. Beliefs, experiences, and "ultimate evidence"

Sometimes a person cites one belief as a reason for another. We take evidence to be what provides epistemic reasons. Thus it may seem that one belief can be evidence for another belief. We see no strong reason for resisting this claim, but it is important to distinguish between "ultimate" evidence and "intermediate" evidence.

Some philosophers have argued that only believed propositions can be part of the evidence one has. Their typical ground for this claim is that only believed propositions can serve as premises of arguments. Our view differs radically from this one. We hold that experiences can be evidence, and beliefs are only derivatively evidence. Examples intuitively support that we have experiences as evidence. Your evidence for the proposition that it is warm where you are typically includes your feeling of warmth, your evidence for the proposition that you are frustrated by being stuck in the heat in a traffic jam typically includes a palpable sense of your own frustration, your evidence for the proposition that the car in front of yours in the traffic jam is red typically includes your visual experience of how the car looks, and so forth. It is not just other propositions that you believe that contribute to your justification. The experience itself contributes. Experience is our point of interaction with the world—conscious awareness is how we gain whatever evidence we have.

---

[5] This is not to say that seeing a pig is what we shall call (just below, in Section 1.3) a person's "ultimate evidence"—evidence one has for which one need not have evidence. When one sees that a pig is there, one has evidence that one sees a pig there.

Furthermore, all ultimate evidence is experiential. Believing a proposition, all by itself, is not evidence for its truth. Something at the interface of your mind and the world—your experiences—serves to justify belief in a proposition, if anything does. What we are calling your "ultimate evidence" does this without needing any justification in order to provide it.

Memory often helps to justify, of course. Simply remembering a proposition can provide evidence for further propositions. This may seem to be a case in which a believed proposition—the one remembered—is ultimate evidence. But that is not quite right. There is something else involved in memory or an experience of remembering that contributes to justification. We take this to be a plain fact of introspective psychology. There is a clear difference between a thought or image that happens to become conscious, and one that presents itself as being recalled. We hold that this latter sort of impression can be an element of one's non-doxastic evidence for the proposition.

1.4. Evidence and the possession of evidence

Evidentialism holds that a person's doxastic justification is a function of the evidence that the person has. One might think that the way to understand this is first to define, or characterize, what evidence *is*, and then to explain what it is for a person to *have* a particular bit of evidence. But this is a mistake. It is not the case that something just is, or is not, evidence. To see why this is true, consider, for example, your current perceptual experience. Is this experience evidence? The best answer seems to be that it is evidence for you, but it is not evidence for the rest of us. It is part of your evidence for the proposition that you are reading an essay on epistemology. But your experience itself is not evidence for the rest of us. Experiences we would have if you were to describe your experience could be part of our evidence, but our grasp of your experience is indirect. There is no correct non-relational answer to the question "Is it justifying evidence?" Perhaps there would be no harm in saying that something is justifying evidence (*simpliciter*) if it is evidence for someone. However, nothing is gained by saying this either. All the epistemic work that we attempt to do with justifying evidence relies on evidence that someone has. Thus, on our usage, evidence is always evidence someone has.

One useful way to identify what we take to be a person's evidence at a time is to say that it is the information or data the person has to go on in forming beliefs. Your focal visual experiences of the word tokens in this chapter constitute paradigm examples of someone's evidence. There are extremely hard questions about what exactly a person has to go on at any given time. The central issue has to do with information stored in one's memory. At any moment one has some items in consciousness that can guide one's beliefs as well as a lot of information stored in memory. Some of this stored information is readily accessible, in the sense that it would immediately come to mind if one were to think about a relevant topic. Other information would come to mind only if one engaged in a long process, such as psychotherapy, designed in part to recover suppressed memories.

Versions of evidentialism can be developed that differ over what they count as one's evidence at a time. Some restrictive versions count only one's current conscious states. Some inclusive versions count everything stored in one's memory. Moderate views count some but not all stored information. The extreme views have a kind of theoretical neatness, but they are burdened with implausible consequences. The most restrictive view seems to imply that you are not justified in believing simple, obvious, and well-known truths that you are not currently thinking about. The most inclusive views imply that beliefs well supported by everything that you are thinking about can be unjustified because they are undermined by deeply buried memories that could be recovered only through extensive psychoanalysis. Moderate views have more intuitively satisfying implications, but they are difficult to formulate in any precise way.

It seems best not to take any narrow stand on the extent to which information that one has some potential to retrieve is part of the evidence that one has. A main source of support for evidentialism is its capacity to account for intuitive epistemic judgments. People vary in what they find intuitively justified for a person at a time. These varying judgments are correlated with varying judgments about what evidence the person has at the time. (The two of us often differ between ourselves about these matters and each of us often differs with himself about them over time.) It is a strength of evidentialism that it encompasses variants concerning what counts as a person's evidence that bear out these differing intuitions about justification. If there are any decisive arguments that resolve these differences, then there is a version of evidentialism within this range that accords with the conclusion of those arguments. The difficulty of specifying which retrievable information is part of one's current evidence does not call into question the idea that it is evidence that determines epistemic status. To the contrary, it makes clear a way in which some familiar terms of epistemic evaluation are vague or obscure.

1.5. Necessity and contingency

It is common to think of evidential relations as contingent. Consider a simple example. Suppose that you know that Smith owns a pink Corvette and you see a pink Corvette parked in Smith's usual spot in the office parking lot. It is natural to say that your observations provide evidence that Smith is in the office. Of course, this is only contingently evidence for this conclusion. This is not just because it is contingent matter that Smith is in his office given this evidence. That is, it is not just that this is not entailing evidence. Rather, the point is that it is only a contingent matter that this kind of car in this spot in the lot has anything to do with Smith at all. Smith could have driven a Yugo and kept it parked at the service station. The Corvette evidence could have been evidence for Jones's presence, since she could have been the one to drive such a car and park it in that location. These clear contingencies might be thought to argue that evidential relations are contingent matters.

On our view, evidential relations are necessary. The evidence described above about Smith, by itself, is not evidence that Smith is in the office. Instead, the described information is part of a larger body of evidence, and it is this body of evidence that is actually your evidence that supports the conclusion about Smith's whereabouts. One reason for thinking about supporting evidence in this demanding way is that it prevents overcounting. It would be a mistake to think that learning that there is a pink Corvette in the lot is some evidence for Smith's being present and that the information about Smith's automobile ownership is additional evidence for that conclusion. It is the combination of the two that provides one reason for the conclusion. In the absence of any such combination, neither item of information on its own would be any reason at all for one to believe the conclusion. Once the combination is adequately spelled out, it is intuitively a reason someone has for the conclusion under any possible circumstances where a person has that evidence. This includes circumstances in which one has additional defeating evidence, rendering one not justified in believing the conclusion.

It is possible to understand the credibility of the views of those who say that evidential relations are contingent. Salient elements of a necessarily supporting body of evidence for something are themselves acceptable to call "evidence" for that thing. These salient elements may be, by themselves, only contingently reasons for that conclusion. Though we deny that this "evidence" always supports on its own, this use of the word is a practical way to identify key components of the supporting evidence. It is likely that a full theory could be worked out that endorses this way of speaking as literally true. It is clearer to treat the evidential support relation as a necessary relation and to explain apparent counterinstances to the necessity, as we just did. Thought experiments support this necessity. In any case, where everything that might be credibly counted as a person's evidence for a proposition could have been possessed by one who had no reason to believe the proposition, intuitively the person does not actually have supporting evidence for the proposition.

2. Kinds of evidence

2.1. Perceptual evidence

Ordinary perceptual judgments are often justified. For a typical singular perceptual judgment to be justified one must have a suitable perceptual experience as evidence, and some background conditions must be satisfied as well. One needs some conceptual competence suitable for applying concepts in external world perceptual beliefs, and perhaps one needs memories about how ordinary things ordinarily appear, and perhaps one also needs some general view of one's situation that does not too flagrantly conflict with the content of the belief. (There are important epistemic issues about the ingredients of this background. But we are now pursuing an issue that permits them to be set aside.)

Suppose that some such background is in place. Suitable perceptual experience is prominent in acquiring justification for any particular perceptual belief. For instance, when the belief is that *that* is a tree (B1), typically one has visual experiences, E1—En, that consist in visual qualities, some of which are arranged in some treeish fashion, as viewed from some apparent perspective. E1—En are an important part of one's evidence for B1. E1—En are one's "ultimate" perceptual evidence for B1; one needs no evidence for E1—En, and one needs no additional current experiential evidence to justify B1. If the background is in place and one has no grounds for doubting one's faculties or mistrusting the apparent situation, then one is justified in believing B1.

A line of inquiry that leads us to think that E1—En are typical of our "ultimate" perceptual evidence is the series of Socratic questions familiar from Roderick Chisholm's work.[6] If one is asked, "What justifies you in believing

---

[6] Roderick Chisholm, *Theory of Knowledge* (2nd edn., Englewood Cliffs, NJ: Prentice Hall, 1977), 18—20.

B1?", a satisfactory answer is, "I see that tree." If one is asked, "What justifies you in believing that you see that tree?", a satisfactory answer is, "It looks to me as though that's a tree." If one is asked, "What justifies you in thinking that it looks to you as though that's a tree?", a satisfactory answer is to ascribe to oneself experiences of treeish visual characteristics, such as E1–En, and to add background information that gives one reason to think that E1–En are characteristic of how a tree looks.[7] All the answers so far given cite facts about justification that will already be present when B1 is perceptually justified. If one is asked, "What justifies you in believing that you are experiencing those treeish characteristics?", something different is true. The content of the answer may cite evidence that one did not already have when B1 was initially perceptually justified. For instance, a satisfactory answer would be that, in an attempt to answer the previous question, one has become reflectively aware of the characteristics. But until that point, the answers to the Socratic questions cited facts that were present as one's evidence for B1. This line of inquiry traces evidence that one had for B1 back to E1–En, and nothing beyond them need have been present in order for B1 to be perceptually justified. E1–En are at the beginning of the line.

Here are two important intuitive epistemic features of E1–En. First, they can be evidence for a proposition without one's having evidence for them. So they can stop a regress of justification, as the intuitive answers to the sequence of Socratic questions illustrates. Second, E1–En are elements of the interface of one's mind and the rest of the world. They are ways in which the world most conspicuously intrudes into one's conscious life. Perhaps they are "conceptualized" and perhaps they are non-conceptual. We will not resolve that difficult issue. Either way, intuitively they are the most transparent states of which we are aware. They come closest to presenting themselves as they are. Nothing available to introspection mediates between them and us. This is why they can justify without needing justification.

2.2. A priori evidence

Sometimes the mere contemplation of a proposition results in one becoming justified in believing it. It is possible to argue for reliabilist explanations of this, holding that our reliability in some domains accounts for our justification

---

[7] Chisholm's account does not explicitly include this last element.

in those domains. It is also possible to argue that some propositions are self-evident, in the sense that mere adequate contemplation of them necessitates one's having justification for them. On this view, necessarily if one adequately considers one of these simple propositions, one is justified in believing it. We accept neither of these views. We believe that sometimes when a person contemplates a proposition, the person acquires evidence supporting its truth. It is not necessarily the case that everyone gets this sort of a priori evidence by contemplating the same propositions. Just as some people have more acute visual faculties, some may be better able to get the evidence for some truths than others in this a priori way.

The nature of the evidence people acquire in the way just described is elusive. We will leave open many details and say only the following. In considering propositions that are the best candidates for immediate a priori justification, one becomes conscious of something about the relations among the concepts employed in considering the proposition. This non-doxastic awareness of conceptual relations provides the evidence. Thought experiments can provide a different sort of a priori justification. Intuitive judgments about hypothetical particular examples can gain evidence from awareness of conceptual relations, as before. But philosophical principles that are properly generalized from thought experiments are not supported by such conceptual evidence. The a priori evidence for the principles supports them in a broadly inductive way.

2.3. Memory and inference

We accept the intuitively plausible view that memory, inference, and intro-spection are additional sources of evidence and they can provide justification for beliefs. Details about these sources and general theories about how they work would be extremely valuable. However, the general picture is similar to that of perception. In particular, recalling a proposition is evidence that the proposition is true. (We said a bit more about the nature of memorial evidence above.) Properly inferring a proposition from others that are justified is evidence that the inferred proposition is true. (We say a bit more about inferential support below.) In all cases it is plausible to hold that these sources provide justification only when a suitable background is in place. Exactly what constitutes that background is a difficult matter we will not attempt to resolve here. Whatever exactly the background is, it is a matter of evidence. That is, the difficult issue concerns the nature of the background evidence one must have for these sources to provide justification.

3. Evidential support

An evidentialist might adopt any of a variety of views concerning the epistemic support relation—that is, the relation that holds between a body of evidence and a proposition when it is true that a person having that body of evidence is justified in believing that proposition. One way to express a view about evidential support is by formulating epistemic principles identifying what epistemic status believing a proposition has in specified circumstances. Some of these principles will apply to cases of inferential justification—that is, cases in which a person believes a proposition as a result of inferring it from other propositions the person believes. We here distinguish several of these views and give some reasons for favoring the approach to explaining this relation that we prefer. We leave it as the most promising approach, however. It is something to be elaborated on another occasion.

3.1. Evidential proportionalism

According to this view, every body of evidence bears some logical or objective probabilistic relation to each proposition: the evidence entails the truth of the proposition or makes it probable to some degree or entails or probabilizes the denial of the proposition. These relations are matters of deductive and inductive logic (broadly conceived).[8]

We reject this view. We think it ties epistemic relations too closely to logical relations. Specifically, it suggests a kind of logical omniscience that justified believers need not have. A person may know some propositions that logically entail some proposition that the person scarcely understands and surely does not know to follow from the things she does know. The logical route from what she knows to this proposition may be complex and go beyond her understanding, or even the understanding of any person. In our view, the person is not then justified in believing the consequence, even though it is entailed by her evidence. It is noteworthy that, to become justified in believing the proposition, she has to learn something new—namely, its logical connection to her evidence. Thus, in this case, the entailing evidence is not justifying evidence. Something more is needed. People frequently have this something more in the case of simpler logical connections.

---

[8] For discussion, see Alvin Goldman, *Epistemology and Cognition* (Cambridge, MA: Harvard University Press, 1986), sect. 5.2.

The same thing can be true in cases of evidence that confers only logical probability on a conclusion. Where this probabilistic relation is beyond the person's understanding, the person may not be justified to any degree in believing a proposition made probable by the evidence.

Thus, evidential support is not simply a matter of entailment or probabilistic connections.

3.2. Subjectivism

A second possible view about the evidential support relation is that evidence E supports P for person S just in case S believes that E entails or makes sufficiently probable P. There is room for variation on exactly what the content of S's belief about the relation between E and P must be, but the idea of subjectivism is that the support relation depends upon S believing that a suitable relation holds between E and P.

We reject this account for two reasons. For one thing, it implies a meta-level requirement that we reject—namely, that justified belief in all cases requires believing that some suitable objective relation holds between one's evidence and the content of one's beliefs. There can be knowledge and justified belief in the absence of any such beliefs about evidential relations. Children and unsophisticated believers provided clear examples of this, and even sophisticated believers often lack explicit beliefs about the connections between their evidence and their conclusions.

Furthermore, merely believing that the relation obtains is too weak a requirement. Were it sufficient, wild and unjustified beliefs to the effect some evidence supports a conclusion would then render justified those conclusions. As we noted earlier, there are cases in which justifying evidence must include a belief about the connection between some scientific evidence and a conclusion. In the cases in which justification for a conclusion does depend upon a belief that the evidence is properly related to that conclusion, then this belief about the connections must itself be justified. But, on pain of an intolerable infinite regress, actual belief in such a connection cannot be required in all cases.

Thus, evidential support is not simply a matter of belief (or even justified belief) in logical or probabilistic connections.

3.3. Non-doxastic seemings

Sometimes, when someone reflects on some evidence, it is appropriate to say that it "just seems" to the person that it supports a conclusion. A possible view about evidential support makes significant use of these "seemings", holding that E supports C for a person S provided it seems to S that E has a proper logical or probabilistic relation to C.[9] Its seeming to S that E supports P is a non-doxastic state, not a belief that E supports P. As a result, this view avoids our objection to the subjectivist view just discussed. It is also important to note that a seeming is not the sort of thing that needs justification. So, if a seeming justifies, then it is capable of stopping a regress of justifiers that are in need of justification.

The view that justification results from non-doxastic seemings can be formulated in a way that renders it compatible with our claim that evidential relations are necessary. Rather than regarding the evidential support relation as relativized to believers, one can regard the seeming state as part of the evidence and hold that, necessarily, anyone who has a certain body of evidence, including the seeming, is justified in believing the same propositions.

This theory has some welcome implications, since it provides a way to account for the justification of much that we are inclined to regard as justified. One can say that typical perceptual experiences seem to the perceiver to support ordinary propositions about the world, that typical memorial experiences seem to support belief in the propositions they are about, that the premises of simple arguments seem to support their conclusions, and so on.

Nevertheless, we do not find this view satisfactory. For one thing, these non-doxastic seemings are not necessary for justification. When one has a fully articulated good reason to believe something, then the conclusion is justified whether one has the additional non-doxastic seeming state or not. Furthermore, the existence of these non-doxastic seeming states is doubtful. It is easy enough to identify spontaneous beliefs about connections between propositions. It is easy enough to identify feelings of confidence about these beliefs. But it is at least quite difficult to discern any state other than a belief or a level of confidence that can be properly characterized as its seeming to one that E supports P.

3.4. Epistemic principles

Another view about the epistemic support relation asserts special epistemic principles of the sort Roderick Chisholm long defended. These principles state,

---

[9] For a defense of a view according to which seemings in general provide prima facie justification for their contents, see Michael Huemer, *Skepticism and the Veil of Perception* (Lanham, MD: Rowman and Littlefield, 2001).

for instance, that, if certain psychological conditions obtain, then particular propositions are justified. For example, if a person had certain perceptual experiences, then the person was justified in believing particular propositions about the world; if the person had certain memory experiences, then believing the contents of those memories was justified; if a person observed another person behaving in a particular way, then the person was justified in believing that the other person was in particular mental states; and that, if a person observed certain states of the world, then the person was justified in believing particular ethical propositions. Chisholm held that these principles were not special cases of more general logical principles. They were special epistemic principles.

What is distinctive, and troubling, about Chisholm's view is not so much the specific claims he made about what justifies what. His distinctive and troubling claim is that these principles do not derive from any more fundamental or more general ones.[10] It is difficult to resist the thought that these are principles designed to ratify the beliefs that Chisholm thought were justified. Even if one agrees with Chisholm's judgment about these matters, there is a troubling arbitrariness and specificity about his choice of principles. This can best be seen by considering contested cases. Some will say that certain kinds of religious experiences provide justifying evidence for propositions about the existence and nature of God. Others deny this. Chisholm's view seems to imply that one side or the other is right in this dispute, but there are no more fundamental principles to resolve the dispute. Either such experiences just do justify the corresponding propositions or they just do not, and that is all there is to it.

In our view, if perceptual and memorial experiences are justifying (with the proper background in place), then, there is something about them that makes this the case. If religious experience shares this feature, then it, too, is justifying. If it does not, then it is not. There must be a more illuminating truth about why the experiences are justifying.

3.5. Best explanations

We believe that the fundamental epistemic principles are principles of best explanation. Perceptual experiences can contribute toward the justification of propositions about the world when the propositions are part of the best explanation of those experiences that is available to the person. Similarly, the truth of the contents of a memory experience may be part of the best

---

[10] See, e.g., Chisholm, *Theory of Knowledge*, 64–7.

explanation of the experience itself. Thus, the general idea is that a person has a set of experiences, including perceptual experiences, memorial experiences, and so on. What is justified for the person includes propositions that are part of the best explanation of those experiences available to the person. Likewise, one's inferences justify by identifying to one further propositions that either require inclusion in one's best explanation for it to retain its quality or enhance the explanation to some extent by their inclusion.

There are important details of this account that are yet to be developed. In particular, we need an understanding of best available explanation that does not include too much. It may be that the best scientific explanation of a person's current experiences includes detailed scientific theories or distant logical consequences that the person does not understand. Such an explanation is not available to the person. A precise account of this availability is difficult to develop.

The best available explanation of one's evidence is a body of propositions about the world and one's place in it that make best sense of the existence of one's evidence. This notion of making sense of one's evidence can be equally well described as fitting the presence of the evidence into a coherent view of one's situation. So it may be helpful to think of our view as a non-traditional version of coherentism. The coherence that justifies holds among propositions that assert the existence of the non-doxastic states that constitute one's ultimate evidence and propositions that offer an optimal available explanation of the existence of that evidence.

One's justification for a proposition can be of various strengths. Correspondingly, one's evidence varies in the strength of its support of different propositions. According to our explanatory coherence view of evidential support, this variation in strength of support derives from differences in how well the supported propositions explanatorily cohere with one's evidence.

4. Objections

4.1. Entailing perceptual evidence?

John McDowell can be interpreted as suggesting that there are crucial items of non-doxastic evidence that our account omits.[11] Read in this way, his view

---

[11] McDowell has been so interpreted by Duncan Pritchard and Ram Neta, in "McDowell and the New Evil Genius", *Philosophy and Phenomenological Research*, forthcoming. They use the phrase

presents a strikingly different account of perceptual evidence. When one sees that *that*'s a tree, the view implies that one has as evidence the perceptual state of seeing that *that* is a tree (PS1) for the proposition *that's a tree* (B1). PS1 is factive; it cannot exist unless B1 is true. The suggestion is that, when we are in PS1, we have PS1 as entailing evidence for B1 and we can know B1 by believing it on the basis of that evidence.[12] There is no appeal here to what we count as the ultimate evidence—the experiential states E1−E*n*.

We do not deny that there is a sense in which PS1 is evidence that one sometimes has for B1. We are mentalist evidentialists. That is, we think that one's justifying evidence supervenes on the totality of one's mental states. Since PS1, the factive mental state of seeing, is not present when one is visually deceived, our view allows that one has PS1 as evidence in the veridical case and not when one lacks when deceived. Although a person may have the factive mental state as a reason in the veridical case, one does not *need to have as a reason* any such state for B1 to be justified. We deny that PS1 *strengthens* one's justification for B1 over what one has in cases that are otherwise maximally similar except that PS1 does not exist. That is, when B1 is visually justified for one, it is so justified by a body of evidence that prominently includes ultimate evidence like E1−E*n* (in the presence of some suitable background of the sort previously described). When PS1 exists, belief that it exists is ultimately justified by the likes of E1−E*n*. The evidence on the basis of which the belief that PS1 exists can be known need not include the entailing evidence of PS1 itself.

Here are a couple of reasons for doubting that it is PS1, instead of E1−E*n*, that ultimately justifies B1 in ordinary cases of knowing B1 by visual perception. First, PS1 has a justifying strength that intuitively derives from its relation to E1−E*n*. It will be helpful to compare cases in which one sees a tree with cases in which one is deceived by a mere tree façade. If PS1 were ever one's ultimate evidence for B1, then PS1 would be available as *entailing* evidence when one saw a tree and was in state PS1. When PS1 did not obtain, as when one was deceived by a tree façade, one would have no entailing evidence on behalf of B1. Yet,

---

"empirical reason" for what we are here calling evidence. One brief basis for this reading can be found in John McDowell, "Knowledge and the Internal Revisited", *Philosophy and Phenomenological Research*, 64/1 (2002), 97−105.

[12] This claim is independent of the claim that people who have veridical perceptions are in states disparate from those of victims of deception. For all that has been said so far, it may be that in veridical cases the likes of E1−E*n* are present along with PS1, or it may be that in veridical cases the likes of E1−E*n* are not present.

intuitively, one has equally good evidence for B1 in both cases. If the evidence is the same in both cases, then is it no wonder at all that the evidence is equally good. If PS1 were what ultimately justified in the veridical case but not in the façade case, then there would be no straightforward explanation of the equal quality of the evidence.

Second, suppose that one did happen to guess correctly that one was seeing a mere tree façade (B2). Intuitively, one would *not* know B2, and one would *not* have good evidence that B2 was true. Yet one would be in a relational state (PS2) that related one to a tree façade in just the way that PS1 relates one to a whole tree in the veridical case.[13] This state PS2 seems to be as good a candidate for being an ultimate justifier, on the approach attributed to McDowell, as does PS1 in the perceptual case. But, again, the belief that one is seeing a tree façade would be *un*justified, in spite of one's being in PS2. This difference in justifying capacity of such similar states is a liability of the attributed approach. The difference supports the thought that neither PS1 nor PS2 is as transparent to awareness as are the likes of E1−E*n*. The latter thus have better claim to being fundamental evidence than does PS1 or PS2. It is simpler and more unified to think that in both cases the evidence that explains why one is justified, and the strength of the justification, is what we count as the ultimate evidence. Again, PS1 still may be evidence that one has when one has the perceptual knowledge. But its evidential status derives from one's having the ultimate evidence of perceptual experience. PS1 does not enhance one's justification for B1 beyond what the ultimate evidence provides.

4.2. Only knowledge as evidence?

Timothy Williamson identifies one's evidence with one's knowledge.[14] He argues for this identification. Our view allows that some evidence is knowledge. But some of Williamson's arguments jeopardize the conception of evidence that we are proposing here. We will respond briefly to the arguments.

One argument with negative implications for our view is this. "If one's evidence were restricted to the contents of one's own mind, it could not play the role that it actually does in science. The evidence for the proposition that

---

[13] PS2 would not be the *perceptual* state of seeing that *that* is a tree façade, because that perceptual state is knowledge entailing and the guess would not be knowledge.

[14] See Timothy Williamson, *Knowledge and its Limits* (Oxford: Oxford University Press, 2000), ch. 9. All page references in the text are to this work.

the sun is larger than the earth is not just my present experiences or degrees of belief".[15]

We note initially that Williamson has reason to hope that this argument fails. What Williamson's own view implies is that one's evidence is restricted to the contents of one's mind. Again, his view is that one's evidence is one's knowledge, and in the initial chapters of *Knowledge and its Limits* he goes to considerable lengths to argue that knowledge is a mental state.

In any case, the argument does fail. In our view, one's evidence is restricted to the contents of one's mind. But, contrary to the claim of the first sentence, our topic—the justifying evidence that one has at a time—does not play the role of "the" evidence of science. There is no reason to think that the two are the same. We take it that the scientific evidence is something like the publicly accessible reliable indicators that are recognized by science. Again, we think this has an understandable connection to the justifying evidence. The scientific evidence is particularly useful in acquiring justifying evidence. But the two are clearly different.

Williamson also argues that there are central theoretical functions of the ordinary concept of evidence that require evidence to be propositional in form (pp. 194–7). This does not directly dispute our position. Our view is that one's ultimate evidence is non-doxastic. It includes items that are rightly described as perceptual experiences, but we need not deny that all evidence is propositional. A visual experience as of something blue against a white background might consist in an awareness of propositions to the effect that certain visual qualities are arranged in a certain configuration. Still, we would prefer to leave open the propositional status of ultimate evidence.[16] To this end, we will argue for the failure of Williamson's arguments.

Williamson cites the role of evidence in inferences to the best explanation and in probabilistic reasoning. Here is his reasoning in the former case: "where evidence does enable us to answer a question, a central way for it to do so is by inference to the best explanation. Thus evidence is the kind of thing which hypotheses explain. But the kind of thing which hypotheses explain is propositional. Therefore evidence is propositional" (pp. 194–5). In the course

---

[15] Williamson goes on to consider whether including as well the evidence that others have yields the evidence of science and he contends that it does not. See ibid. 193.

[16] For one thing, the exact form of the propositions is problematic. For instance, are they all first-person propositions about how one is experiencing, or are they typically only about the contents of the experiences?

of defending the premise in this argument claiming that what hypotheses explain is propositional, Williamson mentions the topic of explaining events. He says that a request to "Explain WWII" is a request to explain why the Second World War occurred or had some distinctive feature. The latter are clearly propositions to the effect that the Second World War occurred or had the feature. We note that precisely the same can be said about explaining non-propositional candidates for evidence. If a sensory experience is an event, a state of affairs, or some other non-propositional entity, that is no barrier to its serving as a legitimate topic of inference to the best explanation. A request to explain the evidence consisting in an experience can equally be understood as a request to explain why the experience occurred, obtained, or had some other feature.

The same goes for the subject matter of probabalistic reasoning. Williamson writes: "probabilistic comparisons of hypotheses on the evidence depend on the probabilities of the evidence on the hypotheses. But what has probability is a proposition; the probability is the probability *that* . . . At least, this is so when probability has to do with the evidential status of beliefs, as now . . ." (p. 196) We respond that in the probability case too, the evidence can be equally well understood as non-propositional experiences, or the like. "The probability on the evidence" can be harmlessly understood as the probability on the proposition that the evidence occurred, existed, or the like. Indeed, Williamson himself says that this is what we mean in speaking of this sort of probability of an event—we mean the probability that the event occurred. There is no good reason to deny the same treatment to "the probability on the evidence".

Finally in this vein, Williamson discusses using evidence for choosing between hypotheses on the basis of various kinds of reasoning: "in choosing between hypotheses in these ways, we can only use propositions which we grasp. In those respects, any evidence other than propositions which we grasp would be impotent" (p. 197). Once again, this is no good reason to think that the evidence itself is propositional. Propositions to the effect that the evidence exists, or the like, can serve to state the reasons the evidence gives that adjudicate among hypotheses. We conclude that these arguments do not defend the propositional status of evidence.

Again, Williamson holds that all evidence is knowledge. This conflicts with the plausible idea that much perceptual evidence consists in non-doxastic sensory states, an idea that fits well with our view of ultimate evidence.

Williamson defends his view that perceptual evidence is restricted to known propositions. We shall argue that the defense fails.

Williamson acknowledges that a simple proposition, such as the proposition asserting that a certain mountain that one sees is pointed in shape, "does not begin to exhaust [one's] present perceptual experience", nor does any further verbal description capture the richness of the experience in words. Williamson denies that this fact undermines his view. He proposes that the experiential evidence about a mountain's shape that one acquires by looking at it can be conveyed by pointing and saying, "It is that shape" (pp. 197–8). This is supposed to be well suited to expressing a proposition that one knows.

This demonstrative account is highly problematic. It seems both too specific and too external. A natural thought is that one is demonstrating a shape of part of the mountain's surface. Perhaps the demonstrated shape is a two-dimensional geometrical feature of the surface of the mountain—the configuration of a line along the mountain's surface that is perpendicular to the angle of view. But any such configuration would have numerous small details that are not seen. One does not know anything so specific about the mountain's surface. Some shape that does not exactly follow the surface is thus needed. Yet it is not at all clear that, by simply pointing at a mountain and saying "that shape", one could designate any such shape—what would determine exactly where the line goes?

In any case, Williamson's view is that no specific shape is demonstrated. He claims: "That shape must be unspecific enough to give my knowledge that the mountain is that shape an adequate margin for error in the sense of Chapter 5" (p. 198). This claim is obscure. It is not at all clear either what an unspecific shape is, or how one would manage to demonstrate anything other than a specific shape by a use of "that shape" while pointing at a mountain.

The problems increase in the case where one is under the illusion that one sees a mountain. Williamson proposes that the perceptual evidence one gets in such cases is the knowledge that the mountain appears to be that shape. He gives some attention to the issue of whether ordinary perceivers have the concept of appearance needed to grasp this proposition. But he does not discuss the interpretation of the noun phrases in his expression of the knowledge: "the mountain" and "that shape". When it is only an illusion that one sees a mountain and in fact one sees no physical object, it is quite doubtful that "the mountain" expresses any descriptive concept that both is on the subject's mind (consciously or otherwise) and contributes to expressing a true proposition. It is yet more doubtful that under such circumstances any shape (specific or otherwise) is designated by using "that shape" in an attempt to demonstrate a mountain's shape. Without such a shape, the proposition is not true and hence it is not known.

Even if there is some suitable proposition in illusory cases, it is doubtful that the proposition satisfies the doxastic condition on knowledge.[17] Williamson contends that people know some propositions that they do not consider. He does not give any other reason to think that one believes all the perceptual experience propositions that formulate what is intuitively one's perceptual evidence in non-veridical perceptual cases. The hypothesis that all who have deceptive perceptual evidence have some suitable doxastic attitude toward all these appearance propositions is a highly doubtful empirical claim. The need for this claim is a severe liability of the view that only knowledge is evidence.

5. Conclusion

We have described the approaches we favor to the nature of evidence and evidential support. We have elaborated the approaches to various extents and defended them against some objections. Work remains to be done. We hope to have done enough in support of our preferred version of evidentialism to show that the further work is worth doing.

[17] The needed attitude may not be exactly belief. But some sort of positive doxastic appraisal is necessary. Many philosophers have noted the limited extent of our appearance beliefs. See, e.g., John Pollock, *Contemporary Theories of Knowledge*, (Totowa, NJ: Rowman and Littlefield, 1987), 61–3.

5

Experiential Justification

Anthony Brueckner

This chapter is about the justification of perceptual beliefs. I begin by considering various theories of justification. In light of this discussion, I argue that the most attractive view of perceptual justification is that perceptual beliefs are justified in virtue of their relation to propositional-content-bearing experiences. I then discuss a problem for this attractive view.

1. Perceptual beliefs and theories of justification

At a first pass, we could say that *perceptual beliefs* are those beliefs that are *caused by perceptual experiences*, such as seeing a red cup and hearing a cat purr. But this characterization seems both too narrow and too wide: too wide because seeing a red cup can in some strange way cause one to believe that $2 + 3 = 5$ (presumably not a perceptual belief), and too narrow because a perceptual belief that a red cup is present can be caused by a hallucination (which we might well not want to count as a *perceptual* experience). A characterization in terms of the propositional content of the belief will be problematic as well, since a belief with the content *that a red cup is present* could well be caused in multifarious ways that, intuitively, would preclude the belief from counting as perceptual (say, caused by testimony, or by a brain lesion). Maybe the best way to proceed is to count hallucinatory and illusory experiences as *perceptual* experiences in virtue of their phenomenological similarity to veridical perceptual experiences, and to count the perceptually generated belief that $2 + 3 = 5$ as a perceptual belief issuing from a flawed perceptual system. Then we can adhere to the initial characterization of perceptual beliefs as those caused by perceptual experiences.

We can raise the question: when, if ever, do perceptual beliefs amount to knowledge? We can also raise the related question: when, if ever, are perceptual beliefs justified? Another related question will concern us here: supposing that perceptual beliefs are sometimes justified, *how* are they justified? *In virtue of what* are justified perceptual beliefs justified?

The last question about the justification of perceptual beliefs induces questions regarding another categorization: of *theories of justification*. One kind of theory is *coherentism*, according to which *all* justified beliefs—perceptual and otherwise—depend for their justification upon their relations to *other* beliefs. According to what we will call *pure coherentism*, all justified beliefs depend for their justification *entirely* upon their relations to other beliefs.[1] On this view, the Davidsonian Dictum holds true: nothing can justify a belief but another belief.[2] Perceptual experience, then, plays no role in the justification of perceptual beliefs, though of course experience plays a *causal* role in the generation of perceptual beliefs. More precisely: the only possible role that perception can play in the justification of beliefs is that of constituting the *subject matter* of beliefs *about perception*. On a highly overintellectualized view of perceptual justification, beliefs about experiences play a starring role in the justification of perceptual beliefs such as my belief that a red cup is present. On such a view, I cannot become justified in holding cup-beliefs unless I have some pertinent beliefs about my experiences "as of cups".[3] On *anyone's* view, beliefs about experiences *can* play at least a *supporting* role in the justification of cup-beliefs. The unusually intellectual justified believer can form beliefs about his experiences "as of cups" until the cows come home, and these beliefs can lend justificatory support to his cup-beliefs.

On what we will call *impure coherentism*, perceptual experiences, and not just beliefs, can themselves play a justificatory role, but this can occur

---

[1] We will follow the terminological lead of James Pryor's "There Is Immediate Justification", in M. Steup and E. Sosa (eds.), *Contemporary Debates in Epistemology* (Oxford: Blackwell, 2005).

[2] See Donald Davidson, "A Coherence Theory of Truth and Knowledge", in E. LePore (ed.), *Truth and Interpretation: Perspectives on the Philosophy of Donald Davidson* (Oxford: Blackwell, 1986). The Dictum has its roots in the work of Sellars and Quine.

[3] I place the phrase in scare quotes because it is not clear what it means. An answer will be given later in a discussion of whether experiences have propositional content.

only in conjunction with beliefs.[4] For example, Stewart Cohen has put forward a view according to which experiences can provide justification for perceptual beliefs in conjunction with beliefs about the reliability of one's experiences.[5]

On each version of coherentism, the justification of believer S's belief B1 by its relations to others of his beliefs can be thought of in several different ways. According to what we will call the *linear conception*, a belief is justified in virtue of its being a member of a chain of inferentially related beliefs. On what we will call the *finitary* version of the linear conception, justification-chains are always finite. This means that a given justified belief will always occur at least *twice* in a justification-chain. For example, S's belief B1 is justified by his belief B2, B2 is justified by his belief B3 . . . and his belief Bn is justified by B1. So B1 figures in its own justification. How does this conception apply to the justification of perceptual beliefs? It is not at all clear. One simple possible exemplification of finitary linear coherentism regarding perceptual beliefs would be this: my belief that this cup is red is justified by my belief that I have experience "as of a red cup", and the latter belief is justified by the former. On finitary linear coherentism, justification-chains will often have a more complex structure than that considered so far. For example, S's belief B1 might be justified by his beliefs B2 and B3, B2 by B4 and B5, B3 by B6 and B7 . . . In such a justification-tree, B1 will occur at least once in each branch of the tree.

On the *infinitary* version of the linear coherentist conception endorsed by Peter Klein, each justification-chain will contain an infinite number of justified beliefs, forming either a treelike structure or a simpler non-treelike structure as first sketched above.[6] On this conception, a given belief will *not* occur twice in a simple justification-chain or justification-tree: no belief will figure in its own justification.

The other possibility for a coherence theory of justification is for the theorist to adopt a *holistic* conception of the structure of justification. On this conception, we do not employ the notions of a justification-chain or a justification-tree—an ordered series of beliefs, or ordered treelike structure

[4] See also Pryor, "There Is Immediate Justification".

[5] See Stewart Cohen, "Basic Knowledge and the Problem of Easy Knowledge", *Philosophy and Phenomenological Research* (2002).

[6] See Peter Klein, "Human Knowledge and the Infinite Regress of Reasons", in J. E. Tomberlin (ed.), *Philosophical Perspectives*, 13 *(Epistemology)* (Oxford: Blackwell, 1999).

of beliefs, which beliefs stand in justificatory relations. Instead, we hold that a belief is justified just in case it is a member of a sufficiently coherent system of beliefs held by a believer. In contrast to the linear conception, holists hold that no particular subset of beliefs of one's belief system is the source of one's justification for one's believing that, say, this cup is red.[7]

So we can divide theories of justification according to how they answer the question: do beliefs always need to figure in the justification of beliefs? Coherentists answer "Yes", and *foundationalists* answer "No". According to foundationalism, some beliefs are justified independently of their relations to other beliefs. There are many versions of foundationalism. One way of dividing them up involves the notion of a *justifier*. Suppose that S's belief B1 is justified. We can ask: in virtue of what property of things, or of what state of affairs, is B1 justified? This is a question about the *source* of S's justification for his belief B1. If there is a property or state of affairs that plays such a justificatory role, then we will call that property or state of affairs the *justifier* of B1. Let us call beliefs that are justified independently of their relations to other beliefs *foundational* beliefs. According to one possible version of foundationalism, foundational beliefs have no justifiers. This is a peculiar position, which, to my knowledge, has no takers.[8] So let us set it aside. On a more plausible version of foundationalism, if S's belief B1 is justified, then it has some justifier. We can make one last distinction: *traditional* foundationalism has it that justifiers of foundational beliefs are always *token mental states* (other than beliefs).[9] Examples of such justifiers would be: a memory, a rational intuition, a perceptual experience. According to *non-traditional* foundationalism, justifiers of foundational beliefs are *never* token mental states. Examples of non-traditional foundational justifiers would be: the reliability of a belief-forming process, the proper functioning of a module of one's cognitive system, the mere fact that a belief is held, and the intellectual virtue of the believer.[10]

---

[7] See, e.g., Laurence BonJour, *The Structure of Empirical Knowledge* (Cambridge, MA: Harvard University Press, 1985). One prima facie consequence of holism is that all of one's beliefs are justified if any of them is.

[8] Note that the view that a foundational belief somehow justifies itself—is its own justifier—is not an example of the view in question.

[9] That is, the property of having a token mental state, or the state of affairs of the occurrence of a token mental state.

[10] See Alvin Goldman, "What is Justified Belief?", in G. S. Pappas (ed.), *Justification and Knowledge* (Dordrecht: D. Reidel, 1979), Alvin Plantinga, *Warrant: The Current Debate* (Oxford: Oxford University Press, 1993), Gilbert Harman, *Change in View* (Cambridge, MA: MIT Press, 1986), and Ernest

For the remainder of this chapter, we will consider a traditional foundationalist approach to the justification of perceptual beliefs. We will consider the view that *perceptual experiences* are the justifiers of those foundational beliefs that are perceptual beliefs (as opposed to, say, the *rationally intuited* belief that $2 + 3 = 5$, if that is foundational).

2. An application of the foregoing categorization

We can, in an interlude, use the foregoing fairly standard categorization of theories of justification to raise some questions about the influential epistemological views of Timothy Williamson.[11] According to Williamson, all evidence is propositional in character. Evidence always takes the form of *believed propositions.*[12] Any proposition that one knows (and hence believes) is part of one's body of evidence for further beliefs. Conversely, any (believed) proposition that counts as part of one's body of evidence must be among the propositions one knows. As Williamson says, $E = K$ (where 'E' denotes one's evidential beliefs, and 'K' denotes one's knowledge). Perceptual beliefs are justified if they are beliefs that amount to knowledge. According to Williamson, perceptual experiences are never justifiers for one's perceptual beliefs. This is because experiences are obviously not (believed) propositions. So he rejects traditional foundationalism. Now, if only (believed) propositions can be justifiers, then there are just two possibilities for Williamson's view of the justification of perceptual beliefs. The first possibility is to adopt the peculiar version of foundationalism that we set aside. This is the view that there are foundational beliefs (such as perceptual beliefs) that are justified while lacking justifiers. The second possibility is to adopt some form of coherentism. The first possibility is not open to Williamson unless he rejects his thesis that *all justification is evidential.* That thesis requires that every justified belief has an evidential justifier that comes in the form of a justified belief constituting a piece of knowledge, given $E = K$. The second *coherentist* possibility

Sosa, "Knowledge and Intellectual Virtue", in his *Knowledge and Perspective* (Cambridge: Cambridge University Press, 1991).

[11] See Timothy Williamson, *Knowledge and its Limits* (Oxford: Oxford University Press, 2000).

[12] Williamson actually conceives of one's evidence as consisting in *propositions.* But he allows that, since the evidential propositions in question are *known*, they are also *believed.*

is never even explicitly considered by Williamson in *Knowledge and its Limits*. So it is something of a mystery as to what Williamson's view of perceptual justification exactly is.[13]

3. Experiential justification

Let us return to our traditional foundationalist. *How*, according to him, do perceptual experiences justify perceptual beliefs? Why exactly is my experience "as of a red cup" a justifier for my belief that a red cup is present? A fairly simple-minded answer would be that the perceptual belief is caused by my experience, and my experience, we will suppose, is caused by a red cup that is present. One prima facie problem with this answer is that it leaves us with no rationale for holding that perceptual beliefs that are caused by illusory or hallucinatory experiences can be justified beliefs. If no red cup causes my experience "as of a red cup", then it looks as if our proposed answer would have us hold that my hallucinatorily induced perceptual belief that a red cup is present is unjustified (and similarly for all hallucinatorily induced perceptual beliefs). One might think that that negative finding is correct, however. We will return to this issue below. A second problem with the proposed answer arises as follows. Suppose that a red cup causes my experience "as of a red cup", and suppose that that experience in turn causes a belief that a green rat is present. On the proposed answer, why exactly does this causal sequence *fail* to generate justification for my perceptual rat-belief? We need to fill out the fairly simple-minded answer to our question about how experiences justify perceptual beliefs in such a way as to distinguish between the case of the cup-belief (justified) and the rat-belief (unjustified).

One way to begin to fill out the answer under consideration is to raise the further question: are perceptual experiences properly regarded in the Kantian manner as *representations*? One version of the "Yes" answer to this question is to say that perceptual experiences are representations in virtue

---

[13] For discussion of Williamson's view of perceptual justification, see my "Knowledge, Evidence, and Skepticism according to Williamson", *Philosophy and Phenomenological Research* (2005). See also my "E = K and Perceptual Knowledge", in P. Greenough and D. Pritchard (eds.) *Williamson on Knowledge* (Oxford: Oxford University Press, forthcoming).

of having *propositional content*.[14] A second version of the "Yes" answer is to say that perceptual experiences are representations even though they do *not* have propositional content. An example of the second sort of view can be found in the work of Tyler Burge.[15]

For Burge, representational states have two different sorts of content: propositional and non-propositional. Beliefs have propositional content, while perceptual representations have non-propositional content. Both states can be *veridical*: beliefs are veridical when their propositional *truth conditions* are satisfied; perceptual experiences are veridical when their non-propositional *correctness conditions* are satisfied (as we find in the cases of good maps and accurate photographs).

For Burge, the relation between a perceptual experience and an associated perceptual belief is not like the relation between a reason for belief and a belief. Reasons have propositional content, and perceptual experiences do not. When I believe that there is fire on the basis of the reason that, as I believe, there is smoke and where there is smoke, there is fire, my reason-based belief is *justified*. Things are different in the case of perceptual belief, according to Burge. When I believe that a black cat is approaching on the basis of a perceptual experience of a cat, I have an *epistemic entitlement* (rather than an internal, reasoned-based justification) to rely upon the non-propositional perceptual representation in forming the belief. The relation between the experience and the belief is not like that between a justifying reason and a justified belief, according to Burge. To think otherwise, he says, is to think of the move from perception to belief as being too much like *inference*. So Burge is not moved by the Davidsonian Dictum.[16]

In contrast to Burge, a number of philosophers hold the view that perceptual experiences are representations that *do* have propositional content. This view on the face of it provides the beginnings of a response to the intuitive idea behind the Davidsonian Dictum that only beliefs can be justifiers. If an

[14] See, e.g., Pryor, "There is Immediate Justification", Bill Brewer, *Perception and Reason* (Oxford: Oxford University Press, 1999), and Michael Huemer, *Skepticism and the Veil of Perception* (Lanham, MD: Rowman and Littlefield, 1999).

[15] See Tyler Burge, "Perceptual Entitlement", *Philosophy and Phenomenological Research* (2003).

[16] Burge gives a sort of transcendental argument for the existence of perceptual entitlement. For a critical discussion, see my "Content Externalism, Entitlement, and Reasons", in Sanford Goldberg (ed.), *Internalism and Externalism in Semantics and Epistemology* (Oxford: Oxford University Press, 2007).

experience has a propositional content, as does a belief, then the experience is to that degree *belief-like*. An experience would then in a sense be *in the space of reasons* and hence, on the Davidsonian view, would be a candidate for being a justifier of a perceptual belief.[17]

But at first blush it is not at all clear whether experiences have *determinate* propositional content. I am looking at a red cup sitting on a blue tablecloth. Does my visual perceptual experience have the propositional content *that there is a red cup on the table? That there is a red cup on the blue tablecloth? That there is a red cup on the left half of the blue tablecloth?* While it is relatively clear how to specify the propositional content of a *sentence* that is uttered in a context, it is not at all clear how to do this for a perceptual experience. Perhaps the specification should be done in terms of the perceptual beliefs that are caused by the experience. For example, if someone sees the red cup on the blue tablecloth but lacks the concept of a tablecloth, then he will not be caused to believe that there is a red cup on the blue tablecloth. Thus it will be wrong to attribute the content *that there is a red cup on the blue tablecloth* to his visual experience.

Before thinking a bit more about the view that experiences are propositional-content-bearing justifiers of perceptual beliefs, let us pause to consider the ugly visage of skepticism about the very existence of perceptual justification. We have been proceeding as if it is obvious that many (perhaps most?) perceptual beliefs are justified (and hence are candidates for amounting to knowledge). We have been asking: given that there is perceptual justification, what is its source? What are the *mechanics*, so to speak, of perceptual justification? The Cartesian skeptic about the possibility of knowledge about the external world would obviously balk at this philosophical procedure. James Pryor is a writer who has both (1) defended the conception of experiences as propositional-content-bearing justifiers, and (2) sought to employ this conception in defending an anti-skeptical epistemology of perceptual justification. Let us explore the conception in question in the context of Pryor's views on skepticism about perceptual justification.

---

[17] See John McDowell, *Mind and World* (Cambridge, MA: Harvard University Press, 1994) for a discussion of "the space of reasons".

4. Pryor

In "The Skeptic and the Dogmatist", James Pryor attempts to present a novel answer to skepticism regarding the possibility of perceptual justification.[18] I will begin by discussing Pryor's reconstruction of the skeptic's reasoning. He thinks that the following principle lies at the heart of the skeptic's case:

SPJ If you're to have justification for believing p on the basis of certain experiences or grounds E, then for every q which is "bad" relative to E and p, you have to have antecedent justification for believing q to be false—justification which doesn't rest on or presuppose any E-based justification you may have for believing p. (p. 531)

Let us note some features of SPJ. The principle is neutral as to what the putative justification for *p* is supposed to consist in: experiences versus grounds, which are presumably beliefs of evidential propositions. Further, for our purposes, we need not settle the question of precisely what counts as a "bad", justification-threatening *q*. Where *p* is the proposition that I have hands, suffice it to say that the skeptical hypothesis that I am dreaming (which is *compatible* with *p*) and the Evil Genius and brain in a vat hypotheses (which are *incompatible* with *p*) are all counted by Pryor as bad.

The skeptic argues that I lack the *antecedent justification* for rejecting such bad *q*s that is demanded by SPJ. This is because, according to Pryor's skeptic, this rejection would need to "rest in part on some perceptual justification ... [I] have for believing things about the external world" (p. 530). According to Pryor and his skeptic, no a priori, non-perceptual grounds are available to do the job; so only perceptual grounds of some sort can meet SPJ's demand. Pryor argues that, since my reasons for rejecting the bad *q*s must be "partly perceptual", they would therefore have to "rest on or presuppose" my alleged *E-based* justification for believing *p*. By SPJ, then, this alleged justification for believing *p* turns out to be merely apparent, not genuine. This is because I do *not* have *antecedent* justification for believing the bad *q*s to be false,

---

[18] James Pryor, "The Skeptic and the Dogmatist", *Nous* (2000). All page references in the text are to this article.

justification that is independent of my putative E-based justification for believing p.[19]

One problem with this formulation of the skeptic's reasoning is that my E-based perceptual justification for p ($=$ I have hands) will involve specific experiences "as of my having hands" (or perhaps, as SPJ seems to allow, beliefs about such experiences—on a non-foundationalist approach). It is therefore not at all obvious that whatever perceptual reasons I claim to have for rejecting a bad q—say, the hypothesis that I am in a vat—would have to "rest on or presuppose" my perceptual justification E for believing p. For all that has been said, my grounds for rejecting that bad q might involve my experiences as of others' testimony regarding my normal, embodied status. *Such* grounds do not in any straightforward way "rest on" the experiences as of my having hands (or my beliefs about these experiences) that constitute E. Accordingly, in order to give the skeptic a run for his money, SPJ would need to be amended so that a different constraint is placed upon justifying grounds for rejecting a bad q: we might require, for example, that such grounds must not "rest on or presuppose" justification *of the same type*, or *having the same source*, as my alleged E-based justification for believing p.

Now let us look at Pryor's way of answering the skeptical reasoning. He adopts "dogmatism about perceptual justification", and this allows him to deny SPJ, the backbone of the skeptic's case:

According to the dogmatist, when you have an experience as of p's being the case, you have a kind of justification for believing p that does *not* presuppose or rest on any other evidence or justification you may have. You could have this justification even if there were *nothing* else you could appeal to as ampliative, non-question-begging evidence that p is the case. Hence, to be justified in believing p, you do *not* need to have the antecedent justification the skeptic demands. You do not need to have evidence that would enable you to rule the skeptic's scenarios out, in a non-question-begging way [i.e., in a way that does not appeal to E or an E-like justification]. (p. 532)

According to Pryor, my perceptual justification for believing that p does not involve *evidential beliefs* or *reasons* at all. My perceptual belief that p is justified simply in virtue of my having an experience (or several) "that represents

---

[19] This reasoning has its roots in Barry Stroud, *The Significance of Philosophical Scepticism* (Oxford: Oxford University Press, 1984). For further formalization and critical discussion, see Crispin Wright, "Skepticism and Dreaming: Imploding the Demon", *Mind* (1991), and my "Problems with the Wright Route to Skepticism", *Mind* (1992).

p as being the case" (p. 519). In general, content-bearing experiences by themselves justify beliefs with *matching contents*. Thus, it is not required that my perceptual justification for believing that p somehow involve evidential beliefs or reasons of the sort specified in SPJ: beliefs or reasons that enable me to exclude bad skeptical qs without "resting on or presupposing" the type of justification I have for believing that p. Instead, my perceptual justification for believing that p derives from my experiences whose contents represent that p.[20, 21]

5. A difficulty for Pryor-style views of perceptual justification

My main worry about Pryor's position—and, in general, the view that content-bearing experiences are perceptual justifiers—concerns the question of whether, on this view, I have justification for rejecting the bad skeptical qs—whether I have justification for believing their denials.[22] Pryor wants to distinguish his position from that of the *Relevant Alternatives Theorist*. According to such a theorist, it is possible that I should have perceptually based justification for believing that this is a zebra while lacking justification for rejecting the "bad" alternative hypothesis that it is a cleverly disguised mule, or a dreamed or hallucinated zebra. This is because those alternatives to its being a zebra are not *relevant* alternatives (by some standard of relevance). According to the view under discussion, one's justification for believing that p (= I have hands) only needs to be strong enough to justify rejection of the *relevant* alternatives to p—the relevant hypotheses that are incompatible with p.[23]

---

[20] So an experience "as of a red cup sitting on the table" is an experience whose propositional content is *that a red cup is sitting on the table*. Going back to another loose end from earlier: even if an experience with the latter content is hallucinatory, the experience still justifies the belief that a red cup is sitting on the table in virtue of its matching propositional content.

[21] According to Pryor, the justification that an experience provides for one's belief that p is prima facie justification. This is justification that is sufficient for knowledge provided that (a) all other conditions for knowledge are met, and (b) the experiential justification remains *undefeated*.

[22] Note that I can have justification for believing not-q even if I do not in fact believe not-q: to say that I have justification for believing not-q is to say that, if I were to believe not-q upon considering the matter of whether or not q is the case, then my belief would be justified.

[23] See Fred Dretske, "Epistemic Operators", *Journal of Philosophy* (1970), the locus classicus of Relevant Alternatives Theory.

Pryor does not accept Relevant Alternatives Theory. This strongly suggests that he holds that, when one has perceptual justification for believing p, one also has justification for rejecting bad skeptical alternatives to p. If he held that one need not have justification for such rejection in order to have justification for p, then he would have a simple response to the skeptic's deployment of SPJ: one need not have the special sort of justification for rejecting bad qs that is required by this principle because one need not have justification *of any sort whatsoever* for rejecting them. However, Pryor instead presents the more complex, "dogmatic" answer to the SPJ-based reasoning that is under discussion.

In general, Pryor shows no inclination to reject the following plausible Closure Principle for justification that is denied by the Relevant Alternatives Theorist:

CL1 If S has justification for believing that α, and α entails β, then S has justification for believing that β.[24]

A related principle is:

CL2 If S has justification for believing that α in virtue of possessing justifier j, and α entails β, then S has justification for believing that β in virtue of possessing j.

In other words, if j is a source of justification for α (for S), then j is also a source of justification for the entailed β (for S).

Assuming, then, that Pryor holds that when one has perceptual justification for believing that p ($=$ I have hands), one also has justification for rejecting bad skeptical alternatives to p, we may ask: what is the source of the *latter* justification? Unfortunately, Pryor does not discuss this question in any detail. The only answer that is suggested by his overall view is this: that which perceptually justifies one in believing p also justifies one in rejecting the bad qs.[25] Consider again the earlier example. Suppose that I am perceptually justified in believing *that I have hands* ($= p$) in virtue of having experience E "as of p"—that is, having experience as of having hands. On the answer that is suggested by Pryor's overall view, my having E also justifies me in believing, say, that I am not a brain in a vat.

---

[24] See again n. 21 above.

[25] Pryor seems to endorse the pertinent instances of Cl2 in n. 35 of "The Skeptic and the Dogmatist". He says that your justification for an ordinary perceptual belief "gives you justification for believing" that a skeptical hypothesis such as that I am in a vat is false.

I will now argue that, on Pryor's conception of perceptual justification, it is quite unclear how my having E could justify me in rejecting bad skeptical hypotheses such as that I am envatted. The problem applies to all views according to which experiences justify perceptual beliefs in virtue of having propositional contents. As we have seen, Pryor maintains that experiences have propositional content: "some propositions are such that we see or seem to see that they are so" (p. 538). There is a policeman writing me a parking ticket as I run toward him, but, according to Pryor, it is not clear that my current perceptual experiences have the content *that there is a policeman*. That proposition is (probably) not *perceptually basic*, since it is not "about manifest observable properties of objects in the world" (p. 539). I see that the proposition is true in virtue of seeing that there is a blue-coated figure and of having certain background evidence about police uniforms. According to Pryor, our experiences provide us with immediate justification for believing those propositions that our experiences *basically represent* to us, such as the proposition *that there is a hand.*[26] Which propositions are perceptually basic may vary with the degree of a perceiver's conceptual sophistication, so that, for example, for an artist, the proposition *that this is a German expressionist painting* may be perceptually basic.

In the light of these remarks, it seems obvious that Pryor would hold that, for the average person, the proposition *that I am not a brain in a vat* is *not* perceptually basic. Only philosophical sophisticates have the requisite concepts. Even in the case of a vat aficionado such as myself, it is hard to see how it can be part of the very content of my experience E (as of having hands) that I am not a brain in a vat. Surely my experience as of having hands does not have the representative content *that I am not the sum of two primes*. Neither would it seem to have the content *that I am not a brain in a vat*.

If this is right, then, even though E's content is such as to provide me with justification for believing that I have hands, E's content does *not* provide me with justification for believing the entailed proposition that I am not a brain in a vat.[27] As we saw earlier, if Pryor maintains that *nothing* justifies me in rejecting

---

[26] I am ignoring some nuances of Pryor's view here, since he thinks that it is up to cognitive psychologists to settle the question of whether propositions like *that there is a (complete) hand* are perceptually basic for us, or, instead, propositions like *that there is a facing flesh-colored surface of such and such a shape* (p. 539).

[27] Some writers have wondered how one's experiences (content-bearing or not) could possibly justify belief of the denial of skeptical hypotheses. Given an acceptance of CL1, they are moved to

that bad skeptical hypothesis (so that I am *not* justified in rejecting it), then his overall position is like that of the Relevant Alternatives Theorists, with whom he claims to part company.

There is another possibility for Pryor, which does not seem to be very attractive either. Suppose that he agrees with the foregoing analysis of his view: that which justifies me in believing that I have hands (namely, E) *fails* to justify me in believing the entailed consequence that I am not a brain in a vat. Even so, Pryor may say that even though E fails to justify me in believing that I am not in a vat ($=$ not-q), the proposition that I have hands ($= p$), once justified for me by its relation to E, itself *becomes available as evidence* for believing further propositions. E justifies p, and, even though E does *not* justify the entailed not-q, p *itself* justifies not-q (in virtue of entailing it).[28] On this view, we hold on to CL1 (rejecting Relevant Alternatives Theory) while rejecting CL2. Whenever S has justification for believing some α, he will also have justification for believing an entailed β (this justification flowing from α itself, which has become available as evidence). This is Cl1. But S's justifier for believing that α need not be identical to his justifier for believing that β. This is the denial of Cl2.

I have criticized this conception of the structure of justification elsewhere, and I will not repeat my objections here.[29] The basic intuitive oddnesss of the conception is that it seems to involve a mysterious generation of justification *ex nihilo*. If E is my entire source of justification for p, and E is not sufficient to justify a belief of not-q, then the claim that p itself (once justified) yields justification for not-q seems to involve manufacturing justification out of thin air. On the other hand, if one finds Pryor's answer to the SPJ skeptic to be promising, then this would be reason to take seriously the foregoing counterintuitive picture of the structure of justification. This picture would explain how it can both be true that (1) my experiential justifier for p fails to justify not-q, and yet (2), consistently with Cl1, I *do* have justification for not-q.

---

countenance the existence of some sort of a priori justification for believing the denials in question. See, e.g., Stewart Cohen, "How to be a Fallibilist", *Philosophical Perspectives* (1988), and Crispin Wright, "Some Reflections on the Acquisition of Warrant by Inference", in Susana Nuccetelli (ed.), *New Essays on Semantic Externalism, Skepticism, and Self-Knowledge* (Cambridge, MA: MIT Press, 2003).

[28] See, e.g., Peter Klein, *Certainty* (Minneapolis: University of Minnesota Press, 1981), and his "Skepticism and Closure: Why the Evil Genius Argument Fails", *Philosophical Topics* (1995) for such a view.

[29] See my "Skepticism and Epistemic Closure", *Philosophical Topics* (1985), and "Klein on Closure and Skepticism", *Philosophical Studies* (2000).

6. Conclusion

So we have a problem for the view that experiences are perceptual justifiers. We have in the end a *dilemma* for this view. On the first horn of the dilemma, we suppose that experiences have propositional content. As we have seen, this conception has the great virtue of answering the coherentist challenge embodied in the Davidsonian Dictum that only beliefs can play the role of justifiers. Suppose that we hold on to Cl2, rejecting both Relevant Alternatives Theory and Klein's strategy of accepting Cl1 while denying Cl2. We are then forced into the implausible position of maintaining that an experience bearing the content *that I have hands* provides justification for the belief that I am not a brain in a vat. That is, if we hold on to Cl2, then we must say that that which justifies my belief that I have hands (namely, my content-bearing experience as of having hands) also provides justification for believing the entailed proposition that I am not a brain in a vat, notwithstanding the fact that the experience's content is not *that I am not a brain in a vat*.

On the second horn of the dilemma, we again hold on to both Cl1 and Cl2. But we deny that perceptual justifiers have propositional content. This allows us to avoid the implausible claim of the first horn regarding how experiential content provides justification for believing that I am not a brain in a vat. But on this horn, we are left with no answer to the challenge of the Davidsonian coherentist. If experiences do *not* justify perceptual beliefs in virtue of bearing propositional contents that match those of the perceptual beliefs (since experiences do not bear contents at all), then *in virtue of what* do experiences constitute perceptual justifiers?

If both horns seem problematic, then the following unattractive moves are available: (A) deny that experiences are justifiers of perceptual beliefs and embrace coherentism, (B) deny Cl1, say, by adopting Relevant Alternatives Theory, and finally (C) hold on to Cl1 and follow Klein in denying Cl2.

6

Skepticism and Perceptual Knowledge

Ernest Sosa

Dreams pose a deeper skeptical paradox than brains in vats or evil demons. In what follows we take up that paradox. A heterodox conception of dreams is first defended in preparation for our first resolution. A second resolution is then based on a conception of knowledge as apt belief, as belief whose correctness is attributable to the believer's epistemic competence or virtue.

1. Varieties of skepticism

Skepticism takes surprisingly many forms. The Pyrrhonian skeptic suspends judgment by using tropes that counter any reasons offered in favor of belief. Academic skeptics, by contrast, are more assertive, if only by claiming that we know nothing, either in general, or in some large department of common sense or science. The world around us is said to lie beyond our ken, for example, as do the minds of our neighbors, and the realm of morality. Any attempt to refute such global claims will likely beg the question, by relying on implicit claims about the realm in question. Since our skeptic is claiming that such assumptions must lie beyond our ken, it would beg the question to appeal to them in arguing against him.

Irrefutable does not mean true. Take the global claim that we know nothing at all. If refuting such a skeptic requires adducing some premise, to do which is implicitly to claim knowledge of its truth, then we are bound to beg the question. The radical boldness of our global skeptic makes him dialectically irrefutable, but that does not prove him right.[1]

Such varieties of skepticism are less problematic than the variety of main interest to us here. At the heart of common sense, our skeptic claims to find a commitment that precludes knowledge, either in general or in some main department. According to this commitment, a belief can amount to knowledge only if it is *sensitive*, only if, *had its content been false, then it would not have been held by that believer.* You can know that you see a hand, for example, only if, *had you not seen a hand, you would not have believed that you saw one.*

2. Skepticism, sensitivity, and safety

If such a sensitivity requirement is indeed at the core of common sense, this puts the skeptic in a good position. Belief that one is not radically misled turns out to be constitutionally insensitive. Indeed, radical scenarios are constructed to secure precisely this result. If you were now a brain in a vat being fed coherent experiences, for example, that would not stop you from believing that you were *not* radically deceived.

In response one might try strengthening the requirement as follows.

Basis-relative sensitivity. A belief constitutes knowledge only if, *had it been false, then the believer would not have held it on the same basis on which he actually holds it.*

But this is no help unless we externalize perceptual bases for belief. Suppose you believe that *p* because you see that *p* and you take this at face value. You see that here is a hand, for example, and you believe accordingly on that basis. Such a belief *will* satisfy the requirement of basis-relative sensitivity: had its content been false, then, trivially, it could not have had a *factive* basis, since any such basis has to be veridical.

---

[1] Besides, if the very making of a claim commits also to knowledge of what is claimed, then the global skeptic contradicts himself. True, the skeptic might retreat to the more defensible claim that ordinary knowledge of the world around us is beyond us, without putting in question the armchair reasoning that leads us to that philosophical posture.

However, that externalist response to the skeptic[2] has quite implausible consequences. Thus, consider a normal perceiver and his counterpart BIV, who reason in just the same way, and who enjoy qualitatively identical total conscious states, over the whole of the relevant interval. That being so, the two of them would seem *equally justified* in their perceptual beliefs. If the BIV in particular is thus epistemically justified, however, then factive seeing cannot be required for justified visual belief. Such a requirement would be met by the normal perceiver but not by the BIV. Deprived of factive perception, BIVs must base their justified beliefs on something more internal than that.

Actually, BIV science fiction is not required for our point. A perfectly ordinary case will make it equally well. A perceptual belief that one faces a red surface might be entirely justified, for example, even if what one sees is really a white surface illuminated with red light. One is justified in taking the surface to be red, nevertheless, provided one has no reason whatsoever to suspect the quality of the light. One is justified in holding that perceptual belief, even if one's visual experience is not veridical, and one does not factually see that the surface is red.

If the relevant epistemic bases are thus internal, this resurrects the skeptical paradox. Had one been radically deceived, after all, one would still have believed *on the same internal basis* that one was *not* radically deceived.

The appeal to factive perceptual states falls short, therefore, in resolving our skeptical paradox.

A better response to the skeptic begins by noting that subjunctive conditionals do not contrapose,[3] which suggests requiring not sensitivity but safety, as follows.

> *Basis-relative safety.* A belief cannot constitute knowledge if the believer might too easily have so believed on the same basis while his belief was false. (Alternatively, in order to know one must believe on a certain basis, possibly the null basis, where so believing on such a basis has a strong enough tendency to be right.)

---

[2] Found in John McDowell, *Mind and World* (1996), and in Timothy Williamson, *Knowledge and its Limits* (2002), both published by Oxford University Press.

[3] For example, if I were to open my kitchen faucet, it would be false that water would flow while the main house valve was closed. But consider the contrapositive of this conditional: namely, that, if water flowed out of the faucet while the main valve was closed, then water would not flow. This contrapositive would be obviously false, showing contraposition to be invalid for such conditionals.

Safety does not serve the skeptic as does sensitivity. Belief that one is not radically deceived is insensitive. But a belief can be safe despite being insensitive. This is because scenarios of radical deception are outlandish, remote possibilities *not* liable to occur (not too easily). Therefore, a belief that one is not radically deceived is safe despite being insensitive: *not* too easily might one have been radically deceived. Belief that one is not radically deceived would tend to be correct. The possibility of radical deception is so outlandish that one's belief to the contrary would tend to be correct.

3. Why the dream scenario is special

Our line of reasoning is effective against the usual run of radical skeptical scenarios, such as the brain in a vat, the evil demon, the Matrix, and so on. Only the dream scenario stands apart. Dreams being so common, the possibility that one dreams is not outlandish. Therefore I cannot defend the safety of my belief that I am awake by adducing how remote is the possibility that I go wrong in so believing. Too easily for comfort I might have been not awake but only dreaming.

There are those who defend common sense against the sensitivity-wielding skeptic by rejecting closure. Even if we do not know ourselves to be free of radical scenarios, it is argued, we can still know about hands and fires. But this has very implausible consequences, as is well known. Moreover, no similar strategy would work against the safety-wielding skeptic, since he can use the dream scenario for a direct attack on ordinary perceptual beliefs. Take a belief that one sees a hand, or a fire. Too easily might one form such a belief on its usual experiential basis, while only dreaming. So it is not a safe belief. This does not depend on any assumption of closure.

That is why the dream scenario has a distinctive importance by comparison with the familiar radical scenarios. It is not outlandish, for one thing; what is more, it threatens our perceptual beliefs *directly*, not by way of closure.[4]

That does require a certain orthodox conception of dreams, however, according to which beliefs and experiences in our dreams are real beliefs and

---

[4] Alternatively, one might argue that dreams are relevant (close) alternatives by analogy to the fake barns example. Just as the spatial/temporal proximity of enough possible fake barn encounters creates a problem for the belief that one perceives a barn, so the spatial/temporal proximity of enough possible dreams creates a problem for the belief that one perceives an external reality.

experiences hosted not only in the dream but also in actuality, while we dream. Only thus would our ordinary perceptual beliefs be threatened by the possibility that we might believe the same on the same experiential basis in a realistic dream.

Is that really how we should conceive of our dreams?

4. Dreams: The orthodox conception

Are dreams made up of conscious states just like those of waking life except for how they fit their surroundings? The orthodox answer is affirmative. Dream states and waking states are thought to be intrinsically alike, though different in their causes and effects.

That conception is orthodox in today's common sense and also historically. Presupposed by Plato, Augustine, and Descartes, it underlies familiar skeptical paradoxes. Similar orthodoxy is also found in our developing science of sleep and dreaming.[5] Despite such confluence from common sense, philosophical tradition, and contemporary sleep science, the orthodox view is deeply flawed, or so I will argue, before suggesting a better view. To dream is to imagine, not to hallucinate.[6]

Dreams-based skepticism stands out because the dream possibility is too close for comfort. If while dreaming we have real beliefs based on real phenomenal experiences, then a normal perceptual judgment could always be matched by a subjectively indistinguishable, similarly based judgment, made while one dreams. Too easily, then, we might now have been dreaming in forming our perceptual beliefs. On the orthodox conception, a dreaming subject might form such a belief in his dream, and thereby in reality. No doubt it would be a false belief, based on illusory phenomenal experience. Any given perceptual belief, or one intrinsically just like it, might thus too easily have been false though formed on the same experiential basis.

---

[5] In his *Dreaming: An Introduction to the Science of Sleep* (Oxford and New York: Oxford University Press, 2002), 108, Allan Hobson writes: "[Positron emission tomography studies] . . . show an *increase* in activation of just those multimodal regions of the brain that one would expect to be activated in hallucinatory perception . . . . In other words, in REM [Rapid Eye Movement] sleep—compared with waking—hallucination is enhanced."

[6] But I need only the weaker thesis that to dream is more like imagining than like hallucinating, and in particular that dreaming is like imagining in certain respects to be indicated below.

Fortunately, the orthodox conception is not beyond question. A lot rides epistemically on just how dreams are constituted.

5. What are dreams made of?

Do the characters in my dreams have beliefs and intentions? They do in general, but do I myself also have them as protagonist in my dream? Unquestionably I do believe and intend things *in my dream*.[7] In my dream I am conscious, I assent to this or that, I judge or choose.[8] This all happens *in the dream*, of course, but does it thereby *really* happen, albeit while I dream? This simple question is easy enough to grasp, but surprisingly hard to answer.

When something happens *in my dream*, reality tends not to follow suit. When in my dream I am chased by a lion, this poses no threat to my skin. No physical proposition about the layout of the world around me is true in actuality just because it is true in my dream. What about mental propositions about how it is in my own mind? Must any such proposition be true in actuality whenever it is true in my dream? No, even if *in my dream* I believe that a lion is after me, and even if *in my dream* I intend to keep running, *in actuality* I have no such belief or intention. What is in question is the *inference* from <In my dream I believe (or intend) such and such> to <In actuality I so believe (or intend)>.

My exposition relies heavily on distinguishing between two expressions: 'in my dream' and 'while I dream'. From the fact that *in my dream* something happens, it does not follow that it happens *while I dream*. From the fact that in my dream I am chased by a lion, it does not follow that while I dream I am chased. Moreover, from the fact that while I dream something happens, it does not follow that it happens in my dream. From the fact that while I dream it rains and thunders, it does not follow that in my dream it rains and thunders.

At any given time nearly all one's beliefs remain latent. A belief might be manifest when formed, or it might occasionally rise to consciousness from

---

[7] Here I distinguish between first-person participation in the dream and third-person participation, as when one sees oneself do something as if in a movie or on a TV screen. One can figure in one's movie as a victim of a recent knockout, and would not thereby undergo any present experience.

[8] I here use 'affirmation' for conscious assent to a propositional content and 'volition' for conscious assent to a possible course of action (including simple actions, even, as a limiting case, those that are basic and instantaneous).

storage. To make one's belief explicit is to *judge* or *assent* or *avow*, at least to oneself.[9] The same is true of one's intentions, few of which surface at any given time. One does, of course, retain countless beliefs and intentions while asleep and dreaming. Among these are intentions recently formed: to stop by the library the next day, for example; and beliefs recently acquired: that the weather will be fine in the morning, say. If so, then what one knows as one dreams is that one is in bed; one lay down in the knowledge that one would be there for hours, and this knowledge has not been lost. *Lying in bed until morning* is what one intended through most of the day, even as one thought about other things, as one had dinner, and so on. That was still one's intention as one lay down, and there is no reason to suppose that it was lost as one fell asleep. One does not lose one's intentions for the coming morning. One retains intentions as to what one *will* do upon awakening. One retains, as one drifts off to sleep, beliefs about the layout of the room: the location of one's shoes, for example, or the alarm clock, and so on. It is hard to see how one could then concurrently believe that one is being chased by a lion, rather than lying in bed, with the shoes a certain distance and direction from where one lies.

Granted this for states of belief and intention, with their crucial functional profiles, perhaps conscious episodes are different. These one may perhaps *really* undergo *while* dreaming whenever one does so *in one's dream*. Conscious assent to a proposition does not guarantee that it is really believed, nor does conscious assent to a course of action guarantee the corresponding intention. One might even consciously assent to the opposite of what one really believes, or intends. Actions speak louder than words; louder than conscious assents, too. A deep-seated prejudice might be disavowed sincerely while still surviving, firmly entrenched. Similarly, a belief might survive in storage while consciously disavowed in a dream. Conscious affirmations and volitions might thus contradict stored beliefs and intentions, and dreams may provide just a special case of that general phenomenon. The fact that one retains stored beliefs and intentions while dreaming thus seems compatible with real affirmations and volitions to the contrary, made not only in one's dream but thereby also in reality, while dreaming.

What then of propositions about your own *current conscious states*, whether conscious experiences or conscious assents? Even if you do not while dreaming

---

[9] However, as will emerge, one might judge, or affirm or avow something that one does not believe, and even something that one disbelieves.

really *believe* that you are then chased by a lion, perhaps you do still consciously *affirm* it. If in a dream one is in a certain *conscious* state, is one then *actually* in that state, while dreaming? If in my dream I make a conscious choice, do I thereby really make that choice, while dreaming?

In a dream you may covet thy neighbor's wife, in the dream a sultry object of desire. Do you then violate the biblical injunction? If you go so far as to succumb, are you then subject to blame? Having sinned in your heart, not only in your dream, but in actuality, you could hardly escape discredit. Is one then blameworthy for choices made in a dream? That has near-zero plausibility, about as little as does blaming a storyteller for his misdeeds as protagonist in a story spun for a child. (One might blame him for telling such a story to such an audience, but this is different; one does not thereby blame him for doing what he does *in the story*.)

If while dreaming one does *actually* assent to misdeeds, even to crimes, does its being just a dream protect one from discredit? That seems implausible. If sudden paralysis prevents you from carrying out some deplorable intentions, this does not protect you from discredit, from the full weight of the biblical injunction. How then can you be protected by the disengagement of your brain from the external causal order? How then can you be protected by the disengagement of your inner mental life, as in a dream?

Is dreaming perhaps like being drunk or drugged? These disabling conditions lighten responsibility. Perhaps when dreaming you do make conscious choices, while your disabling state lightens your responsibility. Is *that* why we do not blame people for sins in their dreams? No, it is not that one is *less* responsible for what happens in one's dream. Rather, one is not responsible in the slightest.

Dreams seem more like imaginings, or stories, or even daydreams, all fictions of a sort, or quasi-fictions. Even when in a dream one makes a conscious choice, one need not do so in actuality. Nor does one necessarily affirm in reality whatever one consciously affirms in a dream.

What then of current *phenomenal* experiences? Does their presence in a dream entail their real presence in the conscious life of the dreamer, albeit while he dreams? Here at least, it may be thought, we can plausibly draw the line. But consider the consequences. In respect of such experiences it is supposedly just as if a lion is after me. Yet I may form neither the belief that this is so nor the intention to escape. Am I not now deserving of discredit? Even if such a belief and such an intention are formed *in the dream*, they are not thereby formed *in actuality*, despite the actual experiences that would seem to require them in anyone rational. If the phenomenal experiences in dreams *are* real experiences, while dream beliefs are not real beliefs, then every night we are guilty of massive irrationality or epistemic vice.

Or so it seems at first thought. When we watch a movie, however, we undergo phenomenal experiences without being at fault for failing to take them at face value. We use them rather in an exercise of "make believe", in which our imagination is guided by what we see on the screen and hear from the sound system. We do have real visual and auditory experiences (as we do also when we view a documentary, or the nightly news), but we have switched off our cognitive processing for the duration of the film, so that we can immerse ourselves willingly in the offline illusion. And there is no irrationality in this. Similarly, then, while vividly dreaming, we may indeed enjoy phenomenal experiences, just as we do at the movie theater, though our cognitive processing is switched off, enabling our immersion in the imaginative illusion of the dream.

We do not here need to choose between these two options on phenomenal experience. What is important for epistemology, as will emerge, is that in dreaming we do not really believe; we only make-believe.[10]

6. Dreams and skepticism

Have we here found a way to defend our perceptual knowledge from the skeptic's dream argument? Even if we might just as easily be dreaming that we see a hand, this does not entail that we might now be astray in our perceptual beliefs. For, even if we might be dreaming, it does not follow that we might be thinking we see a hand on this same experiential basis, without seeing any hand. After all, what happens in a dream does not thereby really happen. So, even if I had now been dreaming, which might easily enough have happened, I would not thereby have been thinking that I see a hand, based on a corresponding phenomenal experience.

---

[10] My view on dreams is thus virtually the opposite of Colin McGinn's in his recent *Mindsight* (Cambridge, MA: Harvard University Press, 2004), where it is argued that, in dreaming, we have real beliefs but not real percepts (as opposed to certain objects of imagination, called 'images'). By contrast, I think that, in dreaming, we have no real beliefs but may well have real percepts (as we do in watching a movie or a play).

That disposes of the threat posed by dreams for the safety of our perceptual beliefs. Does it dispose of the problem of dream skepticism? It does so if dreams create such a problem only by threatening the safety of our perceptual beliefs. *Is* that the only threat posed by dreams? No, arguably our conception of dreams gives rise to an even more radical form of skepticism.

If dreaming is just imagining, then traditional formulations of radical skepticism, Descartes's included, are not radical enough. The possibility that we dream now threatens not only our supposed perceptual knowledge but even our supposed introspective knowledge, our supposed takings of the given. It is now in doubt not only whether we see a fire, but even whether we *think* we see a fire, or *experience* as if we see it. Just as we might be dreaming we perceive a fire without really doing so, so *in a dream* we might affirm the cogito and have experience as of a fire without *in reality* affirming or experiencing any such thing. If dreams pose a problem for our perception of our surroundings, then on the imagination model they equally pose a problem for our apprehension of the given.

That means we should look long and hard before buying that skeptical line. Elsewhere I rebut it, and defend our knowledge of the given and of the cogito, and even our knowledge, when awake, that we are awake. I argue that in the end we can just as well declare <I think, therefore I am awake> as <I think, therefore I am>. But there is no room here for those arguments. Instead, I propose now to take a step back for a better look at our ordinary knowledge and what it requires. So far we have been assuming that knowledge requires the basis-relative safety of its constituent belief. And dreams pose a skeptical problem because they pose a problem for the safety of our perceptual beliefs. Is that requirement beyond question? Must our perceptual knowledge be safe?

In defending against the skeptic we had rejected a requirement of sensitivity in favor of a less demanding requirement of safety. Perhaps we should instead require something even less demanding. In what follows I will argue for a view of our knowledge that requires neither sensitivity nor safety.

7. Animal knowledge as apt belief

When an archer takes aim and shoots, that shot is assessable in three respects.

First, we can assess whether it succeeds in its aim, in hitting the target. Although we can also assess how accurate a shot it is, how close to the bull's-eye, we here put degrees aside, in favor of the on/off question: whether it hits the target or not.

Second, we can assess whether it is adroit, whether it manifests skill on the part of the archer. Skill too comes in degrees, but here again we focus on the on/off question: whether it manifests relevant skill or not, whether it is or is not adroit.

A shot can be both accurate and adroit, however, without being a success creditable to its author. Take a shot that in normal conditions would have hit the bull's-eye. A gust of wind may divert the arrow so that, in conditions thereafter normal, it would miss the target altogether. However, a second gust may next guide it to the bull's-eye after all. The shot is then accurate and adroit, but not accurate *because* adroit. So it is not apt, and not creditable to the archer.

An archer's shot is thus a performance open to the AAA structure: accuracy, adroitness, aptness. So are performances generally, at least those that have an aim, even if the aim is not intentional. A shot succeeds if it is aimed intentionally to hit a target and does so. A heartbeat succeeds if it helps pump blood, even without intending to do so.

Maybe all performances have an aim, even those superficially aimless, such as ostensibly aimless ambling. Performances with an aim, in any case, admit assessment in respect of our three attainments: namely, accuracy, or reaching the aim; adroitness, or manifesting skill or competence; and aptness, or reaching the aim *through* the adroitness manifest. The following will be restricted to performances with an aim.

Some acts are performances, of course, but so are some sustained states. Think of those live motionless statues that one sees at tourist sites. Such performances can linger, and need not be constantly sustained through renewed conscious intentions. The performer's mind could wander, with little effect on the continuation or quality of the performance.

Beliefs too might thus count as performances, long-sustained ones, with no more conscious or intentional an aim than that of a heartbeat. At a minimum, beliefs can be assessed for correctness independently of any competence that they may manifest. Beliefs can be true by luck, after all, independently of the believer's competence in so believing, as in Gettier cases.

Beliefs fall under the AAA structure, as do performances generally. We can distinguish between, first, a belief's accuracy, that is, its truth; second, its adroitness, that is, its manifesting epistemic virtue or competence; and, third, its aptness, that is, its being true *because* competent.[11]

Animal knowledge is essentially just apt belief.

Let us consider more closely our archer's shot. There are at least two ways in which that shot might fail to be safe: I mean, two ways in which the archer might then easily have released that arrow from that bow aimed at that target while the shot failed. The following two things might each have been fragile so as to deprive that shot of safety: (*a*) the archer's level of competence, for one; and (*b*) the appropriateness of the conditions, for another.

Thus, (*a*) the archer might have recently ingested a drug, so that at the moment when he aimed and shot, his blood content of the drug might easily have been slightly higher, so as to reduce his competence to where he would surely have missed. Or else (*b*) a freak set of meteorological conditions might have gathered in such a way that too easily a gust might have diverted the arrow on the way to the target.

In neither case, however, would the archer be denied credit for his fine shot simply because it is thus unsafe. The shot is apt and creditable even if its aptness is fragile in the ways described. What is required for the shot to be apt is that it be accurate because adroit, successful because competent. That it might too easily have failed through reduced competence or degraded conditions renders it unsafe but not inapt.

So we have seen ways in which a performance can be apt though unsafe. Moreover, a performance might be safe though inapt. A protecting angel with

---

[11] Compare: "We have reached the view that knowledge is true belief out of intellectual virtue, belief that turns out right by reason of the virtue and not just by coincidence." (Sosa 1991, p. 277) Also: "What in sum is required for knowledge and what are the roles of intellectual virtue and perspective? . . . [One] must grasp that one's belief non-accidentally reflects the truth [of the proposition known] through the exercise of such a virtue." (Sosa, 1991, p. 292). Also: "We need a clearer and more comprehensive view of the respects in which one's belief must *be non-accidentally true* if it is to constitute knowledge. Unaided, the tracking or causal requirements proposed . . . permit too narrow a focus on the particular target belief and its causal or counterfactual relation to the *truth* of its content. Just widening our focus will not do, however, if we widen it only far enough to include the process that yields the belief involved. We need an even broader view." (Sosa (1997), from the sections entitled "Circular Externalism" and "Virtue Epistemology"; emphasis added.) That broader view, as explained soon thereafter, puts the emphasis on the subject and on the subject's virtues or competences. And it is made clear that the belief must be non-accidentally true, and not just non-accidentally present. The view developed in the present chapter, is essentially that same view, now better formulated, based on an improved conception of aptness, and explicitly amplified to cover performances generally.

a wind machine might ensure that the archer's shot would hit the bull's-eye, for example, and a particular shot might hit the bull's-eye through a gust from the angel's machine, which compensates for a natural gust that initially diverts the arrow. In this case the shot is safe without being apt: it is not accurate *because* adroit.

In conclusion, neither aptness nor safety entails the other. The connection that perhaps remains is only this. Aptness requires the manifestation of a competence, and a competence is a disposition, one with a basis resident in the competent agent, one that would in appropriately normal conditions ensure (or make highly likely) the success of any relevant performance that it may issue. Compatibly with such restricted safety, the competence manifest might then be fragile, as might also the appropriate normalcy of the conditions in which it is manifest.

8. Apt belief and the problem of dreams

The bearing of those reflections on the problem of dreams is now straight-forward. True, on the orthodox conception dreams do pose a danger for our perceptual beliefs, which are *un*safe through the proximity of the dream possibility, wherein one is said to host such a belief on the same sensory basis while dreaming. However, what dreams render vulnerable is only this: either the perceptual competence of the believer or the appropriate normalcy of the conditions for its exercise.

The dreamer's experience may be fragmentary and indistinct, so that his sensory basis may not be quite the same as that of a normal perceiver. Recall Austin's "dreamlike" quality of dreams, and Descartes's idea that dreams are insufficiently coherent. However, the dreamer's reduced or lost competence may blind him to such features of his experience, features that would enable him to distinguish dreaming from perceiving. Sleep might render one's conditions abnormal and inadequate for the exercise of perceptual faculties. The proximate possibility that one is now asleep and dreaming might thus render fragile both one's competence and also, jointly or alternatively, the conditions appropriate for its exercise. That is how the possibility that one is asleep and dreaming might endanger our ordinary perceptual beliefs, making them unsafe. But this is just one more case where safety is compromised while aptness remains intact.

Ordinary perceptual beliefs might thus retain their status as apt, animal knowledge, despite the nearby possibility that one is asleep and dreaming. Ordinary perceptual beliefs can still attain success through the exercise of perceptual competence, despite the fragility of that competence and of its required conditions. However unsafe a performer's competence may be, and however unsafe may be the conditions appropriate for its exercise, if a performance does succeed through the exercise of that competence in its proper conditions, then it is an apt performance, one creditable to the performer. Knowledge is just a special case of such creditable, apt performance. Perceptual knowledge is unaffected by any fragility either in the knower's competence or in the conditions appropriate for its exercise. The knower's belief can thus remain apt even if the proximity of the dream possibility renders it unsafe.

9. Conclusion

In summary, some skeptics find a paradox at the heart of common sense. If you are to know that p, they argue, you must believe it sensitively, in that, if it had been false, you would not have believed it. Or at least you must believe it on a basis such that, if it had been false, you would not have believed it on that basis. This denies us knowledge that we are not misled victims of a radical skeptical scenario. Our belief that we are not misled envatted brains, for example, is one that lacks sensitivity. If that were our plight, we would still take ourselves to be normal perceivers of a normal scene before us.

A first response is to replace the sensitivity requirement with its safety counterpart, where the safety of a belief requires only that believing on such a basis one *would* then be right. A belief can thus be safe without being sensitive, since subjunctive conditionals do not contrapose. Though more adequate than the sensitivity requirement, this requirement of safety is still inadequate. We still face the skeptic's paradox, given that dreams are a common enough fact of life, unlike the usual run of outlandish scenarios. Dreams threaten the safety of our ordinary perceptual beliefs, since too easily might our perceptual beliefs have been false though similarly based on phenomenal experience, as supposedly happens in our dreams.

I offer two ways to meet this threat. First, I argue that dreams do not contain beliefs, and hence do not threaten the safety of our ordinary perceptual beliefs.

Second, I argue that, in order to be knowledge, a belief needs to be neither sensitive nor safe; it needs rather to be apt—that is, correct in virtue of manifesting the believer's epistemic competence exercised in its appropriate conditions.

Consider indeed performances generally, not just intellectual performances such as judgments or beliefs. Your pertinent skill and competence, and your relevant circumstances for their exercise, can both be sufficiently fragile to render your performance unsafe. In spite of that, it may still be apt, however, still a performance creditable to you as an attainment of your own. Knowledge is simply such apt performance in the way of belief. Knowledge hence does not require the safety of its contained belief, since the belief can be unsafe because of the fragility of the believer's relevant competence or circumstances, while it is nonetheless apt, nonetheless attributable to the believer's competence manifest in its appropriate circumstances.

The bearing of those reflections on the problem of dreams is now straightforward. True, on the orthodox conception dreams do pose a danger for our perceptual beliefs. The dream possibility is too close for comfort, since one is said to host beliefs on the same sensory basis while dreaming. However, what dreams render vulnerable is only this: either the perceptual competence of the believer or the appropriate normalcy of the conditions for its exercise.

When we sleep and dream, then, our circumstances are inappropriate for the manifestation of our perceptual competence. Hence, even assuming that we do have perceptual beliefs in our dreams, these cannot then be apt, since, even if and when they accidentally hit the mark of truth, they fail to do so in a way creditable to the believer's competence. But this does not affect our perceptual beliefs in waking life, which remain apt.

Animal knowledge is hence equivalent to apt belief, which resolves our skeptical paradox.[12]

---

[12] And promises, moreover, a solution for the Gettier problem, the problem that beliefs can be true and justified without being knowledge. Why do such beliefs fall short? Because they are not apt, despite being true and justified. Here is an early statement of this view: "We have reached the view that knowledge is true belief out of intellectual virtue, belief that turns out right by reason of the virtue and not just by coincidence." (E. Sosa, *Knowledge in Perspective* (Cambridge: Cambridge University Press, 1991), 277.) The view has now been developed beyond the present capsule statement, in my recently published *A Virtue Epistemology* (Oxford University Press, 2007).

7

Knowledge-Closure and Skepticism

Marian David and Ted A. Warfield

> Uncovering difficulties in the details of particular formulations of [the closure principle] will not weaken the principle's intuitive appeal; such quibbling will seem at best like a wasp attacking a steamroller, at worst like an effort in bad faith to avoid being pulled along by the skeptic's argument.
>
> (Robert Nozick, *Philosophical Explanations* (1981), 206)

Leopold enters his dining room and seems to see a chair in front of him. Does Leopold know that there is a chair in front of him? The following informal skeptical argument attempts to show that he does not:

> Leopold does not know that he is not a brain in a vat inhabiting a chairless world.

Early versions of various parts of this chapter were presented by one or both of us in colloquia at the University of Rochester, the University of Cincinnati, Florida State University, and the University of Notre Dame. We jointly presented a substantial portion of this material at a workshop on Lotteries, Closure, and Skepticism at the University of Missouri. We thank our audiences and hosts on these occasions. We have received generous feedback on this project from many philosophers and apologize for not thanking all of them by name here. We do want to thank especially Robert Audi, E. J. Coffman, Earl Conee, Thomas Crisp, Richard Feldman, and John Hawthorne for helpful feedback and valuable advice. Our deepest debt is to Leopold Stubenberg, who provided insightful and skeptical feedback while tolerating more discussion of this material than even a good friend should have to endure.

If Leopold does not know *that*, then he does not know that there is a chair in front of him.

So, Leopold does not know that there is a chair in front of him.

This argument is valid. Its first premise might be defended on the grounds that the particular skeptical hypothesis involved—the hypothesis that he is a brain in a vat inhabiting a chairless world—is well chosen so that Leopold does not know it to be false. Alternatively, it might be defended on the general grounds that agents like Leopold cannot possibly know any skeptical hypotheses to be false. In this chapter we will not have much to say about this first premise. We will mostly be concerned with the argument's second premise and with some issues pertaining to the argument's conclusion.

The second premise of the argument might be defended by invoking some principle of *epistemic closure*. Although there are other ways to defend the second premise, this type of defense seems to be the best known and most prominent one. We will discuss it at length. We intend to examine skeptical arguments that are based on epistemic closure principles.[1]

The conclusion of the argument is that one agent (Leopold) does not know one thing (that there is a chair in front of him). This conclusion is not immediately troubling. Many agents do not know many things. The argument is supposed to be worrisome because it seems obvious that a similar and equally plausible argument could be given for the conclusion that any typical agent does not know any typical proposition ordinarily thought to be known by the agent on perceptual grounds. In other words, the argument concerning Leopold and the chair is supposed to be worrisome because it is seen as an argument from arbitrary instance to the quite general conclusion that all human agents lack all perceptual knowledge. We will pay some attention to the details of how the generalization from Leopold and his chair to human agents and perceptual knowledge in general might go.

We begin in Section 1 with some preliminary remarks about epistemic-closure principles, knowledge-closure principles in particular, and the role of knowledge-closure principles in skeptical argumentation. After discussing

---

[1] One apparently alternative defense of the second premise invokes an *underdetermination* principle, making use of the idea that Leopold's evidence underdetermines the "chair hypothesis" vis-à-vis the skeptical hypothesis; see, among others, Brueckner (1994), and Cohen (1998).

some implausible knowledge-closure principles and identifying two key problems for such principles in Section 2, we move on in Sections 3 and 4 to discuss more plausible knowledge-closure principles and their possible use in skeptical argumentation.

1. Preliminaries

An epistemic closure principle is a principle asserting that, if an agent stands in some epistemic relation, say the relation of knowing, to a proposition, then the agent also stands in that epistemic relation to further propositions connected in some specified way to the first proposition. The epistemic relation is then said to be "closed" under the specified connection. For example, the following principle expresses the closure of knowledge under entailment (that is, necessary consequence, strict implication):

Closure 1:   For all S, all p, all q: if S knows p, and p entails q, then S knows q.

This says that, for all agents S, and propositions p and q, if S knows p, and if p entails q, then S knows q. Note that epistemic principles, like philosophical principles in general, are traditionally intended as necessary truths. So the principle should be understood to fail unless it holds with necessity. We will sometimes follow general custom and suppress initial quantifiers as well as references to the agent; we will also use obvious symbols and insert clarifying parentheses. (We will, when necessary, present the arguments in "full-dress" detail.) The short version of Closure 1 will then look like this:

Closure 1 $(Kp$ and $(p$ entails $q)) \rightarrow Kq$.

Some (but not all) skeptical arguments employ a knowledge-closure principle. Here is an example of a skeptical argument that employs Closure 1. Actually, it is just an argument sketch representative of how closure-based arguments are frequently portrayed in the literature on closure and/or skepticism. Consider the following skeptical hypothesis: h = you are the victim of an evil demon who is leading you into falsely believing all of the things you take yourself to know via perception; for example, the demon is misleading you into believing that there are chairs in the room when in fact there are not. Let c = the proposition that there are chairs in the room; let ∼h = the denial of the skeptical hypothesis just sketched—that is, the proposition that you are *not* the victim of an evil demon who . . . The skeptic then argues as follows:

P1 $(Kp \text{ and } (p \text{ entails } q)) \rightarrow Kq$

but

P2 $\sim K \sim h$

hence

3   Either $\sim Kc$ or $\sim(c \text{ entails } \sim h)$

but

P4   c entails $\sim h$

hence

5    $\sim Kc$

Premise P1 is just Closure 1. Premise P2 claims that you do not know that the skeptical hypothesis is false (perhaps you cannot, perhaps you simply do not). This is the skeptic's key claim—one might, of course, challenge this claim, but that would be a topic for another paper. Step 3 follows from P1 and P2. Premise P4 is supposed to be obvious. The conclusion, 5, follows from 3 and P4. If sound, an argument along these lines might be taken to show that agents such as us do not know the humdrum propositions we take ourselves to know via perception, such as the proposition that there are chairs in the room.

The basic strategy behind this type of skeptical argument is this. First employ a general epistemic principle the non-skeptic is committed to, then use a skeptical hypothesis to turn the principle against the non-skeptic. It is crucial to the success of this strategy that the non-skeptic really be committed (at least implicitly) to the general epistemic principle in question. This is *not* the case for the sample argument given above (we mention it for purposes of illustration only). The simple closure principle it employs, Closure 1, is easily seen to be false: people do not know all the necessary consequences of what they know. The argument, though valid, is unsound. But perhaps there is a more promising closure-based skeptical argument around the corner. Such an argument would have to employ a closure principle that is not easily seen to be false, and it would have to lead (through at least arguably sound steps) to an interesting skeptical conclusion.

Here we will focus on closure principles involving one epistemic notion: *knowledge*. We will not discuss closure principles involving justification, or warrant, or rationality, or other epistemic notions. We do not mean to suggest that discussing such closure principles would not be worthwhile, or that such a discussion would not be of relevance to skeptical argumentation. We focus on closure principles involving knowledge because most discussions of closure-based skepticism turn on closure principles involving knowledge, and also because we like knowledge and want to think about knowledge and knowledge-skepticism. Also, we tend to think that knowledge is somewhat easier to handle than notions like justification or rationality. The latter are ambiguous in ways in which knowledge is not (if the notion of knowledge is ambiguous, it is less ambiguous than the other notions).

Our central question is this: are there any plausibly true epistemic closure principles concerning knowledge that figure centrally in arguably sound skeptical arguments with interestingly strong conclusions? There are several angles from which one might approach this question. One might first try to formulate a plausible skeptical argument and then ask what closure principle, if any, the argument employs. Alternatively, one might look directly at closure principles, asking of each candidate principle whether it is vulnerable to counterexample; if not, one might go on, asking whether a skeptical argument using the principle looks promising. We will adopt this latter approach.

Most (but again, not all) contemporary discussions of skepticism involve knowledge-closure principles, so it seems that quite a few epistemologists believe that the answer to our question is: "Yes, there are indeed plausible knowledge-closure principles that figure centrally in arguably sound skeptical arguments with interestingly strong conclusions." It turns out, however, that authors whose main concern is with skepticism often invoke implausible closure principles when discussing closure-based skeptical arguments. Sometimes they even invoke a principle they themselves acknowledge to be false, adding a footnote to the effect that the principle would have to be modified somehow to make it immune to counterexample. On the other hand, authors who explicitly discuss closure principles tend to focus on providing counterexamples against some such principles or on protecting them from alleged counterexamples. Their discussions are usually motivated by a background concern with skepticism, but they almost never include even minimally detailed consideration of how, if at all, the most plausible closure principles might figure in a specific skeptical argument. We expect that others who are familiar with the relevant literature have occasionally wondered about this situation and have thought that someone should try to sort out what exactly is going on with knowledge-closure principles and skepticism.

It is, after all, possible to smell a rat here. One might reasonably suspect that there are not that many true closure principles at all and that the few plausible ones will be of less use to the skeptic than it initially appeared while the ones that would clearly be of use to the skeptic will not be plausible. This suspicion motivates our discussion. Though we are inclined to agree with Feldman (1995: 487) that "some version of the closure principle . . . is surely true", this does not force us to believe that the true version(s) of the principle will be useful in a skeptical argument. This is an issue that depends on the details. So, *pace* Nozick (see the passage with which we began this paper), we intend to quibble about the details of closure principles because the details may well matter to the formulation and evaluation of a specific skeptical argument.[2] Though a few authors have looked into some of the relevant issues,[3] the main issues that concern us here have not been addressed in sufficient detail and have certainly not been resolved. We do not promise to resolve them here, but we do intend to take some steps towards a resolution.

2. Implausible principles

Closure 1, recall, claimed that knowledge is closed under entailment (necessary consequence); that is, it claimed that one knows the necessary consequences of what one knows:

Closure 1 $(Kp$ and $(p$ entails $q)) \rightarrow Kq.$

This principle is false for at least two reasons. First, and most obviously, the principle implies that you believe all the necessary consequences of what you know, and this is clearly implausible. Vast numbers of propositions are entailed by what you know, far too many to believe them all. Second, assume you *do* believe q; and assume, in addition, that q is a necessary truth. Necessary truths

---

[2] Nozick himself argued, implausibly, that closure principles fail as a consequence of details of his analysis of knowledge; see his (1981: ch. 3.2). This argument is no more plausible than Nozick's widely rejected analysis of knowledge. Additionally, the details of Nozick's argument that Closure fails given his account of knowledge are mistaken. See Warfield (2004) for a discussion of this issue.

[3] Two early discussions are Klein (1981), and Brueckner (1985).

are trivially entailed by any proposition. So, according to Closure 1, you are guaranteed to know q as long as you know a single truth. Surely, that is much too lenient: you might believe q for bad reasons; or you might believe it in the face of strong (albeit misleading) evidence to the contrary, evidence that you are unable to defeat. If you did this, you would not know q, even though it is entailed by something you know. Closure 1 is invitingly simple but false: it cannot serve in a successful skeptical argument.

We have just seen that Closure 1 suffers from at least two problems. It seems natural to begin to respond to these problems by adding a requirement to the effect that the agent must have at least "noticed" the relevant entailment. This leads to the following well-known closure principle saying that knowledge is closed under *known* entailment:

Closure 2 (Kp and $K(p$ entails q)) $\rightarrow$ Kq.

The skeptical argument employing Closure 2 goes roughly like this (where again c = some bit of alleged perceptual knowledge and $\sim$h = the denial of the skeptical hypothesis):

P1   (Kp and $K(p$ entails q)) $\rightarrow$ Kq
P2 $\sim$K$\sim$h
3     $\sim$Kc or $\sim$K(c entails $\sim$h)
P4   K(c entails $\sim$h)
5     $\sim$Kc

Although Closure 2 is the best-known and most widely discussed epistemic-closure principle, it is still false. It is the principle one usually finds in discussions of closure-based skepticism, sometimes with an accompanying footnote indicating that it would have to be modified somehow to make it immune to counterexample.[4]

Closure 2 faces two problems. Here is the first problem. One can fail to believe q, despite knowing p and knowing that p entails q. One might not have "put two and two together" and done the inference (knowledge of an entailment does not guarantee that one actually draws the inferences it underwrites), and one might not otherwise believe q. Call this the "belief problem".

Here is the second problem. We call it the "warrant problem". Let us bracket the belief problem and pretend agents who know p and know that

---

[4] Cf. Nozick (1981: 47–8); Vogel (1990: 13); Cohen (1999: 62).

p entails *q* also believe *q*. Closure 2 requires not merely that *q* be believed; it requires that *q* be *known*. Consistent with knowing *p* and knowing that *p* entails *q*, however, one might believe *q* for terrible reasons (and perhaps in the presence of relevant defeaters, and so on). While the belief problem raises the psychological issue whether we will find all the beliefs Closure 2 predicts we will find, the warrant problem raises the epistemic issue whether such beliefs, even where they are found, will have the required epistemic status to count as knowledge.

Before we turn to principles that directly address these problems, we want to take a look at some relatives of Closure 2 that we will ignore in our subsequent discussion. Feldman (1995: 488) discusses a principle about the "transmission of justification" that, reformulated as a principle about the "transmission of knowledge", would look like this:

Closure 3 $K(p \text{ and } (p \text{ entails } q)) \rightarrow Kq$.

Evidently, Closure 3 does not solve the belief problem; and it does not solve the warrant problem either. Still, there might be something to be said for it. Note first that Closure 3 should not be any worse off than Closure 2, for it is plausibly taken to be entailed by Closure 2.[5] In addition, it looks as though Closure 3 ought to be a bit safer than Closure 2, for Closure 3 does not obviously entail Closure 2. Now consider the rule

R1 $Kp \text{ and } K(p \text{ entails } q) \rightarrow K(p \text{ and } (p \text{ entails } q))$.

Rule R1 is a restriction of a more general rule, the so-called conjunction rule, according to which Kx and Ky together entail $K(x \text{ and } y)$, for any propositions *x* and *y*—a rule that figures prominently in various versions of the lottery paradox and has been contested.[6] Since R1 is a restriction of this contested conjunction rule, R1 itself might be considered questionable. Now, though Closure 3 does not obviously entail Closure 2, the combination of R1 with Closure 3 does obviously entail Closure 2. In view of this, one might suspect Closure 2 of implicitly relying in some manner on the questionable R1. If this is a serious worry for Closure 2—we are not sure whether it is—Closure 3 will be preferable: although it does not begin to address the belief problem

---

[5] This assumes, as is plausible, that knowledge of a conjunction entails knowledge of each conjunct. Hence, the *antecedent* of Closure 3 entails the *antecedent* of Closure 2; hence, Closure 2 entails Closure 3. For any two principles with the same consequent, if the antecedent of one entails the antecedent of the other, then the other entails the one.

[6] The original presentation is in Kyburg (1961).

and does not do much by way of addressing the warrant problem, it at least avoids a potential difficulty.

Closure 3 allows us to illustrate how modifications to closure principles may significantly affect their utility for skeptical argumentation. (This is a bit artificial because Closures 2 and 3 both face difficulties that suffice for their not being useful to the skeptic, but the illustration should prove useful nonetheless.) A skeptical argument employing Closure 3 would *begin* like this:

P1 $K(p \text{ and } (p \text{ entails } q)) \rightarrow Kq$
P2 $\sim K \sim h$
3 $\sim K(c \text{ and } (c \text{ entails } \sim h))$
P4 $K(c \text{ entails } \sim h)$

But now it is unclear how the skeptic is to get from this point to the desired conclusion "$\sim Kc$". An epistemic principle underwriting the step from 3 and P4 to "$\sim Kc$" would be:

P5 $\sim K(p \text{ and } (p \text{ entails } q)) \rightarrow \sim Kp \text{ or } \sim K(p \text{ entails } q)$

which, together with 3, allows the skeptic to derive the disjunction "$\sim Kc$ or $\sim K(c \text{ entails } \sim h)$", which in turn gets him to "$\sim Kc$" by premise P4.

But principle P5 is logically equivalent to the rule R1. So the skeptic seems to weaken his argument, making it vulnerable to the charge of relying on a questionable rule. Moreover, if a skeptical argument based on Closure 3 relies on R1 anyway, then the switch from Closure 2 to Closure 3 is ultimately pointless: with R1 available, the sole ground for suspicion about Closure 2 that motivated switching to Closure 3 has been removed (since R1 and Closure 3 together entail Closure 2, any worry about the latter is a worry about the conjunction of the former). To make a strong argument, the closure-based skeptic needs the best closure principle he can get. Since Closure 3, *qua* closure principle, appears to be somewhat safer than Closure 2, the skeptic might consider it to be a preferable starting point. But, in order to employ it in his argument, he needs to rely on a vulnerable rule combined with which Closure 3 offers no improvement over Closure 2 for skeptical purposes. The skeptic might as well have stuck to Closure 2: the net gain in plausibility of the argument based on Closure 3 seems to be zero.

In what follows, we will ignore variants of closure principles that, in the manner of Closure 3, combine two occurrences of the K-operator in the antecedent into one. Though they might be somewhat safer than their "distributed" siblings, this gain in safety will be offset by the need to complicate the skeptical argument when employing such a principle.

Let us briefly look at another relative of Closure 2. We have noted that Closure 2 is the most prominent knowledge-closure principle by far. We have also noted that it is typically introduced as an improvement over Closure 1. But one might well wonder what exactly motivates moving from Closure 1 to Closure 2, rather than

Closure 4 $(Kp$ and $(p$ entails $q)$ and $B(p$ entails $q)) \rightarrow Kq,$

which would seem to be an alternative way of accommodating the idea that, in order to know q, when q is entailed by something one knows, one must have "noticed" the relevant entailment. Why is Closure 2 so prominent while Closure 4 is never mentioned? Sure enough, Closure 4 suffers from the belief problem (and the warrant problem); but so does Closure 2. Is there anything Closure 2 can do that Closure 4 cannot do?

Here are three considerations. First, say an agent knows p and believes correctly that p entails q but does not know this because the agent holds the entailment belief based on hearsay rather than understanding and/or reflection. Such an agent might be said to fail to know q on the grounds that she will be unable to defeat (misleading) evidence against (p entails q) and/or against q. An agent who knows p and *knows* that it entails q, on the other hand, should be better positioned (in principle) to defeat such misleading evidence; so Closure 2 seems better than Closure 4. Second, what exactly is it to believe that p entails q? Say some agent believes that p entails q but does not believe that, necessarily, if p is true then q is true. Is this possible? Well, why not? Does the agent know q? One might think she does not have sufficient grasp of the concept of entailment really to know q, given what she has to go by. As a remedy one might propose this: though it is possible to believe that p entails q while having a defective grasp of the concept of entailment, it is not possible to *know* that p entails q while having a defective grasp of the concept of entailment; so Closure 2 once again seems better than Closure 4. Third, Closure 2 does not appear to entail Closure 4, whereas Closure 4 trivially entails Closure 2.[7] So Closure 2 appears to be the safer principle. In what follows, we join the general custom of neglecting Closure 4.

---

[7] Because the antecedent of Closure 2 trivially entails the antecedent of Closure 4; see n. 5.

3. Plausible principles (*a*): Strengthening the antecedent

We now want to return to the main line of the chapter. Closures 1–4 share a consequent—namely K*q*—that gets the principles into trouble with the belief problem. There is nothing in the antecedents of any of these four principles guaranteeing that *q* is believed, and, without believing *q*, one does not know *q*. Searching for a closure principle that is not clearly false, one can pursue two general strategies. One can (*a*) build belief in *q* into the antecedent of a candidate closure principle, or (*b*) weaken the consequent of a principle so that it does not require belief in *q*. We will now explore these moves in some detail. In this section we consider option (*a*). In Section IV we consider option (*b*).

Let us first consider a simple principle that aims to avoid the belief problem by building belief in *q* into the antecedent of Closure 2:

Closure 5 (K*p* and K(*p* entails *q*) and B*q*) $\rightarrow$ K*q*.

Though Closure 5 indeed sidesteps the belief problem, it does nothing to address the warrant problem: it says nothing at all about one's reasons for believing *q*. What if, for example, one knows *p*, knows that *p* entails *q*, and believes *q*, but believes *q* not because of *p* and the entailment but rather for some problematic reason? For example, what if I know that there are at least nine people in the room (I started counting and stopped at nine), and I know that this entails that there are at least seven people in the room, and I believe that there are at least seven people in the room but not because of the inference or the counting but rather because I *always* believe that there are at least seven people in the room when I am in the room. Though the example is somewhat frivolous, it should be clear that, in this sort of situation, where one does not base believing *q* on proper grounds for believing *q*, it looks like one does not know *q*.

The obvious response is to build an appropriate basing relation clause into the antecedent of Closure 5. The result will be a principle similar to:

Closure 6 (K*p* and K(*p* entails *q*) and B*q* based on deduction from *p* and (*p* entails *q*)) $\rightarrow$ K*q*.

We will not offer a detailed exploration of various difficulties concerning the nature of the basing relation. But a few remarks seem to be in order.

It should be noted that the inserted clause about the basing relation, "B*q* based on deduction from *p* and (*p* entails *q*)", is a bit ambiguous. It can be understood in at least two different ways, reflecting two views about deduction and about what sorts of beliefs Closure 6 expects the epistemic agent to hold. More precisely, the clause can be understood to imply either (i) or (ii):

(i) *S* believes *q*, and *S* believes *p*, and *S* believes that (*p* entails *q*), and *S* believes *q* based on deducing it from her belief *p* together with her belief that (*p* entails *q*).

(ii) *S* believes *q*, and *S* believes that (*p* and (*p* entails *q*)), and *S* believes *q* based on deducing it from her belief that (*p* and (*p* entails *q*)).

Reading (ii) demands, as it were, more by way of beliefs from the agent than what is already involved in K*p* and K(*p* entails *q*). It expects the agent to have put together into one conjunctive belief the two beliefs involved in these two bits of knowledge. Accordingly, it assumes a picture of deduction where the agent deduces her belief *q* from her conjunctive premise-belief that (*p* and (*p* entails *q*)). Reading (i) demands less from the agent. It does not expect that she has put together the beliefs involved in K*p* and K(*p* entails *q*) into a single conjunctive premise-belief. Accordingly, it assumes a picture of deduction where the agent deduces her belief *q* from two premise-beliefs, without expecting her to have put the two together into a single premise-belief. On the face of it, reading (i) seems preferable: since it expects less from the agent, the resulting version of Closure 6 will apply to a wider range of cases than a version incorporating reading (ii). We therefore select the first reading.[8]

All the principles preceding Closure 6 are easily understood as making synchronic claims, saying that an agent possesses as piece of knowledge *q* at a time *t* provided the agent satisfies a certain condition at that same time *t*. Although Closure 6 as a whole should also be understood in this way, it must be noted that the clause about the basing relation complicates matters because it carries with it an implied reference to a time earlier than *t*. An agent who is at a time *t* in the state of believing *q* *based on deduction* from premises *p* and (*p* entails *q*) will typically have entered that state by way of an inference that began at a time prior to *t* at which the agent did not yet believe *q*. Moreover, the basing clause should be understood to imply that the agent already knew the

---

[8] If one preferred a variant of Closure 6 that employs a single K-operator in the manner of Closure 3, then reading (ii) would seem the better choice.

premises at that prior time; otherwise the clause would probably not remove the problems it was designed to remove.

We note, finally, that Gilbert Harman has argued repeatedly (e.g. 1973: ch. 10) that it is at best misleading to talk about deduction as if it were a psychological inference process. We do not wish to engage this issue here. We assume that Closure 6 can be interpreted (or, if need be, reformulated) so as to avoid any mistaken views about the nature of deduction.

Some have thought that Closure 6 is beyond criticism. Does it not merely say that one knows what one (properly) deduces from what one knows? And is this not so obvious as to be beyond criticism? Well, those are two questions. The answer to the first is "Yes—although, to be more precise, Closure 6 actually says that one knows what one has (properly) deduced from what one knew and still knows". The answer to the second question is "No, this is not so obvious as to be beyond criticism".

Closure 6 may run into trouble with cases of epistemically *overdetermined* beliefs. I know that this is a chair, and I know that if this is a chair it cannot fly away, and I believe on the basis of these two bits of knowledge that the chair will not fly away. Additionally, however, I believe that the chair will not fly away because I believe that its wings are broken (and also because I believe that my crystal ball revealed to me that it will not fly away).[9] Admittedly, this is again a frivolous example. Perhaps the following is more realistic. Pretend I am a thorough logician and, whenever I can manage, I like to provide two independent proofs of every theorem I prove. On one occasion I knowingly deduce a theorem, T, from known starting assumptions but also independently manage to "deduce" it fallaciously from mistaken starting assumptions. Do I know T? And what if I used additional bad proofs?

We are not quite sure what to make of cases like this—much seems to hang on exactly how one understands the difficult notion of believing one thing "on the basis of" some other things. Much seems to hang, that is, on further detailed issues about "the basing relation" left unsettled by our brief discussion earlier. Perhaps whether one knows depends in part on relevant counterfactuals expressing what one would believe if the other reason(s) were subtracted out and/or on the firmness of belief that comes from each

---

[9] The conditional in this example is not obviously a strict conditional. We occasionally use examples of this form where in our judgment nothing of consequence turns on the precise modal strength of the conditional. Examples more clearly involving strict conditionals can easily be substituted at a cost of additional complexity in the presentation.

individual source of belief. It may well be worth exploring these issues about overdetermination, closure, and the basing relation in some detail.[10] But when searching for a plausible closure principle, it is perhaps best to avoid such complexities and consider a slightly modified candidate:

Closure 7   (Kp and K(p entails q) and Bq *solely* based on deduction from p and (p entails q)) → Kq.

We think there are challenges even to this extremely plausible-looking principle. Here we will merely gesture at three of them. There might be agents with weird global defeaters; in particular, agents who satisfy the antecedent of the principle even though they believe (and for subjectively quite compelling reasons) that deduction is not a good way of adding beliefs.[11] There might be incoherent agents; in particular, agents who satisfy the antecedent, hence believe q, but also incoherently believe $\sim q$: Can one really know q while believing $\sim q$? And there is also a quite different challenge deriving from cases caught up in epistemic paradox.[12] Though we take these challenges quite seriously, we acknowledge that they involve relatively arcane issues. We will not pursue them at this point.

There are principles intuitively "in between" Closure 6 and Closure 7 that might also be of interest. An example of such a principle is:

Closure 6.5   (Kp and K(p entails q) and (Bq based on deduction from p and (p entails q)) and $\sim$(Bq based on some "defective reason")) → Kq.

If one interprets the "no defective reason" clause broadly enough, this principle avoids the "bad" overdetermination cases facing Closure 6 and allows for more flexibility in the antecedent than is allowed by the antecedent of Closure 7. On the downside, because of the "no-defective-reason" clause, Closure 6.5 is rather more vague than Closure 6 and Closure 7. Still, it might be considered preferable to both. Note, however, that the challenges to Closure 7, briefly hinted at in the previous paragraph, will be equally relevant to the evaluation of Closure 6.5—and, of course, to Closure 6 as well.

[10] See VanArragon (2001: ch. 2).

[11] They might be faithful but somewhat confused students of Vann McGee, the author of "A Counterexample to Modus Ponens"; see McGee (1985).

[12] See Maitzen (1998) for an extensive discussion of closure and epistemic paradox. In David and Warfield (manuscript and forthcoming) we discuss these and some other challenges.

We have now identified three closure principles (Closures 6, 6.5, and 7) that appear to be sufficiently plausible to make it worth asking whether they are of use in a skeptical argument. Though Closure 6 is rather more vulnerable than Closures 7 and 6.5 (which are themselves not beyond challenge), it is not obviously false. Since it is also the least cumbersome of the three, we will begin by asking how it performs in a closure-based skeptical argument.

Let us first look at an argument sketch starting from Closure 6 that proceeds along the lines of the argument sketches given earlier—we abbreviate the cumbersome locution "based on deduction from" to "bod from":

Argument Sketch

P1 Kp and $K(p$ entails $q)$ and Bq bod from p and $(p$ entails $q) \rightarrow Kq$
P2 $\sim K \sim h$
3   $\sim Kc$ or $\sim K(c$ entails $\sim h)$ or $\sim (B \sim h$ bod from c and $(c$ entails $\sim h))$
P4 $K(c$ entails $\sim h)$
P5 $B \sim h$ bod from c and $(c$ entails $\sim h)$
C1 $\sim Kc$

This way of representing the skeptical argument, though useful for indicating the argument's overall structure, has some shortcomings. Most importantly, rendering the conclusion as "$\sim Kc$"—where "c" is said to stand for some bit of alleged perceptual knowledge and the reference to agents is entirely suppressed—tends to downplay the conclusion the skeptic ought to be aiming for. When the "specter of skepticism" is raised, the skeptical threat is described as being of a very general nature. Skeptical arguments are supposed to threaten us with the strong general conclusion that we (that is, all human agents) lack all knowledge of an interesting sort (all empirical knowledge, or all perceptual knowledge); they are supposed to show that we do not know the empirical or perceptual propositions we think we know. Thus, the conclusion the skeptic really ought to be aiming for must say that no human agents know any proposition of some interesting class C:

7. $\forall S, \forall p \in C: \sim SKp.$

For present purposes we should think of class C, the class of propositions the skeptic is targeting, as the class of "perceptual propositions"—where perceptual propositions are, very roughly, propositions about our (alleged) environment (including our own bodies) that we typically believe or disbelieve (if we believe or disbelieve them at all), based, at least in part, on how our (alleged) environment looks, sounds, tastes, smells, or feels to us. Whether this class can actually be specified in a more precise and satisfying manner is a difficult issue. We will sidestep it for now, noting that the task of specifying C will fall to the skeptic.[13]

The skeptic under consideration here operates with a skeptical hypothesis, say some version of the evil-demon hypothesis, which is extracted from a larger skeptical scenario—a scenario that "explains", through the machinations of some evil demon, how it might have come about that we hold our perceptual beliefs, based on how things perceptually appear to us, even though these beliefs are all false. Skeptical hypotheses extracted from such a scenario are designed to attack our *perceptual* beliefs. They are not designed to attack beliefs that are concerned exclusively with our own conscious states or with simple logical matters. This accounts for the restriction to propositions of class C. Moreover, such skeptical hypotheses are designed to attack our perceptual *beliefs*. They are not designed to attack propositions we do not believe, for they offer an explanation of why we hold the perceptual beliefs we hold compatible with their being false. So the skeptic will try to reach his ultimate conclusion, 7, via a slightly weaker lemma,

6. $\forall S, \forall p \in C: SBp \rightarrow \sim SKp,$

which says that no human agents know any propositions of class C they believe. The more general conclusion, 7, follows easily from 6 by the principle that no one knows anything they do not believe.

Having identified the conclusion the skeptic ought to be aiming for, we should be able to turn the above argument sketch into a more carefully spelled-out general argument. It is usually taken for granted that this involves interpreting the argument sketch as attempting to establish the general skeptical conclusion, 7, by way of arguing from "arbitrary instances" (arbitrary human agents and arbitrary perceptual beliefs held by such agents). Before we look and see how this is supposed to go, we must address an additional wrinkle that comes up with respect to the fourth step of the argument sketch.

Premise P4 of the argument sketch says "K(c entails $\sim$h)". Since knowledge entails truth, this premise requires that it must be true that (c entails $\sim$h).

---

[13] This is somewhat disingenuous. After all, the philosophical skeptic is (usually) not a real person but rather the metaphorical personification of our own skeptical worries. Consequently, the premises of a serious skeptical argument must be premises that we ourselves are initially inclined to accept: in the end, the skeptic's tasks are our tasks.

But this means that as soon as we try to generalize over "c" we must address a preliminary issue glossed over in the argument sketch. Is the skeptic going to use a single skeptical hypothesis, such that each perceptual belief entails the denial of this hypothesis? Or is he going to use many different skeptical hypotheses, each one tailored to suit the specific perceptual belief at hand? In other words, the skeptic might be thinking along the lines of

There is a skeptical hypothesis that makes trouble for every perceptual belief;

or he might be thinking along the lines of

For every perceptual belief there is some trouble-making skeptical hypothesis.

Since the skeptic might try either option, we shall have to distinguish between two types of skeptical strategy, depending on what sort of hypotheses the skeptic wants to employ.

Let us first consider the strategy of the *general skeptical hypothesis*. A skeptic pursuing this strategy wants to advance a single skeptical hypothesis such that each perceptual belief, each belief in a proposition of class C, entails the denial of this hypothesis. Interestingly, it is not entirely straightforward to extract from a skeptical scenario a skeptical hypothesis that will do this job. The following is a somewhat rough proposal:

H   There is an evil demon who makes it the case that human agents tend to hold beliefs committing them to the view that there are material objects even though there are no material objects.

The idea is that our perceptual beliefs all entail the proposition that there are material objects, which of course entails the denial of H.[14]

The proposal is a bit rough. There may well be perceptual beliefs that do not entail the existence of material objects. For example, various conditional beliefs and/or negative beliefs might depend epistemically on how things perceptually appear to us, thereby counting as perceptual beliefs, but might not themselves entail the existence of any material object, even if they are based on beliefs that do. If so, a skeptic employing hypothesis H will be forced to somehow restrict C, the class of propositions he is targeting, which would of course weaken

---

[14] The skeptical hypothesis Descartes considers in the first Meditation appears to be a general hypothesis much like H; cf. *Meditations*, AT VII, p. 21.

the skeptical conclusion. (One might note in passing that propositions that explicitly mention material objects, say the proposition that there are chairs in the room, entail the proposition that there are material objects only under the assumption that material objects (chairs) are necessarily material objects: though this seems eminently plausible, it might still be noteworthy that a skeptic employing H relies on this assumption.) Rather than going into other worries one might possibly have about hypothesis H, we turn to the skeptical argument that employs H.[15]

A more carefully worked-out skeptical argument that (a) is based on Closure 6, (b) proceeds along the lines indicated by the argument sketch given above, (c) employs a single general skeptical hypothesis like H, and (d) aims at the general skeptical conclusion saying that human agents do not have any perceptual knowledge (do not know the propositions of class C), will go like this:

Argument A

P1 $\forall S, \forall p, \forall q$: SKp and $SK(p$ entails $q)$ and SBq bod from p and (p entails q) $\rightarrow SKq$

P2 $\forall S$: $\sim SK\sim H$

3 $\forall S, \forall p$: $\sim SKp$ or $\sim SK(p$ entails $\sim H)$ or $\sim(SB \sim H$ bod from p and (p entails $\sim H$))

P4 $\forall S, \forall p \in C$: $SBp \rightarrow SK(p$ entails $\sim H)$

P5 $\forall S, \forall p \in C$: $SBp \rightarrow SB \sim H$ bod from p and (p entails $\sim H$)

6 $\forall S, \forall p \in C$: $SBp \rightarrow \sim SKp$

7 $\forall S, \forall p \in C$: $\sim SKp$

---

[15] What about other candidates for playing the role of the general skeptical hypothesis? They are not easy to find. Take the hypothesis that we are all dreaming: it is not easy to come up with any perceptual beliefs that *entail* the denial of this hypothesis. Or take the hypothesis that there is an evil demon who makes it the case that all our perceptual beliefs are false—call it H1: "There is an evil demon who makes it the case that ($\forall S, \forall p \in C$: if SBp, then p is false)." Our perceptual beliefs, beliefs in propositions of class C, will not entail the denial of H1. To see this, consider a particular proposition, c, say the proposition that there are chairs in the room, and assume that it belongs to C and that some person S believes it. Proposition c of course entails that c is not false. But that is not enough. To entail the denial of H1, c would have to entail the denial of the conditional "if c ∈ C and SBc, then c is false"; that is, it would have to entail the conjunction "c ∈ C and SBc and c is not false"; but it does not. Take, finally, the hypothesis that we are brains in a vat. This skeptical hypothesis is significantly less general than H: only perceptual beliefs entailing that our bodies are more than just our brains will entail the denial of the brains-in-a-vat hypothesis. Anyway, the problems we are about to raise for skeptical arguments employing H also arise for arguments employing this considerably less general skeptical hypothesis.

Argument A is clearly valid. If it were sound, it would establish the strong conclusion the skeptic is aiming for. But the argument is not sound. On the contrary, premises P4 and P5 are ridiculously false.

Consider premise P4. Is it plausible to suggest that human agents know of each one of their perceptual beliefs that it entails the denial of the skeptical hypothesis? This ascribes all sorts of entailment beliefs to agents (who hold perceptual beliefs), and it is perfectly clear that typical agents do not have all these entailment beliefs. It is still more clear that it is not the case that all agents have all these entailment beliefs about the perceptual propositions they believe—it is even doubtful that most of the agents who happen to be aware of the skeptical hypothesis (that is, philosophers) have a large number of such entailment beliefs. Consider premise P5. It says that all agents (who hold perceptual beliefs) believe the denial of the skeptical hypothesis, $\sim$H, and believe it based on deduction from each of their premise-belief pairs p and (p entails $\sim$H), for every perceptual proposition p they believe. This ascribes all the entailment beliefs already ascribed by premise P4 to all agents. In addition, it ascribes beliefs in the denial of the skeptical hypothesis to all agents holding any perceptual beliefs. In addition, it maintains that each agent's belief in the denial of the skeptical hypothesis is radically overdetermined, being based on each of the premise-belief pairs p and (p entails $\sim$H), for each of the agent's perceptual beliefs p. Is any of this plausible? The answer is obvious: it is not at all plausible.

Let us look at the version of Argument A that takes the slightly safer principle Closure 7 as its starting point. The only place where this will make a difference is premise P5—the difference being that Closure 7 will make things worse. The Closure 7 version of P5 requires that, for *each* of their perceptual beliefs p, agents believe the denial of the skeptical hypothesis, $\sim$H, *solely* on the basis of deduction from the premise-pairs p and (p entails $\sim$H). For any agent holding more than a single perceptual belief p, this is not even logically possible.

What about the version of Argument A that starts with Closure 6.5? Again, this can only make a difference at premise P5. The Closure 6.5 version of P5 is not as absurd as the Closure 7 version. It is, however, still worse than the Closure 6 version, for it requires that agents believe $\sim$H based on deduction from the premise-pairs p and (p entails $\sim$H), for each of the agents' perceptual beliefs p, and that they do not also believe $\sim$H based on any defective reason.

Let us now consider the strategy of the *particular skeptical hypotheses*. Judging from the literature on closure principles and their role in skeptical arguments, this strategy appears to be the preferred one. Authors who discuss this topic typically make use of some argument sketch, albeit one based on Closure 2 rather than the Closure 6, 6.5, or 7. They select some perceptual proposition, say the proposition that there are chairs in the room, supposed to be believed by some agent. They then extract from the skeptical scenario a skeptical hypothesis tailored to suit the particular belief under consideration—for example, a hypothesis to the effect that the evil demon through his machinations makes it look to the agent as if there are chairs in the room even though there are not.[16]

The recipe for constructing such a particular skeptical hypothesis is this. Take a particular agent, S, and a particular proposition, c, say the proposition that there are chairs in the room. Assume c belongs to the skeptic's target class, C, and assume S believes c. The particular skeptical hypothesis corresponding to c for S is:

H⟨S, c⟩ There is an evil demon who misleads S into believing c even though c is false.

Hypothesis H⟨S, c⟩ is "the particular skeptical hypothesis corresponding to c for S" because it applies to particular S and because proposition c itself occurs within the formulation of the hypothesis—actually, the hypothesis says explicitly that c is false. Note that, in virtue of this feature, our proposition c trivially entails the denial of H⟨S, c⟩. But note also that most other propositions from the target class C, propositions that are logically independent from c, will not entail the denial of this hypothesis. To reach a general skeptical conclusion, one covering all beliefs from C, the skeptic will need a different particular hypothesis, H⟨S, p⟩ for each proposition p in the target class C. Thus, a skeptic who pursues this strategy and wants to give a general argument, based on Closure 6, for the conclusion that we do not have any perceptual knowledge will have to make use of

Argument B

P1 $\forall S, \forall p, \forall q$: SKp and $SK(p$ entails $q)$ and SBq bod from p and $(p$ entails $q)$ → SKq

---

[16] For some authors whose remarks indicate that they tend to think of closure-based skepticism in terms of the strategy of particular skeptical hypotheses, see: Dretske (1970); Nozick (1981: 204–11); Klein (1992: 459); Feldman (1995: 487); Cohen (1999: 85, n. 31).

P2.1 $\forall S, \forall p \in C: \sim SK \sim H\langle S, p\rangle$

3.1 $\forall S, \forall p \in C: \sim SKp$ or $\sim SK(p$ entails $\sim H\langle S, p\rangle)$ or $\sim (SB \sim H\langle S, p\rangle$ bod from p and $(p$ entails $\sim H\langle S, p\rangle)$

P4.1 $\forall S, \forall p \in C: SBp \rightarrow SK(p$ entails $\sim H\langle S, p\rangle)$

P5.1 $\forall S, \forall p \in C: SBp \rightarrow SB \sim H\langle S, p\rangle$ bod from p and $(p$ entails $\sim H\langle S, p\rangle)$

6    $\forall S, \forall p \in C: SBp \rightarrow \sim SKp$

7    $\forall S, \forall p \in C: \sim SKp$

Argument B is a bit more complicated than Argument A and even more implausible. Its crucial premises, P4.1 and P5.1, assume, quite absurdly, that agents believe all the denials of the particular skeptical hypotheses corresponding to their perceptual beliefs and believe all the entailments from their perceptual beliefs to the corresponding denials of the particular skeptical hypotheses. That is, they ascribe to agents lots of beliefs involving denials of lots of different particular skeptical hypotheses, which is even more implausible than the beliefs ascribed to agents by the corresponding premises of Argument A.

The Closure 6.5 version of premise P5.1 again makes things a bit worse by requiring in addition that agents must not have any defective reasons for their beliefs in all the denials of the particular skeptical hypotheses.

The only point where the strategy of the particular skeptical hypotheses makes a small positive difference compared to the strategy of the general skeptical hypothesis is with respect to the Closure 7-based version of the argument. Closure 7's version of P5.1 will say that, for each of their perceptual beliefs p, agents S believe $\sim H\langle S, p\rangle$, and that each of these beliefs in $\sim H\langle S, p\rangle$ is based *solely* on one pair of premises—a different pair for each denial. At least this is not impossible, although it is of course still quite absurd.

One might object that a skeptic who pursues the strategy of the particular skeptical hypotheses is not committed to the view that there is a single skeptical argument, like Argument B, establishing in one stroke that all the perceptual beliefs of all agents fail to constitute knowledge; instead, the skeptic is merely committed to the view that for each perceptual belief of each agent there is some skeptical argument establishing, by way of a particular skeptical hypothesis, that the agent does not know the proposition corresponding to the hypothesis. Fair enough, but it will not make a difference: most of the arguments envisaged by this response will be unsound, ascribing to agents beliefs they do not hold.

We pause for a moment to reconsider a point about the format used here to represent closure-based skeptical arguments. The point questions the adequacy of representing perceptual beliefs in terms of a skeptical target class C of perceptual propositions p believed by agents S. One might reasonably object (and Robert Audi has so objected) that this is inadequate because the adjective "perceptual" is not plausibly construed as picking out a property of propositions; instead, it modifies the relation of *believing* that holds between agents and propositions. In other words, there are no perceptual propositions as such: pretty much any proposition, whatever its nature or content, can be believed by an agent on perceptual grounds (namely, by testimony).[17]

At first it looks as though accommodating this objection should require only relatively mechanical changes in Arguments A and B: replace all occurrences of the restricted quantifier "$\forall p \in C$" by unrestricted "$\forall p$"; and replace all occurrences of "SBp" by "$SPBp$", saying that S perceptually believes p. (Both arguments would then directly proceed to the conclusion "$\forall S, \forall p : SPBp \rightarrow \sim SKp$", saying that all agents fail to know any proposition they perceptually believe.) On second thoughts, however, accommodating the objection presents a bit more of a problem—a problem for the skeptic, that is, in coming up with a skeptical hypothesis. Take the skeptic who wants to employ a single general skeptical hypothesis. If pretty much any proposition can be believed on perceptual grounds, including necessary truths, the skeptic must produce a skeptical hypothesis whose denial is entailed by any necessary truths that happen to be believed by sundry agents on perceptual grounds (namely, by testimony). No hypothesis along the lines of H will do this job. Moreover, any candidate hypothesis must immediately face the objection that it is not a possible hypothesis, since its denial, being entailed by a necessary truth, must be a necessary falsehood. The difficulty remains essentially the same for a skeptic who wants to employ different skeptical hypotheses, each one tailored to suit a particular proposition believed by an agent on perceptual grounds, including any necessary truths believed on perceptual grounds. We leave this difficulty unresolved and return to the main line of the paper.

We have seen that Closures 6–7, however plausible they might be as closure principles, will not take the skeptic to the general conclusion that no one has

---

[17] The already somewhat tortuous yet still rather imprecise characterization of C given earlier (see the paragraphs following the Argument Sketch) is not, it seems, good enough to forestall this objection.

any perceptual knowledge via worked-out versions of the standard sketch of closure-based arguments—that is, via arguments like A or B. The attempt to strengthen the antecedent of some relatively simple closure principle in order to handle the belief and warrant problems just forces the skeptic to make a number of additional assumptions when trying to reach the skeptical conclusion $\sim SKp$ in its general form. The additional assumptions are rather difficult to defend.

The problem we have been belaboring for the last few pages, let us call it the "generalization problem", will always arise to various degrees for arguments proceeding along the lines considered so far—with the only exception being arguments based on the clearly flawed principle Closure 1 and perhaps suitably chosen cousins of Closure 1. All other closure principles strengthen Closure 1's antecedent in ways that force the skeptic to ascribe problematic beliefs to agents. The generalization problem arises with respect to all these principles and the rough rule seems to be: the safer the principle the more severe the problem.

We note that the generalization problem, though somewhat neglected, is a rather obvious one. Part of the reason why it is not given the attention we think it deserves might be this. While it is usually acknowledged that Closure 1 is not an acceptable principle (the preferred candidate usually being the slightly more plausible Closure 2), there seems to be a tendency to forget about this point and inadvertently to revert back to Closure 1 when it comes to thinking about the skeptical argument that is supposed to be based on "the" closure principle.

So far we have been arguing that closure principles with a strengthened antecedent will not allow the skeptic to reach the general conclusion that we do not have any perceptual knowledge by way of a closure-based argument like the ones considered above. However, this does not quite show that such principles are of no use at all to the skeptic. Maybe an argument based on a closure principle can be useful to the skeptic by taking him part of the way, where the other part must then be covered by some additional consideration.

To get a better picture of the two-stage strategy we have in mind here, turn back to the Argument Sketch based on Closure 6 given earlier. Instead of interpreting it as a sketch of an argument by arbitrary instance, which involves ascribing to agents lots of beliefs about skeptical hypotheses they do not hold, why not apply it to just a few (non-arbitrary) agents who are aware of skeptical hypotheses? Or, even better, apply it just to one agent, say, to *me*—after all, I am aware of skeptical hypotheses. One of the perceptual propositions I believe is that there are chairs in the room. Applying the argument just to myself and this particular proposition, so the idea would go, I must conclude that I do not know that there are chairs in the room; and now comes the additional step: "If I don't know *that*, then I don't know any perceptual proposition; and if *I* don't know any perceptual proposition, then no one knows any perceptual proposition."

Before considering the crucial additional step that constitutes the second stage of the overall argument, one should note that the first stage is already a bit difficult. Yes, I am aware of the skeptical hypothesis, h, be it the general hypothesis or the particular hypothesis corresponding to the proposition that there are chairs in the room. I believe that this proposition, call it c, entails $\sim$h and, let us assume, I know that it does. Thus, premise P4 of the closure-based argument applied to me and my perceptual belief c seems fairly safe. But what about premise P5? It says that I believe $\sim$h based, at least in part, on deduction from my belief c together with my belief that c entails $\sim$h. Do I? I find this rather difficult to tell. If it is supposed to mean that I would not believe $\sim$h if I did not believe c and (c entails $\sim$h), or that the strength of my belief in $\sim$h would then be less than it is now, it feels wrong. But again: it is hard to tell. And it does not get any easier when I ask myself, *à la* Closure 6.5, whether I have any defective reasons for believing $\sim$h. One thing that is very clear to me, though, is that I do not believe $\sim$h based *solely* on c and (c entails $\sim$h); so Closure 7 is out of the running. Assuming that you are roughly like me, we can observe that the first shot at the new, two-stage strategy tends to bog down at the first stage.

But maybe one can cut through this problem by reshaping the original idea behind the two-stage strategy. Turn to one of the general closure-based arguments, say Argument A. It does not establish the general skeptical conclusion that no agent has any perceptual knowledge. But it is not implausible to maintain that it establishes a still general but weaker, *conditional* conclusion:

CA If $SK(p$ entails $\sim$H) and $SB \sim$H bod from p and (p entails $\sim$H), *then* $\sim SKp,$

which, note, is to be taken as a general principle applying to all agents, S, and all propositions, p, such that $p \in$ C and SBp.

Evidently, for this principle to hold it does not matter whether there are any agents who actually believe that p entails $\sim H$, or believe $\sim H$ based on deduction from p and (p entails $\sim H$). The principle circumnavigates these issues by conditionalizing on the problematic premises P4 and P5 of Argument A. The principle does not, of course, conditionalize on the other two premises of Argument A. So it depends on the relevant closure principle—that is, on Closure 6 (though analogous principles depending on Closure 6.5 or Closure 7 could easily be formulated)—and it depends on the skeptic's contention that no one knows $\sim H$. (The modal status of CA is somewhat unclear. Since Argument A is valid, the principle could safely be declared to be necessary, if the two premises it depends on were clearly necessary. The relevant closure principle, let us assume, is necessarily true if true at all. But it is not clear whether the same can be said for the premise that no one knows $\sim H$; it is not even clear whether the skeptic typically takes this premise to be a necessary truth.)

CA is, of course, not the strong unconditional conclusion the skeptic is aiming for. It does not say that no one has any perceptual knowledge. All it says is, roughly speaking, that agents who satisfy CA's antecedent do not know the perceptual propositions that satisfy CA's antecedent.[18] The skeptic needs more than this. And he might maintain that he can get it. With CA in hand, he might want to proceed to the second stage of his argument by making the following additional claim:

Claim Principle CA shows that (actual or possible) agents who satisfy the antecedent of CA do not know any perceptual propositions that satisfy the antecedent of CA; but if *such* agents do not know *these* perceptual propositions, then no agent knows any perceptual proposition.

An observation may help to clarify the status of this Claim. Even if the skeptic could not get anything more than the conditional conclusion CA,

---

[18] We apologize for this awkward rendering of CA. It is tempting to paraphrase CA as saying, roughly, that agents who satisfy the antecedent have *no* perceptual knowledge. But note, there is no quantifier corresponding to the "no" in CA's consequent. CA's consequent applies to (exactly) agents and propositions that pair-wise satisfy the antecedent: it is not easy to put this fluently. Also, since the full CA is a universal generalization, it is not quite right to talk about its antecedent/consequent. What this talk refers to is the antecedent/consequent of the part of CA that is explicitly exhibited above.

this would not by itself amount to an argument *against* skepticism. That is, even if the skeptic could show nothing more than that agents who satisfy CA's antecedent fail to know the relevant propositions, that would not show that agents who do not satisfy CA's antecedent do know the relevant propositions (that the skeptic can show $\sim SKp$ only for agents satisfying the antecedent does not show that we can establish that *only* agents satisfying the antecedents are such that $\sim SKp$). This much is surely right and should be kept in mind by anyone who wishes to resist closure-based skepticism. However, the skeptic's Claim does much more than just making this observation. It says in effect that, because agents who satisfy the antecedent do not know the perceptual propositions that satisfy the antecedent, no one knows any perceptual proposition.

So, what about this Claim? It is a curious one. Note that we would not normally be inclined to reason thus: "Everything that is both F and G is not K; so, Everything is not K." The skeptic's Claim, however, does seem to embrace this sort of reasoning. Of course, with the help of a further premise, a premise of the form "Everything that is *not* both F and G is not K either", the desired result would be immediately forthcoming. But no such further premise is available to the closure-based skeptic under consideration here.[19] So, to defend his Claim, the skeptic would have to point to a special feature—some special property of CA—that makes this sort of reasoning acceptable in this special case. What feature could that be? Well, if the skeptic could make a case for the idea that (actual or possible) agents who satisfy the antecedent of CA are somehow ideally situated, epistemically speaking, with respect to the relevant perceptual propositions, that is, with respect to the perceptual propositions from which they have deduced the denial of the skeptical hypothesis, then he might be able to conclude that, if such agents do not know these propositions, no one knows any perceptual propositions. But it is hard to see how such a case should be made. On the face of it, there is nothing in the antecedent of CA suggesting that agents satisfying it are in an especially good epistemic position with respect to the relevant propositions.

One might even try to argue the contrary, making use of the idea that knowledge is vulnerable to *defeat*: that is, a person who knows p can lose that

---

[19] Getting the relevant "further premise" would require the skeptic to show for all agents S and all propositions p, such that that $p \in C$ and SBp: *if* it is *not* the case that $SK(p$ entails $\sim H)$ and $SB \sim H$ bod from p and (p entails $\sim H$), *then* $\sim SKp$.

knowledge upon acquiring a defeater for the reasons or grounds on which that knowledge was based. It is not very clear to anyone what "acquiring a defeater" amounts to. But it might be held that to acquire a defeater it is sufficient, at least under certain circumstances, that the person has considered it—toyed with it mentally—even if she does not believe it, or even disbelieves it. If so, one could respond to the skeptic by arguing that agents who satisfy the antecedent of CA are agents who are in an epistemically *bad* position with respect to *p*. They have toyed with H and, even though they disbelieve H, they have thereby acquired a defeater for *p*: you know less by reflecting more.

We will not go any further into this issue. We are satisfied if we have managed to show that even the best knowledge-closure principles (of the "strengthened-antecedent" type) are of more limited use to the skeptic than one might have thought initially. Even assuming that Closures 6, 6.5, or 7 are plausible principles—and, of course, always granting that we do not know skeptical hypotheses to be false—the best the skeptic can do based on these principles alone is to get to a conditional conclusion such as CA. To get any further, the skeptic needs to support something like his additional Claim, and this seems to require a new argument, an argument we have not seen yet.

Before we leave this section, we want to return, once more, to general closure-based arguments derived from the Argument Sketch given above and discuss a skeptical strategy that is not quite covered by Arguments A or B. Remember the general skeptical hypothesis

H   There is an evil demon who makes it the case that human agents tend to hold beliefs committing them to the view that there are material objects even though there are no material objects.

Earlier we looked at an argument, Argument A, which requires the assumption—an assumption that is not entirely trivial—that each of our perceptual beliefs entails the denial of H. One may have noticed that there are other propositions entailing the denial of H. In particular, there is the general proposition

X   There are material objects.

This proposition has the advantage that it trivially entails the denial of H. A skeptic might want to make use of this proposition in a Closure 6 (or 6.5 or

7)-based argument. To do so, he needs an argument different from Argument A or B. For Closure 6, the new argument would go like this:

Argument C

P1. $\forall S, \forall p, \forall q$: SKp and $SK(p$ entails $q)$ and $(SBq$ bod from p and $(p$ entails $q)) \rightarrow SKq$

P2. $\forall S$: $\sim SK \sim H$

3. $\forall S, \forall p$: $\sim SKp$ or $\sim SK(p$ entails $\sim H)$ or $\sim(SB \sim H$ bod from p and $(p$ entails $\sim H))$

P4.2 $\forall S$: $SBX \rightarrow SK(X$ entails $\sim H)$

P5.2 $\forall S$: $SBX \rightarrow SB \sim H$ bod from X and $(X$ entails $\sim H)$

6.2 $\forall S$: $SBX \rightarrow \sim SKX$

7.2 $\forall S$: $\sim SKX$

Argument C concludes that no one knows the proposition that there are material objects.[20] It does better than Arguments A and B because it ascribes fewer beliefs to agents. Indeed, it seems that there are agents, mostly philosophers, who do hold the beliefs ascribed by premises P4.2 and P5.2. However, the argument is still unsound, because it ascribes these beliefs to all agents who believe that there are material objects, not just to philosophers. Moreover, there is also the worry whether agents who do believe X, and (X entails $\sim H$), and believe $\sim H$ really believe the latter based on deduction from the former, as maintained by P5.2.

Of course, the conclusion of Argument C, that no one knows that there are material objects, though an interesting skeptical conclusion in its own right, is not the conclusion the skeptic is ultimately aiming for; it is not the conclusion that no one has any perceptual knowledge. What is the skeptic's plan for reaching that conclusion?

The most obvious plan that comes to mind would be to argue that no one knows any perceptual proposition because no one knows X. That is, the most obvious plan would be to employ Closure 6 again, this time in an argument modeled on A, but with the second premise of Argument A replaced by the conclusion of argument C:

P1. $\forall S, \forall p, \forall q$: SKp and $SK(p$ entails $q)$ and SBq bod from p and $(p$ entails $q) \rightarrow SKq$

---

[20] For an author who discusses closure-based skepticism along the lines of Argument C, see Brueckner (1985: p. 89–90).

7.2 $\forall S : \sim SKX$

3. $\forall S, \forall p : \sim SKp$ or $\sim SK(p$ entails X) or $\sim (SBX$ bod from p and $(p$ entails X))

P4.3 $\forall S, \forall p \in$ C: $SBp \rightarrow SK(p$ entails X)

P5.3 $\forall S, \forall p \in$ C: $SBp \rightarrow SBX$ bod from p and $(p$ entails X)

6. $\forall S, \forall p \in$ C: $SBp \rightarrow \sim SKp$

7. $\forall S, \forall p \in$ C: $\sim SKp$

Premises P4 and P5 of this argument are a bit more plausible than the corresponding premises in the original version of A. Surely, it is more likely that agents holding perceptual beliefs also hold the relevant beliefs involving X than that they hold the relevant beliefs involving $\sim$H. Note, however, that it is still quite implausible to maintain that such agents believe X based on deduction from p and $(p$ entails X), for each of their perceptual beliefs p. Moreover, the resulting *overall* argument—Argument C combined with this continuation—does not appear significantly more plausible than Argument A.

An intriguing alternative to this way of continuing Argument C might be to continue not with an argument based on Closure 6, but with an argument based on a closure principle that goes all the way back to Closure 1; more precisely, to an alternative way of strengthening the antecedent of Closure 1 that we have not considered yet:

Closure 1A $(Kp$ and $(p$ analytically entails $q)) \rightarrow Kq$.

For those who still believe in analyticity, this will be a good candidate for a plausible closure principle, provided they are prepared to construe "analytic entailment" in a certain manner. First, the notion of analyticity must make sense as applied to propositions, and not just to linguistic entities like sentences. Second, the relation of analytic entailment must be taken to imply that one cannot possibly believe the analytically entailing proposition without believing the entailed proposition. Third, the relation of analytic entailment must be taken to imply that one cannot possibly know the analytically entailing proposition without knowing the entailed proposition.

If there is analytic entailment, and if it can be construed in this way, then Closure 1A does not raise the belief and warrant problems for the range of propositions to which it applies. What is this range? There are the seemingly trivial, "decompositional" candidates—for example, the proposition that Audumla is a brown cow analytically entails the proposition that Audumla is a cow.[21] Then there are the "standard" candidates—for example, the proposition that Leopold is a bachelor analytically entails the proposition that Leopold is unmarried. But the sort of cases needed by the skeptic are a bit different still. The skeptic who wants to continue Argument C with a closure argument based on Closure 1A must maintain that all perceptual propositions, such as the proposition that there are chairs in the room, analytically entail the proposition that there are material objects. These candidates for analytic entailment are not at all like the brown cow/cow cases, nor are they quite like the bachelor/unmarried cases; they are cases of "philosophical analyticity".[22]

Of course, *post* Quine, pretty much everything about analyticity is contentious, with candidates of philosophical analyticity surely being the most contentious. Note also that even friends of analyticity might well oppose the idea that analytic entailment (especially the philosophical variety) can be construed in the manner required—namely, as implying that certain propositions cannot possibly be believed without believing certain other propositions and cannot possibly be known without knowing these other propositions.[23] Moreover, a skeptic who is prepared to take on the anti-analyticity camp and to defend the required construal of analytic entailment still faces the problem that the first leg of his overall argument, Argument C, appears to be unsound.

Closure 1A is perhaps the "leanest" closure principle with strengthened antecedent whose skeptical potential is worth exploring. Let us mention, for comparison, what would be the "fullest" closure principle of this sort. It would be a principle taking care of any challenges one might come up with even for Closures 6.5 or 7 by restricting the antecedent to agents who believe

---

[21] But even such decompositional inferences must be handled with care: the proposition that John has some counterfeit money does not analytically entail the proposition that John has some money.

[22] It is noteworthy that Moore in his "Proof of an External World" (1939), which is well known primarily for its last few pages, actually spends most of his time on what appears to be an attempt to show that the proposition that this is a hand analytically entails the proposition that there is an external world. Moore, it seems, assumed that the skeptic would pursue the two-part strategy of first employing Argument C and then Argument A but with Closure 1A instead of Closure 6.

[23] For example, Devitt (1996) argues, roughly, that analytic entailment should rather be understood in terms of a disposition to infer the entailed proposition. On this construal, Closure 1A will not be of much help to the skeptic presently under consideration.

q solely based on deduction from *p* and (*p* entails *q*) and for whom "nothing goes wrong" (epistemically speaking) in so believing *q*:

Closure 8   (K*p* and K(*p* entails *q*) and B*q* solely based on deduction from *p* and (*p* entails *q*) and "nothing goes wrong") → K*q*.

This closure principle should be the safest of the "strengthened-antecedent" family. Of course, the safety is paid for by the considerable (excessive?) vagueness of the "nothing-goes-wrong" clause, which gestures towards potential challenges to Closures 6.5 and 7 and stipulates that none of them apply.

It is clear that Closure 8 will not be of use in a skeptical argument in the style of Argument A or B. Such arguments will have the special problems noted for arguments based on Closure 7 (concerning the "solely-based-on" clause) and they will suffer from an exacerbated form of the problems noted for arguments based on Closure 6.5; that is, they will require a premise to the effect that nothing at all goes wrong (epistemically speaking) with agents who believe *q* based on. . . . Of course, a conditional principle might be derived, analogous to principle CA but incorporating all elements of the antecedent of Closure 8. This would then, again, require supplementation along the lines of the skeptical Claim mentioned earlier.

Our main question, we said, is this: are there any plausibly true epistemic closure principles concerning knowledge that figure centrally in arguably sound skeptical arguments with interestingly strong conclusions? What is our answer so far? Well, we have found some knowledge-closure principles (of the strengthened-antecedent variety) that are at least not clearly false. But no such principle, we have argued, will by itself take the skeptic to the strong conclusion that no one has any perceptual knowledge: as far as knowledge-closure principles of this sort are concerned, there is, one might put it, no skeptical argument that is both sound and "pure". At best, strengthened-antecedent knowledge-closure principles help the skeptic reach a sub-conclusion that needs to be supplemented with an additional Claim, the status of which is unresolved. We think that non-skeptics have little to fear from strengthened-antecedent knowledge-closure principles.

4. Plausible principles (*b*): Weakening the consequent

The closure principles discussed in Section 3 all try to avoid the belief problem and the warrant problem by strengthening the antecedent of Closure 1 in various ways. We now consider the second major strategy for avoiding these problems facing knowledge-closure principles: weakening the consequent. All principles discussed in this section respond to the belief problem by weakening the consequent of the principle so that it does not imply belief. The more plausible principles respond to the warrant problem with well-chosen strengthenings (compared to Closure 1) of the antecedent and/or further weakenings of the consequent of the principle.

Let "K*" stand for a relation weaker than knowing: let it stand for the relation of "being positioned to know" or "being in a position to know" where these locutions are understood not to imply belief in the proposition in question. Being "positioned to know" that Leopold is in the room does not imply that one believes that Leopold is in the room. Perhaps a closure principle making use of this "K*" device will be of use to the skeptic in formulating a plausible closure principle for use in a serious and challenging skeptical argument. Closure principles of this weakened-consequent variety have not been discussed much in the literature on skepticism nor have they been discussed much in the literature on closure principles. Our discussion in this section is therefore a bit tentative as we feel our way into relatively uncharted territory.

Incidentally, principles of this weakened-consequent type are not really knowledge-closure principles as standardly understood. They are not even *closure* principles, because they do not say that one and the same property (for example, knowledge) is closed under some relation. We will explore these principles despite this fact, because they naturally arise when reflecting on the problems with strengthened-antecedent principles.

In the previous section we discussed problems arising for skeptical arguments using closure principles with cluttered antecedents. We will keep these problems in mind while searching for a weakened-consequent closure principle. We therefore begin this discussion with the leanest relevant closure principle making use of K*:

Closure 9   (Kp and (p entails q)) $\rightarrow$ K^*q.

This says that (necessarily) all agents are positioned to know propositions entailed by propositions they know.[24] With its lean antecedent, this principle, if plausible, would be well suited for serving in a skeptical argument for the

---

[24] Equivalently: necessarily, for all agents S, and all propositions p and q, if S knows p and if p entails q, then S is positioned to know q.

general conclusion that no one has any perceptual knowledge. Two immediate issues arise, however.

The first issue arising as we begin this discussion of weakened-consequent closure principles is this. The point of introducing the "positioned to know" terminology and "K*" is so that the consequent of a closure principle using this notion is strictly *weaker* than the consequent of a closure principle with the standard "Kq" consequent. Because of this, the key skeptical premise in a skeptical argument (before, $\sim$K$\sim$SH; now, $\sim$K* $\sim$SH) must be strictly *stronger* when using a closure principle of this new type. Where before the skeptical argument began with the claim that we do not know the denial of the skeptical hypothesis, the argument must now begin with the claim that we are not even positioned to know this denial. Anti-skeptics tempted to respond to the skeptic by claiming that we do know the denial of the skeptical hypothesis will be even more tempted to argue that we are at least positioned to know this denial. If the skeptical claim becomes very strong (because, for example, the interpretation of "positioned to know" makes the consequent of the closure principle exceptionally weak), it may well become inevitable that the anti-skeptic will want to make this move. For now, however, we generously set this issue aside.[25]

The second and perhaps most obvious issue arising because of the introduction of the "positioned-to-know" terminology is this. Serious evaluations of principles involving "K*" and arguments employing these principles will depend upon how "positioned to know" is understood. We will discuss several readings of this phrase in this section. We will argue that many natural readings of "positioned to know" are clearly of no use in skeptical argumentation. Additionally we will argue that some natural readings lead to serious interpretative and internal difficulties with the notion of "positioned to know" itself. Though we will identify a few not wholly implausible readings of "positioned to know" and will find at least one skeptical argument worth discussing, we will find nothing promising for the skeptic in this section.

Before taking up these issues, however, we pause briefly to announce a partial shift in methodology. Recall that near the beginning of this chapter we chose

[25] We set this promising anti-skeptical move aside not because we are not willing to make it. We do think that a promising anti-skeptical strategy could be found by arguing that we know (or are at least positioned to know) the denial of the skeptical hypothesis. We set this issue aside in order to keep our focus on those parts of the skeptical argument intimately featuring knowledge-closure principles.

a strategy of looking for plausible closure principles and then evaluating their possible use in skeptical argumentation. Because of our work and progress in Section 3, we are now familiar with several problems closure-based skeptical arguments can encounter even when they employ plausible-looking closure principles. It seems wise to apply this knowledge now by keeping one eye on the eventual form of the skeptical argument while searching for a plausible weakened-consequent closure principle. This methodological shift began when we observed above that the antecedent of Closure 9 makes it a good candidate for overcoming some of the concerns raised in the previous section's discussion of strengthened-antecedent closure principles. The shift will allow us to avoid a full investigation of all possible weakened-consequent closure principles. Guided by this more focused methodology, we will now explore a few general issues involving "positioned to know", (K^*), and closure principles employing this notion. After doing this we will move on fairly quickly to formulate the most knowledge-skeptic-friendly closure principles employing K^*. We will explain why the skeptical arguments using these most knowledge-skeptic-friendly principles do not seem to help skeptic's cause.

In order to evaluate Closure 9 and other weakened-consequent closure principles we must at least begin to fill in some content for the "positioned-to-know" locution. Understandably, we encounter some difficulty at this point in our inquiry. There is no standard analysis of what it is to be "positioned to know"—something that we can plug into the principle. Additionally, it seems clear that the phrase "being positioned to know" is in many ways vague and slippery. Perhaps we can safely stipulate the following two basic components involved in the understanding of this locution. First, if one knows something, then one is positioned to know it (knowing is the limit case of being positioned to know—one is especially well positioned to know what one knows). Second, one is positioned to know p only if p is true.[26] Beyond

---

[26] This second point might not do justice to all possible understandings of the "positioned-to-know" locution. Perhaps just as I am poised to enter a room I am "positioned to know" that someone is in the room even though no one is currently in the room (my being in the room upon entry will imply that someone is in the room and upon entry I will be quite well positioned to know that I am in the room). As a part of this discussion of knowledge-closure principles, however, we do not see any reason to worry about examples like this one. If for some reason we do not see we should worry about examples like this one, we could modify our claim to read: one is positioned to know only what is (or would be if/when believed) true.

these two fairly minor points, it is not immediately obvious even what sort of analysis of "positioned to know" is most worth exploring, let alone what specific analysis merits attention.

As we have noted, the weakened-consequent strategy is introduced in an attempt to avoid the belief problem that plagues standard formulations of knowledge-closure principles. Since this problem concerned the possible absence of a belief in q in earlier closure principles, perhaps it is natural to begin with an "all-but-belief" interpretation of K^*. On this reading, one is positioned to know something if and only if one has *at least* everything required for knowing it except belief—that is, $K^* = K$ minus B.[27] This reading has the following advantage: because on this reading K^*q is differentiated from Kq only by the psychological issue of whether belief is present, the key skeptical claim (namely, $\sim K^* \sim SH$) is on this reading only barely stronger than in the strengthened-antecedent arguments ($\sim K \sim SH$). For this reason and because of its overall simplicity, this natural first reading of K^* is somewhat attractive.

Given this natural interpretation of K^*, however, Closure 9 suffers from at least two difficulties. First, just as Closure 1 made it too easy to know necessary truths, Closure 9 appears to make it too easy to be positioned to know necessary truths. If Closure 9 is true, anyone who knows anything will be thereby positioned to know all necessary truths. Second, and more generally, Closure 9 seems to make it too easy to be positioned to know things (whether necessary or contingent). It does not seem plausible that an agent who knows p is thereby positioned to know any entailed proposition q, because this would imply that the agent is positioned to know q even if the agent does not even believe that q is so entailed.

These reflections lead, unsurprisingly, to a weakened-consequent principle modeled on Closure 2:

Closure 10   (Kp and $K(p$ entails q)) $\rightarrow K^*q$.

This is probably the sort of principle that most advocates of the "weakening-the-consequent" strategy have in mind.[28] On the face of it, Closure 10 looks

---

[27] Using "warrant" in Plantinga's sense, one could say that S is positioned to know p iff p is for S a warranted truth (whether or not SBp). We take no stand here on whether "warrant" implies "truth": if it does, the explicit inclusion of truth in this claim does no harm. Strictly speaking (because knowing is a way of being positioned to know on our understanding), $K^*p = Kp$ or K minus B, but this can be safely ignored for present purposes.

[28] Cf. Cohen (1999: 84 n. 14); Klein (2000: 110).

as though it takes us at least a step in the direction of a superficially plausible closure principle. Whatever its merits *as a closure principle*, however, Section 3 teaches us that problems will arise if one uses this principle in a skeptical argument. Note that, in addition to its weakened consequent, this principle involves a relevantly strengthened antecedent. A skeptic attempting to employ this principle in a general skeptical argument will be caught ascribing to agents all sorts of entailment beliefs involving the denial of skeptical hypotheses that typical agents are unlikely to hold. We illustrated this fact in Section 3 in some detail and will not do so again here. This is an important reminder that those looking for a knowledge-closure principle for use in a skeptical argument must strive to keep the antecedent of the closure principle as uncluttered as possible.

Another serious difficulty for those interested in using principles such as Closure 9 and Closure 10 for skeptical purposes should be noted. Given the somewhat rough "all-but-belief" interpretation we have suggested for K^*, the most natural way to understand K^* is as a disguised conditional. K^*q on this reading amounts to a conditional, $(Bq \rightarrow Kq)$, of some strength or other: material, counterfactual, or strict. Interpreting the K^* of Closures 9 and 10 in this way is not a promising strategy for the skeptic to pursue. Depending on the strength of the conditional, Closures 9 and 10 interpreted in this way are equivalent to, or imply, principles identical to (or relevantly like) those we have already seen and rejected.

For example, on this interpretation of K^*q and reading the embedded conditional as a material conditional, the superficially appealing

> Closure 10 $(Kp \text{ and } K(p \text{ entails } q)) \rightarrow K^*q$

is equivalent to

> Closure 5 $(Kp \text{ and } K(p \text{ entails } q) \text{ and } Bq) \rightarrow Kq,$

which was shown to be false in Section 3. On the stronger, counterfactual or strict, readings of the embedded conditional, Closure 10 will imply Closure 5 and will therefore be false. For completeness, note that, on the material reading of K^*q,

> Closure 9 $(Kp \text{ and } (p \text{ entails } q)) \rightarrow K^*q$

is equivalent to

> Closure 9′ $(Kp \text{ and } (p \text{ entails } q) \text{ and } Bq) \rightarrow Kq,$

which is a weakened antecedent version of, and therefore implies, Closure 5. Because Closure 5 is false, Closures 9′ and 9 are false and therefore useless to the skeptic. On the stronger readings of the conditional embedded in K*q, Closure 9 implies Closure 9′, which implies the false Closure 5; so, again, Closure 9 is false.[29]

It seems that the skeptic will have to look at different interpretations of K* or look beyond Closure 9 and Closure 10 or both. Let us first consider a case for introducing a new Closure principle. Remember that Closure 9 is problematic as a principle because it says *nothing* about one's epistemic status relative to (p entails q) and therefore seems to make it too easy to be positioned to know various things. Closure 10, on the other hand, seems a bit more promising as a principle, because it specifies that S knows that (p entails q). However, using Closure 10 in a skeptical argument will be problematic because the argument will implausibly assume universal belief in (p entails q). So it seems natural for the skeptic to consider a principle located intuitively "in between" Closure 9 and Closure 10—namely, one that invokes the K* operator in the antecedent, applying it to (p entails q):

Closure 11　(Kp and K*(p entails q)) → K*q

Closure 11 says that one who knows p and is (at least) positioned to know (p entails q) is thereby (at least) positioned to know q.[30] This is intended to help the skeptic avoid attributing problematic entailment beliefs when running his argument while also at least partially addressing the worry that the principle might make it too easy to count as being positioned to know things. Closure 11 might on these grounds be thought to be the most promising principle we have seen so far.

Closure 11 is, from a *structural* point of view, quite promising when looking ahead to the issue of general skeptical argumentation. But one thinking that Closure 11 is promising *on the current interpretation of K** is mistaken. First a minor problem: Closure 11 may well be too close to Closure 9 and might therefore inherit some of the difficulties facing Closure 9. Specifically, Closure 11, like Closure 9, may make it too easy for one to count as positioned to know

---

[29] The strict reading of the conditional embedded in K*q is not viable. Take Closure 10. Say subject S knows p and knows that p entails q. Surely, it does not follow that in every world if S believes q then he knows q. We mention this reading here only because a strict conditional may have a roll to play in other readings of K*.

[30] The "at-least" parentheticals are redundant reminders that we are understanding "positioned to know" in a way implying that one way of being positioned to know something is to know it.

something. Consider an agent who knows p and is *merely* positioned to know that (p entails q) (but who does not even believe, let alone know, that this entailment holds). Given Closure 11, this agent counts as positioned to know q, but this seems too generous. It seems that, rather than being positioned to know q, our agent is at most positioned to be positioned to know q ("two epistemic steps away", whatever exactly that might mean). This is at least some sort of non-trivial difficulty for Closure 11.

Now, however, we turn to a substantially larger problem for Closure 11 on the current reading, which shows that we *must* consider new readings of K^*. Compare Closure 11, with Closure 10:

Closure 11   (Kp and $K^*(p$ entails q)) $\rightarrow K^*q$

Closure 10   (Kp and $K(p$ entails q)) $\rightarrow K^*q$

Though Closure 11 is structurally superior to Closure 10 because of its weaker antecedent, Closure 11 cannot possibly be of use in a skeptical argument on the current interpretation of K^*. This is because Closure 11 is a weakened-antecedent version of Closure 10, which implies that Closure 11 is true only if Closure 10 is true. But we showed a short while ago that Closure 10 on the current reading of K^* implies the implausible Closure 5:

Closure 5   (Kp and $K(p$ entails q) and Bq) $\rightarrow Kq$,

which shows that this reading of Closure 10 is false. It follows that this reading of Closure 11 is also false and must be rejected as well.

Strictly speaking, of course, what we reject in rejecting Closure 11, and Closure 10 for that matter, are these principles with K^* interpreted in the "all-but-belief" manner we have to this point adopted. It seems that someone looking for a plausible weakened-consequent closure principle for possible use in skeptical argumentation must do one or both of the following: (*a*) choose a different interpretation of K^*; (*b*) choose a closure principle structurally different from both Closure 10 and Closure 11. With an eye on skeptical argumentation, we are confident that best move for the skeptic at this point is to choose option (*a*) but reject option (*b*). In particular, we suggest that the skeptic should stick with Closure 11 and search for a more useful interpretation of K^*.

Structurally, after all, Closure 11 has some nice features that tell against choosing option (*b*). Indeed, from the point of view of the structure of the overall skeptical argument, Closure 11 has *all* the features the skeptic is looking for. The sketch of a skeptical argument using Closure 11 is familiar and in some ways promising. Using the same abbreviations as before, the sketch of a skeptical argument using Closure 11 looks like this:

P1 $(Kp \text{ and } K^*(p \text{ entails } q)) \rightarrow K^*q$
P2 $\sim K^* \sim h$
3    $\sim Kc \text{ or } \sim K^*(c \text{ entails } \sim h)$
P4 $K^*(c \text{ entails } \sim h)$
5    $\sim Kc$

Here the first premise is simply Closure 11. Set aside for now how exactly to understand K^* in this principle and reflect on other features of the argument. The second premise is the skeptic's now strengthened central claim: one is not even positioned to know the denial of the skeptical hypothesis. As noted earlier, as one weakens the interpretation of K^*, this key skeptical claim gets stronger, but assume for now that the skeptic will find a good defense of this stronger claim. If the skeptic can find an interpretation of K^* on which the closure principle looks strong and P2 is still defensible, the skeptic's overall argument looks somewhat promising. Premise 4 in this argument sketch modestly claims that all agents are "positioned to know" these entailments and does not claim that all agents actually know them. Here the skeptic might promisingly appeal to the fact that the entailments in question are straightforwardly recognizable by anyone with the relevant concepts. The entailments in question are simple conceptual matters: one reflecting on the relevant propositions will easily see and come to know that (or be able to come to know that), for example, there being a chair in front of one entails the denial of any skeptical hypothesis explicitly stating that there are no chairs or no material objects.

Alternatively, while searching for an improved interpretation of K^*, a skeptic might want to stick with Closure 10. If he does this (and assuming such an interpretation is available), the fourth premise of his argument sketch will implausibly attribute the relevant entailment beliefs to all agents. To avoid this problem, he will then be forced to conditionalize on this premise in a way familiar from Section 3. His immediate conclusion will be only that, for all agents S and all perceptual propositions p, if S knows that (p entails $\sim h$) then S does not know p. The overall argument will then require a second stage in which this sub-conclusion is supplemented by an additional premise—namely, a variant of the claim called Claim in Section 3. Because we have already said what we have to say about such two-stage skeptical arguments and because Closure 11 seems to promise a one-stage argument not in need of an additional premise, we will focus our attention on Closure 11.

Because the sketch of the skeptical argument using Closure 11 is so clean, we think the skeptic's best move is to stick with the form of Closure 11 and attempt to avoid the problems we have pointed out for Closure 11 above by reinterpreting "K^*". We have considered and rejected the "all-but-belief" interpretation of K^*, which interpreted K^* as some sort of modal conditional linking belief to knowledge. What alternatives are available?

Two types of readings appear worth investigating. Though this does not seem especially promising, one might want to consider a diachronic conditional reading of K^*. And one might want to consider various "all (for knowledge) but X" readings related to, but strictly weaker than, the "all-but-belief" reading considered above. Readings of this latter sort analyze "position to know" as some sort of regular conditional (strict, counterfactual, or material), but this time with a fuller antecedent. Instead of "K^*q" being read as "$Bq \rightarrow Kq$", on this new suggestion "K^*q" is read as "$(Bq \,\&\, X) \rightarrow Kq$" with some suitably chosen substitution for X. We now consider both of these possibilities, beginning with the diachronic reading.

The simplest and natural diachronic reading takes "K^*q" to be short for "if the agent now adds q to her beliefs, she will thereby come to know q". This simple diachronic reading faces obvious difficulties related to the issues discussed in detail in Section 3 concerning the basing relation: whether our agent knows q upon acquiring this belief depends upon, among other things, the specific reasons for which belief in q was adopted. Consider an agent who knows both p and that (p entails q). If this agent then comes to believe q, but, on the basis of wholly defective reasons, the agent will not thereby come to know q. This problem should be familiar by now, as should the obvious strategy for attempting to address the problem. The obvious strategy for dealing with this problem is to enrich the diachronic reading in ways analogous to the antecedents of Closure 6 and Closure 7. SK^*q, on this enriched reading, would be read as something like:

> if S now comes to believe q via and based upon proper inferential grounds from S's beliefs p and that (p entails q), then S knows q.

We have two critical observations about this proposed enriched diachronic reading of K^*.

First, diachronically adding a belief in q to one's belief set might have contingent effects that cause trouble for one's overall epistemic state. Perhaps for at least some agent, the addition of Bq brings with it additional epistemic baggage that eliminates knowledge that p or prevents one from knowing or even being positioned to know that (p entails q). Adding Bq even in the right sort of way might, across the time involved in a diachronic reading of this exercise, destroy or defeat one's evidence for q (and/or for "p entails q"). The problem is that closure principles are supposed to be necessary truths, but the claims made by closure principles employing the diachronic interpretation of K* depend on contingent facts about the psychological make-up and/or epistemic make-up and/or environment of agents across time periods. Surely in at least one possible case these factors will interfere in a way that provides a counterexample to any closure principle interpreted by understanding "positioned to know" in this way. It is hard to see how diachronically interpreted closure *principles* can withstand this criticism.

Second, though this specific diachronic reading of K*q might fit well in the *consequent* of principles like Closure 10 (in which "K*" occurs only once and in the consequent), it provides no *general* understanding of "positioned to know" and no understanding of "positioned to know" adequate for both occurrences of "K*" in

Closure 11   (Kp and K*(p entails q)) $\rightarrow$ K*q.

The present reading of K* does not make good sense of Closure 11's consequent because it assumes that the agent believes that (p entails q), while the antecedent of the principle provides only for the agent's being positioned to know this entailment. If our agent does not even believe that (p entails q), she can hardly count as positioned to know q partly by virtue of an entailment belief she does not have. Perhaps this difficulty can be avoided by envisaging a multi-step diachronic process along these lines: "if the agent now adds (p entails q) to her belief set and then adds q to her belief set by deducing it from her beliefs that p and that (p entails q), she will then know that q." This suggestion might help with the present problem, but it leaves us with a bigger one.

The bigger problem is that we have no *general* understanding of K*. Surely there are ways to be positioned to know things that do not involve deduction from premise beliefs of the form p and (p entails q). Compare the "K*" in the consequent of Closure 11 with the one in the antecedent. Our present reading was tailored to suit the former, K*q. That reading cannot apply to the "K*" in the antecedent of Closure 11: apparently that appearance of "K*" must still be read in the original way (if she now adds belief in the entailment to her belief set,[31] she will then know it). We are left with a bifurcated understanding of K*: we have no general understanding of "positioned to know". Call this the "bifurcation problem".

The interpretation of Closure 11, on this bifurcated understanding of K*, will be true if and only if the following multi-step diachronic conditional is true:

> Necessarily, IF S is such that she knows p and such that (if she now adds (p entails q) to her belief set she will know that p entails q), THEN S is such that [if she does now add (p entails q) to her belief set and then also adds q to her belief set based on deduction from her belief that p and her belief that (p entails q)] she will then know q.

Though this reading of Closure 11 is far from perspicuous, we do think it is the best available reading for one pursuing what now seems clearly to be an ill-advised diachronic reading of "positioned to know". This multi-step diachronic reading only makes the first problem we discussed for the enriched diachronic approach more serious. On this reading, there are multiple steps at which various things can go epistemically wrong in one's attempt to reach knowledge that q (defeaters can be acquired, evidence lost, and so on). It is quite implausible to suggest that no actual or possible agent's path to Kq would be blocked somewhere along the way in one of these ways.[32] We see no hope for finding a plausible weakened-consequent closure principle involving diachronic conditionals.

We turn now to regular (non-diachronic), conditional readings of "positioned to know", but this time with an eye on readings weaker than the "all-but-belief" reading discussed above. For now, we bracket the bifurcation problem and focus on the K* in the closure principle's consequent, K*q, interpreting it as some type of conditional with a fuller antecedent than simply "Bq". We examine readings that read "K*q" as "(Bq & X) → Kq", where X is some specified additional condition(s) on believing q. We will consider three substitutions for X, all somewhat familiar from our discussion in Section 3,

---

[31] The agent would presumably be required to do this on the basis of non-defective conceptual reasoning. We set aside this difficulty though it is a non-trivial complication for the skeptic.

[32] Recall, once again, that, in the full-dress version of the skeptical argument, the argument will feature a necessity operator out front and universal quantification over all agents.

and we will consider various readings of the conditional. Here are the three relevant readings of "K^*q":

(i) "K^*q" means "Bq based on deduction from p and (p entails q) $\rightarrow Kq$".

(ii) "K^*q" means "Bq solely based on deduction from p and (p entails q) $\rightarrow Kq$".

(iii) "K^*q" means "Bq solely based on deduction from p and (p entails q) and 'nothing else goes wrong' $\rightarrow Kq$".

We first raise a problem for two of these three readings. Then we move on to note two serious problems that apply to all three readings. We end the discussion in this section with a final possible maneuver by the skeptic hoping to use a weakened-consequent closure principle in a general skeptical argument.

We begin with a problem for readings (i) and (ii), but not reading (iii). For what should by now be a familiar reason, Closure 11 under readings (i)/(ii) implies the truth of Closure 6/Closure 7 from Section 3.[33] In Section 3 though we acknowledged that Closures 6 and 7 are among the most plausible knowledge-closure principles; we also pointed out that they may well be false. If Closures 6 and 7 are *false*, then the principles formed by interpreting Closure 11 with reading (i) and (ii) are also false. We will therefore offer a brief reminder here of objections one might have to Closures 6 and 7.[34]

Closure 6 has trouble with overdetermination cases. Where S believes q both for intuitively good reasons (for example, because of deduction from known "premise beliefs" of the form p and (p entails q)) and bad reasons (for example, because it is Tuesday or because a wholly unreliable witness testified to the truth of q) but believes q most firmly and confidently on the basis of the bad reasons it seems implausible to suggest that S knows q. Closure 7 seems to have serious trouble at least with cases involving "global defeaters"—the most relevant case is one in which agent S satisfies the antecedent of Closure 7 but additionally believes (on the basis of apparently powerful evidence) that deduction is a horrible way, from the epistemic point of view, to add beliefs. Perhaps S believes that this is true of deduction at least on this occasion (the

---

[33] This holds on any interpretation of the conditional embedded in K^*q. For example, Closure 11 read with (i) implies a variant of Closure 6 with K^*(p entails q) in the antecedent. This variant is a weakened-antecedent version of, and therefore implies, Closure 6.

[34] See David and Warfield (manuscript and forthcoming) for further discussion of possible counterexamples to Closure 6 and Closure 7.

occasion of adding q to his belief set). Perhaps S's normally quite reliable Doctor has informed S that his deductive reasoning powers should not be trusted for the next hour because of medication S has taken, and the Doctor supports this by showing S some simple poorly answered logic questions that the Doctor says she administered to S the last time S took the medication in question. For these reasons, and others mentioned in Section 3, one might think that Closures 6 and 7 are false, and that therefore Closure 11 interpreted with either modal reading of (i) or (ii) is also false.

Closure 11 under reading (iii), however, cannot be criticized in this way. Under this reading, Closure 11 implies Closure 8. And, as we pointed out in Section 3, Closure 8, though imprecise, must be true: all counterexamples have been stipulated away. We therefore cannot dismiss Closure 11 interpreted under (iii) on the grounds that it implies a false closure principle. We therefore need an alternative criticism of this reading of this principle. We have two criticisms of this reading, and these criticisms also serve as additional criticisms of Closure 11 interpreted under readings (i) and (ii).

First, these readings all seem to make it far too easy to be "positioned to know" something. That is, the readings all seem to overascribe being "positioned to know". This is most easily illustrated with the strongest reading, reading (iii) of the three available readings. Notice that reading (iii), with its conditional taken as strict, says that I am positioned to know q if and only if it is true that:

Necessarily, if I believe q solely on the basis of deduction from p and (p entails q) and nothing else goes wrong, then I know q

(the counterfactual reading replaces the necessity operator with counterfactual "were I to believe q . . ." in the antecedent and "I would know q" in the consequent). Because "nothing else goes wrong" is being read in such a way as to bracket all possible counterexamples to principles like Closure 7, it seems that on this reading one is going to be ruled to be "positioned to know" any proposition at all, so long as one satisfies the existential presuppositions of (iii)—specifically, so long as one does believe both p and (p entails q). Most notably, this means that one is going to be judged to be "positioned to know" some q even when it is true that, were one to believe q, it would be on the basis of bad reasons, in the face of multiple sources of defeat, and despite a global defeating belief concerning the method of belief formation in question.

The problem is that the powerful antecedent of this reading ("nothing goes wrong") abstracts away from the sometimes messy real epistemic contexts that agents occasionally find themselves in. Sometimes we fail to be "positioned to know" things precisely because our overall epistemic context is problematic (defeaters are present, our belief-forming mechanisms are not working well, and so on). The modal conditional readings of (i)–(iii) abstract away from these problems and rule us "positioned-to-know" propositions we clearly are not positioned to know. These readings are therefore inadequate readings and cannot be of use in a skeptical argument.

Second, notice that none of readings (i)–(iii) of K* under consideration permit a univocal reading of "K*" as it appears in both the antecedent *and* consequent of Closure 11. Readings (i)–(iii) are at best attempts to interpret the "K*" of Closure 11's *consequent*. This type of difficulty arose in the above discussion of diachronic readings of "positioned to know", and, as in that discussion, it seems that a bifurcated understanding of the two "K*" appearances is nearly inevitable. Still further, notice that, even as applied solely to the "K*" of Closure 11's consequent, readings (i)–(iii) make use of the earlier introduced notion of "based on deduction from" that presupposes that agents have the beliefs mentioned in the "based on deduction from" clause of the principle. Notice that this means that the unpacking of K^*q in Closure 11's consequent will require that S have the entailment belief (p entails q). The antecedent of the principle specifies only that S is positioned to know this entailment, and this clearly does not imply believing it. This, too, seems to almost force the skeptic to a theoretically unpromising bifurcated understanding of "positioned to know".

We have said that the skeptic is "almost forced" to an unhappy bifurcated understanding of "positioned to know". We close this section with two ways that a skeptic might try to avoid this problem.

First, the skeptic might propose that we leave the interpretation of "K*" in the antecedent of the closure principle (largely) unanalyzed.[35] This would

---

[35] We note only that it will have to be understood as something like "either the agent knows the entailment or would believe it solely on the basis of good and sufficient reasons (and therefore would know it)". It might seem as if the skeptic is not on terrible ground here given that knowledge of the relevant entailments should be rather easily and cleanly a priori accessible even to agents who have not previously thought about the skeptical hypotheses. But, as skeptics so regularly remind us, appearances can be deceiving. Trouble probably reappears when we are reminded that the universally quantified and modally strong version of the skeptic's principle is going to have to

lead to a presentation of the following familiar skeptical argument sketch, with intuitive defenses of the premises inserted:

P1 $(Kp$ and $K^*(p$ entails $q)) \rightarrow K^*q$ Closure 11 (interpreting K^*q with, e.g., (iii))

P2 $\sim K^* \sim h$ Can't know this

3 $\sim Kc$ or $\sim K^*(c$ entails $\sim h)$

P4 $K^*(c$ entails $\sim h)$ Easy to know this (unanalyzed K^*)

5 $\sim Kc$

P1 here is simply Closure 11 with the "K^*" of "$K^*(p$ entails $q)$" left unanalyzed and "K^*q" interpreted under reading (iii). Premise 2 is the standard skeptical pivot point. P4 is not interpreted using any of the "all-but-belief-and-X" understandings of "K^*" now in play. Instead, the "position-to-know" locution at this step in the argument is left unanalyzed, and the premise is defended with an intuitive appeal to how easy it is to know or at least be positioned to know the straightforward entailments relation specified in P4.[36] But, even if we were inclined to grant the skeptic a free pass on the unanalyzed "K^*" of the antecedent of Closure 11, this skeptical approach suffers from the reliance on the "all-but-belief-and-X" readings of "K^*" criticized above. We do not think that this is a promising route for the skeptic.

Second, and lastly, the skeptic might try to avoid the problems encountered in analyzing "position to know" (both the bifurcation problem and the substantive problems facing readings (i)–(iii)), by trying to push the skeptical argument along without specifying *any* particular interpretation of "positioned to know". It is worth seeing that this approach is not as completely disastrous as it initially sounds. In addition, it is good to see that the approach may well be needed.

The approach may well be needed because of the challenges and open questions facing the other skeptical strategies we have explored. We have seen that both the strengthened-antecedent principles of Section 3 and the weakened-consequent principles explored so far do not lead immediately

---

face up to cases in which, e.g., the agent in question will need first to acquire some new concepts before it is safe to credit her with the entailment beliefs needed for having the knowledge in question. Additional trouble might be found in cases involving conceptual confusion (temporary or permanent).

[36] The point would be generalized in defense of the relevant full-dress universally quantified premise of the more formal skeptical argument of which this is a sketch. As discussed in the previous note, this generalization is not wholly unproblematic.

to a powerful and general skeptical argument. The weakened-consequent principles of this section, however, do seem to be structurally advantageous to the skeptic. We have already seen that there are complications involved in specifying a meaning of "positioned to know" that will serve in a skeptical argument using this type of principle. Perhaps, then, the skeptic would find it worthwhile to see what happens if one tries to press on with a skeptical argument of this type in the absence of any precise (or even imprecise) account of what it is to be "positioned to know" something. We shall show first that this is not an immediate disaster, but we shall go on to show that in the end the approach gets no further than the other approaches we have explored.

The form of the argument is familiar enough. Here is the argument sketch one last time:

P1	$(Kp$ and $K^*(p$ entails $q)) \rightarrow K^*q$	Closure 11 (unanalyzed K^*)
P2	$\sim K^* \sim h$	Can't know this (though unanalyzed K^*)
3	$\sim Kc$ or $\sim K^*(c$ entails $\sim h)$	
P4	$K^*(c$ entails $\sim h)$	Easy to know this (unanalyzed K^*)
5	$\sim Kc$	

In the absence of a particular interpretation of "positioned to know", how is the skeptic to defend (P2) and (P4) of this argument?

Well, all along we have been conceding (P2) of the skeptical argument. The intuitive and not wholly implausible idea behind (P2) is that the skeptical hypothesis is well chosen so that one cannot know its denial (or that it is at least very hard to know its denial). As we have mentioned earlier, the more one weakens the consequent of the argument's first premise, the more tempting it becomes to deny the second premise. In the absence of an analysis of "K^*", we are left in the dark as to the strength or weakness of (P2). But, in the spirit of cooperation, let us concede the intuitive plausibility of the premise despite this and see what else can be said about this argument.

What about (P4)? The above discussion of the bifurcation problem suggested that the "K^*" of this premise (and the consequent of the first premise) would, to be understood, require a different interpretation of "positioned to know" than is used in the antecedent of the first premise. The present suggestion avoids this issue by abandoning the goal of achieving an understanding of the premise beyond whatever intuitive understanding we can get from it in its unanalyzed state. This might not lead to a devastating problem for the skeptical project, because the conceptual matters of concern in the antecedent of the principle are propositions that all agents with the relevant concepts are at least plausibly thought to be "positioned to know".[37] Pretend that we grant the skeptic a free pass on this premise as well. Having a moment ago decided not to challenge (P2), would this mean conceding some sort of overall victory to the skeptic?

We grant, for purposes of discussion, that, even in the absence of an analysis of "positioned to know", it seems plausible that we are not positioned to know the denial of suitably chosen skeptical hypotheses. And we grant, for purposes of discussion, that, even in the absence of an analysis of "positioned to know", it seems plausible that we are in a position to know the conceptually necessary entailment beliefs involved in the skeptical argument. With this much conceded for purposes of discussion, the skeptic might seem to have managed to confront us with an at least superficially plausible general skeptical argument, using a weakened-consequent closure principle.

This verdict is premature. Even conceding the plausibility of (P2) and (P4) of the skeptical argument sketch, the argument has one further substantive premise: (P1), the Closure Principle itself. What are we to make of *this* premise given on the assumption that the skeptic embraces the suggested "no-analysis" reading of "K*"? The skeptic must be hoping that the principle will seem quite compelling despite (or perhaps because of) the lack of clarity about "positioned to know". The skeptic's idea is probably the following. If one knows p and is rather well positioned to know (p entails q), because it is a simple entailment relation, then of course one is positioned to know q. After all, one is well positioned to know the entailment of q by p and, already knowing p, is at least well positioned simply to put these two "premise beliefs" together and infer q.

We see no other way for the skeptic to offer purely intuitive support for (P1) of this skeptical argument sketch (which just is the "no-analysis" version of Closure 11). In the absence of a specification of the meaning of "positioned to know", this is the only sort of support to which the skeptic can appeal. This support is inadequate to the skeptic's task. The skeptic appeals to the intuition that one knowing p and knowing (or being positioned to know) that (p entails q) could simply put these bits of knowledge together and come to know q. On this basis the skeptic hopes that we will concede the first

---

[37] Though see nn. 36 and 37.

premise. Note, however, that this support sounds exactly like an overt appeal to either Closure 6 or Closure 7. The imprecision about which principle is involved is simply a function of the informality of the skeptical reasoning being discussed. We have already seen that Closure 6 and Closure 7 are at least "arguably false". They are, for that reason, not the sort of principles that can be comfortably leaned upon in an intuitive defense of (P1) of the current skeptical argument sketch. We conclude that even quite generously conceding (P2) and (P4) of the skeptical argument sketch does not lead to an apparent skeptical victory. A skeptic attempting to press on with a weakened-consequent closure-based skeptical argument is left with no solid intuitive support for the closure principle (unanalyzed Closure 11) appearing as the argument's first premise.

Having rejected this possible skeptical strategy, we see no further way for the skeptic to offer a plausible skeptical argument using a weakened-consequent knowledge-closure principle. Perhaps this represents a failure of imagination on our part. This territory is not, after all, as clean and well understood as the strengthened-antecedent family of strategies discussed in Section 3. But we trust that we have done enough to show that the ball is squarely in the court of those who think that there is a promising skeptical argument somewhere in this neighborhood.

5. Conclusion

Well-chosen sketches of closure-based skeptical arguments appear to present non-skeptics with the beginnings of a serious challenge to typical knowledge claims. It is uncontroversially true, however, that the knowledge-closure principles employed in these simple argument sketches are not immediately and obviously suitable for use in a general and powerful skeptical argument. We have explored a wide range of possible and natural attempts to produce plausible knowledge-closure principles that might be of service in such a skeptical argument.

Principles discussed in Section 3 (the strengthened-antecedent principles) are the easiest to generate, understand, modify, and defend. But these principles do not by themselves lead to a powerful skeptical argument, and the additional theses needed to reach a general skeptical conclusion using these principles (for example, Claim) have not been adequately explored in the literature.

Principles discussed in Section 4 (the weakened-consequent principles) are not as easy to understand, generate, and defend. This is because of ambiguities and uncertainty about possible interpretations of the key notion of being "positioned to know" something and because philosophers have done little work on the "positioned-to-know" locution. Principles of this sort are, from a structural point of view, more promising principles for use in general skeptical argumentation. Upon closer analysis, however, these principles tend to be much more closely connected to their strengthened antecedent cousins than an initial inspection would reveal. Our exploration of these connections leads us to the conclusion that many weakened-consequent knowledge-closure principles are no more useful to the skeptic than their strengthened-antecedent cousins. The weakened-consequent principles that are not so tightly connected to the strengthened-antecedent family are the least-well-understood principles and therefore at least appear to be the most promising leads in the pursuit of a strong skeptical argument using a knowledge-closure principle. But our investigation of these principles has also failed to find a principle of clear use to the skeptic.

We conclude that, in the absence of a significant advance on behalf of the skeptic, knowledge-closure-based skeptical arguments do not lead us directly to skepticism.

References

Brueckner, A. L. (1985), "Skepticism and Epistemic Closure", *Philosophical Topics*, 13: 89–117.

—— (1994), "The Structure of the Skeptical Argument", *Philosophy and Phenomenological Research*, 54: 827–35.

Cohen, S. (1998), "Two Kinds of Skeptical Argument", *Philosophy and Phenomenological Research*, 58: 143–59.

—— (1999), "Contextualism, Skepticism, and the Structure of Reasons", *Philosophical Perspectives 13: Epistemology*, 57–89.

David, M. and T. Warfield (forthcoming), *One Skeptical Argument*.

—— —— (manuscript), "Six Possible Counterexamples to One or Two Closure Principles".

DeRose, K. (1995), "Solving the Skeptical Problem", *Philosophical Review*, 104: 1–52.

Devitt, M. (1996), *Coming to our Senses*. Cambridge: Cambridge University Press.

Dretske, F. (1970), "Epistemic Operators", *Journal of Philosophy*, 67: 1007–23.

Feldman, F. (1995), "In Defence of Closure", *Philosophical Quarterly*, 10: 487−94.

Harman, G. (1973), *Thought*. Princeton: Princeton University Press.

Klein, P. (1981), *Certainty: A Refutation of Skepticism*, Minneapolis: University of Minnesota Press.

—— (1992), "Scepticism, Contemporary", in J. Dancy and E. Sosa, eds., *A Companion to Epistemology*, Oxford: Blackwell, 458−62.

Kyburg, H. (1961), *Probability and the Logic of Rational Belief*, Middletown: Wesleyan University Press.

McGee, V. (1985), "A Counterexample to Modus Ponens", *Journal of Philosophy*, 82: 462−71.

Maitzen, S. (1998), "The Knower Paradox and Epistemic Closure", *Synthese*, 114: 337−54.

Moore, G. E. (1939), "Proof of an External World"; repr. in *Philosophical Papers*, London: Allen and Unwin, 1959.

Nozick, R. (1981), *Philosophical Explanations*, Cambridge, MA: Harvard University Press.

VanArragon, R. (2001), 'Externalism, Skepticism, and Relevant Alternatives,' doctoral dissertation, University of Notre Dame.

Vogel, J. (1990), "Are there Counterexamples to the Closure Principle?", in M. D. Roth and G. Ross, eds., *Doubting*, Dordrecht: Kluwer Academic Publishers, 13−27.

Warfield T. (2004), "When Closure Does and Does Not Fail: A Lesson from the History of Epistemology", *Analysis*, 64, 35−41.

8

Intuition and Modal Error

George Bealer

Modal intuitions are not only the primary source of modal knowledge but also the primary source of modal error. An explanation of how modal error arises—and, in particular, how erroneous modal intuitions arise—is an essential part of a comprehensive theory of knowledge and evidence. But, more than that, such an explanation is essential to identifying and eliminating modal errors in our day-to-day philosophical practice. According to the theory of modal error given here, modal intuitions retain their evidential force in spite of their fallibility, and erroneous modal intuitions turn out to be in principle identifiable and eliminable by subjecting intuitions to properly conducted a priori dialectic and theory construction. And, thus, the classical method of intuition-driven philosophical investigation is exonerated.

I begin with a summary of certain preliminaries: the phenomenology of intuitions, their fallibility, the nature of concept-understanding and its relationship to the reliability of intuitions, and so forth. This is followed by an inventory of standard sources of modal error. I then go on to discuss two specific sources: the first has to do with the failure to distinguish between metaphysical possibility and various kinds of epistemic possibility; the second, with the *local* misunderstanding of one's concepts (as opposed to out-and-out misunderstanding, as in Burge's original arthritis case). The first source of error,

I am very grateful to Davor Bodrozic, Daniel Demetriou, Nick Kroll, David Liebesman and, especially, John Bengson and Dan Korman for insightful comments and discussion.

though much discussed of late, is I believe widely misunderstood; fortunately, it turns out to be comparatively easy to untangle and poses little threat to intuition-driven philosophical investigation. Discussion of the second source, by contrast, has been absent from the philosophical literature. This source of modal error, and the potential to overcome it, has wide-ranging implications for philosophical method. The failure to understand these sources of modal error has recently led to skeptical accounts of intuition and modal error, which are, I will show, ultimately self-defeating.

1. Intuition as a guide to possibility

First some comments on the nature of intuition. By intuitions we mean *seemings*: for you to have an intuition that *p* is just for it to *seem* to you that *p*.[1] Here 'seems' is understood, not in its use as a cautionary or "hedging" term, but in its use as a term for a genuine kind of conscious episode. For example, when you first consider one of de Morgan's laws, often it neither seems true nor seems false; after a moment's reflection, however, something happens: it now just seems true. This kind of seeming is *intellectual*, not experiential—sensory, introspective, imaginative.

Intuition is different from belief: you can believe things that you do not intuit (e.g., that Paris is in France), and you can intuit things that you do not believe (e.g., the axioms of naive set theory). The experiential parallel is that you can believe things that do not appear (seem sensorily) to be so, and things can seem sensorily in ways you do not believe them to be (as with the Müller–Lyer arrows). Moreover, intuition is typically prior to belief in the order of discovery and evidence: until Putnam we did not even have beliefs about twin earth, but directly upon encountering the example most of us had the intuition that there would be no water on twin earth and only thereafter formed the associated belief. Now, since intuition is analogously different from other psychological attitudes (judging, guessing, imagining, etc.) and from common sense, I believe there is no choice but to accept that intuition is a *sui generis* propositional attitude.

---

[1] I owe this point to George Myro. Here and in certain other places I use propositional variables, e.g., '*p*' where sentential variables, e.g., 'A' are strictly speaking called for. Confusion should not result.

The sort of intuitions relevant to the a priori disciplines are *rational* intuitions (intuitions that present themselves as necessary), not *physical* intuitions. According to traditional usage, "thought experiments" appeal, not to rational intuitions, but to physical intuitions (and the like). Here one constructs hypothetical cases about which one tries to elicit, say, intuitions deriving from one's implicit mastery of relevant physical laws—as, for example, in Newton's bucket thought experiment: is it physically possible for the fluid to remain perfectly flat? Not according to physical intuition. Is it metaphysically possible? Of course. Unlike physical intuition, rational intuition derives from one's understanding of one's concepts, not of empirical laws. Does this imply that a priori knowledge is always the result of *conceptual analysis*? No, not unless the latter includes various necessities that traditionally were thought to be synthetic, not analytic.

The set-theoretic paradoxes establish an important moral, namely, that intuition can be fallible and a priori belief, revisable—contrary to early modern epistemological dogma. We must therefore embrace the alternative tradition—reaching from Plato to Gödel—that recognizes that a priori justification is fallible and holistic, relying respectively on dialectic and theory construction.

It is our standard epistemic practice to count intuitions as evidence, or reasons, absent special reason not to do so (much as we count ostensible sense perceptions as evidence absent special reason not to do so). But (I argue) we have no such special reason in the case of intuitions. Moreover, if we denied, without any special reason, that intuitions are evidence, we would land in an epistemically self-defeating situation, and, therefore, there is no rational alternative but to accept intuitions as evidence. Finally, since modal intuitions are not, in respects relevant to evidential status, different from nonmodal intuitions, they in particular must be accepted as evidence. (I have defended each of these points elsewhere and will just assume them here.[2] I will, however, provide a discussion in §8 of the self-defeating nature of denying the evidential status of intuition as it arises in the context of modal error and scientific essentialism.)

These conclusions raise two questions. First, *why* are intuitions evidence (reasons)? The answer lies in a reliabilist theory of basic sources of evidence.

---

[2] For detailed arguments, see George Bealer, "The Incoherence of Empiricism", *Aristotelian Society*, supplementary volume, 66 (1992), 99–138, and other papers mentioned below.

(Reliabilist theories of nonbasic sources of evidence, on the other hand, face standard counterexamples.) Contingent reliabilist theories of basic sources of evidence, according to which there is a contingent nomological tie between the deliverances of such sources and the truth, are open to counterexamples: for instance, contrary to contingent reliabilism, telepathically generated guessing would not count as a basic source of evidence even if it had a nomologically reliable tie to the truth. The explanation, rather, is provided by *modal reliabilism*—the doctrine that there is a certain kind of qualified modal tie between basic sources of evidence and the truth. Intuition (like phenomenal experience) meets this condition.

Second, why should there be a qualified modal tie between intuitions and the truth? The explanation is provided by an analysis of what it is to understand one's concepts. The intuitive idea underlying the analysis is that the identity of one's concepts is manifested in the intuitions involving those concepts that one would have as one approaches cognitively ideal conditions (intelligence, attentiveness, memory, etc.). According to the resulting explanation, the qualified modal tie between intuitions and the truth does not have a supernatural source (as perhaps it does in Gödel's theory of mathematical intuition); rather, it is simply a consequence of what it is to understand the concepts involved in one's intuitions.

I have defended these positions in other work.[3] Here I will be concerned to explain how erroneous modal intuitions arise. The indicated analysis of understanding concepts will play a critical role in my account of modal error. I will return to it after dealing with three further preliminaries.

2. Concrete-case intuition, conceivability, and metaphysical versus epistemic possibility

2.1. Concrete-case intuition

Theoretical intuitions often play a central role in philosophical debates. Consider, for instance, the theoretical intuitions many people have that free will and determinism are incompatible or that causal closure entails

---

[3] See, e.g., George Bealer, "Philosophical Limits of Scientific Essentialism," *Philosophical Perspectives* 1 (1987), 289–365; "A Priori Knowledge and the Scope of Philosophy", *Philosophical Studies* 81 (1996), 121–42; and "A Theory of the A Priori", *Philosophical Perspectives* 13 (1999), 29–55.

epiphenomenalism. Theoretical intuitions, however, are typically far more fallible than concrete-case intuitions—much as observations that are heavily theory-laden are much more fallible than those that are not. (This is why in controversies over physical measurement, disputes are typically adjudicated by comparatively non-theory-laden observations such as where the arrow is pointing on the dial or where the endpoints of a rod are on the yardstick.) In contemporary philosophy, it seems that some people are content to found their philosophical theories on a few central theoretical intuitions rather than concrete-case intuitions. This practice lacks historical perspective. The history of philosophy is littered with examples of philosophers no less brilliant than our contemporaries who founded their philosophy on small families of theoretical intuitions which they found especially compelling. The list is embarrassingly long—ranging from Parmenides to Berkeley and Hume, Spinoza and Leibniz, Hegel and Bradley, and on to Schlick and Ayer. To one group of philosophers, certain theoretical principles can seem self-evident whereas to an opposing group the opposites can seem just as compelling. Left at this level, a "battlefield of endless controversies," as Kant puts it, is inevitable.

The only solution is to defer to concrete-case intuitions. (This is so even in the case of widely held general principles such as the transitivity of the part/whole relation and perhaps the law of excluded middle or even Leibniz's Law.) This is not to say that these intuitions will themselves be in harmony; the point is that significant overlapping collections of them are in sufficient harmony to adjudicate the dispute. We witness success at this in an impressive list of cases that we now all take for granted. For example, the perceptual-relativity refutation of phenomenalism; the Spartan-pretender refutation of logical behaviorism; the defective-instrument refutation of instrumentalism; the unrepeatable-events refutation of the inductivist theory of justification; and on and on. It is, however, only hubris to think that at just this point in history our theoretical intuitions are at last reliable.

2.2. Conceivability

Many philosophers take conceivability and inconceivability to be the primary guide to possibility.[4] I think this is a mistake—well, unless when you say

---

[4] For a more detailed discussion of conceivability, see George Bealer, "Modal Epistemology and the Rationalist Renaissance", in Tamar Szabo Gendler and John Hawthorne (eds.), *Conceivability and Possibility* (New York: Oxford University Press, 2002), sect. 1.2.

'It is conceivable that p', all you are saying (at least conversationally) is that you have an intuition that p is possible; and when you say 'It is inconceivable that p', all you are saying is that you have an intuition that it is impossible that p. If so, a lot of confusion would be avoided if we simply talked about possibility and impossibility intuitions. The same goes for 'imaginable' and 'unimaginable'.

Suppose, however, that this easy idiomatic gloss on 'conceivable' and 'inconceivable' is not correct and that these terms are instead taken at face value as literal expressions of certain modal facts: it is conceivable that p iff it is possible for someone to conceive that p; it is inconceivable that p iff it is not possible for someone to conceive that p. Then we have a pair of problems. First, unlike intuitions of possibility and impossibility, conceivability and inconceivability would not be suited to play their reputed evidential role in modal epistemology. That it is possible, or impossible, to conceive that p is itself a modal fact. But in order for someone to acquire evidence (reasons), something must *actually happen*: a datable psychological episode must *occur* (the occurrence of a sensation, an introspective or imaginative experience, a seeming memory, an intuition). Modal facts do *not* occur. Nothing *happens* when something is conceivable or inconceivable. So something's merely being conceivable or inconceivable cannot provide anyone with evidence (reasons) for anything.

Second, our beliefs about what is conceivable, or inconceivable, can be highly inferential and are often theoretical. True, one way you can come to believe that it is possible for someone to conceive that p is for *you actually* to conceive that p. But why should your conceiving that p provide you with evidence that p is possible? I can see no reason why it should unless conceiving that p involves intuiting that p is possible. (Stephen Yablo himself says, "In slogan form: *conceiving involves the appearance of possibility*."[5]) But then one is right back to relying on modal intuitions. The moral is simple: talk of conceivability and inconceivability invites (avoidable) confusion. The same goes for imaginability and unimaginability.

---

[5] Stephen Yablo, "Is Conceivability a Guide to Possibility?", *Philosophy and Phenomenological Research*, 53 (1993), 5. In support of the centrality of modal intuition, Yablo tells us that "modal intuition *must* be accounted reliable if we are to credit ourselves with modal knowledge . . ." ("The Real Distinction between Mind and Body", *Canadian Journal of Philosophy*, supp. vol. 16 (1990), 179).

2.3. Metaphysical possibility and epistemic possibility

The modal expressions 'could', 'can', 'might', and 'possible' are used in diverse ways which fall into two broad classes: epistemic and nonepistemic. (An analogous division holds for 'must' and 'necessary'.) In modal logic, metaphysics, and philosophy of language and mind, the primary focus is on a certain form of nonepistemic necessity—in Kripke's words, necessity *tout court*. Kripke christened this necessity 'metaphysical necessity'.

To illustrate some of the epistemic uses of 'could', consider any thinkable necessary truth *p*.[6] The first use is the 'could'-of-ignorance: absent what we deem to be adequate evidence (or adequate justification) one way or the other about *p*, we can truly say, "It could be that *p*, and it could be that not *p*. We just do not know yet." (For example, this can be truly said of Goldbach's Conjecture.) But once we have adequate evidence (justification) one way or the other, what was meant in speaking *that way* can no longer be truly said. Second, there is the 'could'-of-less-than-complete-certainty: if we have less than complete certainty about *p* (even if we have adequate evidence, or justification, for *p*), we can still truly say, "We still could be mistaken; we know we can be wrong about almost anything." (For example, even though we now have a proof of Fermat's Last Theorem, this can still be truly said of it.) Third, there is the 'could'-of-qualitative-evidential-neutrality (as I will call it): for a posteriori necessities, we can often truly say, "It could have turned out that *p*, and it could have turned out that not *p*." And this is so, even though, meant this way, this cannot be said of any traditional a priori necessities. For example, meant this way, 'Whether Hesperus was Phosphorus could have turned out either way' would be true, even though when meant the same way 'Fermat's Last Theorem could have turned out either way' would be false. (Of course, there is a corresponding use of 'It could turn out either way'.)

---

[6] Importantly, these uses of 'could' need not correspond to distinct *literal meanings*; it is enough that they be standard uses of the term in the sort of ordinary contexts relevant to modal epistemology. The ensuing discussion of these epistemic uses of 'could', while inspired by Kripke's comments in *Naming and Necessity* (Cambridge, MA: Harvard University Press, 1980, 103—5, 140—4), departs from Kripke insofar as he evidently did not regard these uses as established standard uses of 'could' in ordinary language. For a more detailed discussion of these uses, as well as a critique of various alleged uses of 'could' (e.g., the alleged 'could'-of-"logical"-possibility), see my "Modal Epistemology and the Rationalist Renaissance" (77—9).

A few semi-formal remarks about these epistemic uses of 'could' might be helpful. Suppose someone intends the 'could'-of-ignorance when uttering the sentence 'It could be that p' in some relevant conversational context.[7] Then, the asserted proposition would be the proposition that results when an associated propositional operation $\Diamond_{ignorance}$ is applied to the proposition p. (In symbols: $\Diamond_{ignorance}\ p$.) The truth conditions of the resulting proposition would be as follows: the proposition that $\Diamond_{ignorance}\ p$ is true iff it is unknown whether p.

The 'could'-of-less-than-complete-certainty may be represented with the operator '$\Diamond_{uncertainty}$'. The truth conditions would be: the proposition that $\Diamond_{uncertainty}\ p$ is true iff it is not completely certain that p.

Finally, the 'could'-of-qualitative-evidential-neutrality may be represented with '$\Diamond_{q\text{-}e\text{-}n}$'. The truth conditions (inspired by Kripke's comments in *Naming and Necessity*) would be: the proposition that $\Diamond_{q\text{-}e\text{-}n}\ p$ is true iff it is possible for there to be a population c with attitudes toward p and it is possible for there to be a population c' whose epistemic situation is qualitatively identical to that of c such that the proposition p', which in c' is the epistemic counterpart of p in c, is true.[8]

(Contrast the foregoing with the untenable account of epistemic possibility offered by David Chalmers.[9])

Note that in each of these three biconditionals the proposition denoted by the left-hand side (e.g., that $\Diamond_{q\text{-}e\text{-}n}\ p$) need not be *identical* to that which is expressed by the associated right-hand side; indeed, in many cases they are intuitively different. This feature allows the above account to avoid various difficulties that undermine other accounts of epistemic uses of 'could'. A case in point is Kripke's account of the 'could'-of-qualitative-evidential-neutrality,

---

[7] Here and certain other places I use single quotation marks where, strictly, corner quotation marks are required.

[8] In symbols: $\Diamond(\exists c)[\text{Attitudes}(c, p)\ \&\ (\exists c')(\exists p')[\text{QualitativelyIdentical}(c', c)\ \&\ \text{Counterparts}(< p', c' >, < p, c >)\ \&\ \text{True}(p')]]$

[9] David Chalmers, "Does Conceivability Entail Possibility?", in Szabo Gendler and Hawthorne (eds.), *Conceivability and Possibility*, 145–200. For instance, on Chalmers's account 'It could turn out that A' is true iff it is not metaphysically possible for an ideally rational being to know a priori that not A (see, e.g., pp. 157 and 162). Likewise for 'It is epistemically possible that A'. But such accounts are mistaken. Is it *epistemically* possible—would you say that it could turn out epistemically—that there are no beliefs? Certainly not. But it is not metaphysically possible for any being to have a priori knowledge that there are beliefs. So, Chalmers's account wrongly implies that it is epistemically possible—it could turn out epistemically—that there are no beliefs.

for as we will see, the above account sidesteps various problems confronting Kripke's account.

3. Understanding concepts

Let us return to the prospect (mentioned in §1) of an analysis of what it is to understand a concept. There is a weak nominal sense in which a person can be said to possess a concept:

A subject possesses a given concept at least nominally iff the subject has natural propositional attitudes toward propositions which have that concept as a constituent content.

Possessing a concept in this sense is compatible with what Tyler Burge calls *misunderstanding* and *incomplete understanding* of a concept ('misunderstanding' for cases where there are errors in the subject's understanding of the concept and 'incomplete understanding' for cases where there are gaps).[10] Possessing a concept in the nominal sense is also compatible with, for example, having propositional attitudes merely by virtue of the attribution practices of third-party interpreters. But possessing a concept in such ways, or modes (merely nominally, incompletely, erroneously, and so forth), is very different from *genuinely understanding* the concept. The goal is to analyze this notion.

The intuitive idea behind the intended analysis of understanding is that the identity of one's concepts is manifested in the intuitions involving those concepts that one would have as one approaches cognitively ideal conditions. Specifically, for target concepts c and relevant hypothetical test cases p involving c,[11] if the subject understands c and the auxiliary concepts involved in p, as the subject approaches ideal cognitive conditions (intelligence, attentiveness, memory, etc.), the subject's intuitions regarding the applicability of c to p become increasingly *truth-tracking*. That is, as the subject approaches ideal cognitive conditions, it would be increasingly the case that, for such c and p, the subject would have the intuition that c applies to p if and only if c really does apply to p. If the subject did not have such truth-tracking

[10] Tyler Burge, "Individualism and the Mental", *Midwest Studies in Philosophy*, 4 (1979), 73–122.
[11] A hypothetical case p involving c is a proposition of the form: it is possible that, for some x, x is in such and such concrete hypothetical situation and x falls under the concept c in that situation.

intuitions, the right thing to say would be that either the subject does not genuinely understand one or more of the concepts involved, or the subject's cognitive conditions are not really those indicated, or some other such (perhaps presently unforeseeable) defeater is present.[12]

On this picture, when a subject's mode of understanding shifts to genuine understanding from, say, an incomplete and incorrect understanding, there is an associated shift in the subject's intuitions—in both *quantity* and *quality*. The quantity grows because one's understanding is no longer incomplete, that is, the gaps in one's understanding responsible for the "don't knows" are filled. The quality improves because one's understanding is no longer erroneous, that is, errors in one's understanding are corrected.

Intuition thus bears a qualified modal tie to the truth. The indicated tie does not have a supernatural source; rather, it is simply a consequence of what it is to understand the concepts involved in one's intuitions. Genuine understanding of one's concepts consists in possessing them in a mode such that at the end of a certain idealized intuition-driven process (conducted in ideal cognitive conditions and during which the chosen test propositions are all genuinely understood) converges on relevant necessary truths in a certain fashion. The analysis of understanding one's concepts thus implies that (and, hence, explains why) there should be such a tie to the truth at the end of a priori theorizing.

A common criticism of using the analysis of understanding to explain intuition's tie to the truth is that it amounts to invoking a "dormitive virtue," which is either unacceptably mysterious or viciously circular.[13] The objection fails, however, for in the present context the explanandum is a modal fact—i.e., intuition's qualified *necessary* tie to the truth. And necessities call for a very different sort of explanation from that called for by contingencies. In the explanation of necessities, it is wholly appropriate to articulate essences, and it is of the essence of the understanding of concepts that intuitions involving those concepts be correct (given ideal cognitive conditions, notably intelligence). This is compatible with its being of the essence of intelligence to have the complementary property. In fact, this complementarity is paradigmatic of functionally

---

[12] I should emphasize that this is only a rough sketch of the final analysis; it omits crucial details and the supporting justification. For a detailed discussion and defense, see "A Theory of the A Priori".

[13] See, e.g., Paul Boghossian, "Knowledge of Logic", in Paul Boghossian and Christopher Peacocke, *New Essays on the A Priori* (Oxford: Clarendon Press), 229–54.

definable families of basic properties. Thus, if the contemplated criticism should work against the proposed explanation of intuition's tie to the truth, it should by parity work against these other functional definitions (and implicit-turned-direct definitions and perhaps impredicative definitions generally). But plainly this is not so. Evidently, then, it is safe to make use of the analysis of understanding in order to explain intuition's qualified modal tie to the truth.

4. Modal error

I have emphasized that intuition is fallible—but not so fallible as to undermine it as a source of evidence. To assure ourselves that this is so, it is appropriate to inventory the sorts of error to which modal intuition succumbs and to explain what is going wrong. This, in turn, would help us to identify what conditions need to be optimized in order to eliminate, or least confine, modal intuitional errors.

Many modal intuitional errors have the same etiology as nonmodal intuitional errors. Consider, for example, the following five sources:

Cognitive deficiency. Some errors have their origin in cognitive deficiencies (intelligence, attentiveness, etc.). For example, such deficiencies explain why many people initially have the erroneous modal intuition regarding the Barber Paradox (i.e., that it is possible for someone to shave all and only those who do not shave themselves).

Conflation. Some errors are born from a failure to take note of various conceptual or logical distinctions. We see this, for example, in Galileo's paradox of infinity (which is based on the common intuition that there cannot be as many odd numbers as there are natural numbers); here two concepts of equinumerosity are conflated, namely, the concept of one-to-one correspondence and the concept of proper inclusion.

Misunderstanding. Some errors have to do with out-and-out misunderstanding of one's concepts—as, for example, in the case of the positive intuition Burge's arthritis man would have if asked whether it is possible to have arthritis in the thigh.

Underdescription and context-sensitivity. Some errors arise from underdescription of the case under consideration or from inattention to relevant contextual factors (including Gricean pragmatic factors and context-dependent norms involved in the specification of the case).

Theoreticality. As discussed in §2, theoretical intuitions (as opposed to concrete-case intuitions) are typically more vulnerable to error, much as theory-laden observations are.

In what follows, I want to focus on two particularly thorny sources of modal intuitional error: the first has to do with the failure to distinguish between metaphysical possibility and various kinds of epistemic possibility; the second, with the *local* misunderstanding of one's concepts (as opposed to out-and-out misunderstanding, as in Burge's original arthritis case). Untangling these two types of modal error plays a pivotal role in the defense of scientific essentialism (hereafter SE)—for example, in the defense of the thesis that water, gold, and so forth are natural kinds having microscopic (or otherwise hidden) a posteriori essences. Our discussion of the first source of modal error (§§5–6) is wholly concerned with people, like Kripke himself, who have pro-SE modal intuitions but who also report having apparently anti-SE modal intuitions. Our discussion of the second source of modal error (§7) is instead concerned with people who have anti-SE intuitions but who simply lack pro-SE intuitions.

5. Modal error and rephrasal strategies

All successful arguments for SE rely on intuitions, for example, intuitions concerning Aristotle and the teacher of Alexander, water and the water-like stuff on twin earth, and so forth. Indeed, careful reflection on the structure of such arguments (discussed in §6.2 below) reveals that without the evidential support of intuitions SE would be unjustified.[14] But there is a prima facie problem with the reliance on intuition, for Kripke and those who share his pro-SE intuitions also have a host of apparently anti-SE intuitions, for example, the intuition that it could have turned out that some samples of water contained no hydrogen. Kripke, of course, was well-aware that he needed to deal with this problem in order for his defense of SE to succeed. He did so by developing an account of such apparent errors in modal intuition.

---

[14] To be sure, certain contemporary advocates of SE might wish to abandon the intuitional defense of SE altogether. But this results in an essentially unstable position: absent intuition, radical empiricist Quineanism about modality, not scientific essentialism, is the result. (This difficulty will play a role in §8.) In the present context, we will only be concerned with philosophers who do not wish to abandon intuition-driven philosophical method.

Our discussion of such modal errors will proceed by presenting, and then assessing, Kripke's account.

So what are Kripke and those who share his pro-SE intuitions to make of the apparent conflict? Bear in mind that this group includes not just proponents of SE but also critics. Proponents of SE have two responses.

First, they could simply declare that anti-SE intuitions are mistaken whereas their own pro-SE intuitions are correct. But critics of SE could simply meet this response by claiming that things are the other way around. The result would be a stalemate.

The second response is, of course, to try to resolve the apparent conflict. The leading general strategy for doing this follows Kripke in deeming the widespread conflict among our intuitions to be only an appearance. All, or most, of our intuitions are correct. (Indeed, Kripke tells us, "I think [intuition] is very heavy evidence in favor of anything, myself. I really don't know, in a way, what more conclusive evidence one can have about anything, ultimately speaking."[15] Kripke also seems to believe that our intuitions must be on the whole correct if scientific essentialism is to be based on adequate evidence.) Despite their correctness, however, many are *misreported*. When we rephrase our (apparently) anti-SE intuitions to make them consistent with our pro-SE intuitions, we succeed. But, of course, this is not enough. Two further requirements (not discussed by Kripke) must be met. First, when opponents of SE try to rephrase the pro-SE intuitions to make them consistent with the apparently anti-SE intuitions, they fail, thus provisionally breaking the impending stalemate in favor of SE (see below for an illustration). Second, it must be the case that there is not some further, equally plausible, rephrasal strategy that is asymmetric in this way, but this time favoring anti-SE rather than pro-SE. For, if there were such a rephrasal strategy, the impending stalemate would be restored.

Kripke and his followers have used two rather different rephrasal strategies. The first turns on an alleged equivocation involving a confusion about features of our epistemic situation. According to this strategy, when we report our pro-SE intuitions (e.g., twin-earth intuitions), what we say is strictly and literally true; but when we report our apparently anti-SE intuitions, we confuse ordinary possibility with the possibility of a certain kind of epistemic situation. For example, when we say 'It could have turned out that some

[15] *Naming and Necessity*, 42.

samples of water contained no H_2O', what we say is strictly and literally false. The intuition is true but incorrectly reported. Kripke develops this idea in connection with the Hesperus/Phosphorus example:

> Now this seems very strange because in advance, we are inclined to say, the answer to the question whether Hesperus is Phosphorus might have turned out either way. And so it's true that given the evidence that someone has antecedent to his empirical investigation, he can be placed in a sense in exactly the same situation, that is a qualitatively identical epistemic situation [to ours], and call two heavenly bodies 'Hesperus' and 'Phosphorus', without their being identical. So in that sense we can say that it might have turned out either way.[16]

Generalizing from these examples, we arrive at the following schema. The true thing incorrectly reported by 'It could have turned out that A' is correctly reported by the following sentence: It is possible that a population of speakers in an epistemic situation qualitatively identical to ours would make a true statement by asserting 'A' with normal literal intent. Consider the true intuition that we incorrectly report with 'It could have turned out that there were samples of water containing no H_2O'. The rephrasal comes out true because in the envisaged population of speakers 'water' might not name water but rather XYZ (or 'H' might not name hydrogen but perhaps X instead). When rephrased thus, the original apparently anti-SE intuition is plainly consistent with the thesis that, necessarily, water $= H_2O$.

Kripke's second rephrasal strategy is this.[17] Suppose that 'R_1' and 'R_2' are co-designating rigid designators whose designatum was fixed by the nonrigid (i.e., contingent) designators 'D_1' and 'D_2', respectively. When we report an apparently anti-SE intuition with 'It could have turned out that $R_1 \neq R_2$', our intuition is correct but misreported. It is correctly reported with 'It is possible that $D_1 \neq D_2$'. On its standard narrow-scope reading, the latter sentence is consistent with the SE thesis that, necessarily, $R_1 = R_2$. For 'D_1' and 'D_2' are only contingently co-designating. For example, on this proposal 'It could have turned out that water $\neq H_2O$' might be rephrased as: 'It is possible that the clear thirst-quenching stuff $\neq$ the such-and-such chemical compound'. The latter is consistent with the thesis that, necessarily, water $= H_2O$, for there is

---

[16] *Naming and Necessity*, 103–4.

[17] It is the second rephrasal strategy, not the first, that plays a pivotal role in Kripke's argument (in *Naming and Necessity*) against the identity theory in philosophy of mind. This argument is critically assessed in George Bealer, "Mental Properties", *Journal of Philosophy*, 91 (1994), 185–208.

a possible situation in which there is a unique clear thirst-quenching stuff that is not a such-and-such chemical compound.

Both rephrasal strategies are flawed. First, let us consider two problems with the second rephrasal strategy. (I will criticize the first strategy in §6.1.)

(1) It is based on the thesis that, when we report an intuition with 'It could have turned out that $R_1 \neq R_2$', often the true thing we have in mind is strictly and literally reported with 'Possibly, $D_1 \neq D_2$', where 'R_1' and 'R_2' are names and 'D_1' and 'D_2' are descriptions. But Kripke, of all people, should not be proposing that, when we make use of a proper-name sentence in ordinary conversation (even if the sentence happens to be of the form 'It could have turned out that $R_1 \neq R_2$'), we have in mind something *descriptive*. After all, the situation is *phenomenologically and behaviorally indistinguishable* from situations in which we have in mind something *nondescriptive* (as, for example, when Kripke asserts his well-known thesis 'If Hesperus $=$ Phosphorus, then it is not possible that Hesperus $\neq$ Phosphorus'). For Kripke to deny this would be *ad hoc* and implausible. Hence, the rephrasal strategy itself is implausible.

(2) It can be shown that this rephrasal strategy does not even accomplish the goal of breaking the impending stalemate between our apparently conflicting pro- and anti-SE intuitions. Specifically, this rephrasal strategy lacks the requisite asymmetry property (described above). For one can wield it so as to sustain the original force of prima facie anti-SE intuitions and to deflate the original force of the pro-SE intuition reports, thereby rendering our prima facie pro-SE intuitions consistent with the rejection of SE. The following recipe provides one way of doing this. Adopt the traditional description theory of names. Hold that names occurring in reports of anti-SE intuitions *are* being used strictly and literally and that they express *nonrigid* descriptive content. Hold that names occurring in reports of pro-SE intuitions are *not* being used strictly and literally and that they are being used to express *rigid* descriptive content. (e.g., this rigidity could be the result of implicitly understood actuality-operators.) The rephrasal strategy can thus be used to affirm anti-SE just as effectively as it can be used to affirm pro-SE. Hence, the impending stalemate is not broken.

One advantage of the first rephrasal is that, unlike the second, it does have the requisite asymmetry. Because our anti-scientific-essentialists are Lockean internalists, they are committed to holding that the meaning of 'water' and other relevant expressions cannot differ across populations of speakers in qualitatively identical epistemic situations. Accordingly, they must hold that their rephrasal of the pro-SE intuition report *entails* the pro-SE report itself.

(Consider the apparently pro-SE intuition reported with 'Possibly, there is a twin earth such that . . . the clear thirst-quenching samples are not samples of water'. When the first rephrasal strategy is applied, such anti-scientific-essentialists must hold that this intuition is true but incorrectly reported; it is correctly reported with 'It is possible for there to be a population of speakers in an epistemic situation qualitatively identical to ours who would make a true statement by asserting "There is a twin earth such that . . . the clear thirst-quenching samples are not samples of water" with normal literal intent'. But, given their Lockean internalism, these anti-scientific-essentialists must hold that such a population of speakers would mean what we mean with 'The clear thirst-quenching samples are not samples of water'. If so, this rephrasal entails that it is metaphysically possible that there be a twin earth such that . . . the clear thirst-quenching samples are not samples of water.[18] Consequently, our anti-scientific-essentialists are committed to holding that the rephrasal has the same pro-SE force as the original report.) By contrast, scientific essentialists are not traditional internalists, so they are free to hold that the meaning of 'water' and other relevant expressions can differ across populations of speakers in qualitatively identical epistemic situations. So when the original intuition seems to have an anti-SE force, they are free to hold that that force is deflated upon rephrasal. The impending stalemate is thus broken in their favor.

No known competing rephrasal strategies have the requisite asymmetry.[19] I have space to show why for just one of these strategies, though the other cases are very similar. This strategy, which is advocated by Thomas Nagel, Michael Levin, and Crispin Wright, involves the idea of imaginative projection, as I will call it.[20] The idea is that when we assert 'It could have turned out that

---

[18] After all, the rephrasal is equivalent to 'It is possible for there to be a population of speakers in an epistemic situation qualitatively identical to ours in whose language there is a *true* sentence synonymous to the English sentence "There is a twin earth such that . . . the clear thirst-quenching samples are not samples of water" ', and this sentence plainly entails the original report 'There is a twin earth such that . . . the clear thirst-quenching samples are not samples of water'.

[19] Chalmers's approach would have the requisite asymmetry but, as we saw (in note 9), is unsatisfactory on other grounds.

[20] Thomas Nagel ("What Is It Like to be a Bat?", *Philosophical Review*, 83 (1974), 435–50). Michael Levin ("Tortuous Dualism", *Journal of Philosophy*, 92 (1995), 314–23). Crispin Wright, ("The Conceivability of Naturalism", in Szabo Gendler and Hawthorne (eds.), *Conceivability and Possibility*, 437–8). Christopher Hill critically assesses the imaginative projection strategy in "Imaginability, Conceivability, Possibility and the Mind-Body Problem" (*Philosophical Studies*, 87 (1997), 65–72).

water $\neq$ H$_2$O', the true thing we have in mind is: it is possible to imagine what it would be like to uncover evidence that would show that water $\neq$ H$_2$O. But this rephrasal strategy fails because it lacks the requisite asymmetry. Specifically, opponents of SE can use it to deflate their prima facie pro-SE intuitions just as effectively as advocates of SE can use it to deflate their prima facie anti-SE intuitions. Consider, for example, the pro-SE twin-earth intuition reported by 'It could have turned out that there is a twin earth macroscopically like earth but where the water-like samples would not be water'. By applying the present rephrasal strategy, opponents of SE would arrive at the following: it is possible to imagine what it would be like to acquire evidence showing that a certain macroscopic duplicate of water (e.g., XYZ) is not water. (For example, I can imagine what it would be like for such evidence to emerge in the course of a partly scientific and partly philosophical investigation.) Since the imaginability of such a scenario does not entail that it is metaphysically possible for there to be a macroscopic duplicate of water that is not water, this rephrasal deflates the original pro-SE intuition. So stalemate would ensue. Ironically, this rephrasal strategy turns out to be as much a threat to SE as it is an aid.[21] (The resulting dialectical situation thus resembles that which confronts advocates of skeptical accounts of modal error, to be discussed in §8.)

6. Modal error and epistemic possibility

6.1. No conflict

I used to think that the upshot of the discussion in §5 was that Kripke's first rephrasal strategy (and no other) successfully deflates our prima facie anti-SE intuitions and thus reconciles the apparent conflict.[22] But I have come to think that this assessment of the situation is mistaken.

---

[21] Wright does not introduce this strategy in an effort to defend SE; in the context in which he proposes the strategy, he curiously just assumes the truth of SE and aims to use the strategy to disarm Cartesian-style modal arguments against the identity theory. But given that SE does not apply to a variety of philosophically important topics (e.g., logic, mathematics), as discussed in §6.2, the applicability of SE to any particular subject is not settled in advance. Rather, it must be settled on a case-by-case basis, for SE fails to apply to a great diversity of a posteriori correlations (see note 32 for examples). Therefore, Wright may not base his defense of the a posteriori identity theory on SE without eliciting intuitions showing that SE applies to mental properties. The same dialectical point applies mutatis mutandis to Levin and, evidently, Nagel.

[22] Cf. Bealer, "Mental Properties".

To repeat, Kripke holds that there is a genuine conflict between his thesis that, say, it is necessary that Hesperus = Phosphorus and the ordinary assertion that it could have turned out that Hesperus was not Phosphorus.[23] Kripke takes there to be a conflict because he believes that '[I]t *could have turned out that p* entails that *p* could have been the case'.[24] And he believes that, if conflicts like this cannot be resolved, his argument for SE would be foiled. His resolution is to hold, that all, or most, of our intuitions are correct and that the apparent conflict among our intuitions is only an illusion resulting from the fact that the sort of prima facie anti-SE intuitions we have been discussing are *misreported*. The inaccurate statement 'It could have turned out that *p*' is accurately stated thus: 'It is possible that a population of speakers in an epistemic situation qualitatively identical to ours would make a true statement by uttering "*p*" with normal literal intent'.

But this sort of metalinguistic rephrasal is untenable because of familiar problems concerning fine-grained intensional content. For example, it runs afoul of the Langford–Church translation test. Church describes this test thus: "[W]e may bring out more sharply the inadequacy of [an analysis] by translating into another language . . . and observing that the two translated statements would obviously convey different meanings to [a speaker of the other language] (whom we may suppose to have no knowledge of English)."[25]

Likewise, Kripke's rephrasal runs afoul of analogues of the sorts of considerations raised by Tyler Burge and Stephen Schiffer against metalinguistic rephrasals of propositional-attitude reports.[26] For instance, Burge raises several objections (pp. 94–9) to metalinguistic rephrasals of the belief that his arthritis man forms when the doctor tells him, "You cannot have arthritis in the thigh." Here are three examples. First, like Church, Burge objects that the metalinguistic reformulations prevent the relevant beliefs from being shared across language communities (p. 96). Second, upon hearing what the doctor told him, arthritis man forms a belief (naively, the belief that he cannot have arthritis in the thigh) that results in great relief—indeed, a dissipation of his fears (p. 95). But this relief is plainly not produced by a belief about the semantics of English (concerning the reference of the English word 'arthritis'). Third,

---

[23] Kripke, *Naming and Necessity*, 103–5, 140–4.   [24] Ibid. 141–2.

[25] Alonzo Church, "On Carnap's Analysis of Statements of Assertion and Belief ", *Analysis*, 10 (1950), 98.

[26] Burge, "Individualism and the Mental". Stephen Schiffer, *Remnants of Meaning* (Cambridge, MA: MIT Press, 1987).

and relatedly, when *occurrent* mental events are at issue, arthritis man "may be brought up short by a metalinguistic formulation of his just-completed ruminations, and may insist that he was not interested in labels" (p. 97). Schiffer raises additional considerations. For example, he complains that the specialized semantical concepts required for satisfactory metalinguistic paraphrases are simply too sophisticated to enter into the contents of an ordinary person's beliefs (p. 68). These objections clearly generalize to Kripke's metalinguistic rephrasal strategy.

There is, however, an extremely simple alternative assessment of the situation, which now seems to me to be correct. Kripke held that there is no conflict in the intuitions at issue, but there is a conflict in the reports of those intuitions. The alternative response is simply to deny that there is conflict even in the reports. When we say (in the relevant situation) that it could have turned out that Hesperus was not Phosphorus, we are simply not contradicting the SE thesis that it is necessary that Hesperus = Phosphorus. Why? Because we are just employing an established epistemic use of 'could', namely, the 'could'-of-qualitative-evidential-neutrality. As we saw in §2, this use of 'could' simply does not collide with the metaphysical use. End of story. Kripke took there to be a conflict in the *reports* of our prima facie pro- and anti-SE intuitions (insofar as he believed that "*it could have turned out that p* entails that *p* could have been the case"). True enough—there is a conflict when the uses of 'could' are the same. That is, 'It could have turned out that Hesperus ≠ Phosphorus' and 'It could not be the case that Hesperus ≠ Phosphorus' are outright contradictory when 'could' is used the same way in both sentences. But in the context of Kripke's discussion his first and second uses of 'could' are simply not the same. So goes the alternative assessment. As soon as we see this, the appearance of conflict between the reports (as well as the intuitions expressed by them) vanishes.[27]

Remember that at this stage of the dialectic we are concerned with those who do in fact have the relevant pro-SE intuitions and who are concerned with what to do about the prima facie conflict between these intuitions and the apparently anti-SE intuitions. A philosopher in this position might hold that my alternative assessment of the apparent conflict is all well and good, but nevertheless wonder how we are to be sure whether we have

---

[27] Thus, just as in the case of Galileo's Paradox, Kripke's present puzzle arises from failing to notice a relevant distinction: as soon as we see it, we see that there was never a contradiction.

an intuition of a metaphysical possibility or an epistemic possibility, say, qualitative epistemic neutrality. In "Modal Epistemology and the Rationalist Renaissance," I proposed a test for exactly this purpose.

Suppose you are considering the modal status of one of the classic hypothetical-case propositions p (e.g., that Aristotle was not the teacher of Alexander, that Phosphorus is not visible in the morning, that there is water on twin earth). Typically, for the philosophical purpose at hand, you may bypass the question of whether p is metaphysically possible and consider instead whether p is a contingent proposition. Therefore, one may without loss recast our question in that idiom. And since a survey of cases shows that 'contingent'—unlike 'possible', 'could', and so forth—does not have an epistemic reading, one need no longer worry about the possibility of equivocation. Consequently, concerning the twin-earth case, philosophers who share Kripke's apparently pro-SE intuitions may shift their attention to the intuition that the twin-earth proposition is a contingent proposition—that is, the intuition that it is contingent whether there is a twin earth macroscopically, but not microscopically, like earth where there is a water-like stuff which is not genuine water.[28] But they may not do this for the epistemic possibility that water could have turned out not to be H_2O. The sort of philosopher that we are presently concerned with simply lacks the intuition that the proposition that water is not H_2O is a contingent proposition.

Thus we find that our first potential source of modal error—the alleged confusion of epistemic and metaphysical possibility—is relatively easy to untangle. In fact, in its most famous instances, it was not a source of error at all. The only error in those instances was in thinking that any of the relevant modal intuitions (either the apparently anti-SE or the pro-SE intuition) must have been erroneous in the first place.

6.2. Semantic Stability

For a certain important class of propositions, apparently anti-SE intuitions cannot be disarmed in the way just discussed. I have in mind propositions that are *semantically stable*.[29] Very roughly, a proposition p is semantically stable iff

---

[28] Or the intuition that it is contingent whether there is a twin earth macroscopically but not microscopically like earth where there is a water-like stuff and, *if* all actual samples of water are H_2O, *then* these twin-earth samples are not genuine water.

[29] I first introduced the notion of semantic stability, together with the following account, in "Mental Properties".

no proposition besides *p* itself can play exactly the same cognitive role for our twin-earth counterparts as *p* plays for us. More precisely,

> For thinkable *p*, *p* is semantically stable iff, necessarily, if *p* plays some cognitive role in the mental life of a community c, then it is necessary that, for any other community c' in qualitatively the same epistemic situation as c, no proposition can play that role other than *p* itself.

Expressions have (or lack) a corresponding sort of epistemic invariance.[30] Natural kind terms are paradigmatic semantically unstable terms—'water', 'gold', 'heat', 'beech', 'elm', etc. By contrast, the core vocabulary of the a priori disciplines—logic, mathematics, philosophy—is semantically stable: 'some', 'all', 'and', 'if', 'is identical to', 'is', 'necessarily', 'possibly', 'true', 'valid', '0', '1', '+', '÷', 'property', 'quality', 'quantity', 'relation', 'proposition', 'state of affairs', 'object', 'category', 'conscious', 'sensation', 'pleasure', 'pain', 'emotion', 'think', 'believe', 'desire', 'decide', 'know', 'reason', 'evidence', 'justify', 'understand', 'explain', 'purpose', 'good', 'fair', 'ought'.

A successful argument that SE holds in a particular case (e.g., necessarily, water $=$ H_2O) consists of two steps.[31] First, pro-SE intuitions are elicited supporting the thesis that the proposition at issue is an a posteriori necessity: in all known cases, these intuitions either are or can be reworked into twin-earth style intuitions. Second, one shows that prima facie anti-SE intuitions (e.g., the intuition that it could have turned out either way whether water $=$ H_2O) can be disarmed but that, when anti-scientific-essentialists attempt to do the same for prima facie pro-SE intuitions (i.e., the intuitions elicited in step one), they fail. Note, however, that, although this two-stage defense of SE succeeds for natural-kind identities like 'Water $=$ H_2O', *both* steps fail in the case of semantically stable terms.

Let t be a semantically stable term. In connection with the first step, consider the t-analogue of the twin-earth argument for 'water'. We are to contemplate the possibility of another planet (or world) macroscopically like earth (the

---

[30] Although, for ease of expression, I will take the liberty to pass back and forth between the metalinguistic notion and the objectival notion, the objectival notion is basic and the metalinguistic notion is a derived notion defined in terms of it. Identifying the objectival notion as basic allows the stable/unstable distinction to be uniformly and economically extended to all categories of entity. In addition, it allows us to consider situations in which there are conscious beings but no natural languages. And it requires no caveat about ambiguity; after all propositions, concepts, properties, and so forth are not ambiguous.

[31] Here and elsewhere I will suppress existence conditions when they are not pertinent.

actual world) but microscopically different. We are to consider the items *here* to which t applies, and we are then to ask whether, intuitively, t would fail to apply to the corresponding items *there* (which, by hypothesis, are microscopically different). The question is outlandish if t is a core term from logic, mathematics, or metaphysics (see the examples given above). Take, for instance, 'property'. There are properties here; could there fail to be properties there?!

The same thing holds if t is a core term or concept from epistemology, philosophy of mind, ethics, and so forth. Consider, for example, the concept of thinking. First, we are to suppose that on earth all and only thinking beings have a certain microstructure say, "T-fibers" (which are composed ultimately of hydrogen, oxygen, carbon, etc.). Consider a twin earth on which our Doppelgängers display "thinking"-behavior exactly like ours. It turns out, however, that, whereas our thinking—and our associated "thinking"-behavior—co-occurs with firing T-fibers, the "thinking"-behavior of our Doppelgängers co-occurs instead with firing T_{te}-fibers (composed ultimately of X, Y, Z, etc.). Would we say that these creatures are thinking? To be sure, we would not be *certain* that they are; macroscopic behavioral criteria never entail that a mental predicate applies. Nevertheless, *it would not be counterintuitive to say that they are thinking*. Note the contrast with water. It would be counterintuitive to say that samples of XYZ on twin earth are genuine samples of water. This intuition is the essential first step of the SE argument concerning 'water'. The analogous intuition concerning 'thinking' is simply *missing*! Accordingly, the essential first step of the argument that SE applies to 'thinking' cannot even get off the ground. The general thesis is that this essential first step in the argument for SE fails for semantically stable terms.[32]

---

[32] Someone might think that even though this essential step in the argument for SE fails, considerations of simplicity create a presumption in favor of SE. But this is not so. Even if in the actual world the atmosphere of every planet were chemically just like earth's, we would not say that in a nonactual world a twin-earth would have no atmosphere if it were enveloped by *pure* oxygen. It would be preposterous to hold that simplicity creates a presumption in favor of restricting the term 'atmosphere' to the familiar mixture of gases on earth. Since there is no presumption in favor of SE for this and a large, remarkably diverse family of other, prima facie functional terms (e.g., soil, shelter, fuel, drink, and so forth), uniformity supports the conclusion that there is no presumption in favor of SE in the case of other prima facie functional terms like 'thinking'—unless some reason independent of simplicity (e.g., genuine evidence or outright argument) can be given for taking 'thinking' to be different. For a detailed discussion (and additional examples), see Bealer "Philosophical Limits of Scientific Essentialism".

Now for the second step in the SE argument. When we try to disarm the prima facie anti-SE intuitions concerning semantically unstable propositions (e.g., that it could have turned out that water $\neq H_2O$) as we did in §6.1, we succeed. But in the case of analogous prima facie anti-SE intuitions concerning semantically stable propositions, this strategy always fails.

Though this may be seen on a case by case basis, it is also a consequence of the following general principle:

> For semantically stable propositions p, if it could (epistemically) have turned out that p, it is metaphysically possible that p.

In slogan form, for semantically stable propositions p: epistemic possibility entails metaphysical possibility. (In symbols, $\Diamond_{q-e-n}p \rightarrow \Diamond p$.) This principle follows directly from (i) the definition of semantic stability and (ii) the truth conditions (given in §2.3; see also §§5–6.1) for the epistemic use of 'it could have turned out' needed for the defense of SE.[33]

Thus, when it comes to semantically stable propositions, our epistemic-possibility intuitions are a good guide to metaphysical possibility. So, if you are in doubt about the reliability of metaphysical-possibility intuitions but not the associated epistemic-possibility intuitions, the latter may without loss play the role formerly played by the former. The chance that we might be mistaking intuitions of epistemic possibility for intuitions of metaphysical possibility poses no threat: even if we are, no error would result since intuitions of the epistemic possibility entail the corresponding metaphysical possibility for semantically stable propositions.[34]

Clearly, then, the standard routine for disarming prima facie anti-SE intuitions fails in the case of our semantically stable prima facie anti-SE intuitions.

[33] This principle is the basis for the argument against the identity theory I give in "Mental Properties". Some people mistakenly believe that Kripke articulates this principle and indeed that his argument against the identity theory in *Naming and Necessity* is based on it; but examination of the text shows that this is plainly not so. See note 17 above.

[34] All the same points hold for "mixed" intuitions of the sort discussed above. All we need to do is replace the semantically unstable component with a necessary condition of this semantically unstable element that is semantically stable. As long as the substitute semantically stable concept is sufficiently specific, we will have the intuition that the new proposition is epistemically possible if we had the intuition that the original proposition was. And, again, the epistemic possibility would entail the metaphysical possibility.

The upshot is that neither stage of the argument for SE goes through for semantically stable concepts and propositions.[35]

This brings us back to the main thread of our discussion of modal error. At the close of §4 we isolated two sources of modal error with special bearing on SE: the first concerned the failure to distinguish between metaphysical and epistemic possibility; the second, the local misunderstanding of one's concepts. In §5 we began our investigation of alleged modal errors having to do with the first source. In §6.1 we completed this investigation, showing that the supposed instances of such modal errors identified by Kripke in his defense of SE simply were not genuine errors at all. In the course of §6.2 we considered a reconstruction of the two-step argument for SE as it applies to the standard class of semantically unstable propositions (that water $= H_2O$; etc.). This reconstruction enables us to see more clearly where the resolution given in §6.1 fits into the larger argument for SE (namely, in step two).

Our discussion of the first source of modal error focused on people, like Kripke himself, who have pro-SE modal intuitions but who also report having anti-SE modal intuitions. By contrast, our discussion of the second source of modal error will focus on people who have anti-SE modal intuitions but simply lack pro-SE modal intuitions. We now turn to this discussion.

7. Modal error and local misunderstanding

Stephen Yablo presents an account of modal error—specifically, how anti-SE modal intuitions can be in error.[36] Yablo is not concerned with errors resulting from conceptual illusions, limitations on intelligence, inattentiveness, and so

---

[35] Scientific essentialism therefore provides us with no reason to doubt the possibility of a priori knowledge of semantically stable modal truths. What could block this possibility? Evidently, nothing could unless there are necessary cognitive limitations, notably on intelligence. If correct, these considerations suggest the following, which I call the *Semantic Stability Principle*: For knowable semantically stable propositions p, if p is necessary, p is knowable a priori. Given that the central truths of the a priori disciplines are semantically stable necessities, the Semantic Stability Principle implies the more circumscribed principle that the knowable central truths of the a priori disciplines are knowable a priori. This is just the traditional rationalist thesis of the Autonomy of the A Priori Disciplines.

[36] Yablo, "Is Conceivability a Guide to Possibility?" Yablo's discussion is stated in the idiom of 'conceivability' and 'inconceivability'; I will be reformulating it in what follows in the idiom of possibility and impossibility intuitions, whose use we defended in §2.1.

forth. Nor is he concerned with the above problem (on which Kripke spent so much time)—namely, the problem of reconciling our metaphysical and epistemic intuitions, which (I have argued) were correctly reported in the first place and were never in conflict. Yablo's underlying concern is rather with full-fledged errors in intuitions about metaphysical possibility.

Yablo holds that these errors have two potential sources, in each case mistaken *beliefs*:

(a) mistaken a posteriori beliefs (e.g., someone who mistakenly believes that Hesperus ≠ Phosphorus might have the intuition that Hesperus could outlast Phosphorus), or

(b) mistaken beliefs regarding the relationship between such a posteriori beliefs and associated modal truths (someone might deny that, if Hesperus = Phosphorus, then necessarily Hesperus cannot outlast Phosphorus).

I am here less interested in class (a), for practiced dialecticians have the ability to proceed using exclusively "pure" a priori intuitions, namely, those that survive even under the hypothesis that such a posteriori beliefs (both pro- and con-) are unjustified or mistaken.[37]

How do people come to have erroneous modal intuitions belonging to the second class? Yablo's answer is that they are somehow produced by underlying class (b) beliefs, which by hypothesis are false. But it is plausible that at least some people have class (b) beliefs that are based, ultimately, on relevant concrete-case intuitions. But since such a person's class (b) beliefs are by hypothesis false, presumably a number of the intuitions upon which these false beliefs are based must themselves be false. What explains why *these* intuitions go wrong? If the explanation is that they too are produced by false class (b) beliefs, we go round in a circle. It seems, therefore, that we need something besides, or at least in addition to, Yablo's belief-based explanation of class (b) intuition errors.

An example will help to bring out the same point, but in another way. Suppose two empirically well-informed, dialectically skilled philosophers have conflicting concrete-case SE intuitions. For example, suppose that, upon first

[37] In fact, by exercising this ability in the context of pure a priori philosophizing, one's natural-kind intuitions will actually diminish in number by virtue of this ability—for instance, against the background of the hypothesis that all and only water on earth is composed of H_2O, the intuition that necessarily water contains hydrogen; and against the hypothesis that water samples on earth have a highly disuniform composition, the intuition that water could have lacked hydrogen—thereby all but eliminating disagreements of the sort associated with class (a).

considering the twin-earth example, Hilary Putnam had the intuition that the samples of XYZ would not be water whereas Rudolph Carnap, upon hearing the same example, had the contrary intuition.[38] How are we to explain this?

According to Yablo's explanation, Putnam's and Carnap's beliefs—specifically, their class (a) and class (b) beliefs—must at the time in question be relevantly different. But surely this need not be so. Surely we may suppose that at the time in question both men were empirically well-informed and that both believed the prevailing anti-essentialism of the day (in particular, both believed that water $=$ H_2O and that this fact is only contingent). In spite of this, they have opposing intuitions about the twin-earth case. As it stands, Yablo's account does not explain why this occurs.

We are thus in need of something besides (or in addition to) Yablo's belief-based explanation of class (b) intuition errors. Our analysis of what it is to understand a concept might provide the missing pieces. The simplest explanation in this vein would be that either Putnam or Carnap outright *misunderstands* the concept of being water. In some cases, this is no doubt the right explanation, but surely not in the case of Hilary Putnam or Rudolph Carnap: these eminent philosophers of science did not outright misunderstand the everyday concept of being water!

A more plausible explanation is that, in spite of having a full underlying mastery of the concept, Carnap *locally misunderstands* it. That is, he has a local (i.e., in principle temporary) disruption of his otherwise full understanding of the concept. This is analogous to the sense in which a patient would be given a clean bill of health at his annual check-up, despite his having a cold at the time of the check-up—the patient's health is locally (temporarily) disrupted, but his standing health is impeccable.

An example might help to illustrate this phenomenon of local misunderstanding.[39] A student, musing about prime numbers, reports having the intuition that -3 is a prime number, and from this he concludes that in the definition of prime number the domain is not restricted to natural numbers but includes all integers, negative as well as positive. Fortunately, he also has a firm intuition that primes are divisible only by themselves and one, and he

---

[38] We may in addition suppose that Carnap has the further intuition that it is contingent whether water contains hydrogen. In view of our "contingency test" from §6.1, this would serve to show that his initial intuition concerns metaphysical possibility not some kind of epistemic possibility.

[39] This example is based on an exchange that occurred in one of my classes.

has the intuition that every negative integer, $-n$, is the product of itself and the number one and is also the product of n and -1. From this he rightly infers that negative integers cannot be prime. Then, he has the intuition that 3 is prime but that $3 = 1 \times 3$ and $3 = -1 \times -3$. From this and the conclusion he just reached, he then infers that only natural numbers are permitted in the definition of prime. In view of this performance, the student plainly *understood* the concept of being prime all along. What went wrong early on was that he suffered a *local* lapse in his understanding of his concept of a prime number. Using only an a priori process, however, he was able to correct this lapse *on his own*, therein manifesting his underlying mastery of the concept.

Carnap is evidently in a somewhat similar situation. Not only does he have the intuition that, on twin earth, samples of XYZ would be water, he also would (if asked) have the corresponding mistaken categorial intuition that water is a macroscopic stuff (individuated by its macroscopic properties)—as opposed to a compositional stuff (individuated by its composition). But this categorial misunderstanding is (we may suppose) only *local*: it is correctable by Carnap *on his own* (without the aid of any auxiliary empirical information) using the a priori (dialectical) process, specifically, by careful examination of further cases, say, *other* sorts of twin-earth cases (e.g., the diamond/cubic zirconium twin-earth case[40]), and by systematization of the results. That is, left entirely to his own a priori devices, Carnap would in the fullness of time become a scientific essentialist. (So too, given the patient's standing good health, his infection will in the fullness of time be cured by his own bodily resources, without any external intervention.)

Having identified the phenomenon of local misunderstanding, we are now in a position to complete a previously missing step in our dialectic concerning SE. For, in addition to resolving (or dissolving) the apparent conflict among our own intuitions, a full defense of SE requires assuring ourselves that we are not subject to relevant local misunderstandings. The line of reasoning given above shows how we are to go about establishing that there is no such local misunderstanding underlying our pro-SE intuitions.

The general point is that, at least in a large family of cases, the quality of one's understanding of one's concepts holds the key, not only to the correctness

---

[40] The diamond-appearing samples on twin earth are samples of cubic zirconium (the comparatively cheap material from which fake diamonds are commonly made on earth). Would Carnap really have had the intuition that those samples are diamonds?! Certainly not.

of one's intuitions, but also to their incorrectness; furthermore, whether or not that understanding has only lapsed locally is the key to whether or not it is correctable a priori. And this also explains a related, historically important phenomenon. For, presumably, if Carnap has the intuition that in the twin-earth example the samples of XYZ would be water, he would likewise have the intuition that the proposition that puddles of water contain hydrogen is a contingent proposition. In fact, just about everyone prior to the advent of SE had this intuition. The source of this remarkably widespread modal error is the very same local misunderstanding as in the Carnap example.

Local misunderstanding was of course a primary target of Socratic elenchus and is responsible for especially recalcitrant instances of Plato's problem of *doxa*. The phenomenon is ubiquitous in philosophy, and for that reason has significant implications for philosophical method. Amongst other things, before one is entitled to declare a philosophical conclusion final, one must always first assure oneself that one has not been the victim of local misunderstanding. And it should be borne in mind that local misunderstanding can be deeply hidden so that the dialectical recovery is long and hard. But ultimately it is a great boon to philosophy, for it allows us to tolerate colliding intuitions without having to abandon our classical method of intuition-driven philosophical investigation.

The more immediate moral of this discussion is thus that, besides Yablo's class (a) and class (b) belief-based intuitional errors (on the supposition that Yablo is right about these two sources of local error), there are two other classes:

(c) those resulting from local misunderstanding
(d) those resulting from out-and-out misunderstanding (for example, the sort of modal error Burge's arthritis man would be guilty of, namely, intuiting that it is possible to have arthritis in the thigh).

Of course, analogous conclusions hold for the phenomenon of local lapses in the completeness (vs. correctness) of one's understanding of one's concepts.

8. Skeptical accounts of modal error

We have thus far been considering a model of modal error according to which intuitions retain their evidential force, and according to which errors can in principle be identified and eliminated by subjecting our intuitions to the sort of a priori dialectic sketched above. I mentioned at the start of §5 that certain proponents of SE endorse radical accounts of modal error according to which large families of our modal intuitions are systematically unreliable. In the present section, I will assess a typical, but admirably careful and well-articulated, example—namely, Christopher Hill's account.[41] I will show that this account is ultimately inadequate: it attributes intuitions to a great many people that they simply do not have, and, moreover, it would undermine the evidential basis of SE, leaving proponents of SE in an epistemically self-defeating position. It is worth going into some detail on this matter since all radical accounts fall into similar self-defeat.[42]

Hill is interested in a family of intuitions of the form: it is possible for something to be A and not-B (where, for example, A is a common-sense kind and B is a theoretical kind). Such intuitions are generated as follows:

> [T]here is a class H of psychological mechanisms whose members work as follows: where M is any member of H, M takes two concepts as inputs, and then, provided that it is possible to conjoin each of the concepts with the negation of the other without generating an inconsistency, and provided also that there is no available a posteriori reason to think that the two concepts are necessarily coextensive, M delivers an intuition of possibility as an output.[43]

This is supposed to be a perfectly general account of the mechanism responsible for generating possibility intuitions of the indicated form and, as such, is an adequate account only if it correctly predicts (among other things) which metaphysical possibility intuitions one will have (or lack) concerning commonsense kinds and associated microstructural properties upon consideration of the relevant cases.[44]

---

[41] Hill, "Imaginability, Conceivability, Possibility and the Mind—Body Problem", 65–72.

[42] For example, Levin, "Tortuous Dualism" and Wright, "The Conceivability of Naturalism". For more on the topic of epistemic self-defeat, see Bealer, "The Philosophical Limits of Scientific Essentialism" and "The Incoherence of Empiricism".

[43] Hill, "Imaginability, Conceivability, Possibility and the Mind-Body Problem", 76.

[44] There is an obvious problem with Hill's account as stated that can be avoided by revising the account so that 'the two concepts are necessarily coextensive' is replaced with 'necessarily, the first concept's extension includes the second concept's extension'. Let us suppose that at relevant points this repair is in place.

Various proponents of SE reasonably believe that SE extends to certain commonsense kinds even though they have no specific knowledge of the relevant a posteriori facts (e.g., of their chemical composition). For example, suppose that Saul Kripke (or any other scientific essentialist, e.g., Hill himself) believes that SE extends to various kinds of gemstones—say, rubies—even though he has no specific knowledge of the chemical composition of rubies.[45] In this case, surely Kripke would not have the intuition that it is metaphysically possible that there be rubies containing no aluminum oxide (silicon dioxide, aluminum silicate, or some such). Likewise, he would not have the intuition that it is metaphysically possible that there be rubies that *are* composed of aluminum oxide (etc.). He would simply not have such intuitions one way or the other (see note 37 above). But Hill's account entails that, in the envisaged circumstance, Kripke *would* have the intuition that it is metaphysically possible that there be rubies that contain no aluminum oxide (etc.), for (i) there is no inconsistency (or analytic impossibility, as Hill requires in other passages) in the conjunction of the concept of being a ruby and the negation of the concept of containing aluminum oxide and (ii) given that (by hypothesis) Kripke lacks the relevant empirical knowledge concerning the chemical make-up of rubies, he lacks "a posteriori reason to think that the two concepts are necessarily coextensive." Thus, Hill's account predicts the wrong result. (Of course, Kripke would no doubt have intuitions that it is *epistemically* possible, in one or more of the senses catalogued above, that there be rubies containing no aluminum oxide; but according to Hill's account he should be having the corresponding *metaphysical*-possibility intuitions as well.)

Besides wrongly predicting in this way the modal intuitions people will have, Hill's account lands proponents of SE in an epistemically self-defeating position. Let me explain. After spelling out the mechanisms just discussed, Hill goes on to reject the outputs of a certain subcategory of these mechanisms as highly unreliable:

---

[45] LaPorte ("Chemical Kind Term Reference and the Discovery of Essence", *Noûs*, 30 (1996), 122–3) reports that mineralogists do not consider *all* minerals that share the chemical composition of rubies to be rubies. This, however, does not appear to collide with the SE claim that a *necessary* condition of a mineral's being a ruby is that the mineral have the chemical composition that rubies in fact have. If I am wrong about this, just choose another relevant a posteriori necessity.

[W]e are committed to holding that if M is a mechanism that produces conceivability-based intuitions to the effect that a *physical* commonsense kind is separable from its correlated theoretical kind, then that mechanism is highly unreliable.[46]

But how does Hill know that this mechanism is highly unreliable? Because its outputs conflict with SE. For example, such mechanisms would (for people who lack the a posteriori knowledge of the chemical composition of water samples on earth) take as inputs the concept of being composed of water and the concept of containing H_2O and deliver as output the intuition that it is possible for there to be something composed of water but not containing H_2O. But how does he (or we) know that SE is correct (assuming that the mechanism is unreliable)? Herein lies the self-defeat: for the justification of SE relies on intuitions which, according to this account, are of the sort generated by this highly unreliable mechanism. Thus, the account renders SE unjustifiable—and so too Hill's thesis that the intuitions delivered by the mechanism are unreliable.

To see why, note that there are two ways one might come to know that it is metaphysically necessary that water contains H_2O:

(i) One might follow Kripke and Putnam's method and try to establish it *indirectly* by means of concrete-case intuitions such as twin earth intuitions (cf. step one in §6.2).
(ii) One might bypass such concrete-case intuitions and instead try to establish it *directly* by means of a (theoretical) intuition that it is impossible for there to be water that contains no H_2O (or that it is metaphysically necessary that water contains H_2O).

The dilemma for Hill is that his mechanism stands in the way of our coming to know these modal facts by either route.[47]

Consider the second route first. Of course, those who lack the empirical information that water and H_2O are coextensive will lack a posteriori reason to think that the associated concepts are *necessarily* coextensive. So, according to Hill, the mechanism H will lead such people to have the intuition that possibly there is water that contains no H_2O. Given Hill's mechanism, to avoid having this intuition one must come to possess an a posteriori reason to think that the associated concepts are necessarily coextensive. As a first step, one must

---

[46] Hill, "Imaginability, Conceivability, Possibility and the Mind-Body Problem", 78.
[47] Might there be a third route that relies solely on empirical evidence? No. As discussed below, empirical evidence alone cannot ever serve as evidence that something that is so is metaphysically necessary. See "The Philosophical Limits of Scientific Essentialism" for further discussion.

acquire the empirical information that water and H_2O are coextensive. But, on its own, this does not provide our person with a reason to think that *necessarily* water and H_2O are coextensive. As Kant tells us, "Experience tells us, indeed, what is, but not that it must necessarily be so, and not otherwise." No amount of empirical evidence (i.e., phenomenal experience and sense perception) can ever reveal whether something that is so is necessary; on the contrary, if we limit ourselves to empirical evidence, we are in the position of Quinean radical empiricists and, therefore, should conclude that there simply are no modal truths.[48] So, after learning that water and H_2O are coextensive, how does one go on to know that they are necessarily coextensive?

Suppose that Hill answers that, upon learning that water and H_2O are coextensive, one would straight off have the intuition that it is impossible that water and H_2O not be coextensive and that this intuition would provide one with the requisite reason for thinking that they are necessarily coextensive. But this move is not available to Hill. To see why, recall that, according to Hill's mechanism, after acquiring the empirical information but prior to having the intuition that it is impossible that water and H_2O not be coextensive, one would (upon considering the question) have the intuition that it is possible that water and H_2O are *not* coextensive. Given this, consider what would happen if one considered the question whether it is *possible* or, instead, *impossible* for water and H_2O not to be coextensive. By the present supposition, one would have the intuition that this is *impossible*; and, at the same time, according to Hill's mechanism, one would have the intuition that this is *possible*! That is, one would have simultaneous contradictory intuitions. But, in such an irrational state, one certainly would not have a reason to favor the impossibility intuition, and so one will not have acquired the missing reason for thinking that water and H_2O are necessarily coextensive. If there is no alternate justificatory route to SE, skepticism would be inevitable.[49]

---

[48] Admitting testimony as evidence does not help the Quinean out of this problem, for how did our informants move from phenomenal experience and sense perception to knowledge of what is necessary? As Kripke says, "*Philosophical analysis* tells us that they [i.e., propositions of the type in question] cannot be contingently true, so any empirical knowledge of their truth is automatically empirical knowledge that they are necessary. This characterization applies, in particular, to the cases of identity statements and of essence." (*Naming and Necessity*, 159, emphasis added.) And to know that identity statements and statements of essence cannot be contingently true, nonempirical resources are needed.

[49] Alternatively, suppose that Hill were to suggest that, once one has learned that water and H_2O are coextensive, then (upon considering the question) one would straight off have the

Two final points about this horn of the dilemma. We have been focusing on the issue of commonsense kinds. But analogous considerations would hold if instead we were to focus on the question of whether the associated common nouns are rigid designators. Likewise, analogous considerations would hold if we focused on particulars (and their associated proper names), rather than kinds. There simply is no place Hill can get a foothold from which to justify SE.

Thus, the effort to justify SE via the *direct* route (i.e., bypassing concrete-case intuitions) leads to skepticism. (This is no surprise, for when it comes to theoretical issues already rife with controversy, we have no choice but to turn to our concrete-case intuitions.) This brings us to the other horn of the dilemma, on which one attempts to justify SE using concrete-case intuitions. Most of us came to conclude that it is necessary that water is coextensive with H_2O by reflecting on concrete-case intuitions—for example, twin-earth intuitions. (This was Kripke's route although Kripke himself does not frame his cases in terms of "twin earth" but rather in terms of possible worlds.[50]) In all known cases, the relevant concrete-case intuitions either are twin-earth intuitions or can be reworked into twin-earth style intuitions. But, once again, given Hill's account of modal error, this justificatory route leads to failure. For, just as in the case of the direct route, Hill's account implies that these intuitions are highly unreliable.

For instance, Putnam elicited the intuition that it is possible for the world to be macroscopically as it is in actuality even though the watery stuff is not

---

intuition that they are necessarily coextensive and that this intuition would provide one with the requisite reason for thinking that they are necessarily coextensive. In this case, the same conclusion would result. For, on the assumption that Hill's mechanism M is operative, there would surely have to be a corresponding mechanism H' that generates associated contingency intuitions (vs. possibility intuitions): specifically, whenever one considers the question whether this proposition is *necessary or contingent*, H' would generate the intuition that the proposition that water and H_2O are coextensive is contingent. But given our supposition on behalf of Hill, one would also have the intuition that this proposition is *necessary*. That is, one would have simultaneous contradictory intuitions. So, once again, the missing justification of SE is unavailable, and skepticism would result. The same conclusion holds if Hill were to focus on the conditional: if water and H_2O are in fact coextensive, then they are necessarily coextensive. To see why, suppose someone were to intuit the truth of this conditional. Suppose further that the person knows that water and H_2O are in fact coextensive and that the person considers the question whether this proposition (that water and H_2O are coextensive) is necessary or contingent. Then, the person surely would have the intuition that the proposition that they are coextensive is necessary. Given this, the remainder of the argument in the text goes through just as before.

[50] Kripke, *Naming and Necessity*, 131–3.

H_2O (but rather XYZ). Putnam then elicited the intuition that samples of this watery stuff would not be water. Let us focus on the first of these two intuitions, which is a possibility intuition conjunctive in form. Consider the second conjunct, namely, that the watery stuff is not H_2O. According to Hill, the intuition that it is possible that the watery stuff is not H_2O is generated by a "highly unreliable" mechanism. (After all, watery stuff is a commonsense kind; H_2O is a theoretical kind; there is no relevant analytic connection between watery stuff and H_2O; and we are capable of lacking a posteriori evidence regarding the fact that the actual extension of the commonsense kind watery stuff coincides with the actual extension of the theoretical kind H_2O.) Since this intuition is generated by a highly unreliable mechanism, it is not to be trusted. Now, if someone lacking the relevant a posteriori information has the intuition that it is possible that watery stuff not be H_2O, in almost all instances that person would also have the twin-earth intuition (that it is possible for the world to be macroscopically as it is in actuality even though the watery stuff is not H_2O). But if the former intuition is not to be trusted, neither is the twin-earth intuition. Since this evidently generalizes to pretty much all concrete-case intuitions used to justify SE, SE would lack the missing justification, if Hill's account were correct.

Hill might respond that the watery stuff is not the sort of commonsense kind on which his unreliable mechanism operates; on the contrary, it operates only on genuine "natural kinds" (in some preferred sense). But this only takes us in a circle, for how are we to distinguish natural kinds (in this preferred sense) from other kinds? Presumably, the answer resides in the fact that natural kinds, unlike the other commonsense kinds, are subject to SE.[51] Again, however, the very intuitions required for distinguishing those kinds that are subject to SE from those that are not are generated by a "highly unreliable" mechanism on Hill's account.

Hence, Hill is in a dialectically self-defeating position. By condemning as unreliable such a wide range of our modal intuitions, he has left himself with no evidential basis for the SE claims that he employs in his argument. This result generalizes to other skeptical accounts of modal error. (These points hold in spades for philosophers who would reject intuitions altogether, for

---

[51] In this connection, it is important to remember that there is a very wide range of commonsense kinds to which SE does not apply: for example, atmosphere, dirt, fuel, clothing, and so forth.

how do they propose even to refute logical behaviorism, instrumentalism, phenomenalism, inductivism, and all the other philosophical dinosaurs that they no longer believe in?)

Clearly what one needs in order to justify SE is a more forgiving account of modal error according to which the sort of intuitions needed to establish SE are not condemned as erroneous. This is what I have tried to provide. I have catalogued various standard sources of intuitional error—cognitive deficiency, conflation of one's concepts, out-and-out misunderstanding of one's concepts, underdescription and context-sensitivity, and so forth. I then went on to isolate a largely overlooked source of modal error, which skeptical accounts do not accommodate, namely, the local misunderstanding of one's concepts. Fortunately, even when one's understanding of certain pivotal concepts has lapsed locally, one's larger body of intuitions (given suitably good cognitive conditions) would be sufficiently reliable to allow one to ferret out the modal errors resulting from this lapse in understanding by means of dialectic and/or a process of a priori reflection. As we have seen, this source of modal error, and the capacity to overcome it, has wide-ranging implications for philosophical method—including, in particular, its promise for disarming skepticism about the classical method of intuition-driven philosophical investigation itself.

9

Rational Disagreement as a Challenge to Practical Ethics and Moral Theory: An Essay in Moral Epistemology

Robert Audi

Disagreement in ethical matters is often felt to be more pervasive than disagreement in matters of "descriptive" fact. The latter are taken to include scientific hypotheses as well as propositions about what is observable through the unaided senses. Even apart from this sense of contrast, moral disagreement—roughly, disagreement about what is right or wrong—is widely considered to be both common and sufficiently resistant to rational resolution to constitute a challenge to the objectivity of ethics. The exact extent of moral disagreement in one or another population is a question for social psychology and will not be pursued here. But I will distinguish *kinds* of disagreement in a way that is crucial for properly appraising both the extent and the

Parts of this chapter are revised versions of short sections of *The Good in the Right*, ch. 2, and of "The Foundationalism-Coherentism Controversy: Hardened Stereotypes and Overlapping Theories", in Audi, *The Structure of Justification* (Cambridge: Cambridge University Press, 1993), 117–63. The paper benefited from presentation of an earlier version at Western Michigan University, and for helpful comments on parts of earlier versions I thank Roger Crisp, Nathan King, and Quentin Smith.

epistemological significance of moral disagreement. I will argue that certain kinds of disagreement are compatible not only with the objectivity of ethics but also with the self-evidence of a certain kind of moral principle. Much of what I say applies to disagreement in *any* subject-matter domain, but only the moral domain will be examined in detail.

1. Disagreement on common-sense moral principles

Ethical intuitionism is famous for the claim that certain ordinary moral principles are self-evident.[1] A common objection to this intuitionist thesis is that, if the basic principles of ethics are self-evident, there should be much less disagreement on them.[2] There is much to say in reply to this *dissensus objection*, as I shall call it.

First, it is essential to distinguish the self-evident from the obvious. A self-evident proposition is roughly a truth such that any adequate understanding of it meets two conditions: (1) in virtue of having that understanding, one is justified in believing the proposition (that is, has justification for believing it, whether one in fact believes it or not); and (2) if one believes the proposition on the *basis* of that understanding of it, then one knows it.[3] A self-evident proposition need not be obvious, in the sense that its truth is apparent as soon as one considers it with understanding. Unlike many self-evident propositions (such as complicated logical ones), obvious propositions (even when not self-evident) are normally *compelling*—that is, such that comprehendingly considering them at least typically implies believing them "straightaway".[4]

---

[1] W. D. Ross held this in *The Right and the Good* (1930); I have explicated and argued for the view in detail in *The Good in the Right* (Princeton: Princeton University Press, 2004).

[2] A similar objection is voiced and partially answered by J. R. Lucas, in a paper defending Rossian intuitionism against objections by P. F. Strawson and others. See "Ethical Intuitionism II", *Philosophy*, 46/175 (1971), 1–11, at 5.

[3] Two qualifications will help. First, if the belief is based on anything *other* than understanding the proposition, that understanding must still be a *sufficient* basis (in a sense I cannot explicate now). Second, I take the relevant basis relation to preclude a wayward causal chain: the understanding must not produce the belief in certain abnormal ways. (I assume the belief in question *constitutes* knowledge, but there is no need to build this assumption into the account.) Explication and defense of these points is provided in Audi, "Self-Evidence", *Philosophical Perspectives*, 13 (1999).

[4] The association of the self-evident with the obvious has a venerable history. Consider this passage from Aquinas: "Further, those things are said to be self-evident which are known to be

I refer to propositions we might call *intrinsically obvious*—say, that something exists. Many truths commonly called obvious are, by contrast, *circumstantially obvious*; it is, for instance, normally obvious *to* anyone who has the relevant concepts and focuses on an ordinary oak tree in good light that it has branches. It is intrinsic obviousness that has often seemed necessary for self-evidence.

Second, it is important to see that a self-evident proposition can possess only *mediate self-evidence*. This is a relativized notion, but its variable application makes it a useful supplement to the absolute concept defined above. A proposition, *p*, is mediately self-evident for a person, S, provided S's justification for believing it is achievable only on the basis of (and in that sense mediated by) reflection, conceived as requiring a stretch of a kind of conceptual thinking. The sorts of basic moral principles that are candidates for self-evidence—say, the Rossian principle that we have a prima facie obligation to keep our promises—are (initially) understandable by normal adults only on the basis of reflection. These principles may be far from obvious, and we should not expect ready consensus on them, or even a high degree of consensus after some discussion of them between disagreeing parties. Indeed, given the sophistication needed for adequately understanding 'prima facie', some people have difficulty understanding Ross's principles at all, at least initially. Without adequately understanding them, one has at best little reason to assent to them; with such understanding—given that they attribute pervasive duties to us and are to that extent demanding—one may have some reason to resist assenting them.

My third point here is that, at least among philosophers or the skeptically minded, some hesitation in accepting the principles may come from *thinking* of this as requiring endorsement of their self-evidence, which is after all the status intuitionists have prominently claimed for them, or of their necessity, a property that has commonly been taken to be grasped *in* seeing the truth of a self-evident (or any a priori) proposition. These terms may be seen as labels indicating what one must accept in assenting to the principles. But, despite the naturalness of thinking of the self-evident as having these properties, the second-order proposition that they are self-evident need not *also* be self-evident in order for them to have this status themselves. Indeed, such propositions

true as soon as the terms are known, which the Philosopher (1 *Poster.* iii) says is true of the first principles of demonstration. Thus, when what whole is and what part is is known, it is at once recognized that every whole is greater than its part" (*Summa Theologiae*, I, 2, 1, Obj. 2 & Reply). This formulation does not entail that the self-evident is obvious, but the prominent—or at least the uncontroversial—examples in the literature are of obviously true propositions.

should be expected to be at least commonly *not* self-evident. Knowledge of a proposition's epistemic status is typically inferential and requires both epistemic concepts and a different kind of understanding of it from knowledge of a first-order truth expressed (mainly) in ordinary notions.

It may also be clarifying to stress something a critic of intuitionism can easily miss. The self-evidence of a moral principle—say, that promise-keeping is prima facie obligatory—does not imply, and is not taken by intuitionists to imply, that the corresponding singular moral judgments are self-evident. For instance, that *I* should (all things considered) keep a particular promise is not self-evident (it is not a priori, for one thing). It may be *intuitive* (say, intuitively obvious), but its content is not such as (by itself) to ground its justification or truth. Indeed, given how commonly obligations conflict, disagreement and error in such judgments are quite unsurprising, and they give no support to skepticism about the truth or even the self-evidence of the moral principles in question.

1.1. Two types of agreement concerning reasons

Supposing there is disagreement on the truth or the epistemic or modal status of the Rossian principles, there need not be disagreement about the basic *moral force* of the considerations they cite. For instance, whether or not we accept or even consider the common-sense Rossian principle concerning promising, we might, both in our reflection and in regulating our conduct, take our having promised to do something as a basic moral reason to do it. That we do take it so is indicated by our not considering its reason-giving force to derive from some other reason—say, that non-performance would cause suffering. When we reflect and conduct ourselves in the way that manifests taking such considerations as basic reasons, we exhibit what I call *agreement in reasons*. A parallel point holds for other Rossian principles. We might take the fact that driving through a residential neighborhood in the snow might kill a child at play as a basic reason not to do that: that it may do such an injury is reason-giving apart from any further considerations.

There are at least three levels of response to reasons in such matters: accepting reasons, accepting them *as* reasons, and conceptualizing them as reasons. Let us take these in turn.

Suppose I do something simply because I promised to. I am like a Rossian "plain man". In consciously doing the deed on the ground that I promised to, I manifest my acceptance of promising as providing a reason. That I promised to do the deed is my reason for doing it; and I unselfconsciously accept its reason-giving status. I would indeed be surprised if anyone who knew of the promise asked what reason I have to do it. Second, imagine that a student is late for an appointment and I think it was because he lingered to talk, but he tells me that it was owing to an unexpected illness. I may accept this reason as such; this may be a matter of implicitly contrasting his statement—which constitutes his reason in the relevant sense—with other possible explanations of his lateness and construing his statement as (normatively) excusatory. But, since my concern is only whether I should, for instance, admonish him, I do not need to conceptualize (as opposed to merely comprehending) his statement *as* offering a reason. To engage in such thinking, I must *grasp* the concept of a reason, but I need not *exercise* it.

The third case is broadly philosophical. Suppose I consider the general question whether disliking people is a reason not to recommend them for a job. I am now conceptualizing a variable *as* a reason. My focus is in part the property (or status) of being a reason. My concern is largely abstract. At the first two levels, and especially at the first, we can exhibit agreement with others *in* reasons for action—*operative agreement*, as we might call it—without agreeing *on* reasons—for instance, on their epistemic status as basic or derivative.

There are also at least three cases of agreement on reasons. One is agreement on what *constitutes* a reason in the kind of context in question; this requires conceptualizing some element as a reason, and the case divides into at least two kinds. We may (1) agree on a definition of the notion in question or (2) on instances (though instantial and definitional kinds of agreement often *tend* to coincide.) A second case is agreement on some constitutive *principle* expressing reasons. This may or may not require such conceptualization, since it may be formulated only in terms of, say, duties. But it is general in a way agreement in accepting a reason need not be. A third case is agreement on how much *force* a reason has relative to other considerations; this, too, is general but may or may not require such conceptualization.

1.2. Higher-order agreement regarding reasons

Agreement *on* reasons, then, requires a view about reasons or their status; it is coincidence in certain kinds of beliefs *about* reasons. Agreement in reasons, as where, in order to get popsickles, two children each run to the newly arrived ice-cream vendor on a hot summer day, may not even require the concept of a reason, as opposed to a responsiveness to considerations that constitute reasons, such as a way to satisfy desire for something cool and wet. It is a kind of coincidence in such responsiveness. If it does require the concept of a reason, the agent still need have no general view about the status or varieties of reasons. I can be moved to nurse a wound that someone gets from falling from a bicycle, even if I do not think of the situation as giving me a reason to do it. Nor need I think of it that way in order to answer 'Why are you late?' by citing the sufferer's need for help. I may in fact consider this a good answer, even apart from subsuming the notion of need here under that of a reason for action. I am, to be sure, in a position to appreciate, in an intellectual way, the reason I had and to begin to appraise its force. But no such intellectual reflection is required for responsiveness to such a reason.

Moreover, someone who is like me in behavioral and even inferential responsiveness to reasons may have, or be disposed to offer, a quite different intellectual account of any given reason to which we are similarly sensitive. In elemental cases that present us with moral reasons for action, Kantians and utilitarians may respond in similar ways, each judging that there is, say, an obligation to give a terminally ill patient a true diagnosis, despite their differing accounts of the basis of the obligation. Intuitionism builds on this similarity in responsiveness to reasons, and its appeal is in part due to the sense that, at the level of agreement in reasons, thoughtful people[5] tend to have the makings of a common starting point.

Agreement on reasons seems closely connected with intuitive induction as Ross, Broad, and others saw it. The conceptual progression they portray might in some cases have the following three stages. To see this, consider the grasp of an individual ground as supporting a kind of act, say of promising as calling for doing the promised deed. This grasp is, as manifested in a sense of duty to do the promised deed, a recognition of a reason. As manifested in realizing the

---

[5] One might perhaps say 'civilized' rather than 'thoughtful'. It might be objected, however, that we have no way to identify people as civilized apart from their accepting certain moral standards. I would agree that the notion is vague, but I have in mind mainly complexity of life forms, especially including institutions such as universities and orderly government, activities like the creation of literature and the other arts, and a high level of literacy. Civilized people, conceived as participating in such forms of life, can surely be identified without presupposing their agreement on specific moral standards and probably with at most minimal presuppositions about their moral standards or lack thereof. Even supposing, however, that certain kinds of tribal societies are not civilized in the sense in question, *within* those societies there may still be adherence to all or most of the principles Ross articulated. It is toward *outgroups* of one kind or another that history has seen the grossest departures from those principles.

truth that on the basis of the promise one ought to do the deed, it is at least a minimal recognition of a reason as such—as something that renders one obligated to act. Third, in the richest of the three cases, the grasp of a reason manifests itself in believing the principle that promising always gives rise to prima facie duties. This belief represents one kind of a generalization of the recognition of a reason.

As the examples illustrate, a *commitment* to a view *about* reasons may be implied in taking a consideration *as* a reason. But commitments are not always realized, and this kind may not even tend to be realized unless abstract or philosophical questions arise for the agent. Much moral practice raises no such questions. If there is the kind of wide (though certainly not unlimited) agreement in moral practice that I think there is—a kind of operational as opposed to doctrinal agreement—then the most important kind of consensus needed for the theoretical success of intuitionism as a moral theory is in place.

To be sure, success as a theory is not required for the truth or even the self-evidence of the basic moral principles in question. But it is certainly arguable that the truth and non-inferential justifiability of the relevant principles explains, or at least comes closer to explaining than any competing hypothesis, the high degree of consensus among people in wide segments of their everyday moral practice.[6] Non-inferential justifiability is particularly important here: by contrast with, for instance, first-order principles endorsed by utilitarianism, Kantianism, and divine-command approaches, Rossian principles do not stand in need of justification by derivation from standards or wider principles viewed as grounded independently of them. If, however, the Rossian principles are not only non-inferentially justifiable but also true, then disconfirmation is (other things equal) less likely to occur and more likely to be defeated if it does.

---

[6] This is not to suggest that there cannot be as much consensus on what is justifiable only inferentially. But the only plausible candidates for premises that yield justification are not only consistent with the truth of the Rossian ones but difficult to justify or even understand apart from the Rossian ones—something argued in *The Good in the Right*, ch. 3. Compare Judith Jarvis Thomson's distinction between explanatory and object-level moral judgments, e.g. between the judgment that capital punishment is wrong because it is intentional killing of someone who poses no threat, and the judgment that capital punishment is wrong. See *The Realm of Rights* (Cambridge, MA: Harvard University Press, 1990), 30. I suspect that some resistance to Rossian intuitionism may derive from insufficiently detaching his object-level principles of prima facie duty from his explanatory gloss—prominent in his introduction of the basic duties—construing each as having a particular ground.

2. The wider problem posed by rational disagreement

One might accept most of Section 1 and still hold that dissensus threatens the idea that moral questions admit of objective answers. In morally appraising specific actions, as well as in considering moral principles, conscientious rational persons who find others disagreeing with them often wonder who is right. Suppose we think that, for a belief on some important moral matter, a person who disagrees with us is as rational and generally informed as we. Should we still adhere to our view?

2.1. The epistemic role of consensus

In a critical study of my position, Roger Crisp is inclined toward a negative answer, applicable not only to Rossian principles but also to singular moral judgments. He particularly emphasizes what he calls Sidgwick's consensus condition.[7] In Sidgwick's words:

[d]enial by another of a proposition that I have affirmed has a tendency to impair my confidence . . . the absence of . . . disagreement must remain an indispensable negative condition of the certainty of our beliefs . . . if I have no more reason to suspect error in the other mind than in my own, reflective comparison between the two judgments necessarily reduces me temporarily to a state of neutrality. [*Methods of Ethics,* 7th edn., 1907]

With this in view, Crisp poses a problem for any objectivist moral epistemology:

R (who believes that p) comes across another thinker, S, who asserts not-p. Immediately, according to the consensus condition, this should impair her confidence in p. But . . . unless S's epistemic state is significantly faulty in one or other of these ways, R may well feel that her trust in p has been dented.

In Crisp's example, R is supposed to be justified in believing that S is in roughly as good an epistemic state as R. Should R feel reduced trust here? One difficulty with this case is that confidence is a psychological notion whose bearing on justification is not made clear. The strength of our confidence that *p* may vary quite independently of our degree of justification for believing it. Furthermore, Crisp is thinking of self-evident propositions, which are only

---

[7] See Roger Crisp, "Intuitionism and Disagreement", in Mark Timmons, John Greco, and Al Mele (eds.), *Rationality and the Good* (Oxford: Oxford University Press, 2007). References to this paper are hereafter included parenthetically in the text.

one kind I hold to be (often) intuitively knowable. Even when they are known, however, they need not be believed with "certainty". There are also degrees of justification; hence justification for believing one might not be of the high degree appropriate to certainty.

Crisp raises a related problem, pertinent to any kind of proposition and not undermined by these clarifications. "R . . . has merely to ask herself whether it is possible that another person, in as epistemically good a state as she is, might reasonably hold not-p. If it is, then she should suspend judgement on p." Whatever he thinks Sidgwick may have been committed to saying about this problem for intuitionism, Crisp says that it "rests on a dim view of human epistemic capacities" (p. 33). From his example concerning disagreement about what kind of bird is before two people, it is clear that he takes an epistemically good "state" to include things like visual acuity and favorableness of the light. This notion encompasses a huge number of variables. Background beliefs are included, as are inferential capacities, reliability of memory, and conceptual sophistication. He might grant, then, that we are commonly not justified in believing that someone else is in as good an epistemic position as we.

More important, the fact that it seems very clear to me that (for example) there is a robin before me is some reason to take a person who disagrees *not* to be in as good a position to tell. It might seem that, if we could test every epistemically relevant variable, we might instantiate the unfortunate position Crisp describes. But suppose we conscientiously test every variable we can conceive. Doing so (for the purpose in question) presupposes that we trust our own beliefs enough to make a reasonable comparison of someone else's grounds with our own, now checked out. You must, for instance, ascertain that I discern someone's hurt feelings as clearly as you, if my disagreement is to force you to doubt your judgment that an apology is owed for having hurt them. Now, however, if you finally see, as you list your freshly scrutinized grounds, that I cannot be brought to agree that she has been hurt, you may have *better* reason to think you missed some relevant difference between us than to think you should suspend judgment on the disputed proposition.

In the very act of conscientiously comparing my epistemic situation with yours, you must, in a certain way, trust *your* judgment along the way if you are thereby to arrive at a conclusion you may justifiedly hold. In particular, you must anchor your judgment that I am in a good epistemic position by presupposing some judgments of yours as to, say, whether I am aware of certain elementary perceptible facts. You need not *always* favor your judgment over mine when we disagree, but the confidence you have that I am in a good epistemic position must come from relying on *your* epistemic position, and the strength of *that* position will be confirmed by the entire exercise of reconsidering both positions. Dogmatism is undermined; conviction need not be.

Suppose, however, that conviction is undermined. There are two quite different cases here. We have been considering the one most commonly discussed: suspended judgment together with a kind of cautionary distancing of oneself from the proposition in question. It is also possible to pass from belief to *acceptance*—for instance, where one withholds belief that *p* but resolves to act on *p* unless some good reason not to do so emerges. Acceptance of the non-doxastic kind I have in mind can take various forms. I am thinking of the kinds of cases in which one accepts a scientific hypothesis as both plausible and a good basis for investigation or accepts a person's excuse as a basis for continuing a relationship. Unlike accepting for the sake of argument, this kind is incompatible with *disbelieving p*; but it does not require distancing oneself from *p* in the way suspension of judgment commonly does, and indeed one can pass from belief to acceptance in a gradual and unreflective way that does not require suspension of judgment. Far more could be said about acceptance,[8] but it is important to see that it can be a response to a sense of rational disagreement that can have a lesser impact on one's intellectual and practical life than suspension of judgment as commonly conceived.

2.2. The sources of disagreement and the resources of intuitionism

As stressed above, the claim (common to at least the most prominent versions of intuitionism) that some moral principles are self-evident does not entail their being *obvious*. They need not even be psychologically compelling; considering them with adequate understanding commonly does not entail believing them. Indeed, if one holds background beliefs, or accepts theories, that call for rejecting a self-evident proposition, disbelief may be possible in this same case. It is not always clear, however, that denying a proposition entails disbelieving it, as I think the case of self-deception (among others)

---

[8] I have discussed acceptance in some detail, and referred to various works treating it, in "Doxastic Voluntarism and the Ethics of Belief", *Facta Philosophica*, 1/1 (1999), 87–109, and "The A Priori Authority of Testimony", *Philosophical Issues*, 14 (2004), 18–34.

confirms.[9] Our inferential behavior and our other beliefs are also important for determining what we believe. Let me illustrate this point with respect to the distinction between agreement *on* reasons and agreement *in* reasons.

Suppose a Rossian promissory principle is self-evident and that, correspondingly, it is self-evident that promising to A entails having some reason to A. There is disagreement on both points.[10] But someone who denies that promising to A entails a reason to A may regularly take the making of a *particular* promise to imply such a reason. Might such a person still accept as true someone's denial of having a reason to A, after having promised to A? Suppose so. We would wonder why the denial occurs. Holding a theory requiring this denial is one possible explanation; another—compatible with this one—is an inadequate understanding of some relevant concept, such as that of *having some reason*. This concept embodies defeasibility, which is no easy notion to grasp.

These points are among those that make clear how the kind of self-evidence required by (rationalist) ethical intuitionism is compatible with theoretical and other kinds of opposition to the view. But theoretical opposition applies mainly to disagreement *on* reasons and need not be manifested in disagreement *in* them. This is where Crisp raises further doubts. He grants that there is sufficient consensus on such self-regarding normative principles as Pain ("Non-deserved suffering of any agent that would be caused in or by some action of that agent counts (though not always decisively), for that agent, against the performance of that action by that agent") to provide a sound basis for intuitionism. But he asks, "How should R proceed in philosophy? And how should she live?" (p. 12). In answering, he says, "Once she realizes that these principles fail to meet the consensus condition, it will become clear to her that they have no claim to self-evidence, to being objects of knowledge, or to any directly justified role in her deliberation" (p. 14). Several points are in order.

(1) For reasons already offered, the proposed consensus condition is too strong. But suppose the condition is plausible enough to require suspending judgment on whether Rossian moral principles are self-evident. (2) It does

---

[9] This point is defended in some of my papers on self-deception, esp. "Self-Deception, Rationalization, and Reasons for Acting", in Brian McLaughlin and Amelie Rorty (eds.), *Perspectives on Self-Deception* (Berkeley and Los Angeles: University of California Press, 1988).

[10] The main issue here is the particularlism/generalism contrast; my generalist view is defended, most recently, in "Ethical Generality and Moral Judgment", in James Dreier (ed.), *Contemporary Debates in Ethical Theory* (Oxford: Blackwell, 2006).

not follow from this supposition that the principles have no claim to being *known*; both empirical and certain kinds of a priori principles can be known without being self-evident. (3) It also does not follow that the principles have no non-derivatively justified role in deliberation, say that they must be capable of being backed up by utilitarian or Kantian considerations. Non-inferential justification for believing them would suffice for the kind of defeasible role my intuitionism requires.

3. Epistemic parity and intellectual humility

We gain clarity concerning the implications of disagreement in moral matters if we frame the problem in the light of a conception of *epistemic parity*. The basic idea is this: *A* and *B* are epistemically on a par with respect to a claim provided they are (1) equally rational and (2) equally informed on facts relevant to that claim. In principle, two people could also be epistemically on a par with respect to a general subject matter, such as ethics; but what this would require can be seen by generalizing on the notion as characterized by (1) and (2). When both conditions are satisfied, we may speak of *full* epistemic parity; when only one is satisfied or either is only partially satisfied, we may speak of *partial* epistemic parity; and the latter notion admits of degrees. The case of disagreement on a single proposition will be my focus, and I will begin with an important question.

Can we ever know or even reasonably believe that someone is fully on a par with us *given* a persisting, entrenched disagreement on a matter we have discussed? Let us consider both rationality and information conditions.

Rationality conditions are both multifarious and subtle. One variable is competence in deductive and inductive reasoning. Another is responsiveness to experience, theoretical and practical. A person whose beliefs do not appropriately reflect sensory experience or whose desires do not appropriately reflect pain and pleasure is not rational.[11] A subtle aspect of this matter is what we might call *evidential proportionality*: the extent of fit between one's degree of evidence for a belief and the degree of one's confidence in holding it. More subtle still is insight—for instance, seeing what certain kinds of things are and knowing why certain kinds of events, particularly actions, occur. A great deal

---

[11] This point is defended in Audi, *Architecture of Reason* (Oxford: Oxford University Press, 2001).

could be said to explicate these conditions; but that some such conditions are important for rationality is all I need to claim. The conditions are difficult to clarify, and it may be hard to determine whether they are satisfied; but that favors my overall view, as will soon be apparent.

Information conditions on rationality might seem easy to characterize: they may seem to be just a matter of knowledge of certain facts. But supposing this is so, the issue is how to identify *relevant* facts. What determines relevance of information? Moreover, information includes false propositions, which are admissible in our comparison when they are appropriately evidenced. A further problem is how we should deal with imperfect information? Still another problem is how we know what *non-propositional* evidence someone has, say from sensory experience or memory impressions. Our access to others' total evidence is at best indirect, difficult, and incomplete. Plainly, it may often be difficult or, in practice, impossible, to know or even to have good evidence for thinking that someone is in fact epistemically on a par with one concerning a given issue.

Consider assisted suicide as a case in point. Leave rationality aside and consider just the parity-of-information problem. Is the economic benefit of legalizing the practice relevant? And, if so, how much benefit is needed to constitute a good reason for legalization? What of its influence on treatment? Might the poor be subject to pressure to request assisted suicide because they are draining scarce resources? How are we to weigh religious objections to the practice? May a liberal society take into account that many deeply disapprove of the practice, or would liberal neutrality toward religion call on policy-makers and even ordinary citizens to set this variable aside?

Suppose we could get agreement on all these questions. If disagreement on the morality of legalization persisted, we might attribute it to differences in rationality. For, on the plausible assumption that normative truths are consequential on non-normative factual truths, agreement on the latter should lead rational persons to agree on the former, at least on the (rather large) assumption that the consequentiality relations are not beyond their comprehension and that all these non-normative truths are expressed by the shared, relevant information. To be sure, if normative *beliefs* are determined by (or at least implied by) non-normative beliefs expressing the relevant facts, there would *be* no disagreement in this idealized case. But positing even an implication relation here is plausible only for rational persons, and the implication is at least not likely to hold where deficiencies in rationality affect normative thinking.[12]

Given the difficulty of gaining evidence for full epistemic parity, and given the increase in justification for one's view that is likely to come from pursuing the question, there is no good reason to take dissensus to imply lack of objectivity or even of justification, concerning singular moral judgments. Moreover, lack of consensus itself may be due to differences in either the information or the rationality of disputants. Mere lack of consensus is not necessarily disturbing. Minor errors in reasoning are common, and access to information is typically quite variable, both between persons and for a given person over time. Indeed, where there is no reason to expect something close to full epistemic parity, a good deal of dissensus is to be expected. Reduced confidence may also be a quite sufficient response to plausible dissensus; suspension of judgment may be either unreasonable or at least rationally discretionary.[13]

This conclusion should not be allowed to lead to complacency. The difficulty of determining that someone else is epistemically (at least) on a par with oneself does not imply that we never have justification for thinking it or that we can be easily justified in believing ourselves superior. Particularly in important matters, self-scrutiny is a condition for reasonably maintaining a belief when, as is not uncommon, we think that there is a significant probability that a disputant has full parity with ourselves. The problem is intensified as the number of disputants rises (though not in any simple proportion to their numbers), but it is still quite possible for a person to retain the threatened belief quite rationally. It may be, for instance, that only one of the large

[12] That there is the kind of consequentiality relation mentioned in the text implies the ontic objectivity of moral predications, in the sense that their truth is not dependent on anyone's believing it. This is compatible with certain dispositions to believe it being necessary conditions for its truth: for that truth may be correlated nomically with perception of the relevant facts on the part of rational persons.

[13] My position in this chapter may be consistent with Richard Foley's view that "Insofar as it is reasonable to regard us as exact epistemic peers with respect to the issue, it is reasonable for me to withhold judgment until I understand how one or both of us have gone wrong" (*Intellectual Trust in Ourselves and Others* (Cambridge: Cambridge University Press, 2001), 111). In my view, it is unlikely that we *can* reasonably believe this on the kinds of issues on which there is persisting disagreement after a serious effort at communication on the issue. Moreover, I would be inclined to hold that reduced (or at least minimal) confidence together with continued self-scrutiny might be rational even if we can reasonably believe the parity is exact.

number of disputants has an independent judgment or all may share a mode of reasoning, or an item of information, that is unsound.

Self-scrutiny may, then, leave our initial beliefs in place; but, if it is reasonable for us not to suspend judgment, self-scrutiny and comparison with others may at least reduce our confidence of their truth and our willingness to stake a great deal on them. Even where it is not reasonable to suspend judgment, however, reason may require reduced confidence or, perhaps, passing from belief to a kind of acceptance. Reduced confidence, combined with intellectual vigilance, may permit rational retention of beliefs that skeptics would have us relinquish. Reduced confidence may occur even as self-trust as a general attitude is strengthened by self-scrutiny; but self-trust should not be inflated into skepticism about others' credibility, any more than it should be enervated by disagreement with plausible disputants.[14]

4. Dogmatism

So far, I have made a case for intellectual humility in moral matters but not for moral skepticism. My view implies that dogmatism is to be resisted. Just what dogmatism is, however, is often left unclear. Some account should be given of it to enable us to reject it without losing conviction where we are entitled to have it. The problem is particularly important for ethical intuitionism. As most often understood, it is a foundationalist view and hence open to the charge of dogmatism, often taken to apply to any view that affirms our knowing (or at least being capable of knowing) various propositions for which we can offer no argument.

The problem might be expressed as follows: if one can have knowledge or justified belief without being able to show that one does, and even without having a premise from which to derive the proposition in question, then the way is open to claim just about anything one likes, defending it by cavalierly noting that one can be justified without being able to show that one is (or even to show that p). This kind of defense is often rightly seen to be dogmatic. But

---

[14] For a related treatment of rational disagreement which largely supports mine here, see Thomas Kelly, "The Epistemic Significance of Disagreement", *Oxford Studies in Epistemology*, vol 1. (Oxford: Oxford University Press), 167–96. Another pertinent paper, focusing mainly on moral disagreement, is Sarah McGrath, "Moral Disagreement" (forthcoming).

what is dogmatism? There have apparently been few detailed discussions of it in recent epistemological literature.[15]

4.1. Dogmatism and similar attitudes

I have been referring to dogmatism as an epistemological attitude or stance, not as a trait of personality. I am mainly interested in what it is to hold a belief dogmatically. This is probably the basic notion, in any case: a general dogmatic attitude, like the personality trait of dogmatism, is surely in some way a matter of having or tending to have dogmatically held *beliefs*.[16] Moral beliefs are my chief concern, but dogmatism is subject-matter neutral, and I will thus often speak about it in general terms.

It is instructive to start with some contrasts. Dogmatism in relation to a belief is not equivalent to stubbornness in holding it; for, even where a dogmatically held belief cannot be easily given up, one could be stubborn in holding a belief simply from attachment to it, and without the required disposition to defend it or regard it as better grounded than alternatives. For similar reasons, psychological certainty in holding a belief does not entail dogmatism. Suppose one is both psychologically certain of a simple logical truth *and* disposed to reject denials of it with confidence and to suspect even well-developed arguments against it as sophistical. This does not entail being dogmatic. The content of the relevant belief is important: even moderate insistence on a reasonably disputed matter may bespeak dogmatism; stubborn adherence to the self-evident need not. An attitude that would be dogmatic in holding one belief may not be so in holding another.

Dogmatic people are often closed-minded, and dogmatically held beliefs are often closed-mindedly maintained; but a belief held closed-mindedly need not be held dogmatically: it may be maintained with a guilty realization that emotionally one simply cannot stand to listen to challenges of it, and with an awareness that it might be mistaken. Moreover, although people who hold beliefs dogmatically are often intellectually pugnacious in

---

[15] One exception is the discussion by David Shatz in "Foundationalism, Coherentism, and the Levels Gambit", *Synthese*, 55/1 (1983).

[16] This suggestion may be controversial: an epistemic virtue theorist might argue that the trait is most basic and colors the attitude, and that these together are the basis for classifying beliefs as held dogmatically or otherwise. Most of my points will be neutral with respect to this priority issue.

defending them, such pugnacity is not sufficient for dogmatism. Intellectual pugnacity is consistent with a keen awareness that one might be mistaken, and it may be accompanied by open-minded argumentation for one's view. Nor need a dogmatically held belief generate such pugnacity; I might be indisposed to argue for my beliefs, whether from confidence that I know or from temperament, and my dogmatism might surface only when I am challenged.

4.2. A second-order element in dogmatism

One element all of these possible conceptions of dogmatism have in common is lack of a second-order component. But that component may well be necessary for a dogmatic attitude, at least of the full-blooded kind. Typically, a dogmatically held belief is maintained with a conviction (often unjustified) to the effect that one is right—say, that one knows, is properly certain, or can just see the truth of p. Such a second-order belief is not, however, sufficient for a dogmatic attitude. This is shown by certain cases of believing simple logical truths: these can be held both with such a second-order belief and in the stubborn way typical of a dogmatic attitude, yet not thereby bespeak a dogmatic attitude. It might be held that in this case they would at least be *held dogmatically*; but if the imagined tenacity is toward, say, the principle that if $a = b$, and $b = c$, then $a = c$, one could not properly call the attitude dogmatic. We might better speak of maintaining the belief steadfastly rather than dogmatically.

It might be argued, however, that, even if the only examples of dogmatism so far illustrated are the second-order ones, there are still two kinds of dogmatism: first- and second-order. It may be enough, for instance, that one be *disposed* to have a certain belief, usually an unwarrantedly positive one, about the status of one's belief that p. Imagine that Bill thinks that Mozart is a far greater composer than Haydn, asserts it without giving any argument, and brushes aside arguments to the contrary. If he does not believe, but is disposed to believe on considering the matter, that his belief is, say, obviously correct, then he may qualify as dogmatically holding it. Here, then, there is no actual second-order attitude, but only a disposition to form one upon considering the status of one's belief. I grant that this kind of first-order pattern may qualify as dogmatism; but the account of it remains a second-order one, and it still seems that the other first-order cases we have considered, such as mere stubbornness in believing, are not cases of dogmatism. They may exhibit believing dogmatically, but that does not entail dogmatism as an epistemic attitude or trait of character, any more than doing something lovingly entails a loving attitude, or being a loving person. It appears, then, that at least the clear cases of dogmatically holding beliefs imply either second-order attitudes or certain dispositions to form them.

4.3. Four dimensions of dogmatism

There may be no simple, illuminating way to characterize dogmatism with respect to a belief that p; but, if there is, the following elements should be reflected at least as typical conditions: (1) confidence that p, and significantly greater confidence than one's evidence or grounds warrant; (2) unjustified resistance to taking plausible objections seriously when they are intelligibly posed to one and understood; (3) a willingness, or at least a tendency, to assert p flat out even in the presence of presumptive reasons to question it, including simply the conflicting views of one or more persons whom S sees or should see to be competent concerning the subject matter; and (4) a (second-order) belief, or disposition to believe, that one's belief is clearly true (or certainly true). Note, however, that (i) excessive confidence can come from mere foolhardiness and can be quite unstable; (ii) resistance to plausible objections may be due to intellectual laziness; (iii) a tendency to assert something flat out can derive from mere downrightness of personality; and (iv) a belief that one is right might arise not from dogmatism but merely from conceit, intellectual mistake (such as a facile anti-skepticism), or sheer error. Notice also that the notion of dogmatism is not just psychological, but also epistemic.

Of the four elements highly characteristic of dogmatism, the last may have the best claim to be an unqualifiedly necessary condition, and perhaps one or more of the others is necessary. The four are probably jointly sufficient; but this is not self-evident, and I certainly doubt that we can find any simple condition that is non-trivially sufficient, such as believing that one knows, or is justified in believing, p (which one does believe), while also believing one has no supporting reason for p.[17] This condition is not sufficient because it could stem from a certain view of knowledge and reasons—say, a view on which one never has reasons (as opposed to a basis) for believing simple self-evident

---

[17] Shatz, "Foundationalism, Coherentism, and the Levels Gambit", 107, attributes a similar suggestion to me (from correspondence), and it is appropriate to suggest here why I do not mean to endorse it.

propositions. The condition also seems insufficient because it could be satisfied by a person who lacks the first three of the typical conditions just specified.

Let us work with the full-blooded conception of a dogmatically held belief summarized by conditions (1)–(4). What, then, may we say about the common charge that ethical intuitionism is dogmatic, in a sense implying that it invites proponents to hold certain beliefs dogmatically? This charge has been leveled on a number of occasions against the underlying foundationalism of the view in most forms,[18] and some plausible replies have been framed.[19] The dogmatism charge is more likely to seem cogent if intuitionism is conceived as answering the dialectical regress problem (as, for foundationalism itself, it has often been taken to do[20]). For in this case a (doxastic) stopping place in the regress generated by 'How do you know that *p*?' will coincide with the assertion of a second-order belief, such as that I know that *q*—for example, that there is a window before me; and, since knowledge claims (claims *to know*, as opposed to assertions of what *is* known) are commonly justifiable by evidence, flatly stopping the regress in this way will seem dogmatic. Even if such a claim is itself justified by citing a non-doxastic basis, such as my visual experience of a window, one is still asserting the existence of this state of affairs and hence apparently expressing knowledge: making what seems a tacit claim *to* it, though not actually claiming to *have* it.

4.4. Does ethical intuitionism invite dogmatism?

In ethics perhaps more than in any other realm of discourse, there may be a special need to avoid dogmatism. For ethical disagreements often *must* be

---

[18] The dogmatism charge has been brought by, e.g., Bruce Aune in *Knowledge, Mind and Nature* (New York: Random House, 1967), 41–3, and, by implication, by James Cornman and Keith Lehrer in *Philosophical Problems and Arguments* (2nd edn.; New York: Macmillan, 1974), 60–1. William P. Alston goes so far as to say: "It is the aversion to dogmatism, to the apparent arbitrariness of putative foundations, that leads many philosophers to embrace some form of coherence or contextualist theory . . . " ("Two Types of Foundationalism", *Journal of Philosophy* (1976), 182–3). For recent work supporting the dogmatism charge against ethical intuitionism, see Walter Sinnott-Armstrong, "Moral Relativity and Intuitionism", *Philosophical Issues*, 12: 305–28, and "Reflections on Reflection in Robert Audi's Moral Intuitionism", in Timmons, Greco, and Mele (eds.), *Rationality and the Good*. I reply in part to him in "Reason and Intuition in Thought and Action", in ibid.

[19] See Alston, "Two Types of Foundationalism", for a reply (which supports mine) to the dogmatism charge.

[20] See, e.g., Anthony Quinton, *The Nature of Things* (London, 1973), p. 119. Quinton, it is interesting to note, is sympathetic to the kind of modest foundationalism that would serve as an answer to the problem in his formulation.

resolved, if only by the passing of a law or by one party's prevailing over the other in action. Since intuitionism typically embraces a foundationalist epistemology, we should pay special attention to two different ways in which the regress of justification can be viewed and can be dealt with in practice if it looms up during ethical argument. The first is the difficulty of answering—say, in response to repeated challenges from a skeptic—questions about how one knows, or about what justifies one. This is what I have called *the dialectical form of the regress problem*.[21]

By contrast, consider either the entire body of a person's apparent knowledge, as Aristotle seems to have done,[22] or a representative item of apparent knowledge, say my belief that there is snow outside, and ask on what this apparent knowledge is grounded (or based) and whether, if it is grounded on some further belief, *all* our knowledge or justified belief could be so grounded. This is a structural question about knowledge, not a request for a verbal response in defense of a claim to it. No dialectic need even be imagined; we are considering a person's overall knowledge, or some presumably representative item of it, and asking how that body of knowledge is structured or how that item of knowledge is grounded. Again we get a regress problem: how to specify my grounds without vicious circularity or regress or, on the other hand, stopping with a belief that does not constitute knowledge (or is not justified), or seems only capriciously regarded as knowledge. Call this search for appropriate grounds of knowledge *the structural form of the regress problem*.

---

[21] Chisholm seems to raise the problem in this way when he says, "If we try Socratically to formulate our justification for any particular claim to know ('My justification for thinking that I know that A is the fact that B'), and if we are relentless in our inquiry ('and my justification for thinking that I know that B is the fact that C'), we will arrive, sooner or later, at a kind of stopping place ('but my justification for thinking that I know that N is simply the fact that N'). An example of N might be the fact that I seem to remember having been here before or that something now looks blue to me" (*Theory of Knowledge*, 1966, 2); cf. 2nd edn., 1977, esp. 19–20. In these and other passages Chisholm seems to be thinking of the regress problem dialectically and taking a foundational belief to be second order. To be sure, he is talking about justification of any "claim to know"; but this and similar locutions—such as "knowledge claim", have often been taken to apply to expressions of first-order knowledge, as where one says that it is raining, on the basis of perceptions that one would normally take to yield knowledge that it is.

[22] See *Posterior Analytics*, bk 3. Having opened bk. 1 with the statement that "All instruction given or received by way of argument proceeds from pre-existent knowledge" (71^a1–2), and thereby established a concern with the structure and presuppositions of knowledge, he formulated the regress argument as a response to the question of what is required for the existence of (what he called scientific) knowledge (72^b4–24). (The translation is by W. D. Ross.)

If we raise the regress problem in the structural form, there is much less temptation to consider ethical intuitionism dogmatic. For there is no presumption that, with respect to anything I know, I non-inferentially know that I know it (and similarly for justification). Granted, on the assumption that by and large I am entitled, without offering evidence, to assert what I directly know, it may seem that even moderate foundationalism justifies me in holding—and expressing—beliefs dogmatically. But this is a mistake: there is considerable difference between what I non-inferentially know or justifiably believe and what I may warrantedly *assert* without evidence. It is, for instance, apparently consistent with knowing that p, say that there is music playing, that I have some reason to doubt that p; I might certainly have reason to think that others doubt it and that they should not be spoken to as if their objections could not matter. Thus, I might know, through my own good hearing, that p, yet be unwarranted in saying that I know it, and warranted, with only moderate confidence, even in saying that I believe it. Here 'I believe it' would *express*, but not *claim*, my knowledge; 'I know it' explicitly claims knowledge and normally implies that I have justification for beliefs about my objective grounds, not just about my own cognitive and perceptual state.

Nothing said here implies that one *cannot* be justified in believing what one holds dogmatically. That one's attitude *in* holding p is not justified does not imply that one's holding p is itself not justified. It might be possible, for all I have said, that in certain cases one might even be justified, overall, in taking a dogmatic attitude toward certain propositions. This will depend on, among other things, the plausibility of the proposition in question and the level of justification one has for believing that one is right. But, typically, dogmatic attitudes are not justified, and my intuitionist theory, far from implying otherwise, can readily explain this.

Furthermore, once the pervasive defeasibility of our justification is appreciated and seen to be consistent with intuitionism, then, even if one does think that one may assert the propositions in question without offering evidence, one will not take the attitudes or other stances that are required for holding a belief dogmatically. As the example of my belief about the music illustrates, most of the time one is likely to be open to counterargument and may indeed tend to be no more confident than one's grounds warrant. To be sure, fallibilism alone, even when grounded in a proper appreciation of defeasibility, does not preclude dogmatism regarding at least many of one's beliefs. But it helps in fostering humility, and it is a natural for moderate intuitionists to hold a fallibilistic outlook on their beliefs, especially their empirical beliefs, and to bear it in mind in framing an overall conception of human experience.

Rational disagreement may have many sources. If it should occur between persons who are in a situation of full epistemic parity relative to the proposition at issue, then its persisting through a serious attempt to secure agreement is a reason to believe that neither is justified. If we do justifiedly think we are in such a situation, we may have no rational alternative other than suspending judgment or engaging in self-scrutiny regarding our grounds for holding the belief and at least reducing our confidence to the minimum consistent with retaining it. We have seen, however, that it is difficult for one to amass evidence supporting full epistemic parity with others; this is particularly so because our better access to our own grounds for belief tends to enable us to emerge from a careful comparison of our epistemic situation with that of our disputant with better justification than we initially had for holding the belief in question. Often, of course, we do agree with others. Many who draw skeptical conclusions from the frequency of dissensus do not compare it with the frequency and wide scope of agreement. If there is as much spontaneous, unmanipulated agreement as there appears to be, particularly if, in normative matters, we consider agreement *in* rather than *on* reasons, this is some support for the objectivity of the relevant subject matter and the justification of the shared beliefs concerning it.

Our discussion shows not only that the epistemological significance of disagreement must be assessed in relation to the capacities and information of the disputants; it also focuses attention on different kinds of disagreement. For ethics, the difference between disagreement in reasons and disagreement on reasons is central. The latter is easily explained and does not imply the former. Disagreement in reasons is less common than might be thought (and apparently is often thought). Even when it occurs, however, the case may not be even close to one of full epistemic parity. The effort to see whether someone we disagree with shares the relevant information and is equally rational in appraising it cannot be guaranteed either to make agreement possible or to enable one to be confident that one's own view is correct; but I have seen this positive movement in many cases, and I believe that it tends to occur. Where it does not, one may have to choose between revising one's position and standing one's ground, possibly against more than one disputant. Humility may sometimes favor the former; dogmatism may sometimes underlie the latter. But revision need not be retreat, and retention need not be stubbornness. Intellectual virtue lies in being able to respond to disagreement without either a facile skepticism or a dogmatic self-confidence.

10

Irrationality and Cognition

John L. Pollock

1. The puzzle of irrationality

Philosophers ask, "What should I believe? What should I do? And how should I go about deciding these matters?" These are questions about rationality. We want to know how we, as real cognizers, with all our built-in cognitive limitations, should go about deciding what to believe and what to do. This last point deserves emphasis. Much work on rationality is about "ideal rationality" and "ideal agents". But it is not clear what ideal rationality has to do with real, resource-bounded, agents. We come to the study of rationality wanting to know what *we* should do, and this chapter is about that concept of rationality.

Philosophers, particularly epistemologists, regard irrationality as the nemesis of the cognizer, and they often think of their task as that of formulating rules for rationality. Rules for rationality are rules governing how cognitive agents should perform their cognitive tasks. If asked for simple examples, philosophers might propose rules like "Don't hold beliefs for which you do not have good reasons (or good arguments)", "When you do have a good argument for a conclusion, you should accept the conclusion", and "Be diligent in the pursuit of evidence". Epistemological theories are often regarded as proposing more detailed rules of rationality governing things like inductive reasoning, temporal reasoning, and so forth, and theories of practical reasoning propose rules for rational decision making.

Philosophers seek rules for avoiding irrationality, but they rarely stop to ask a more fundamental question. Why is it possible for humans to be irrational?

We have evolved to have a particular cognitive architecture. Evolution has found it useful for us to reason both about what to believe and about what to do. Rationality consists of reasoning, or, more generally, cognizing, *correctly*. But, if rationality is desirable, why is irrationality possible? If we have built-in rules for how to cognize, why are we not built always to cognize rationally? Consider the steering mechanism of a car. There are "rules" we want it to follow, but we do that by simply making it work that way. Why is cognition not similar? An even better comparison is with artificial cognitive agents in AI. For example, my own system OSCAR (Pollock 1995) is built to cognize in certain ways, in accordance with a theory of how rational cognition ought to work, and OSCAR cannot but follow the prescribed rules. Again, why are humans not like this? Why are we able to be irrational?

The simple answer might be that evolution just did not design us very well. The suggestion would be that we work in accordance with the wrong rules. But this creates a different puzzle. If we are built to work in accordance with rules that conflict with the rules for rationality, how does rationality come to have any psychological authority over us? In fact, when we violate the rules of rationality, and subsequently realize we have done so, we feel a certain pressure to "correct" our behavior and conform to the rules. However, if we are built to act in accordance with rules that lead to our violating the rules of rationality, where does this pressure for conforming to them come from? Their authority over us is not just a theoretical authority described by philosophical ideals. They have real psychological authority over us. Whence do they derive their authority? If evolution could build us so that rationality has this kind of *post hoc* authority over us, why could it not have built us so that we simply followed the rules of rationality in the first place?

It cannot be denied that we are built in such a way that considerations of rationality have psychological authority over us. But we are not built in such a way that they have absolute authority—we can violate them. What is going on? What is the role of rationality in our cognitive architecture? Why would anyone build a cognitive agent in this way? And, by extension, why would evolution build us in this way?

These puzzles suggest that we are thinking of rationality in the wrong way. I am going to suggest that these puzzles have a threefold solution. First, the rules philosophers have typically proposed are misdescribed as "rules for rationality". They play an important role in rational cognition, but it can be perfectly rational to violate them. Second, the reason we can violate them is that we are reflexive cognizers who can think about our own cognition and redirect various aspects of it, and there are rules for rationality governing how this is to be done. But, third, we do still behave irrationally sometimes, and that ultimately is to be traced to a particular localized flaw in our cognitive design.

Having proposed an account of irrationality, we will be able to use that to throw light on rationality. I will urge that the task of describing the rules for rationality is a purely descriptive enterprise, of the sort that falls in principle under the purview of psychology. Still, there is something normative about the rules for rationality, and I will try to explain that. Although, on this account, theories of rationality are empirical theories about human cognition, the nature of reflexive cognition provides philosophers with a privileged access to rational cognition, enabling us to investigate these matters without performing laboratory experiments.

First, some preliminaries.

2. Rationality, epistemology, and practical cognition

Much epistemology is about how beliefs should be formed and maintained. It is about "rational doxastic dynamics". Beliefs that are formed or maintained in the right way are said to be *justified*. This is the "procedural" notion of epistemic justification that I have written about at length in my works in epistemology (Pollock 1987; 1997; Pollock and Cruz 1999). It is to be contrasted with the notions of epistemic justification that are constructed for the sake of analyzing "*S* knows that *P*", an enterprise that is orthogonal to my present purposes.

Procedural epistemic justification is closely connected to rationality. We can distinguish, at least loosely, between epistemic cognition, which is cognition about what to believe, and practical cognition, which is cognition about what to do. Epistemic rationality pertains to epistemic cognition, and practical rationality pertains to practical cognition. Rationality pertains to "things the cognizer does"—acts, and, in the case of epistemic rationality, cognitive acts. In particular, epistemic rationality pertains to "believings". Epistemic justification pertains instead to beliefs—the products of acts of believing. But there seems to be a tight connection. As a first approximation we might say that a belief is justified iff it is rational for the cognizer to believe it. Similarly, practical cognition issues in decisions, and we can say that a decision is justified iff it is the product of rational practical cognition.

It is a commonplace of epistemology that epistemic cognition is not simply practical cognition about what to believe. If anyone still needs convincing of this, note that the logical properties of epistemic cognition and practical cognition are different. For instance, if Jones, whom you regard as a reliable source, informs you that P, but Smith, whom you regard as equally reliable, informs you that $\sim P$, what should you believe? Without further evidence, it would be irrational to decide at random to adopt either belief. Rather, you should withhold belief. Now contrast this with practical cognition. Consider Buridan's ass, who starved to death midway between two equally succulent bales of hay because he could not decide from which to eat. That was irrational. He should have chosen one at random. Practical rationality dictates that ties should be broken at random. By contrast, epistemic rationality dictates that ties should not be broken at all except by the input of new information that renders them no longer ties. So epistemic cognition and practical cognition work differently. And, of course, there are many other differences between them—this is just one simple example of the difference.

On the other hand, a common presumption in epistemology is that epistemic justification is a *sui generis* kind of justification entirely unrelated to practical cognition, and one can study epistemic rationality and epistemic justification without ever thinking about practical cognition. One of the burdens of this chapter will be to argue that this is wrong. I will argue that, for sophisticated cognitive agents like human beings, an account of epistemic rationality must presuppose an account of practical rationality. I will defend this by discussing how epistemic cognition and practical cognition are intertwined. I will suggest that epistemic irrationality always derives from a certain kind of practical irrationality, and I will give an account of why we are subject to that kind of practical irrationality. It turns out that, for what are largely computational reasons, it is desirable to have a cognitive architecture that, as a side effect, makes this kind of irrationality possible. This will be an important ingredient in an account of epistemic rationality, and it will explain why it is possible to hold beliefs unjustifiably, or more generally to be epistemically irrational.

3. Rationality and reflexive cognition

First a disclaimer. One way people can behave irrationally is by being broken. If a person suffers a stroke, he may behave irrationally. But this is not the kind of irrationality I am talking about. Philosophers have generally supposed that people do not have to be broken to be irrational. So, when I speak of irrationality in this chapter, I am concerned only with those varieties of irrationality that arise in intact cognizers.

The key to understanding rationality is to note that not all aspects of cognition are subject to evaluation as rational or irrational. For instance, visual processing produces a visual representation of our immediate surroundings, but it is a purely automatic process. Although the visual representation can be inaccurate, it makes no sense to ask whether it was produced irrationally. We have this odd notion of having control over certain aspects of our cognition and not over other aspects of it. We have no control over the computation of the visual image. It is a black box. It is both not introspectible and cognitively impenetrable. But we feel like we do have some control over various aspects of our reasoning. For example, you are irrational if, in the face of counter-evidence, you accept the visual image as veridical. The latter is something over which you do have control. If you note that you are being irrational in accepting that conclusion, you can withdraw it. In this sense, we perform some cognitive operations "deliberately". We have voluntary control over them.[1]

To have voluntary control over something, we must be able to monitor it. So mental operations over which we have voluntary control must be introspectible. Furthermore, if we have voluntary control over something, we must be able to decide for ourselves whether to do it. Such decisions are performed by weighing the consequences of doing it or not doing it—that is, they are made as a result of practical cognition. So we must be able to engage in practical cognition regarding those mental operations that we perform deliberately. To say that we can engage in cognition about some of our mental operations is to say that we are *reflexive cognizers*. We have the following central connection between rationality and reflexive cognition:

> Rationality pertains only to mental operations over which we have voluntary control. Such operations must be introspectible, and we must be able to engage in practical cognition about whether to perform them.

I will refer to such cognition as *voluntary cognition*. This need not be cognition that we perform deliberately, but we can deliberately alter its course. Rationality pertains only to voluntary cognition.

---

[1] Cf. the discussion of freedom and spontaneity in cognition in McDowell (1994).

4. Q&I modules

Next, another preliminary. In studying rational cognition, philosophers have often focused their attention on reasoning, to the exclusion of all else. But it is important to realize that much of our belief formation and decision making is based instead on various shortcut procedures. Shortcut procedures are an indispensable constituent of the cognitive architecture of any agent that must make decisions rapidly in unpredictable environments. I refer to these as *Q&I modules* (quick and inflexible modules). I have argued that they play a pervasive role in both epistemic and practical cognition (Pollock 1989; 1995). Consider catching (or avoiding) a flying object. You have to predict the trajectory. You do not do this by measuring the velocity and position of the object and then computing parabolic paths. That would take too long. Instead, humans and most higher animals have a built-in cognitive module that enables them rapidly to predict trajectories on the basis of visual information. At a higher level, explicit inductive or probabilistic reasoning imposes a tremendous cognitive load on the cognizer. We avoid that by using various Q&I modules that summarize data as we accumulate it, without forcing us to recall all the data, and then makes generalizations on the basis of the summary (Pollock 1989: 119 ff.).

Although they make cognition faster, Q&I modules are often subject to various sources of inaccuracy that can be corrected by explicit reasoning if the agent has the time to perform such reasoning. Accordingly, our cognitive architecture is organized so that explicit reasoning takes precedence over the output of the Q&I modules when the reasoning is actually performed, and the agent can often learn to mistrust Q&I modules in particular contexts. For instance, we learn to discount the output of the Q&I module that predicts trajectories when (often by using that module) we can predict that the flying object will hit other objects in flight.

5. Practical irrationality

I distinguished between practical rationality and epistemic rationality. By implication, we can distinguish between practical irrationality and epistemic irrationality. Practical irrationality is easier to understand. The explanation turns on the role Q&I modules play in practical cognition. Paramount among the Q&I modules operative in practical cognition is one that computes and stores evaluations of various features of our environment—what I call *feature likings*. Ideally, feature likings would be based on explicit computations of expected values. But they are often based on a form of conditioning instead (see Pollock 1995, 2001, and 2006b for more discussion of this). The advantage of such *evaluative conditioning* is that it is often able to produce evaluations in the absence of our having explicit beliefs about probabilities and utilities. It estimates expected values more directly. But it is also subject to various sources of inaccuracy, such as short-sightedness. Thus, for example, a cognizer may become conditioned to like smoking even though he is aware that the long-term consequences of smoking give it a negative expected value.

Decision making is driven by either full-fledged decision-theoretic reasoning, or by some of the shortcut procedures that are an important part of rational cognition. If a decision is based on full-fledged decision-theoretic reasoning, then it is rational as long as the beliefs and evaluations on which it is based are held rationally. This is a matter of epistemic rationality, because what is at issue are beliefs about outcomes and probabilities. If the decision is based on a shortcut procedure, it is rational as long as it is rational to use that shortcut procedure in this case. And that is true iff the agent lacks the information necessary for overriding the shortcut procedure. So the cognizer is behaving irrationally iff he has the information but fails to override the shortcut procedure. For instance, a person might have a conditioned feature liking for smoking, but know full well that smoking is not good for him. If he fails to override the feature liking in his decision making, he is being irrational. This seems to be the only kind of uniquely practical irrationality (that is, practical irrationality that does not arise from irrationally held beliefs). We might put this by saying that smoking is the stereotypical case of practical irrationality. The smoker is irrational because he knows that smoking has a negative expected value, but he does it anyway.

What makes it easy to understand practical irrationality is that all decision making has to be driven by something, and, if the cognitive system is not broken, these are the only ways it can be driven.

Overriding shortcut procedures is something one can explicitly decide to do. One can engage in higher-order cognition about this, and act on the basis of it. So overriding shortcut procedures is, in the requisite sense, under the control of a reflexive agent. Is the agent who fails to override a shortcut procedure just not doing enough practical cognition? That does not seem quite right. The smoker can think about the undesirable consequences of smoking, and conclude that he should not smoke, but do it anyway. He did all the requisite cognition, but it did not move him. The problem is a failure of *beliefs* about expected values to move the agent sufficiently to overcome the force of the shortcut procedures. The desire to do something creates a strong disposition to do it, and the belief that one should not do it may not be as effective. Then one is making a choice, but one is not making the *rational* choice. Note, however, that one can tell that one is not making the rational choice. Some smokers may deny that they are being irrational, but they deny it by denying the claims about expected values, not by denying that they should do what has the higher expected value.

I have suggested that uniquely practical irrationality always arises from a failure to override the output of Q&I modules, and I have illustrated this with a particular case—the failure to override conditioned feature likings. There is a large literature on practical irrationality,[2] and I do not have time to survey it here. My general focus will be on epistemic irrationality instead. I have not done a careful survey of cases of practical rationality, but I think it is plausible that uniquely practical irrationality always consists of the failure to override the output of Q&I modules. This source of practical irrationality seems to be a design flaw in human beings, probably deriving from the fact that Q&I modules are phylogenetically older than mechanisms for reasoning explicitly about expected values. It is important to retain Q&I modules in an agent archiecture, because explicit reasoning is too slow. In particular, it is important to retain evaluative conditioning, because explicit reasoning about expected values is both too slow and requires too much experience of the world for us to base all our decisions on it. But it appears that evolution has done an imperfect job of merging the two mechanisms.

The upshot is that practical irrationality is easy to understand. My suggestion is that it all derives from this single imperfection in our cognitive architecture. When I turn to epistemic irrationality, I will argue for the somewhat surprising conclusion that it too derives from this same source.

6. Reflexive epistemic cognition

Epistemic irrationality consists of holding beliefs irrationally. We have seen that rationality pertains only to mental operations over which we have voluntary

---

[2] See particularly Kahneman and Tversky (1982).

control. Such operations must be introspectible, and we must be able to engage in practical cognition about whether to perform them. But why would a cognitive agent be built so that it has voluntary control over some of its mental operations? Why not build it so that it follows the desired rules for cognition automatically? What I will now argue is that there are good reasons for building a cognitive agent so that it is capable of such reflexive epistemic cognition.

6.1. Reordering the cognitive-task queue

The simplest form of reflexive cognition is about how to order our cognitive tasks. We always have more cognitive tasks to perform than we can perform immediately. We have multiple new pieces of information to explore, multiple goals to reason about, and so on. We cannot pursue all of these at once, so they go on a queue—the *cognitive-task queue*. They are prioritized somehow and taken off the queue and explored in order of their priority. There must be a default prioritization in order to make this work. However, we can decide to take things in a different order. For example, given two problems, one of which aims at achieving a more important result, the default prioritization might have us look at the more important one first. However, we may know from experience that we are very unlikely to solve the more important problem, and much more likely to solve the lesser problem. We may then decide to look at the lesser problem first. This seems to be a straightforward matter of comparing expected values. So this is a case in which practical cognition can intervene and alter the course of other aspects of cognition. What we are doing is engaging in practical cognition that results in reordering the cognitive-task queue. We are deciding what to think about, and in what order to address problems. The ability to do this seems very important. It makes us more efficient problem-solvers. For instance, when an experienced mathematician or scientist addresses a problem, he can draw on his experience for how best to proceed—what reasoning to try first. An equally bright college freshman may be unsuccessful at solving the problem primarily because he has no special knowledge about how to proceed and so must take things in the default order imposed on his cognitive-task queue.

6.2. Refraining from accepting a conclusion

Consider a second kind of reflexive cognition. We can have an argument for a conclusion, and see nothing wrong with it, but, *without giving up the premises*, we may refrain from accepting the conclusion either because we have independent reason for thinking it is wrong, or because we are simply suspicious of it. What is to be emphasized is that we can do this without giving up the premises, even if the argument purports to be deductive. The liar paradox is an example of this. In the case of the liar paradox, we have a purportedly deductive argument that looks correct—we do not see anything wrong with it—but we *know* the conclusion is incorrect. A very important feature of our cognitive architecture is that we are able to "back out of the problem" without solving it. We do not just go crazy, or believe everything. We "bracket" the reasoning, setting it aside and perhaps coming back to it later to try to figure out what is wrong. But notice that we do not have to come back to it. We can decide that it is not worth our time to try to figure out what went wrong.

The same thing holds when we are just suspicious of the conclusion of an argument. This happens in philosophy all the time. We come upon arguments whose conclusions we find hard to believe. We do not immediately accept the conclusions or reject the premises. We set the arguments aside. Often, when we return to them, we are able to pinpoint flaws.

This also happens in mathematics. In the course of trying to prove a theorem, I might "prove" something that just does not seem right. When that happens, I do not forge on. I set it aside and, if I care enough, try to figure out what went wrong. Something similar happens throughout science. Scientists get evidence for conclusions they find unbelievable, even though they cannot immediately see what is wrong with their data. They do not automatically accept the conclusions. They have the power to set them aside and examine them more carefully later.

If reasoning worked like the steering mechanism on a car, we would have to accept the conclusions of these arguments, but in fact we do not. It is clearly desirable for an agent to be so constructed that it can treat arguments in this more flexible manner. This indicates that the simple rule "When you have a good argument for a conclusion, you should accept the conclusion" is not a genuine rule of rationality. It is perhaps best viewed as a default rule to be followed in the absence of reflexive cognition.

6.3. Errors in reasoning

A third variety of reflexive cognition concerns the fact that we sometimes make errors in reasoning. For instance, mathematicians almost always make mistakes initially when trying to prove complex theorems. Far be it from being the most certain form of knowledge, the results of mathematical reasoning are often among the least certain. This can seem puzzling. If reasoning is a mechanical process, it seems that it should go wrong only when something in the system breaks. For example, in its current implementation, OSCAR cannot make mistakes in reasoning. However, mathematicians are not broken just because they make mistakes. What is going on?

Part of the explanation lies in the fact that mathematicians cannot hold the entire proof in working memory. They have to rely upon longer-term memory to know what the earlier steps of the proof accomplished.[3] Typically, they write the proof down as they go along, but they tend to write it down only sketchily, so they also have to rely upon memory to interpret their notes. All this makes it possible for them to be mistaken about what they have already accomplished, and so they may make new inferences from things they have not actually established. Memory gives us only a defeasible reason for believing what is recalled. Thus the reasoning underlying mathematical proof construction is actually defeasible and reflexive.[4] It is reflexive because mathematicians are reasoning about what their earlier reasoning accomplished (that is, appealing to memory of their earlier reasoning and reasoning defeasibly from that).

Another part of the explanation of mathematical error lies in the fact that mathematicians often "sketch" an argument rather than writing it out in full detail. The sketch asserts that certain things are inferable on the basis of other things without actually working through the argument. This involves some kind of pattern matching or analogical reasoning. It is desirable to allow a cognizer to form beliefs on the basis of such sketches, because actually constructing the full argument is tedious and usually not necessary. In effect, the cognizer is reasoning probabilistically (using the statistical syllogism) in meta-reasoning about the possibility of constructing arguments. So this can also be regarded as a form of reflexive cognition. He is reasoning about what reasoning he could do. Note that this alters the default course of cognition, because that would dictate that the agent not adopt the belief until an argument has actually been produced. This illustrates that the rule "Don't hold beliefs for which you do not have good arguments" is not a correct rule of rationality. It is again at best a default rule pertaining to non-reflexive cognition.

---

[3] See the discussion of this in Pollock (1987: ch. 3) and Pollock and Cruz (1999).
[4] I first gave this account of mathematical reasoning in Pollock (1987).

When we decide whether to accept a conclusion on the basis of a sketch of an argument, this typically involves some deliberation on our part. If it is really important that we get it right, we may be more reluctant to accept it without working out the sketch in more detail. For instance, if we were just curious about whether the theorem is true, a rough sketch may satisfy our curiosity. But if we intend to publish the result or use it to build airplanes or nuclear reactors, we will take more care. This seems to be a matter of practical reasoning about the expected value of accepting the sketch.

Now notice something that will be very important when I discuss philosophical methodology. If an argument sketch is wrong, in order to retract the conclusion on the basis of its being wrong, we have to be able to tell that it is wrong. We check various ways of filling out the sketch, and when they do not work we conclude inductively that the sketch is wrong—that is, that there is no correct argument that fills it out. For this to work, we have to be able to tell that the inference sketched is not licensed by particular explicit arguments constructed using our built-in inference rules, where those arguments are intended to fill out the sketch. So we have to be able to introspect what we did, and we must be able to check its conformance with our built-in inference rules.

It is important to recognize that sketching an argument is not something that only mathematicians do. We can sketch arguments in other contexts as well. Someone might think to himself, "Should I believe in God? Well, something had to create the universe, so there must be a God." Someone else might think, "Well, if there were a God, there wouldn't be so much evil in the world, so there can't be a God." As arguments, these are grossly incomplete, and notoriously difficult to complete. But they certainly can lead to belief. So argument sketches do not have to concern mathematics. We can have argument sketches about anything.

There seems also to be an important connection between sketching arguments and certain aspects of planning. Planning is often said to be "hierarchical" (Sacerdotti 1977). We plan for how to do something using high-level actions. For instance, if I want to get to LA my initial plan might be no more elaborate than "Fly to LA". But to execute this plan, I must plan *how* to fly to LA. I must plan when to go, what flight to take, how to get a ticket, and so on. Hierarchical planning is a good cognitive strategy, because we often have to make decisions quickly without having the information we need to fill in the details. We may not get that information until later—maybe not even until we begin executing the plan. For instance, consider a plan for driving across an unfamiliar city on an interstate highway. We may plan which highway to take, and which turns to make, but we do not plan ahead about which lanes to drive in. We decide the latter as we drive, taking account of the flow of traffic around us.

When we adopt a high-level plan, we are assuming that we can fill in the details later as we get more information. But this is something we can know only inductively. And we often have to begin execution of a plan before we finish working out the details. We might model hierarchical planning as the construction and subsequent expansion of an argument sketch that there is a particular sequence of actions we can perform that will achieve the goal. Alternatively, we might pursue the opposite reduction and think of the construction of argument sketches as hierarchical planning for building a complete argument.

6.4. Forms of reflexive epistemic cognition

The upshot is that there are good reasons for making an agent a reflexive cognizer—enabling the agent to engage in cognition that alters the default course of cognition in various ways. We have seen at least three kinds of reflexive cognition that humans can perform:

- reorder the cognitive-task queue;
- believe something on the basis of a sketch of an argument rather than a full argument;
- refrain from accepting the conclusion of an argument.

Although it is desirable for an agent to be able to cognize in these ways, this also opens the door to epistemic irrationality. That is the topic of the next section.

7. Epistemic irrationality

Rationality pertains only to mental operations that are introspectible and subject to voluntary control. We have seen three examples of how reflexive cognizers make use of voluntary control. Now let us look at how each of these kinds of reflexive cognition can lead to irrationality, and see whether we can characterize the source of the irrationality.

7.1. Reordering the cognitive-task queue

Having the ability to decide what to think about can result in our not thinking about things we should think about. Several familiar forms of irrationality derive from this.

Not thinking about problems for a theory

Given a cherished theory, it may occur to one that certain considerations might generate a problem for the theory (a defeater). There is a temptation not to think about these considerations, so as to avoid discovering that the theory is wrong. But not doing so is, at least often, irrational. The ability to refrain from thinking about the defeaters derives from the more general ability to reorder the cognitive-task queue, so the same reflexive ability that is useful for some purposes enables us to be irrational in others.

Just why is it irrational to avoid thinking about possible problems for our theory? It is practical cognition that allows us to do this. We desire not to be proven wrong, and, given that desire, perfectly correct practical reasoning leads to the conclusion that one way to achieve that is to avoid thinking about the possible problem. If it is irrational not to think about the considerations that might generate a problem for the theory, then the practical cognition must be irrational. If the reasoning from the desire not to be proven wrong is correct, then the only way the practical cognition can be irrational is for it to be irrational to have the desire. Can that be irrational? We can throw light on this by noticing that there is a spectrum of cases in which we fail to think about the possible problem, and in some of these cases we are being irrational, but not in others.

The simplest case is one in which you do not think about the possible problem for your theory just because you do not have time to do so. You cannot do everything. That is why we have a cognitive-task queue. Science and philosophy have to compete for attention not only with other abstract intellectual tasks, but also with doing the laundry and taking out the garbage. Things to think about go on the cognitive-task queue, and may never be pulled off if other more important things keep intervening. You should not give up the theory just because you *might* be wrong. If you had time to think it through, you might well be able to dismiss the problem. Perhaps, without thinking it through, you should hold the belief with a bit less conviction (that is, the probability of there being a defeater might diminish your degree of justification), but you should not simply give it up. So your belief is not automatically unjustified just because you do not think about the possible problem.

In the first case, the reason you fail to think about the problem is that you do not have time, not that you are trying to avoid being refuted. Perhaps that is where irrationality comes in. But consider a second case. Suppose you are a Nobel Prize-winning physicist, famous for constructing the theory that may be challenged by the problem. The award of the Nobel Prize has given you great prestige, and made you able to do good things unrelated to the truth of the theory (for example, collect food for starving refugees from war-torn countries). If it were to become known that the theory is wrong, you would be the subject of ridicule and no longer able to accomplish these good things. Furthermore, you might know that, if you find that you are wrong, you will not be able to conceal it. In this case, you are being perfectly rational in not wanting to be proven wrong, and correspondingly rational in not thinking about the possible problem. If you are being rational in not thinking about the possible problem for the theory, it is presumably rational for you to continue to believe the theory. Is your belief in the theory justified? I would think so. After all, the problem is only a *possible* problem. This case is like the first case in that, if you did think about the problem, you might well be able to dismiss it. So the fact that you avoid thinking about the possible problem in order to avoid being refuted does not automatically render your belief unjustified.

Why should it ever be irrational for you to avoid thinking about the possible problem in order to avoid being refuted? After all, you desire not to be refuted, and, other things being equal, it is rational to try to satisfy your desires. But it is clear that there are cases in which it is irrational. The problem in these cases must be that your desire not to be refuted is irrational. It is natural to suppose that, ordinarily, your desire not to be proven wrong derives from a desire not to *be* wrong (by a kind of evaluative conditioning). Not thinking about the difficulty subserves the end of not being proven wrong, but not the end of not being wrong. So the desire not to be proven wrong is rationally problematic unless it has some other justification (as in the case of the Nobel Prize winner). It is based on a conditioned feature liking that ought to be overridden by your knowledge that it does not actually contribute to the end of not being wrong. In this respect, it is like having the desire to smoke in the face of knowing that smoking is bad for you. So the epistemic irrationality derives from a practical irrationality.

In a case in which it is irrational for you to avoid thinking about the possible problem, but you do so anyway, is your continued belief in the theory irrational? That does not follow, any more than it follows in the other cases. You are doing something wrong—you should check out the possible problem—but, given that you are not going to, it would not be reasonable to give up the theory. After all, you have a lot of evidence for it, and you have not found a *real* problem, only a possible problem. As before, perhaps you should believe the theory with a somewhat lower degree of conviction, but it would be irrational to give it up on the basis of the mere possibility of a problem.

Even though it would be irrational to give the belief up, I am not comfortable saying that the belief is justified. Epistemic justification is about whether we "should" hold a belief. But our normative judgments often have a more complex structure that cannot be expressed in this simple terminology. In cases of irrationality, if asked whether I should hold a belief in certain circumstances, the answer might be, "You shouldn't be in those circumstances, but, given that you are, you should hold the belief." This does not imply "You should hold the belief" *simpliciter*. If you should hold the belief only because it is the best thing you can do given that, irrationally, you got yourself into those circumstances, do we want to say that it is a justified belief? The term "epistemic justification" is a term of art, so we can use it however we want, but this strikes me as a peculiar way to use it. We might say that the belief is *justified on the basis of the evidence that has been considered*, but not justified *simpliciter* because more evidence should have been considered.

One of the main lessons to be learned from this example is that epistemic rationality pertains to more aspects of cognition than epistemic justification. We can talk about a cognizer being rational or irrational in believing something, but also in how he carries out searches for additional evidence and defeaters, and rationality may pertain to other aspects of cognition as well. These considerations impinge on our judgments of justification. Epistemic justification has generally been taken to be the central notion of epistemology, but perhaps that is a mistake. If our interest is in understanding rational cognition, then the central notion should be rationality. In most cases, we can say what we want to say by talking about justified belief. But there may be no clear way to make sense of epistemic justification so that it has enough structure to be useful in talking about complex cases—particularly cases of "contrary-to-duty rational obligations", which are about what you should do given that you are in circumstances you should not be in.

It might be suggested that we can avoid this difficulty by understanding justification as relative to the "available evidence", but I doubt that is a well-defined notion. If the available evidence is just that currently contained in working memory (that is, what the cognizer is explicitly thinking about), it is too restrictive. But, if it includes other beliefs, they will be stored in long-term memory and must be retrieved before they can be used in cognition. Beliefs stored in long-term memory can be retrieved only with varying degrees of difficulty, and retrieval can range from virtually instantaneous to a process that takes hours or days or may fail altogether on any particular occasion. An agent cannot be culpable for not taking account of information that he has not yet been able to retrieve from long-term memory. So there is no obvious way to define a notion of "available evidence" in such a way that a sensible notion of "justified belief" can appeal to it.

Epistemic justification seems to make unproblematic sense in cases that are not contrary-to-duty. Then justified beliefs are those held on the basis of rational epistemic cognition. So "epistemic justification" gives us a useful but rather crude tool for talking about the rationality of epistemic cognition. But in more complicated cases, where we want to know whether a cognizer should retain a belief in circumstances he is in only because he was irrational, talk of epistemic justification may not make clear sense.

Wishful thinking

A familiar form of irrationality is wishful thinking. How is wishful thinking possible? It does not seem that you can make yourself believe something just by wanting it to be true. That is not what happens in wishful thinking. I suggest that it is again a matter of irrationally reordering the cognitive-task queue. Consider example. My teenage daughter has gone to a high-school football game, and it occurs to me to wonder whether she took a jacket. Without really thinking about it, I conclude, "Oh, she must have." What is happening here? It seems I am briefly rehearsing something like the following argument: (1) Most reasonable people would take a jacket; (2) she is a reasonable person; (3) so she took a jacket. Where I am going wrong is in not thinking hard enough about defeaters for this argument. She is a teenager and wants to look cool, and she thinks wearing a jacket is not cool.

What is important about this example is that I am drawing the conclusion on the basis of an argument—not just because I want it to be true. The term "wishful thinking" is a misnomer. You cannot make yourself believe something just by wishing it were true. On the other hand, my wanting it to be true may prevent me from looking for defeaters. Believing the conclusion makes me feel good (or allows me to avoid feeling bad), so this is a reason for not doing anything that might make me disbelieve it.

The practical reasoning involved in this example seems, on the surface, to be rationally correct. Why should I not do it? After all, I want to feel good. However, the desire to believe that my daughter took a jacket derives from a desire for that to be true. I care about my daughter's well-being, and not just about feeling good. Having the belief is not conducive to the truth of what is believed, so this is a rationally criticizable desire. Again, what is wrong here is the practical irrationality of the reasoning leading me not to think about defeaters.

This case differs from the previous case in that this time the belief is intuitively unjustified. In both cases, irrational practical cognition results in our not considering possible defeaters, but in the previous case the belief was initially justified and then a potential defeater occurred. In the present case we adopt the belief on the basis of a defeasible argument supporting it. Whenever we do this, we should immediately consider whether we already have any readily available defeaters. That is a requirement of rationality, and it is what the irrational practical cognition is preventing.

Hasty inference

We often engage in what might be called "hasty inference". For example, I may think about a hypothesis, think briefly about considerations that favor its being true, and then conclude that it is true and quit thinking about it. This is another example of not searching for defeaters.

One variety of hasty inference that has been noted in epistemology (Goldman 1979) is hasty generalization. In hasty generalization, we often think of the cognizer as generalizing on the basis of inadequate evidence rather than ignoring defeaters. But what is wrong with that is that the ignored evidence may contain counterinstances of the generalization, so this is again a matter of not taking adequate account of defeaters. It is made possible by my deciding what to think about. It differs from the previous case, however, in that, instead of intentionally avoiding defeaters, I am being insufficiently careful in searching for them. A plausible suggestion is that such carelessness arises from a desire to be finished with a task (in this case, searching for defeaters), regardless of whether you have completed it correctly. Presumably, the desire to be finished with a task derives, by evaluative conditioning, from the desire to have it accomplished; however, it is not genuinely conducive to the goal of having the task accomplished. So this is analogous to the observation that the desire not to find defeaters is not conducive to the achievement of the desire to be right. In both cases evaluative conditioning leads to desires that we ought to override, and we are being irrational if we do not. Again, the resulting belief is unjustified.

If this is right, then many cases of hasty inference and hasty generalization derive from the phenomenon we have already noticed—reordering the cognitive-task queue in order to achieve irrational desires. However, this is not the only kind of hasty inference, as we will see next.

7.2. Ignoring evidence

Enabling the agent to refrain from accepting a conclusion makes it possible for the agent to refuse to adopt a belief for which he has good reasons, just because he finds the conclusion repugnant. Thus a person may refuse to believe that he has a potentially fatal disease, and thereby refrain from seeking treatment. He does not want it to be true that he has the disease, and that causes him to want not to believe it. This is another case of practical irrationality, susceptible to an analysis similar to that I proposed for wishful thinking. The desire not to believe one has the disease presumably derives from a desire that it not be true, but not believing it does not make it false. Having the desire not to believe it turns on evaluative conditioning and involves a failure to override conditioned desires with explicit knowledge of the values of outcomes. Because refraining from believing he has the disease prevents him from seeking treatment, the expected value of refraining from believing is strongly negative, just as in the case of smoking. Hence it is irrational to ignore the evidence and refrain from holding the belief.

7.3. Inadequate arguments

If we can accept a conclusion on the basis of a sketch of an argument, we can do so on the basis of an inadequate sketch. Consider an example. Suppose you conclude that God does not exist because there is so much evil in the world. You have what seems to be a relevant consideration for your conclusion, but you do not have a complete argument, and it is not obvious how to turn it into an argument. Thinking about it superficially, you think it must be possible to turn this into a good argument, and so, without thinking about it further, you accept the conclusion. Perhaps you are actually justified in thinking there is an argument that can be constructed, but suppose you are not. Then you are being overly hasty.

In a case like this, it seems that you have a weak inductive or analogical reason for thinking there is an argument that can be given. If you think no more about the matter, it seems to me you are justified in your conclusion, albeit weakly. But, if you think just a little more about how to spell out the argument and fail to find a way to do it, that failure should constitute a defeater. We can distinguish several possibilities:

- You fail to accept the defeater (that you cannot fill out the argument) on the basis of the inductive argument supporting it, or you fail to retract the conclusion in light of the defeater, because you want to believe the conclusion. This is irrational, as above, and your belief is unjustified.
- You do not follow up on the matter because you have more pressing things to think about. Then your belief remains weakly justified.
- You fail to accept the defeater on the basis of the argument supporting it because, through intellectual laziness, you just do not think about the matter. This is another case of carelessness, and can be treated as above. Again, your belief is unjustified.

8. A single source for irrationality?

I have argued that the only cognitive acts that can be assessed for rationality are those potentially under the control of reflexive cognition. I called this *voluntary cognition*. I have also shown how reflexive cognition can make possible at least the most commonly cited kinds of epistemic irrationality. I argued that all the varieties of epistemic irrationality I surveyed derive from practical irrationality that occurs in the course of reflexive cognition, and I think this is true in general. So, on this account, epistemic irrationality derives from practical irrationality that occurs in the course of reflexive cognition. And I have suggested, a bit tentatively, that all practical irrationality may also derive from a single source—the failure to override Q&I modules.. This often takes the form of failing to override conditioned feature likings in the face of explicit knowledge about expected values. If this is right, it follows that all irrationality, practical or epistemic, derives from this single source. From this I want to draw some general conclusions about epistemic rationality and epistemic justification.

9. Epistemic rationality and practical rationality

An understanding of epistemic irrationality can, obviously, be employed to give an account of epistemic rationality. Epistemic cognition is rational just in case it is not irrational. I remarked in Section 2 that philosophers have commonly supposed epistemic justification to be analyzable independently of practical rationality. However, at least in those cases where the notion makes clear sense, justified beliefs are those held on the basis of rational epistemic cognition, and the characterization of rationality for epistemic cognition will be dependent, in part, on a characterization of rationality in reflexive cognition. If, for example, we fail to find a defeater for a bit of reasoning because we have irrationally reordered the cognitive-task queue so as to avoid finding it, then we may not be justified in believing the conclusion of the argument. However, the irrationality involved in reordering the cognitive-task queue is practical irrationality. We employ practical reasoning in deciding whether to reorder the cognitive-task queue, and the irrationality of that practical reasoning is what makes our belief unjustified. Thus an analysis of epistemic justification cannot be given independently of an account of practical rationality.

On the other hand, we should not jump to the conclusion that there is no difference between epistemic rationality and practical rationality. As I illustrated in Section 2, they often have quite different logical properties. My conclusion is just that you cannot give an analysis of epistemic rationality without talking about practical rationality. The converse seems equally clear. For example, decisions are based in part on beliefs about your situation. If you hold the beliefs unjustifiably, then your decision is also unjustified. So the analyses of epistemic and practical rationality must form a unified package. We need a single theory characterizing both and saying how they are connected.

It also follows from the present account that much work in epistemology falls short of producing rules for rational cognition. Accounts of how to reason inductively, or how to reason about times and causes, or how to form beliefs on the basis of perceptual input, are not themselves complete rules of rationality. At best, they describe the rules the cognizer should follow in the absence of reflexive cognition. They are "default rules" for how to cognize, but a complete account of rational cognition must not only describe these rules, but also explain how they fit into the more comprehensive architecture for rational cognition that characterizes both how we should reason in the absence of reflexive cognition and also how we should reason and perhaps violate some of these default rules in the course of reflexive cognition.

10. Normative and descriptive aspects of a theory of rational cognition

The most important consequence of this account of irrationality concerns the nature of theories of rational cognition. Let us begin with the question of whether such theories are normative or descriptive. The standard philosophical view has it that theories of rationality are normative, not descriptive. They are about how we *should* cognize rather than about how we *do* cognize. Philosophy constructs normative theories of how to cognize, and psychology investigates what we actually do. The two enterprises are supposed to be largely orthogonal.

But I think this standard view is wrong. On my view, theories of rational cognition are, by and large, theories of how cognition actually works. It is striking, despite all the philosophical talk about irrationality, how rarely people behave irrationally. Almost all our cognition is rational. Given the preceding account of irrationality, we can see why this is the case. On that account, irrationality arises from a single respect in which the human cognitive architecture works less well than we might desire—we find it difficult to override conditioned feature likings. Thus rationality has a much more central role in cognition than the traditional philosophical model supposes. If we confine our attention to those parts of cognition that are subject to rational evaluation, cognition *just is* rational cognition, with the exception that it occasionally goes wrong because of our failure to override Q&I modules. The result is that, for the most part, rules governing rational cognition are just rules describing how cognition actually works. Insofar as cognition does not work that way, it is because of this one glitch in the system. Given a description of the rules for rational cognition and a description of the glitch, we have a complete description of voluntary cognition. Describing voluntary cognition is a descriptive enterprise, potentially under the purview of psychology or cognitive science. And the theory of rational cognition makes up the bulk of that descriptive theory. So it seems to follow that constructing a theory of rational cognition is a descriptive enterprise.

But two questions remain. First, we certainly think of theories of rational cognition as normative—they tell us what we *should* do. How is this to be explained if they are just descriptive theories? Second, I described irrationality as deriving from a glitch in the system. What makes it a glitch rather than just a feature (*à la* Microsoft)? Calling it a glitch implies a value judgment. It assumes that rationality is desirable, and hence the glitch is a bad thing.

I suggest that theories of rationality are both descriptive and normative. In fact, their normativity derives from the descriptive theory. The two observations I just made that were intended to illustrate the normative character of rationality also reflect descriptive aspects of our cognitive architecture. We are so constructed that we fail to override Q&I modules in the face of explicit knowledge of expected values, and hence to behave irrationally. But we are also constructed in such a way that, when we recognize that we have done so, we have a disposition to form the desire to "correct" our cognition—that is, to retract the resulting beliefs and decisions and do the relevant reasoning over again. That is, we have a conative disposition to put a negative evaluation on our behavior and engage in reflexive practical cognition about how to correct the situation. That we have such a conative disposition is just another descriptive feature of our cognitive architecture. The negative evaluation works to combat the conditioned feature liking and reinforces the tendency to behave rationally. This is the sense in which rationality is normative. Of course, sometimes this mechanism is not strong enough to overcome the conditioned feature liking, as in the case of compulsive smokers. But all this is just further description of how our cognitive architecture works. The normativity of rationality merely reflects our tendency to engage in certain kinds of reflexive cognition, and that is an entirely descriptive matter.

If theories of rational cognition are simply descriptions of certain aspects of our cognitive architecture, does that mean we should leave them to the psychologist to construct and confirm? No. First, these are matters that psychologists should, in principle, be able to investigate, but at this point psychologists do not have a good handle on how to do that. Second, it is a feature of our cognitive architecture, employing reflexive cognition as it does, that we have privileged access to the course of our rational cognition. Only voluntary cognition is rational, and what makes it voluntary is that we can monitor it introspectively, reason about it, and alter its course. So, in order for cognition to count as rational, it must be such that we can in principle keep track of what we are doing. We also have to be able to recognize cases in which various kinds of failure occur. In particular, we must be able to discover that an argument sketch cannot be filled out. To do that, we must be able to tell that a particular way of filling it out does not constitute a good argument. This has to be an ability that is built into our cognitive architecture. If we can keep track of what we do, and we can recognize particular cases in which we have made mistakes, then we have the kind of data we need for formulating and confirming theories about when our cognition is not mistaken. We can notice, for example, that we often reason in accordance with *modus ponens*, and we can confirm inductively that we do not regard such reasoning as mistaken. Thus we can confirm that *modus ponens* is a correct rule of reasoning. Of course, this is a particularly simple case. It has, for example, proven much more difficult to discover rules describing the kinds of inductive and probabilistic reasoning that we regard as uncriticizable. But this much is clear. First, the reasoning we perform in this enterprise is straightforward scientific inference to the best explanation. Second, the data to be explained are what we can broadly call "introspective", and pertain both to what the actual course of our cognition is and to the judgments we are built to make about some of its correctness. There is nothing a priori about this enterprise.

11. Voluntary cognition

Rationality pertains only to voluntary cognition. But in what sense is cognition voluntary? Voluntary actions are those driven by practical cognition. Understanding free will in the context of a deterministic system is a notoriously difficult problem. But it is not one we have to solve here. The point is that, however it is to be analyzed, there are things that we do voluntarily. That is what practical cognition accomplishes. We decide to do various things by engaging in practical cognition about what to do. So voluntariness pertains to practical cognition.

It is useful to think of cognition as a virtual machine implemented on our neurological substructure, much as your word processor is a virtual machine implemented on your computer's electronic substructure.[5] We can think of epistemic cognition as a subsidiary virtual machine that, given various inputs, can run by itself. When it does so it is following the default rules of epistemic cognition. In an important sense, epistemic cognition is not voluntary. Where voluntary control comes in is that the epistemic cognition machine has various parameters that we can choose to reset. So the epistemic cognition machine is embedded in the more general practical cognition machine, and, although epistemic cognition can run by itself, practical cognition can tweak it by deciding to interfere in various ways with its default operation. In doing this, practical cognition is also interfering with itself, because the output of epistemic cognition is input to practical cognition—choices are based, in part, on our beliefs about the world.

Machines that are able to alter their own behavior might seem puzzling, but in fact they are not all that unusual. The role of epistemic cognition within practical cognition is similar to the operation of your word processor within your computer's operating system. These are two virtual machines, and the word processor can be thought of as embedded in the operating system. The word processor normally runs by itself, taking input from the keyboard (this is mediated by the operating system) and displaying output on the monitor (this is also mediated by the operating system). But the operating system can intervene in the operation of the word processor. For instance, when memory is low it may prevent the word processor from opening new files. In doing this it is also intervening in its own operation because it is the operating system, not the word processor itself, that creates the window that displays the new file.

So the sense in which epistemic cognition is under voluntary control and hence subject to rational evaluation is simply that epistemic cognition is embedded in and, in various ways controlled by, the more general practical cognition machine. Voluntary control is just what the practical cognition machine does.

12. Conclusions

My strategy has been to throw light on rational cognition by examining irrationality. I argued that practical irrationality derives from a general

---

[5] See Pollock (2008a) for an extended discussion of virtual machines.

difficulty we have in overriding Q&I modules. Epistemic irrationality is possible because we are reflexive cognizers, and hence practical irrationality can affect our epistemic cognition. The upshot is that one cannot give a theory of epistemic rationality or epistemic justification without simultaneously giving a theory of practical rationality.

A consequence of this account is that a theory of rationality is a descriptive theory, describing contingent features of a cognitive architecture, and it forms the core of a general theory of voluntary cognition. Most of the so-called rules for rationality that philosophers have proposed are really just rules describing default (non-reflexive) cognition. It can be perfectly rational for a reflexive cognizer to break these rules.

But rationality is also normative. The normativity of rationality is a reflection of a built-in feature of reflexive cognition—when we detect violations of rationality, we have a tendency to desire to correct them. This is just another part of the descriptive theory of rationality.

Although theories of rationality are descriptive, the structure of reflexive cognition gives philosophers, as human cognizers, privileged access to certain aspects of rational cognition. Philosophical theories of rationality are really scientific theories, based on inference to the best explanation, that take contingent introspective data as the evidence to be explained.

References

Goldman, Alvin (1979). "What is justified belief?", in George Pappas (ed.), *Justification and Knowledge*. Dordrecht: D. Reidel.

Kahneman, Daniel, and Tversky, Amos (1982). *Judgment under Uncertainty: Heuristics and Biases.* Cambridge: Cambridge University Press.

McDowell, John (1994). *Mind and World*. Cambridge, MA: Harvard University Press.

Pollock, John (1987). *Contemporary Theories of Knowledge*. Lanham, MD: Rowman and Littlefield.

_____ (1989). *How to Build a Person: A Prolegomenon*. Cambridge, MA: MIT Press.

_____ (1995). *Cognitive Carpentry*. Cambridge, MA: MIT Press.

_____ (1997). "Procedural epistemology", in Terry Bynum and Jim Moor (eds.), *The Digital Phoenix: How Computers are Changing Philosophy*. London: Blackwell, 17–36.

_____ (2001) "Evaluative Cognition", *Nous*, 35: 325–64.

_____ (2008a) "What Am I? Virtual Machines and Mental States", *Philosophy and Phenomenological Research*, 76, 237–309.

_____(2006b) *Thinking about Acting: Logical Foundations for Rational Decision Making.* New York: Oxford.

_____ and Cruz, Joseph (1999). *Contemporary Theories of Knowledge.* 2nd edn. Lanham, MD: Rowman and Littlefield.

Sacerdotti, E. D. (1977). *A Structure of Plans and Behavior.* Amsterdam: Elsevier-North Holland.

11

Why Epistemology Cannot be Operationalized

Timothy Williamson

1

As advice to enquirers, 'Believe the true' is notoriously useless. It provides no method for believing what it is true. We might try to make the point precise by defining a *method* as a set of rules such that one is, at least in principle, always in a position to know whether one is complying with them. To provide enquirers with methods in that strict sense looks like a good project for epistemology, if not the only one. Such a method need not guarantee true conclusions; it might just make them more likely. Call the attempt to provide such methods *operational epistemology*.

Operational epistemologists may allow some value to non-operational epistemology, in third-personal assessments of enquiry that take into account facts unavailable to the enquirers under assessment. But, they argue, we should also do epistemology in a first-personal way, in which epistemologists think

I thank the Centre for Advanced Study at the Norwegian Academy of Science and Letters for its hospitality during the writing of much of this chapter. Some of the material was presented in various earlier versions at classes in Oxford, at a conference on contextualism at the University of Stirling, the 2006 Formal Epistemology Workshop at Berkeley, the Jean Nicod Institute in Paris, the University of Bristol, the Graduate Center of City University New York and the University of California at Santa Barbara; I thank the audiences for helpful comments.

of the enquirers as themselves. More precisely, it should provide enquirers with guidance that they can actually use, in whatever situation they find themselves. Rationality might be conceived as requiring conformity with the norms of operational epistemology, but not with the norms of non-operational epistemology (such as true belief). Then the thought is that the demands of rationality should be transparent to the agent: ignorance and error as such may be failures, but not failures of rationality.

The injunction to proportion your confidence in a hypothesis to its probability, conditional on what you know, has no place in operational epistemology, for one is not always in a position to know how much one knows. In a situation indiscriminable from one in which one knows something, one may fail to know without being in a position to know that one fails to know. One may also know without being in a position to know that one knows. Operational epistemologists need to work with a notion of evidence on which one is always in a position to know how much is part of one's evidence and how much is not, if they are to propound the injunction that one should proportion one's confidence in a hypothesis to its probability, conditional on one's evidence.

An agent might be built so that its behaviour *fits* a rule even though it is not *guided* by it, because the agent has no epistemic access to whether it is complying with the rule. Fitting may extend beyond purely internal rules, such as performing computations with a specific structure or even having one's perceptual faculties in good working order, to external conditions such as correctly perceiving the state of one's local environment. But operational epistemology as understood here concerns only rules compliance with which is epistemically accessible to the agent.

Call a condition *luminous* if and only if, necessarily, whenever it obtains one is in a position to know that it obtains (given that one is a conscious agent with the relevant concepts). That one is complying with a given method in the sense of operational epistemology is a luminous condition. Thus operational epistemology and the corresponding conception of rationality require the existence of many non-trivial luminous conditions. Of course, luminosity is not itself part of the operational epistemologist's advice; rather, it is a precondition of figuring in any such advice.

In *Knowledge and its Limits* (Williamson 2000: 93–113) I argued that virtually the only luminous conditions are trivial ones, which obtain always or never. Let C be a non-trivial luminous condition, which obtains sometimes but not always. Imagine a process of very gradual change from a case in which C clearly obtains to a case in which C clearly fails to obtain; throughout, the agent is considering whether C obtains. For simplicity, imagine that it is certain for the agent that he or she will undergo such a gradual change in the underlying parameter relevant to C—for instance, felt temperature. Let $t_0, \ldots, t_n$ be a succession of times at very brief intervals from the beginning of the process to the end. Informally, the difference between the agent's situation at t_i and at t_{i+1} is too small to be recognized by the agent; it is below his or her threshold of discrimination. Suppose that C obtains at t_i. Since C is luminous, C obtains at t_i only if the agent is then in a position to know that C obtains. But an agent who is in a position to know that a condition obtains and considers whether it obtains knows that it obtains. Thus the agent knows at t_i that C obtains. Furthermore, I argued for the auxiliary premise that the agent knows at t_i that C obtains only if C does obtain (whether or not the agent knows it) at t_{i+1}. The argument worked by consideration of the way in which knowledge implies a sort of reliably true belief; we need not go into details here. Thus, given the premise that C obtains at t_i, one can deduce that C obtains at t_{i+1}. Since i was arbitrary, the inference works whenever $0 \leq i < n$. By hypothesis, C clearly obtains at t_0. Thus, iterating the inference n times, one finally reaches the conclusion that C obtains at t_n. But that is absurd; by hypothesis, C clearly fails to obtain at t_n. Given that the other features of the example can all be realized, as they can in the relevant cases, what must be given up is the assumption that C is luminous. By contraposition, its luminosity forces its triviality. The triviality of luminous conditions undermines operational epistemology. The operational epistemologist's conceptions of rationality and evidence cannot be satisfied.

Evidently, the anti-luminosity argument rests considerable weight on the reliability considerations underlying the auxiliary conditional premise that the agent knows at t_i that C obtains only if C obtains at t_{i+1}. That premise has indeed been challenged (e.g., by Brueckner and Fiocco 2002; Neta and Rohrbaugh 2004; Conee 2005). The specifics of those challenges will not be discussed here. However, some general remarks may clarify the position, and enable readers to work out for themselves how detailed responses to those critics would go.

First, the auxiliary conditional premise is not intended as a lawlike generalization; it is simply a description of a specific hypothetical process, justified by construction of the example. That the agent knows at t_i is not claimed to *entail* that C obtains at t_{i+1} independently of the continuation of the gradual process at the later time. In particular, it depends on the fact that, by hypothesis, the agent remains alive at the later time.

Second, it is crucial to the example that, again by hypothesis, no sudden drastic change occurs during the process in the basis on which the agent believes that C obtains—that is, in the way in which the belief is formed or maintained, even if the agent is completely unaware of the change. The basis is not confined to phenomena of which the agent is conscious. For instance, one may know and believe on a highly reliable basis at one time, even though, a moment later, without one's realizing it, a mad scientist interferes with one's brain to make the basis of one's subsequent beliefs highly unreliable.

Third, even granted that the basis of belief is inaccessible to consciousness, reliability need not be determined by local properties of the basis. For instance, if someone continues over some time to believe that Lincoln is President on the basis of automatic updating, without receiving further confirmation, the reliability of the basis may depend on whether Lincoln is about to be assassinated.

The main aim of the present chapter is to develop analogues of the anti-luminosity considerations for probabilistic concepts in place of the concept of knowledge. Such analogues generalize the original argument and act as a test of its soundness and significance. For someone might suspect the anti-luminosity argument of exploiting peculiarities of the concept of knowledge, either to conceal a subtle fallacy or to derive a result that, although correct, merely reflects a peculiarity of west European culture or of human folk epistemology more generally. Such a critic may hold that, in order to cut cognition at its joints, we should theorize primarily in terms not of knowledge but of probability, a more sophisticated and graded concept, and one that may seem better suited to the purposes of operational epistemology. However, if we can still establish analogues of the anti-luminosity conclusions even in the new terms, then the original result is shown to be robust after all. More specifically, such generalizations of the original argument show that operational epistemologists cannot survive by formulating their test for an operational method in probabilistic terms.

The relevant concept of probability is *epistemic* or *evidential probability*, probability on one's total evidence. Now in *Knowledge and its Limits* (2000: 209–37) I argued that such evidential probability itself depends on knowledge, because one's total evidence just is the total content of one's knowledge; that is the equation $E = K$. Obviously, to rely on that equation here would violate the point of the exercise. The equation $E = K$ will therefore not be used as a premise in what follows. Probabilistic claims will be assessed in probabilistic terms, without reference to questions of knowledge as such. However, in the upshot, similarities between the anti-luminosity conclusions for knowledge and for probability count against the idea that our epistemological thinking is badly distorted by our focus on knowledge rather than on probability.

2

Non-trivial conditions have been thought to be luminous because they have been regarded as epistemically perfectly accessible to the agent, completely open to view. When such a condition obtains, there should not even be a small non-zero probability that it does not obtain. The picture is that the agent has access to such a condition without the need of mediating evidence, because its obtaining is immediately evident to the agent. Thus the natural analogue of luminosity in probabilistic terms may be defined thus:

(LP)   Condition C is *luminous in probability 1* if and only if in every case in which C obtains, the probability that C obtains is 1.

Such a condition obtains with certainty whenever it obtains at all. 'Probability' in (LP) is to be understood as evidential probability, which is not assumed to be understood specifically in terms of knowledge. In this sense, probability is not objective chance; a natural law may have an objective chance of 1 of obtaining even though nobody has the slightest reason to think that it obtains.

We shall not attribute any purely computational limitations to the agents in question. Although extant forms of would-be operational epistemology tend to make very severe demands on agents' computational capacities, in failing to meet such demands one may be considered to fall short of perfect rationality. By contrast, such a verdict would be quite inappropriate in the sort of cases to be considered here.

As before, imagine a process of very gradual change from a case in which C clearly obtains to a case in which C clearly fails to obtain. It is certain for the agent that he or she will undergo such a gradual change in the underlying parameter relevant to C. Let $t_0, \ldots, t_n$ be a succession of times at very brief intervals from the beginning of the process to the end. Informally, the difference between the agent's situation at t_i and at t_{i+1} is below the agent's threshold of discrimination. Apart from this limit on discrimination, there is no further obstacle to the agent's determining whether C obtains; in particular, the agent's evidence is not positively misleading in any special way. In probabilistic terms, it seems natural to say that it is not certain for the agent at t_i that the situation is not the one that in fact obtains at t_{i+1}, although the agent might not describe the situation like that. It is not certain exactly where one is in the gradual process. Thus, if something obtains at the later time, the epistemic probability at the slightly earlier time that it obtained (at that earlier time) was non-zero.[1] That holds in particular for negative conditions: if something fails to obtain at the later time, the probability at the earlier time that it failed to obtain (at the earlier time) was non-zero. So, if the probability at the earlier time that the condition obtained was one, and the probability then that it failed to obtain was therefore zero, by contraposition the condition obtains at the later time. Hence, for a condition C:

(1_i)   If at t_i the probability that C obtains is 1, then at t_{i+1} C obtains.

Once again, it must be emphasized that (1_i) is merely a definition of a hypothetical process; it does not pretend to be a law of any sort.

Now suppose that C is luminous in probability 1. Then, by (LP):

(2_i)   If at t_i C obtains, then at t_i the probability that C obtains is 1.

Suppose also:

(3_i)   At t_i C obtains.

By *modus ponens* on (2_i) and (3_i):

(4_i)   At t_i the probability that C obtains is 1.

By *modus ponens* on (1_i) and (4_i):

(3_{i+1})   At t_{i+1} C obtains.

By construction of the example:

(3_0)   At t_0 C obtains.

By repeating the argument from (3_i) to (3_{i+1}) n times, for ascending values of i from 0 to $n - 1$, starting from (3_0):

(3_n)   At t_n C obtains.

---

[1] One must exclude trivial indexical ways of specifying conditions such as 'The condition that the time is now', which refer to different conditions at different points in the process.

But (3_n) is false by construction of the example. Thus the premises (1_0), ..., (1_{n-1}), (2_0), ..., (2_{n-1}) and (3_0) together entail a false conclusion. Consequently, not all those premises are true. But it has been argued that (1_0), ..., (1_{n-1}) and (3_0) are all true. Thus not all of (2_0), ..., (2_{n-1}) are true. But all of the latter follow from C's being luminous in probability 1. Thus C is not luminous in probability 1.

In its overall structure, the argument is isomorphic to the original anti-luminosity argument. It provides an extremely general template for arguing that a given condition is not luminous in probability 1. Of course, it is not completely universal, since it does not apply to conditions that always or never obtain: it assumes the possibility of a very gradual process of change that starts with cases in which C obtains and ends with cases in which C does not obtain. Evidently, one that starts with cases in which C does not obtain and ends with cases in which C obtains would do just as well.

Although the argument bears an obvious structural similarity to a sorites paradox, it does not trade on vagueness. In particular, it does not exploit any vagueness in the concept of probability or in the specification of condition C.

The epistemic reading of 'probability' is crucial to the case for the premises (1_0), ..., (1_{n-1}). The case concerns the agent's epistemic limitations, not objective chances. If natural laws and present circumstances determine that the condition obtains at one time, they may still determine that it does not obtain at a very slightly later time. But epistemic probability should also not be confused with pure subjective probability, the agent's credence or degree of belief. For all that has been said, the agent might be irrationally quite certain throughout the process that C obtains, in which case (1_{n-1}) would be false if 'probability' were read as degree of belief. The justification for (1_0), ..., (1_{n-1}) is that, during the gradual process, if C fails to obtain at one time, then it was already not certain on the agent's evidence very shortly before that C obtained then, however subjectively certain the agent was that it obtained. This sort of epistemic probability is far more relevant than pure subjective probability to any normative epistemology or philosophy of science that attempts to get beyond mere criteria of internal coherence.[2]

---

[2] Some hard-line subjective Bayesians will object at this point that the notion of Jeffrey conditionalization suffices for operational epistemology. For criticism, see Williamson (2000: 216–19).

3

Could a philosopher react to the argument of Section 2 by lowering the demand from luminosity in probability 1 to luminosity in probability x, for some real number x strictly between 0.5 and 1? For example, a condition C is *luminous in probability 0.9* if and only if, in every case in which C obtains, the probability that C obtains is at least 0.9. To argue in parallel fashion that C is not luminous in probability x, one would need in place of premise (1_i) the stronger claim that, if at t_i the probability that C obtains is at least x, then at t_{i+1} C obtains. That stronger claim might be hard to support. Formally, in some models, at each of the times $t_0, \ldots, t_n$ the probability that one is at that time is 0.9, with the remaining 0.1 of probability distributed equally among the immediately neighbouring times: such models make every condition whatsoever luminous in probability 0.9 while acknowledging that it is not certain exactly where one is in the gradual process.

As already hinted, such watered-down probabilistic notions of luminosity do not satisfy the motivations for postulating non-trivial luminous conditions in the first place. If it is probable but not certain that my evidence is what I think it is, then my failure to proportion my beliefs to my evidence might reflect my incomplete information about my evidence, and so be difficult to classify as irrationality on the operational epistemologist's conception. If it can be probable without being certain for one that one seems to oneself to see a red patch, then the rule 'Say "I seem to myself to see a red patch now!" when and only when one seems to oneself to see a red patch' cannot be part of a method in the operational epistemologist's sense. Luminosity only in probabilities less than 1 has many of the same philosophical consequences as anti-luminosity. Let us therefore return to the consideration of luminosity in probability 1.

4

The argument of Section 2 has a problematic feature. In explaining what it is, we can start by using times as convenient proxies for the relevant aspects of the situations at those times. Then the argument in effect assumes that, when one is at t_i, there is a non-zero epistemic probability c that one is at t_{i+1} instead. That assumption may look plausible if time is discrete, so that each moment has an immediate predecessor and an immediate successor. But, if time is dense, then there are infinitely many times between t_i and t_{i+1}. Presumably, for each of those intermediate times t, when one is at t_i, the epistemic probability that one is at t is at least as great as the epistemic probability that one is at t_{i+1}. Thus at t_i infinitely many disjoint events (incompatible propositions) have probability at least c, which is impossible because the probabilities of disjoint events must sum to at most 1. The natural assumption is rather that time is continuous and for any two times t and t^*, the probability when one is at t^* that one is at t is 0. Thus premise (1_i) is too strong. If condition C obtains at exactly t_{i+1} but at no other time, then the probability at any time (including both t_i and t_{i+1}) that C does not obtain may still be 1. In continuous probability spaces, probability 1 does not even entail truth.

Of course, what is typically at issue is the agent's information, not about the time itself, but about some aspect of the situation that changes over time, such as the agent's mental state. Hence what really matters is the discreteness or continuity of that aspect rather than of time itself. If time is continuous, some changing aspect of the situation may still be discrete: for example, the number of lights that are on. If time is discrete, some changing aspect of the situation may still take values from a continuous space of possibilities; even if only finitely many of those possibilities are actually realized in a period of finite length, infinitely many other possibilities may be epistemically at least as probable from the agent's perspective. Since many philosophically significant aspects of the agent's situation at least appear to admit of continuous variation, and that appearance cannot simply be dismissed as illusory, we must take the problem of continuous variation seriously. Much of the discussion will continue to be phrased in terms of the agent's information about the time, but it should not be forgotten that this is merely a convenient expository device.

We could try to fix the problem of continuous variation by permitting infinitesimal non-zero probabilities, since infinitely many non-zero infinitesimals can have a finite sum. However, such a reliance on non-standard probability theory would slightly weaken the argument by increasing its burden of assumptions. Let us therefore stick to standard real-valued probabilities and the assumptions that time is ordered like the real numbers and that for any two times t and t^*, the probability when one is at t^* that one is at t is 0.

Another attempted fix would treat the probabilities in question as conditional on the supposition that one is exactly at one of the times $t_0, \ldots, t_n$, while still allowing that time itself is continuous. However, if the (unconditional) probability that one is at a given t_i is 0, then the (unconditional) probability that one is at one of $t_0, \ldots, t_n$ is also 0; we cannot in general assume that probabilities conditional on a supposition of (unconditional) probability 0 are well defined. The technical problem is that the probability of p conditional on q $P(p|q)$ is usually defined as the ratio of unconditional probabilities $P(p\&q)/P(q)$, so that probabilities conditional on a supposition of (unconditional) probability 0 correspond to dividing by 0. One might instead take the conditional probability $P(p|q)$ as primitive and undefined, but that too would slightly weaken the argument by increasing its burden of assumptions.

A more natural approach works with arbitrary brief open intervals of time. Henceforth all talk of times and intervals is to be understood as restricted to times and intervals within the closed interval $[t_0, \ t_n]$, during which the gradual process takes place. The idea is that some short but non-zero length of time ε is such that at any time t^* there is a non-zero probability that one is in any given interval of non-zero duration within ε of t^*: at t^*, one has no certainty as to where one is in that interval. Thus, if t and t^{**} are two times such that $t^* - \varepsilon \leq t < t^{**} \leq t^* + \varepsilon$, then the probability at t^* that one is in the open interval (t, t^{**}) is non-zero. In effect, the quantity ε corresponds to the length of time from t_i to t_{i+1} in the discrete case, which was assumed independent of i (if the duration varied with i, we could simply choose a duration less than the minimum of those lengths for $i = 0, \ldots, n - 1$). Similarly, it was assumed that ε can be chosen small enough to be independent of t^*. This assumption is entirely plausible in the sorts of example with which we are concerned. Over the whole gradual process there is a finite limit to the agent's powers of discrimination; they do not become arbitrarily fine within the interval.

Now suppose that a condition C^* obtains throughout the interval (t, t^{**}) $(t < t^{**})$, and that t^* is in the longer interval $(t - \varepsilon, t^{**} + \varepsilon)$. Hence $t < t^* + \varepsilon$ and $t^* - \varepsilon < t^{**}$, so max $\{t, t^* - \varepsilon\} < \min\{t^{**}, t^* + \varepsilon\}$. Thus C^* obtains throughout the interval of non-zero duration (max$\{t, t^* - \varepsilon\}$, min$\{t^{**}, t^* + \varepsilon\}$), which is within the interval $(t^* - \varepsilon, t^* + \varepsilon)$. Consequently, by what was said in the previous paragraph, the probability at t^* that C^* obtains should be non-zero; as before, knowledge of the time was being used merely as a convenient proxy for knowledge of the conditions obtaining at the time. Now let C^* be the negation of condition C. We have in effect derived this constraint, similar to the contraposed version of (1_i):

(1) If C obtains at no time in a non-empty interval (t, t^{**}), then at no time in the interval $(t - \varepsilon, t^{**} + \varepsilon)$ is the probability that C obtains 1.

Now suppose again that C is luminous in probability 1. Consequently, by (LP), we have this analogue of the contraposed version of (2_i):

(2)   If at no time in the interval $(t - \varepsilon, t^{**} + \varepsilon)$ is the probability that C obtains 1, then C obtains at no time in the interval $(t - \varepsilon, t^{**} + \varepsilon)$.

Combining (1) and (2) yields:

(5)   If C obtains at no time in a non-empty interval (t, t^{**}), then C obtains at no time in the interval $(t - \varepsilon, t^{**} + \varepsilon)$.

But in the examples with which we are concerned, C does not just clearly fail to obtain at t_n; that time was chosen to be well within the period in which C fails to obtain, so that for some small but non-zero duration δ:

(6_0) C obtains at no time in the interval $(t - \delta, t)$.

Applying (5) i times to (6_0) yields this:

(6_i) C obtains at no time in the interval $(t - \delta - i\varepsilon, t + i\varepsilon)$.

By taking i large enough, we therefore derive:

(7)   C obtains at no time in the interval $[t_0, t_n]$.

But (7) is absurd, for by construction of the example C clearly obtains at t_0. Just as in Section 2, this constitutes a *reductio ad absurdum* of the supposition that condition C is luminous in probability 1. Although the argument differs in detail from that of Section 2, its spirit is recognizably the same.

Since the new argument requires an example in which the condition at issue fails to obtain throughout a small open interval, it is inapplicable to a slightly wider range of conditions than the original anti-luminosity argument was. Consider a condition for which between any two moments at which it obtains there is a moment at which it does not obtain and between any two moments at which it does not obtain there is a moment at which it does obtain (the rational and irrational numbers are so related). Such a condition satisfies (1) vacuously. Yet it need not violate luminosity, for on some distributions at every moment it has probability 1 of obtaining. But such curiosities are irrelevant to the original motivations for postulating non-trivial luminous conditions. The conditions at issue, such as seeming to see a red patch, surely can fail to obtain throughout an extended period.

The upshot of this section is that, although the continuity of time slightly complicates the form of the argument that a given condition is not luminous in probability 1, it does not undermine the argument in its philosophically most significant applications.

5

The continuity of time makes it even less promising to replace luminosity in probability 1 by luminosity in a probability strictly between 0.5 and 1 than it was in the discrete case (discussed in Section 3). For consider an example in which condition C supervenes on an underlying quantity q that increases gradually with time; for some constant c, C obtains at a time t if and only if the value of q at t is less than c. Suppose for simplicity that at any time t^* far from the beginning and from the end of the process, if the value of q is in fact x, then the epistemic probability that q is less than x is the same as the epistemic probability that q is greater than x, while the epistemic probability that q is exactly x itself is 0; although the assumption need not hold in all examples, it should hold in at least some. In those examples, the probability at t^* that q is less than x and the probability that q is greater than x are both 0.5. Suppose that, during the gradual process, a long period throughout which the condition C obtains is immediately followed by a long period throughout which C fails to obtain. If t^* is a time in the former period, but close to its end, so that x is less than c, then the probability at t^* that C obtains is in effect the probability that q is either less than x or between x and c, which is 0.5 plus the probability that q is between x and c. By choosing t^* so that x is closer and closer to c, we should be able to make the probability that q is between x and c closer and closer to 0. Consequently, for any real number $\varepsilon > 0$, there should be a time at which C obtains but the probability that C obtains is less than $0.5 + \varepsilon$, in other words, a counterexample to the claim that C is luminous in probability $0.5 + \varepsilon$, because one can choose t^* close enough to the end of the C period for the probability at t^* that q is between x [its actual value] and c to be less than ε.

Under the foregoing assumptions, the best to be hoped for is that, whenever C obtains, the probability that C obtains is greater than 0.5. That is slightly stronger than luminosity in probability 0.5, since it has 'greater than' in place of 'at least'. We can model the stronger claim by supposing that at each time t all the probability is uniformly distributed over the interval $(\max\{t_0, t - \varepsilon\}, \min\{t_n, t + \varepsilon\})$, and that (for some particular condition C) whenever C obtains at a time t it obtains throughout an open interval containing t of length greater than ε. But even the stronger claim is strikingly weak in relation to the original philosophical motivation for postulating interesting luminous conditions. To say that when something is part of one's evidence it is more probable than not for one that it is part of one's evidence falls far short of what would be required for the rule 'Proportion your confidence in a hypothesis to its probability on your evidence' to count as fully operational in the usual sense.

6

An alternative fallback from luminosity in probability 1 uses the mathematical notion of the *expectation* of a real-valued random variable, its mean value weighted by probability. A 'random variable' in this technical sense need not be perfectly random; any function from worlds or states to real numbers (such as the length of a given object in centimetres) constitutes a random variable. Let the agent's probability distribution at time t be P. If the random variable X takes values from the finite set I, then its expectation $E(X)$ at time t is defined by the equation:

(E) $E(X) = \sum_{x \in I} xP(X = x)$.

If X takes values in an infinite set, then the finite sum in (E) will need to be replaced by an infinite sum or integral. For present purposes we may omit mathematical details and harmlessly assume that the expectations with which we are concerned all have well-defined values. Now, even if the agent cannot be certain what the value of X is, the expected value of X may still equal its actual value. Moreover, the equality may be systematic. If the actual value of a variable is always its expected value on the agent's evidence, then the agent seems to have a special probabilistic sort of privileged access to that variable, potentially relevant to the theory of rationality. In such cases, the expected value is a perfect guide to the actual value.

Here is a simple example, which does not pretend to be realistic. Suppose that time is discrete. We model moments of time as the positive and negative integers. The variable T is the time. At each time t, it is equally likely that the time is any one of $t - 1$, t and $t + 1$, but certain that it is one of them: $P(T = t - 1) = P(T = t) = P(T = t + 1) = 1/3$. Consequently, at t, $E(T) = (t - 1)/3 + t/3 + (t + 1)/3 = t$. Thus the expected value of the time is always its actual value, even though one can never be certain what its actual value is.

A similar result holds if time is ordered like the real numbers, provided that at each moment probability is symmetrically distributed over past and future.

A tempting line of thought might seduce one into thinking that such a case cannot arise, at least if the agent has access to permanent features of the epistemic situation. For if one knows at t that the expected time is t, and that the expected time is always the actual time, one can deduce that the time is t, contrary to the original stipulation that at t the epistemic probability that the time is t is only 1/3.

The crucial fallacy in the tempting line of thought is the assumption that the agent is always in a position to know what the expectation of a variable is on its evidence. By the model, at t there is a 1/3 probability that the expectation of the time is $t - 1$ and a 1/3 probability that it is $t + 1$ (although the expectation of the expectation of the time is still t). This uncertainty about the values of expectations derives from uncertainty about the values of probabilities: for example, at t there is a 2/3 probability that there is a 1/3 probability that the time is $t + 1$ (since at both t and $t + 1$ there is a 1/3 probability that the time is $t + 1$), but there is also at t a 1/3 probability that there is probability 0 that the time is $t + 1$ (since at $t - 1$ there is probability 0 that the time is $t + 1$).

One might wonder what use expectations are to an agent who cannot be sure what their values are. But that is just to hanker again after luminosity in probability 1 (in this case, of the expectations), which we have already seen to be unobtainable in the cases that matter. If we really do face uncertainty all the way down, a prospect with which it is by no means easy to be comfortable, then variables whose uncertain actual values always coincide with their equally uncertain expected values might still have a privileged role to play in a sober, watered-down form of operational epistemology. At least they do not seem quite as badly off as variables whose actual values differ from their expected values. More specifically, one cannot operationalize such a rule any further by replacing such a random variable in the rule with its expectation, for the replacement makes no difference.[3]

Amongst the random variables whose expectations we sometimes wish to consider are expectations and probabilities themselves. Indeed, we can regard probabilities as special cases of expectations. For let the *truth value* of A be 1 if A is true and 0 otherwise. Then the probability of A is simply the expectation

[3] Williamson (2000: 230–7) explores uncertain probabilities within a framework based on the concept of knowledge.

of the truth value of A. Thus we shall be concerned with expectations of expectations and probabilities of probabilities. Such higher-order probabilities were already at issue when we considered uncertainty as to the value of the expectation E(T). These higher-order notions need delicate handling. Before proceeding further, it will therefore be prudent to develop a rigorous formal semantic framework for their treatment. It will keep us honest, and prevent us from stumbling into fallacies of equivocation in talk of probabilities of probabilities when many different probability distributions are in play. We can then investigate the significance of the anti-luminosity considerations for variables whose actual and expected values coincide.

7

We first construct a formal language for the expression of higher-order probabilities and expectations. For simplicity, the language does not include quantifiers. Adding them would involve deciding on a policy for handling the tricky problem of quantifying into epistemic contexts such as probability operators create. However, the language does include predicates and singular terms; the latter will all be understood as denoting real numbers.

We define the formulas and terms of the language by a simultaneous recursion:

There are countably many atomic variables X, Y, Z, . . . (informally, denoting real numbers; they correspond to random variables).

For each rational number c there is an atomic constant $[c]$ (informally, denoting c).

If T and U are terms then T $+$ U is a term ($+$ is informally read as 'plus').

If A is a formula then $\neg$A is a formula ($\neg$ is informally read as 'it is not the case that').

If A and B are formulas then A & B is a formula (& is informally read as 'and').

If A is a formula then V(A) is a term (V is informally read as 'the truth value of').

If T and U are terms then T $\leq$ U is a formula ($\leq$ is informally read as 'is less than or equal to').

If T is a term then E(T) is a term (E is informally read as 'the expectation of').

Other truth functors can be introduced as meta-linguistic abbreviations in the usual way. Moreover, 'T = U' abbreviates $T \leq U$ & $U \leq T$ and 'T < U' abbreviates $T \leq U$ & $\neg U \leq T$ (mathematical symbols will be used in both object-language and meta-language since they are being used with the same sense). The expression 'P(A)' for the probability of A abbreviates $E(V(A))$. The inclusion of infinitely many atomic constants is for mathematical convenience only. In particular applications only finitely many such constants are needed.

We must now give a model-theoretic semantics for the language. A model is a triple <W, Prob, F>, where W is a non-empty set, Prob is a function from members of W to probability distributions over W, and F is a function from atomic terms to their intensions, functions from members of W to real numbers. Informally, W is the set of states or worlds; for a world $w \in$ W, Prob(w) is the epistemic probability distribution for the agent at w; if T is an atomic term, F(T)(w) is the value of the random variable T at w. We define the truth value at w of A, val(w, A), and the denotation at w of T, den(w, T), for all worlds w, formulas A and terms T by another simultaneous recursion:

If T is an atomic variable, den(w, T) $=$ F(T)(w).

If c is a rational number, den(w, [c]) $= c$.

If T and U are terms, den(w, T $+$ U) $=$ den(w, T) $+$ den(w, U).

If A is a formula, val(w, $\neg$A) $= 1 -$ val(w, A).

If A and B are formulas, val(w, A & B) $=$ min{val(w, A), val(w, B)}.

If A is a formula, den(w, V(A)) $=$ val(w, A).

If T and U are terms, val(w, T $\leq$ U) $= 1$ if den(w, T) $\leq$ den(w, U) and 0 otherwise.

If T is a term, den(w, E(T)) is the expectation with respect to the probability distribution Prob(w) of the random variable whose value at each world $x \in$ W is den(x, T).

To illustrate the last clause, if W is finite, then:

$$\text{den}(w, E(T)) = \sum_{x \in W} \text{den}(x, T)\text{Prob}(w)(\{x\})$$

When W is infinite, an analogous infinite sum or integral applies. We count <W, Prob, F> as a model only if the expectation den(w, E(T)) is well defined for every $w \in$ W and term T of the language.

This semantics determines truth conditions for statements involving arbitrary iterations of the probability and expectation operators. It was the tacit background to much of the preceding discussion, and can be used to make it precise. One striking effect of the semantics is that the expectation of the expectation of a variable need not be its expectation; in other words, some expectations in some models fall outside the class of random variables whose actual and expected values always coincide. Consider the following model $<W, \text{Prob}, F>$. It has three worlds; $W = \{u, v, w\}$. Informally, think of the worlds close to u as just u itself and v, of the worlds close to w as just v and w itself, and of all worlds as close to v. Then Prob maps each world to the probability distribution that makes all the worlds close to that one equiprobable, and assigns probability zero to any other world. Thus $\text{Prob}(u)(\{u\}) = \text{Prob}(u)(\{v\}) = \frac{1}{2}$ and $\text{Prob}(u)(\{w\}) = 0$; $\text{Prob}(v)(\{u\}) = \text{Prob}(v)(\{v\}) = \text{Prob}(v)(\{w\}) = 1/3$; $\text{Prob}(w)(\{u\}) = 0$ and $\text{Prob}(w)(\{v\}) = \text{Prob}(w)(\{w\}) = \frac{1}{2}$. Treat X as the random variable with these values: $\text{den}(u, X) = F(X)(u) = 8$; $\text{den}(v, X) = F(X)(v) = 4$; $\text{den}(w, X) = F(X)(w) = 0$. It is now elementary to calculate that $\text{den}(u, E(X)) = 6$, $\text{den}(v, E(X)) = 4$ and $\text{den}(w, E(X)) = 2$. Iterating the process, we calculate that $\text{den}(u, E(E(X))) = 5$, $\text{den}(v, E(E(X))) = 4$ and $\text{den}(w, E(E(X))) = 3$. Thus the expectation of the expectation of X differs from the expectation of X at the worlds u and w, although not at v.

A paradox may seem to threaten. For is not one of the most elementary facts that students learn about calculating expectations the equation '$E(E(X)) = E(X)$'? But the expression '$E(E(X))$' conceals an ambiguity. For, since '$E(X)$' is in effect a definite description, a question arises about its scope in the context '$E(E(X))$'. The standard textbook treatment assigns '$E(X)$' wide scope in '$E(E(X))$'; informally, the expectation of the expectation of X is simply the expectation of that constant 'random variable' whose value is always c, where c is in fact the actual expectation of X. This reading is of course perfectly intelligible and legitimate; it makes the equation '$E(E(X)) = E(X)$' trivially correct and does not really raise any issue of higher-order expectations or probabilities. The value of '$E(E(X))$' on the wide scope reading can be calculated on the basis of a single probability distribution. But equally intelligible and legitimate is a reading on which '$E(X)$' has narrow scope in '$E(E(X))$'. The semantics above generates the latter reading and is quite natural. It is this reading that we need in order to raise genuine questions about higher-order expectations and probabilities, and it does not make the equation '$E(E(X)) = E(X)$' trivially correct. The value of '$E(E(X))$' on the narrow scope reading depends on a probability distribution over probability distributions. When we evaluate '$E(E(X))$' at a world w, we evaluate a random variable '$E(X)$'

whose value at a world w^* depends on the probability distribution at w^*, not on that at w.

We can see the difference between the two readings in practice by considering the defining equation for the *variance* of a random variable, '$\text{Var}(X) = E((X - E(X))^2)$'. $\text{Var}(X)$ is supposed to measure how much X is expected to deviate from its mean: the dispersion of X. Consider the example in Section 6 of a random variable whose actual and expected values always coincide. Since the equation '$E(X) = X$' is always certain to be true, the value of $(X - E(X))^2$ is always certain to be 0, so the value of '$E((X - E(X))^2)$' on the narrow scope reading is always 0 too. But of course on the wide scope reading, the value of '$E((X - E(X))^2)$' at any time t, where $E(X) = t$, is calculated in the usual way as $((t - 1 - t)^2 + (t - t)^2 + (t + 1 - t)^2)/3 = 2/3$. Both readings give genuine information, but they given different information. The wide scope reading tells us that, for any number c, if c is in fact the expected value of X then X is expected to deviate from c by a certain amount. The narrow scope reading tells us that it is certain that X will not deviate from its expected value.

Having clarified these matters, let us apply the semantics above to determine whether variables whose actual and expected values always coincide constitute a useful fallback from probabilistic luminosity in the previous senses.

8

Let us start with the simple case in which the set W of worlds is finite. The anti-luminosity considerations trade on the possibility of constructing sorites series between radically different cases. Suppose that such series always exist in W, in this sense:

SORITES   For any $w, x \in W$, there are $w_0, \ldots, w_n \in W$ such that $w = w_0$, $x = w_n$ and for $0 \leq i$, $j \leq n$, if $|i - j| \leq 1$ then $\text{Prob}(w_i)$ $(\{w_j\}) > 0$.

The idea is that at any world it is uncertain whether one is at that world or at one of its immediate neighbours in the series. In particular, for $0 \leq i < n$, $\text{Prob}(w_i)(\{w_{i+1}\}) > 0$ by SORITES. Very roughly, one can get from any world to any world via a chain of worlds each of which is imperfectly discriminable from its predecessor. In this sense, one world is imperfectly discriminable from another if and only if it is not certain for the agent at the latter world that the former does not obtain.

In this setting we can now reconstruct the argument against luminosity. Suppose that we are interested in the value of a term T, and that its expected and actual values always coincide. That is:

(#)   For all $w \in W$, $\text{den}(w, T) = \sum_{x \in W} \text{den}(x, T)\text{Prob}(w)(\{x\})$.

Since W is finite, $\text{den}(w, T)$ attains a maximum value $\max(T)$ at some world w. Let MAX(T) be the set of worlds at which T attains this maximum, $\{x \in W: \text{den}(x, T) = \max(T)\}$. Suppose that $y \in \text{MAX}(T)$, and that the world z is imperfectly discriminable from y: $\text{Prob}(y)(\{z\}) > 0$. Consequently, by (#):

$$\begin{aligned} \max(T) &= \text{den}(y, T) = \sum_{x \in W} \text{den}(x, T)\text{Prob}(y)(\{x\}) \\ &\leq \max(T)(1 - \text{Prob}(y)(\{z\}) + \text{den}(z, T)\text{Prob}(y)(\{z\}) \\ &= \max(T) - (\max(T) - \text{den}(z, T))\text{Prob}(y)(\{z\}). \end{aligned}$$

Thus $(\max(T) - \text{den}(z, T))\text{Prob}(y)(\{z\}) \leq 0$. But $\text{den}(z, T) \leq \max(T)$ and $\text{Prob}(y)(\{z\}) > 0$, so $\text{den}(z, T) = \max(T)$, so $z \in \text{MAX}(T)$. Thus any world imperfectly discriminable from a world in MAX(T) is itself in MAX(T). Consequently, any chain of imperfect discriminability that starts in MAX(T) remains wholly in MAX(T). Hence, by SORITES, any world in W can be reached from a world in MAX(T) by a chain of imperfect discriminability. Therefore, every world in W is in MAX(T). So T attains its maximum at every world in W: in other words, T is constant.

What we have proved is that, in the finite case, SORITES implies that a random variable whose expected and actual values always coincide is trivial, in the sense that its value cannot vary across worlds. But that rules out the variables in which we are most interested, since they do differ in value between worlds (or states) that are joined by a series of imperfectly discriminable intermediaries. In particular, the agent's evidence and mental state vary over such sorites series. We cannot model learning from experience with respect to a random variable that is constant across all epistemic worlds, for then its expectation on the evidence will also be constant across all such worlds. Consequently, at least when the state space is finite, it is useless to postulate an epistemically privileged set of variables whose actual and expected values always coincide. Those variables would exclude everything that can be learnt from new experiences that develop gradually out of old ones.

A similar argument sometimes applies even when the set of worlds is countably infinite, although the condition that the term T attains a maximum value at some world is no longer automatically satisfied. The probability distributions required for SORITES may also be less natural in that case, since one cannot give the same non-zero probability to infinitely many worlds. If the set of worlds is uncountably infinite, SORITES must fail, because at most countably many worlds are imperfectly discriminable in the relevant probabilistic sense from any given world, so at most countably many worlds are linked by a finite chain of imperfect discriminability to a given world. Thus the infinite case requires separate consideration.

An easy generalization is to cases in which, although there are infinitely many worlds, the term T takes values only from a finite set. A more useful generalization is to all cases in which T attains a maximum value without certainty that it does so:

UNCMAX   For some $w \in W$: for all $x \in W$, $\text{den}(x, T) \leq \text{den}(w, T)$, but $\text{Prob}(w)(\{x: \text{den}(x, T) < \text{den}(w, T)\}) > 0$.

By the second conjunct of UNCMAX, $\text{Prob}(w)(\{x: \text{den}(x, T) + 1/n \leq \text{den}(w, T)\}) > 0$ for some natural number n.[4] Let $\text{Prob}(w)(\{x: \text{den}(x, T) + 1/n \leq \text{den}(w, T)\})$ be p; thus $p > 0$. Then

$$\text{den}(w, E(T)) \leq \text{den}(w, T)(1 - p) + (\text{den}(w, T) - 1/n)p = \text{den}(w, T) - p/n < \text{den}(w, T).$$

Thus it is false at w that the actual and expected values of T coincide. Similarly, they fail to coincide when T attains its minimum without certainty that it does so.

A central application of the preceding result concerns cases in which T is itself a probability, so that $E(T)$ is in effect the expectation of an expectation. If T attains the value 1 at some world, that is of course its maximum. Thus, if an event can be certain without being certainly certain, the actual and expected values of the probability of that event do not always coincide.[5]

---

[4] Since $\text{den}(w, E(V(T < [\text{den}(w, T)])))$ and $\text{den}(w, E(V(T + [1/n] \leq [\text{den}(w, T)])))$ are well defined by definition of a model, the probabilities in the argument and UNCMAX are also well defined. The argument that $\text{Prob}(w)(\{x: \text{den}(x, T) + 1/n \leq \text{den}(w, T)\}) > 0$ for some n assumes that Prob is countably additive. If countably non-additive probability distributions are allowed, that derived condition should be used in UNCMAX instead.

[5] In a series of papers, Dov Samet (1997, 1998, 2000) has investigated constraints in epistemic logic related to those examined here. In particular, he considers the 'averaging' axiom that the actual and expected probabilities of an event must coincide (which he takes from Skyrms 1980 and Jeffrey 1992) and shows that in the finite case it implies certainty that if the probability of an event has a given value then it is certain that it has that value. Roughly speaking, Samet's results

One might suppose certainty to imply certainty of certainty, but that is to suppose certainty to be luminous in probability 1, which by earlier results we must expect it not to be unless the standard for certainty is set almost impossibly high. Of course, some philosophers will retort that certainty is an (almost) impossibly high standard for empirical beliefs. If some event cannot attain probability 1, but can attain any probability less than 1, then the preceding argument does not apply to it. However, an event might also attain a maximum probability less than 1. For example, let w and w^* be similar but not perfectly similar worlds, and consider the probability of the condition C that one is at a world more similar to w than w^* is. Other things being equal, that probability will normally attain a maximum at w itself. However, at w, there may well be a positive probability that one is at a world slightly different from w at which the probability that C obtains is less than maximal; then UNCMAX is satisfied. Consequently, at w the expected probability that C obtains is less than the actual probability. As already noted, not even expectations have the epistemic privilege that their expected value is always their actual value.

It might still be tempting to think that, even if probabilities and expectations lack a perfect epistemic privilege, they are still epistemically more privileged than what they are probabilities or expectations of. Thus one might regard the sequence of a random variable, its expectation, the expectation of its expectation, the expectation of the expectation of its expectation, . . . as tending in the direction of ever greater but never perfect epistemic privilege. The trouble with this idea is that the increase in epistemic privilege is typically achieved by the washing-out of empirical evidence. This phenomenon is vivid

concern the hypothesis that the axiom is universally satisfied, whereas the present enquiry is into the hypothesis that a particular event satisfies it. Williamson (2000: 311–15) proves that, on a frame for epistemic logic in which one can know without knowing that one knows or fail to know without knowing that one fails to know, unconditional prior probabilities do not always coincide with the prior expectations of posterior probabilities, where posterior probabilities at a world are the results of conditionalizing prior probabilities on the total content of what one knows at that world. That framework is more restrictive than the present one. To take the simplest case, consider a model with just two worlds, w and x. On the present framework, the event $\{w\}$ could have probability 2/3 at w and probability 1/3 at x. That cannot happen within the framework of Williamson (2000), since conditionalization is either on the whole of $\{w, x\}$, which makes no difference, or on a singleton set, in which case all probabilities go to 1 or 0: thus no event ever has a probability strictly between 0 and 1 other than its prior probability (of course, that result does not generalize to models with more than two worlds). Since that more restrictive framework is justified by the knowledge-centred approach, it cannot be assumed here.

when the number of worlds is finite. Suppose that it is, and that SORITES holds: any two worlds are linked by a chain of imperfectly discriminable pairs. Let T be any random variable. Then it is provable that the sequence T, E(T), E(E(T)), ... converges to the same limit *whichever world one is at*.[6] The original variable T may encode significant information about which world one is at, differentiating some worlds from others, but the process of taking iterated expectations gradually wipes out those differences. Thus the tendency in the direction of epistemic privilege is a tendency in the direction of failing to learn from experience.

As usual, the picture is more complex when the number of worlds is infinite, but it is doubtful that the extra complexities make very much difference to the overall upshot for epistemology. Under realistic assumptions, taking iterated expectations still tends to wipe out empirical differences and thereby undermine learning from experience.

9

The more one tries to privilege something epistemically, the less it can discriminate between different states of the world. Of course, empirical evidence must have *some* epistemic privilege, otherwise there would be no point for the epistemologist in distinguishing it from what it is evidence about. But, if it has too much epistemic privilege, then it no longer discriminates between initially possible outcomes as learning requires. The notion of evidence is held in place, not altogether comfortably, by these opposing pressures. The conception of evidence as the total content of one's knowledge (the equation $E = K$) is a compromise of just the required kind.

---

[6] Proof: one can consider the worlds as states in a Markov chain, with $\text{Prob}(i)(\{j\})$ as the one-step transition probability from state i to state j. Let $p_{ij}(n)$ be the transition probability that one is at j after n steps starting from j. Let $E^0(T) = T$ and $E^{n+1}(T) = E(E^n(T))$. Then, by induction on n, for any n and $i \in W$, $\text{den}(i, E^n(T)) = \sum_{j \in W} \text{den}(j, T)p_{ij}(n)$. But by SORITES the Markov chain is irreducible and aperiodic, so by a standard result about Markov chains (Grimmett and Stirzaker 2001: 232), $p_{ij}(n)$ converges to a limit that is independent of i as n goes to infinity. Consequently, $\text{den}(i, E^n(T))$ also converges to a limit that is independent of i as n goes to infinity. This result subsumes the earlier result that if $E(T) = T$ all worlds in a finite model with SORITES then T is constant.

The considerations of this chapter suggest that the anti-luminosity arguments of *Knowledge and its Limits* are robust. They are not symptoms of an isolated pathological quirk in the ordinary concept of knowledge, 'the epistemology of the stone age'. Rather, they can be replicated from a probabilistic starting point, and reflect the general predicament of creatures with limited powers of discrimination in their attempt to learn from experience. As epistemologists, we need the concept of probability, but the idea that our pervasive fallibility requires that it replace the concept of knowledge is itself the product of residual infallibilistic assumptions, which attribute imaginary epistemic privileges to probability itself. We are fallible even about the best descriptions of our own fallibility. The concept of knowledge is adapted to just such a predicament. In particular, it can demarcate the evidence that conditions evidential probabilities.

By contrast, the operational epistemologist's attempt to work without such 'impure' concepts results in a futile psychologization of the concept of evidence, on which one's evidence is reduced to one's present subjective states. That concept of evidence diverges drastically from what we need to understand the objectivity of the natural sciences, yet still fails to achieve the kind of luminosity that the psychologization aimed to achieve. Like other movements driven by unrealistic idealism disguised as tough-mindedness, the operationalization of epistemology would destroy what it sets out to reform.

References

Brueckner, A., and Fiocco, M. O. (2002). 'Williamson's Anti-Luminosity Argument', *Philosophical Studies*, 110: 285–93.

Conee, E. (2005). 'The Comforts of Home'. *Philosophy and Phenomenological Research*, 70: 444–51.

Grimmett, G., and Stirzaker, D. (2001). *Probability and Random Processes*. 3rd edn.; Oxford: Oxford University Press.

Jeffrey, R. (1992). *Probability and the Art of Judgement*. Cambridge: Cambridge University Press.

Neta, R., and Rohrbaugh, G. (2004). 'Luminosity and the Safety of Knowledge', *Pacific Philosophical Quarterly*, 85: 396–406.

Samet, D. (1997). 'On the Triviality of High-Order Probabilistic Beliefs'. *Game Theory and Information*, REPECc:wpa:wuwpga:9705001.

Samet, D. (1998). 'Iterated expectations and common priors'. *Games and Economic Behaviour*, 24: 131–41.

—— (2000). 'Quantified Beliefs and Believed Quantities', *Journal of Economic Theory*, 95: 169–85.

Skyrms, B. (1980). *Causal Necessity*. New Haven, CT: Yale University Press.

Williamson, T. (2000). *Knowledge and its Limits*. Oxford: Oxford University Press.

12

Epistemology Dehumanized

Panayot Butchvarov

Fundamental disagreements in epistemology arise from legitimate differences of interest, not genuine conflict. It is because of such differences that there are three varieties of epistemology: naturalistic, subjective, and what I shall call epistemology-as-logic. All three have been with us at least since Socrates. My chief concern will be with the third, but I must begin with the first and second, which constitute standard epistemology.

1. Naturalistic epistemology

It seems obvious that epistemology should be naturalistic. Its name is a synonym of "theory of knowledge", the knowledge in question is human, and humans are parts of nature, of its *fauna*. Epistemology naturalized is epistemology humanized: it is about humans. Not only does it ignore god, angels, and extraterrestrials, it ignores even bats. This is why, however, it also lacks the generality and abstraction distinctive of philosophy, which perhaps alone justify its existence alongside the other cognitive disciplines. Humans belong in the subject matter of several special sciences seeking detailed information about such traditional epistemological topics as perception, imagination, memory, and reasoning. This is why naturalistic epistemology is largely programmatic, the substantive work being done by biology and psychology. Quine, who championed it, often mentioned the role of "surface irritations", but wisely left the study of those irritations to neurology. Naturalistic epistemology remains focused on human matters even when straying into non-human biological and non-biological computational states. The intrinsic interest of such states is indisputable, but epistemology considers them mainly for the light they cast on human epistemic states.

Of course, there is a way in which humanity is central in epistemology—namely, that leading to Kant's transcendental idealism and its recent successors—for example, Goodman's irrealism and Putnam's internal realism. How we perceive and understand the world, and thus the world itself as perceived and understood, depend on our faculties of perception and understanding; they depend on *us*.[1] But this is not a proposition of zoology—zoological facts, too, depend on us in this way. It is not a proposition about humans, even though we are humans. It is a virtual tautology. (I shall say more about it at the end of Section 2.) Even astronomy is "humanized" in this sense, but it is about stars and planets, not humans. This is why the proposition implies no relativity to humans, let alone to any particular human culture, age, tradition, language, or writing. Nor does it imply that *everything* depends on our cognitive faculties. Kant pointed out that the notion of things as they are in themselves is not self-contradictory, and a central thesis of his transcendental idealism was that there are such things.[2] If we disagreed, we would be committing ourselves to a peculiar sort of creationism, to epistemic creation *ex nihilo* by humans. Nor is idealism implied, if this is the metaphysical view that only minds and their states exist. Kant vigorously defended both "transcendental idealism" and "empirical realism"—that is, realism with respect to the observable world, finding the two not only compatible but requiring each other. And the distinction between perception and understanding need not be sharp. They are not separate and unequal stages of cognitive development. While a neonate may "see", in the sense that it is not blind, only much later does it see Mother. Mere sensation is at most a necessary prelude to cognition, and itself cognitive only by courtesy. It should not be confused with experience, which Kant described as "a species of knowledge which involves understanding".[3] Kant's view of the understanding

---

[1] I discuss this topic in 'Metaphysical Realism and Logical Nonrealism', in Richard Gale, (ed.) *Blackwell Guide to Metaphysics* (Oxford: Blackwell, 2002), 282–302.

[2] Immanuel Kant, *Critique of Pure Reason*, trans. Paul Guyer and Allen W. Wood (Cambridge: Cambridge University Press, 1998), B xxviii.

[3] Ibid., B xvii.

was mentalistic, his concepts prime examples of what Sartre sarcastically called "inhabitants of consciousness". In this respect its successors, for which the understanding is essentially linguistic, seem superior. We may question the existence of inhabitants of consciousness, but we are not likely to question the existence of language. There is no need, however, to subscribe to the extremist view that all cognition involves language. A prelinguistic child's recognition of Mother does not. But surely any cognition at all developed and distinctively human does.

Naturalistic epistemology may be only programmatic, but the pedigree of the program is impressive. Allowing for the differences in our knowledge of nature, we must concede that much of Aristotle's epistemology was naturalistic. When he described the parts and functions of the soul, he was not doing anything in principle different from what biologists and psychologists do today. And the rationale of the program is impeccable. Surely, human beings are parts of nature. This is why the study of them and of their epistemic states belongs today in the natural sciences. It would be strange to propose to study them non-empirically, in a "philosophical" way. If epistemic states are parts of nature but irreducibly mental, their study would still belong in the natural sciences, though these might then include introspective psychology. Wundt was a scientist, in any reasonable sense of the word. He did not rely only on his own introspective findings, but took seriously and gathered what others reported, engaging also in genuine, not "thought", experiments. Even if human epistemic states were not parts of nature, perhaps by being states of immortal souls, the study of them would not fall wholly outside the natural sciences. Neither Plato nor Aquinas ignored human biology and psychology. An immortal soul is still human because it is the soul of a human being, a certain animal.

If human beings, including their epistemic states, belong in the subject matter of disciplines other than philosophy, the obvious question is what room is left for naturalistic epistemology. Concern over this question explains the shift to a conception of epistemology as just "conceptual", not "factual"—neither about natural facts nor about non-natural facts—and its consequent preoccupation with "definitions", "analyses", or "elucidations" of the "workings of our language". This shift, of course, was not limited to naturalistic epistemology. For much the same reasons, it is distinctive of analytic philosophy as a whole, including analytic ethics.[4] But, if concepts are in nature—presumably, in human brains or languages—they, too, are outside philosophers' competence: there is neurology, as well as linguistics and lexicography. (If they are not in nature—for example, if they are Platonic Forms—then a naturalistic epistemology should have no concern with them.) The study of brain states and words calls not for "definitions" or "elucidations", tested by "intuitions", but for meticulous empirical descriptions and fruitful hypotheses, tested by standard scientific methods. The very idea of aiming at elucidations of brain states is foreign to neurology. As to words, it has been more than half a century since Wittgenstein pointed out that they are not used in accordance with necessary and sufficient conditions, and thus that their uses cannot be captured in definitions. It would be a non-starter to suggest that at least one can study one's own uses of words or the contents of one's own concepts. Even if we allow that someone might own private meanings or concepts, and know introspectively what they are, it is unclear why we should be interested in them.

Epistemology is the theory of knowledge, but the word "knowledge" is ambiguous. It may be understood in two ways: as standing for a disciplinary achievement, as in grammar (Aristotle's favorite example), astronomy, and arithmetic, or for a personal achievement. The first way leads to the philosophy of science and the sociology of knowledge, both understood as seeking accounts of certain collective human activities, and thus as naturalistic. Epistemology took the second way.

That way calls for a further distinction. I may concern myself with *human* personal knowledge. I may ask whether, how, and what knowledge is possible for a human—for me, you, or Jack—given the facts about our common as well as our idiosyncratic cognitive functions and capacities. If so, my epistemological endeavor is still humanized and naturalistic. Or I may concern myself with my knowledge. I may ask whether, how, and what knowledge is possible for *me*, abstracting from the fact that I am human, and ignoring you and Jack. This is the skeptic's question, especially when it concerns the existence of a material world, things "outside us", bodies, including yours, Jack's, and mine. If so, my epistemological endeavor is subjective.

---

[4] See my "Ethics Dehumanized", Proceedings of the Spindel Conference 2002, *Southern Journal of Philosophy*, supplementary volume, and "Saying and Showing the Good", in Heather Dyke (ed.), *Time and Ethics* (Kluwer, 2003).

2. Subjective epistemology

While naturalistic epistemology lacks sufficient generality to be philosophical, subjective epistemology lacks generality altogether. It is baldly and bleakly about only one person—hardly a topic of scientific or philosophical interest, whoever and whatever that person might be. But if when concerned with my knowledge I presupposed, explicitly or implicitly, my humanity, including my body, language, and place on earth or time in history, then my epistemological endeavor would remain humanized and naturalistic, though perhaps narcissistic. It would not be subjective. The term "subjective" should not be understood as a synonym of "mental" or "mentalistic". Quine's rejection of Cartesian epistemology on naturalistic grounds was both too narrow and too wide. It was too narrow because what is characteristic of Descartes's epistemology was not its subject matter, a "thinking thing"—he had to *argue* for its existence—but the exclusive use of first-person indexicals in its defining initial stages. One need not be naturalistically, "scientifically", minded to object to it for that reason. And Quine's rejection of Cartesian epistemology was too wide because in those stages, including the proof of "I exist", it was consistent with a materialist ontology, as Chisholm has suggested.[5] *Pace* Descartes and almost all other philosophers, his *cogito* had no ontological content. If minds were immaterial, your mind would be something objective from my perspective, as God and angels are for the religious person. And my brain, like Chisholm's "microscopic part" of it, would be something subjective, if I could refer to it only as *my* brain. Epistemological ventures, whether Descartes's or Quine's, seldom benefit from ontological adventures.

This is why subjective epistemology is not a capricious narrowing of the subject matter of naturalistic epistemology from all humans to just one. If it were, it would be of no philosophical interest. It arose as a distinct variety of epistemology in order to face the skeptical challenge. The skeptic cannot assume that he or she is human, since being human involves having a body, a part of the material world. Therefore, the subjective epistemologist also cannot make this assumption. It would beg the question against the skeptic. A subjective epistemologist cannot consistently write "An essay concerning human understanding", or "A treatise concerning the principles of human

---

[5] Roderick M. Chisholm, *A Realistic Theory of Categories* (New York: Cambridge University Press, 1996), 99–105.

knowledge", or "A treatise of human nature"—these would belong in naturalistic epistemology, and today in psychology and biology. While there have always been rough equivalents of naturalistic epistemology, subjective epistemology was essentially Cartesian, though it was anticipated by the Greek skeptics, especially Sextus Empiricus. Its *raison d'être* was the project of answering the skeptic. If and when it succeeds, its mission is accomplished, and only naturalistic epistemology and epistemology-as-logic are left.

Naturalistic epistemology does not beg the question against the skeptic by taking its subject matter to be human because it is not concerned with the skeptic's question. In fact, though a "theory of knowledge", it need have little concern with knowledge itself. It is best taken to be concerned with cognition, as this is understood by cognitive psychology and the other cognitive sciences—that is, as the faculty of knowledge. Knowledge is success in the employment of that faculty, but the faculty is of interest even when not employed successfully. Sense perception, imagination, memory, and intelligence are worthy of investigation even when not leading to knowledge. In subjective epistemology, however, only success counts, since as an attempt to answer the skeptic its concern is with the veridicality of cognitive states. Its focus, therefore, must be on knowledge. Alleged cognitive states such as rational, justified, probable, and warranted belief or opinion are at best images of knowledge, and we seek them only as a consolation prize. We seek them when knowledge is absent or impossible, in the hope of finding something still worth having.

This is why, as used in epistemology, "rational", "justified", "probable", and "warranted" are technical terms, usually taken as primitive and thus of obscure meaning and uncertain reference. For example, in everyday usage "justified" is a deontic term, and thus "justified belief", the central phrase in recent epistemological discussion, is a solecism: actions are justified or unjustified, but beliefs are not actions. If told that the phrase stands for belief resulting from reliable processes, this would be a verbal stipulation, far removed from common usage, without discernible rationale, and therefore misleading. Even the word "belief", plain and unadorned by adjectives, is used in current epistemology with questionable sense and reference. "S believes that *p*" (e.g., "S believe that Jones owns a Ford", uttered as contribution to office chatter) functions there roughly as a synonym of the colloquial "S thinks that *p*", and is no more enlightening in philosophy or needed in psychology than the latter. It is not used for expression of religious faith or other commitments, which do have psychological reality and thus are of interest to psychology and, perhaps, to philosophy. The words "rational", "justified", "probable", and "warranted", whether applied to such a phantom belief or to the sentences, statements, assertions, judgments, hypotheses, and so on supposedly expressing it, are often prefaced by the adjective "epistemic". But this makes them even less clear, because in English the noun corresponding to that adjective is "knowledge"—exactly the word they are used to displace. None of them is the natural and traditional word for describing what we might have in cases where we have no knowledge but hope we are not entirely ignorant. That word has been "evidence".

The root of "evidence" is the same as the root of "evident". But to be *evident* is to be *seen* or at least to be readily visible, whether literally or metaphorically, thus *known* or readily knowable, and therefore (if a proposition) *true*. "Seeing is believing," the saying goes, but it usually means that seeing is knowing. Hence, the traditional account of knowledge as apprehension, intuition, awareness, acquaintance. But for our purposes it suffices that being evident entails being known, and we can bracket the question whether being known entails being evident. As we shall see shortly, there is also what has been called the weak sense of "know", and of course there are many other senses.[6] But we need not, and for the reasons mentioned earlier should not, seek a definition of "know", or of any other everyday word.

Often, something is evident not by being seen to be true by itself, but by being seen to follow from something else that is seen to be true. We seldom say, however, that the latter is *evidence* for the former. We seldom call the premises of a valid deductive argument evidence for its conclusion, even if they are evident and the argument has a form as simple as *modus ponens*. Rather, we speak of evidence when what we want to know is neither evident nor seen to follow from anything evident, yet think or hope that something else "supports" it in some other manner. J. L Austin wrote:

The situation in which I would properly be said to have *evidence* for the statement that some animal is a pig is that, for example, in which the beast itself is not actually on view, but I can see plenty of pig-like marks on the ground outside its retreat. If I find a few buckets of pig-food, that's more evidence, and the noises and the smell may

---

[6] The distinction between a weak and a strong sense of "know" was made by Norman Malcolm in "Knowledge and Belief", included in *Knowledge and Certainty* (Englewood Cliffs, NJ: Prentice-Hall, 1963), 58–72.

provide better evidence still. But if the animal then emerges and stands there plainly in view, there is no longer any question of collecting *evidence*; its coming into view doesn't provide me with more evidence that it's a pig, I can now just see that it is, the question is settled.[7]

Austin might have agreed, however, that, when the animal is plainly in view, it is *evident* that it is a pig. And we might add that this is *self-evident*, as long as we mean nothing more than that, though evident, it does not owe its being evident to something else that is evident.[8] Taken literally, of course, the term "self-evident" is a pleonasm, just as "self-seen" and "self-visible" would be. But it serves to mark the important difference between what is evident by itself and what is evident only by being seen to follow from something else that is evident by itself. Even in a *modus ponens* argument with evident premises, the conclusion might not be evident unless *seen* to follow from the premises. It might be evident only in relation to them.

Skepticism and thus subjective epistemology begin with the fact that usually what we want to know is neither self-evident nor made evident by anything else that is evident. We try to render this fact less disconcerting by appealing to something else we hope is relevant to what we want to know. And we call it "evidence", even though it does not make what we want to know evident. This is how Austin used "evidence" in his example. Religion and the law are home of such uses of the word, which often are exquisitely self-conscious, though of course they are common, though less delicate or deliberate, also in the lab and the street. The notion they express is a degenerate offspring of the notion of the evident. But it is understandable and often harmless. We may *need* to know, not merely believe, that God exists, yet recognize that we do not. So we look for "evidences" of his existence. In the courtroom, a verdict of guilt or innocence may be *mandatory*, though neither guilt nor innocence is self-evident or made evident by anything that is self-evident. So we look for something else we hope is relevant to guilt or innocence, and call it "evidence", whether "beyond reasonable doubt" or not, and whether just "circumstantial" or not. If we think such evidence is "strong" enough, we may even say that we *know* that for which it is evidence. Saying this makes explicit our reason for appealing to it in the first place—that is, our desire

---

[7] J. L. Austin, *Sense and Sensibilia* (Oxford: Clarendon Press, 1962), 115, emphasis in original.

[8] This is how G. E. Moore explained what he meant by calling the fundamental propositions of ethics self-evident. See *Principia Ethica* (Cambridge: Cambridge University Press, 1903), preface.

for truth—and provides the appeal with a sort of blessing. How strong the evidence must be to justify saying that we know is never made clear, because it cannot be made clear, given the sort of reasons that lead us to employ such a notion of evidence. As cognitive beings, we seek knowledge because it is truth we want, not mere evidence even if dressed up as "epistemic probability" or "epistemic justification". The idea that such evidence comes in degrees and that possession of it yields an approximation of knowledge, something still worth having when knowledge is absent or impossible, suggests that there can be such a thing as an approximation of truth. But, while truth may be incomplete, irrelevant, or misleading, there is no such thing as two-thirds or 86 per cent truth. Yet this is exactly what the idea of degrees of evidence suggests, and it is made explicit in the vulgar thought of knowledge as belief that is 100 per cent probable.

However, though as cognitive beings it is knowledge that we seek, we are not purely cognitive beings. Those uses of "evidence" and "know" in religion and the law are understandable and defensible, for the reasons mentioned earlier. They are often needed and perhaps mandatory even in the lab and the street: to go about our business we often need and perhaps must think of some judgments as final, *settled*, even if we soon revisit them. In all four, there are practical reasons for resorting to the degenerate notion of evidence. No such reasons exist in epistemology, however, which is neither a religion or a courtroom, nor a lab or the street. Our concerns in it are purely cognitive. This is why in it the degenerate notion of evidence is not harmless. It generates the illusion that what knowledge requires is merely the limit, perhaps only ideal, of a range of degrees of such evidence, of "epistemic probability" or "epistemic justification", and that what falls short of that limit nevertheless might suffice. But it is never made clear what it might "suffice" for, given that it does not suffice for truth, since no practical considerations are relevant. Not surprisingly, it has not sufficed for the skeptic.

In everyday life and thought, the degenerate notion of evidence provides a way of achieving clear epistemic conscience. It is analogous to the degenerate notion of duty, "subjective duty", which provides a way of achieving clear moral conscience. The weak sense of "know" grounded in it is analogous to the weak sense of "ought". If ignorant, as we often are, of what we ought to do, of our "objective duty", we may settle for doing what we *think*, or perhaps just *feel*, we ought to do, for doing our "subjective duty". We may even insist that one always ought to do what one thinks or feels one ought to do. However, just as our real concern as cognitive beings is with truth and therefore knowledge, our real concern as moral beings is with objective duty, with doing what we really ought to do. The weak senses of "know" and "ought" are natural, in view of the scarcity of cases in which we can use "ought" and "know" in their strong senses. There is no need for legislation against them. But we are deeply aware of the difference between the two when facing important matters. We do not say we know we will be alive tomorrow, and thus need no life insurance today, regardless of how healthy and safe we think or feel we are today. And we do not say that our children ought to sacrifice their life whenever they think or feel they ought to.

This is why the strong sense of "know", which requires that what we say we know be self-evident or seen to follow from something self-evident, has been central in subjective epistemology. Self-evidence and what it makes evident are the core of what one has in mind when seeking knowledge about important matters. The attraction of religion is that it promises certainty, not mere probability, about matters of ultimate concern. The attraction of subjective epistemology is similar. Its main topic is also a matter of ultimate concern: whether material things—the earth and the sun, your body and mine—really exist.

However, the principal Cartesian question, which inaugurated modern subjective epistemology, was not "What is knowledge?" This question had been asked before and until recently answered, briefly and informally but sufficiently, in the same way—it is apprehension, grasping, getting hold of the truth, and then steadfastly keeping it. The Cartesian question was whether there is knowledge at all, especially knowledge of a material world. Cartesian epistemology began by taking skepticism seriously, even though hoping eventually to refute it. For this reason, it was essential that its question be expressed with the indexical "I" (or its synonyms and associated forms), that it ask whether *I* have knowledge.[9] And it could not take "I" to refer to the entity to which non-indexical terms, such as "Descartes" and "the author of the *Meditations*", or "PB" and "the author of this paper", refer. If it could, it would be irrelevant to the skeptical challenge because it would beg the question. The skeptic challenges also any claim to knowledge of the existence

---

[9] Bertrand Russell used the suggestive term "egocentric particulars", instead of "indexicals". He wrote: "One of the aims of both science and common sense is to replace the shifting subjectivity of egocentric particulars by neutral public terms" (*Human Knowledge* (New York: Simon & Schuster, 1962), 85).

of human beings, including Descartes and PB. They are parts of the material world. Of course, the skeptic does not say, "There is no material world," only "I do not *know* that there is one." But, if Descartes had *shown* that there is a material world, then *ipso facto* he would have come to know that there is one. And, if the skeptic agreed that Descartes had shown this, then the skeptic would have agreed that there is one. Both were interested in knowledge only as the way to truth.

This is why what was distinctive of Descartes's epistemology was not his initial commitment to the existence of only one entity, or to its peculiar nature (a thinking thing), but his initial use only of indexical expressions without presupposing reference to anything. And this is a cause for concern. When I say that now it is cold here, I am not saying that on 7 November 2002 it is cold in Iowa City, even though on 7 November 2002 I am in Iowa City. Yet neither am I referring to a place other than Iowa City or a time other than 7 November 2002. This causes no geographical or historical problems as long as I am willing to replace "here" with "Iowa City" and "now" with "7 November 2002", or with some other name and date—there would still be a place and a time I am talking about. But, if I am unwilling, then it is unclear that this would be so. I might be like a geographer of *here*, or a historian of *now*.

Nevertheless, there is a difference between indexical and non-indexical expressions. There is a difference between saying "It is cold in Iowa City" and saying "It is cold here" or 'Il fait froid ici'—though not the sort of difference there is between the English and the French sentences, or that between "It is cold in Iowa City" and "It is cold in the university town on the Iowa River"—notwithstanding that all four seem to say the "same thing". It certainly is not just a difference of words. Perhaps this is a reason for thinking that there is an entity or property such as *here* or *hereness*. Perhaps the difference between "It is cold now" and "It is cold on 7 November 2002" is a reason for thinking that there is an entity or property such as *the present* or *presentness*.[10] This reason is more compelling, in view of the seeming connection between the notion of time and the notion of existence. Augustine noted that what does not exist *now* seems to not exist at all, which is not the case with what does not exist *here*; Kant held that, while space is the pure form of outer sense, time is the pure form of both outer and inner sense; Heidegger named his

---

[10] For a detailed argument, see Quentin Smith, *Language and Time* (New York: Oxford University Press, 1993).

classic work *Being and Time*, not *Being and Space*. And throughout the history of philosophy it has been held that there is an overwhelming reason for thinking that there is an entity—the subject, ego, self—that is the primary reference of "I". However, my concern in this chapter is not with these metaphysical and semantical matters, but with the nature of a certain variety of epistemology. I shall argue that subjective epistemology must use "I", or a synonym of it, yet when doing so it can refer to *nothing*, neither to Descartes or plain PB, nor to a thinking thing, his or mine, not because there is nothing to refer to or because of the semantics of "I", but because of the very nature of its project.[11] If so, subjective epistemology has no subject matter and thus, strictly speaking, is not a theory, not even a theory of knowledge. But we must not infer from this that it is a mistake. For "I" does have a use, even if not sense or reference, that cannot be captured by mentioning to what it refers.[12]

John Searle gives the following example. If I make a mess in a supermarket by spilling a bag of sugar on the floor, I may be ashamed, look to see if anyone saw me, and worry about what to do. Whether I use "I" or "PB" does not affect the truth value of the statements I make about the incident, but surely makes an important difference. As Searle says, it is essential to the case that "it is *me* that is making a mess".[13] There *is* a difference between my making a mess and PB's making a mess. For less Anglo-Saxon examples of this sort, such as hearing steps behind me when peeping through a keyhole, we should go to Sartre.

Such a difference is also manifest in a Cartesian context. When asking what if anything I know, I cannot assume the reference of "I" to be PB, even though I am PB. If I write an autobiography using "I", "PB" could replace "I" throughout without change in truth value—there would be a change

---

[11] David Kaplan has distinguished between "pure indexicals", such as "I", which involve no genuine demonstration and do not admit attachment of a noun, and demonstratives, such as "this", which do, e.g., in "this man" ("Demonstratives", in J. Almog *et al.* (eds.), *Themes from Kaplan* (Oxford: Oxford University Press, 1977)).

[12] Following certain remarks by Wittgenstein in *The Blue and the Brown Book* (Oxford: Oxford University Press, 1958), 66–7, G. E. M. Anscombe has argued that "I" is not a referring expression. In using it, she says, "getting hold of the wrong object is excluded, and that makes us think that getting hold of the right object is guaranteed. But the reason is that there is no getting hold of an object at all" ("The First Person", in Samuel Guttenplan (ed.) *Mind and Language* (Oxford: Oxford University Press, 1975), pp. 45–65). Her point is not Hume's. It has nothing to do with what she could or could not "find".

[13] John Searle, *Intentionality* (Cambridge: Cambridge University Press, 1991), 218. But Searle's conclusions are different from mine.

merely in literary genre, from autobiography to biography. There would be no difference in reference, and, if we say there would be difference in "meaning" or "sense", we would be using these as technical terms requiring extensive and inevitably controversial explanation of the distinction between them and "reference". But, whatever we say, in a Cartesian context none of the statements in the biography would be allowable because the truth of all of them would be questioned by the skeptic. Moreover, *pace* Descartes and most Cartesian epistemologists, this would be so even if "I" were replaced with "TT", a name Descartes might have given to the thinking thing the existence of which he thought he had proved. The reason would not be that there is no such thing as TT, or that the proof was unsound, but that referring to TT also would beg the question against a sophisticated skeptic. While Descartes's referring to Descartes would be like his referring to Louis XIII, his referring to TT would be like his referring to Louis XIII's thinking thing. In his celebrated *cogito* argument Descartes inferred that a thinking thing exists, but *which* thinking thing was it? Surely, not Louis XIII's, for Louis XIII, a human though royal being, would not exist if the material world did not.

Could I not say, if I were Descartes, that it was *my* thinking thing? No, because to speak of my thinking thing is to speak of a thinking thing that is related to *me* by a certain relation, presumably the generic relation of having, whatever its species might be, and so I must first find reference for "me"—that is, for "I". Moreover, contrary to Descartes's intentions, I would be implying that I am *not* that thinking thing, that I only bear a relation to it, the generic relation I bear also to my car and my nose, I being what has, and the thinking thing being what is had. And my entering in that relation to TT would be just as questionable as my entering in some relation, say, admiration or distaste, to Louis XIII's thinking thing. The *cogito* was a proof of *my* existence, not of some other thinking thing's existence. Any skeptic worth his salt would forthwith ask, "Why suppose that there is this thing to which supposedly I bear the relation?" The skeptic would ask the question just by being true to his mission, not because of metaphysical prejudice against thinking things or subtle semantical opinions about "I".

It would not help to say that TT is the thinking thing to which only I have access. Even if this is so, and we ignore the unacceptably metaphorical sense of "access" as well as the implied crude distinction between "inner" and "outer", saying this would presuppose an independent answer to the earlier question about the reference of "I". Without answering that question, saying that TT is the thinking thing to which only I have access might be no more relevant or noteworthy than saying that I sniff only with my own nose. The privilege my thinking thing and my nose enjoy endows neither with special significance. *Everyone* has such access only to his or her own thinking thing, just as everyone sniffs only with his or her own nose.

Indeed, not even the most frugal *cogito*, in which one infers only "There is a thinking" from "I think", would be acceptable. *Which* thinking is that? For the reasons already given, we cannot say that it is Descartes's, Louis XIII's, PB's, or even just mine. If we bite the bullet and say it is no one's, we face irrelevance in addition to syntactical absurdity. There may be thousands of such orphaned thinkings. The existence of which one did Descartes infer? Could he just say: *this* thinking, and perhaps name it "T"? But which thinking is *this thinking*? Why suppose that another thinking is not also a *this thinking*? *Pace* Russell, "this" is not a logically proper name but a demonstrative pronoun, and many things, near and distant, past, present, and future, observable and unobservable, can be and often are referred to with it, even by the same person and at the same time—for example, when the person is chatting while typing, double-talking, or speaking with two or more mouths (Descartes could not assume that he had only one mouth). And, presumably, the existence of some orphaned thinkings would be just as questionable for the skeptic as that of Louis XIII's thinkings. The existence of which thinkings, then, would not be questionable? To say "Those of which I am directly aware" would just take us back to problems already discussed.

It is not a principle of logic but surely true that "Someone is F" readily follows from "I am F" only if "I" could be replaced with a name or a non-indexical definite description, even if it is never so replaced and even if we don't, perhaps cannot, know with which name or description to replace it. We readily accept statements employing indexicals because, as a matter of course, we are in principle willing, even if sometimes unable, to replace the indexicals with non-indexicals. We accept statements employing "here" and "now" since usually we are willing to replace these words with, say, "Iowa City" and "7 November 2002". This is true also of "I" in ordinary contexts. "PB" could replace "I" in "I am writing this paper", even if we agree that, as in the examples from Searle and Sartre, the replacement would produce a change not just of words. In some legal documents such replacement would be required. But in a Cartesian context it is prohibited. And, as we have seen, it is only an illusion to think that it would be allowed if we used "TT", or even just "T", in place of "I". In the argument "I think, therefore I am", the pronoun "I" is profligately used twice. Does it have the same reference in the premise and the conclusion, be it to a man, a thinking thing, or a mere thinking? If it does not, the argument is invalid. Does it have reference in the premise at all? If it does not, the argument would again be invalid. If it does, the question against the skeptic is begged.

Descartes did not see that there are these questions because all along he thought he was "directly aware" of a thinking thing and its states. But, even if we ignore our earlier questions about which thinking thing or states he was aware of, a further problem arises, which is fundamental but ignored by Descartes and other subjective epistemologists. If a necessary condition of awareness is that its object exist, then the skeptic would ask whether we are *really* aware of a thinking thing and its states, exactly as the skeptic asks whether we really perceive bodies. On the other hand, if the existence of its object is not a necessary condition of awareness, then the skeptic would question the cogency of any inference to it from the occurrence of the awareness. Descartes thought he might be deceived by God or an evil demon regarding $3 + 2 = 5$, but did not see that if so then he might be deceived also about what he thought he was aware of, "found" in his mind. The failure to see this vitiated Descartes's inferences from the existence of his idea of God to God's existence. Could not God, or at least an evil demon, be deceiving him into thinking that he had that idea? The failure to see that in this way the skeptic could question any appeal to awareness also vitiates twentieth-century appeals to "acquaintance".

It appears that to confront the skeptic without begging the question, the subjective epistemologist must renounce claims to any subject matter. In "I think", the premise of his *cogito* argument, Descartes could not have used "I" to refer to anything, not even to himself, since that he exists was the conclusion of the argument. While naturalistic epistemology has a subject matter too limited to be philosophical, subjective epistemology appears to have no subject matter at all, not even a solitary thinking thing or orphaned thinkings. I have suggested that its *raison d'être* is to meet the challenge of skepticism. Otherwise, there would be no rationale for distinguishing it from naturalistic epistemology, though perhaps including introspective psychology, albeit it would be a naturalistic epistemology concerned, inexplicably, with just one natural object, the epistemic states of only one human being. It must refer to entities only by means of indexical expressions, even if in fact—exactly the fact questioned by the skeptic—they can also be referred to with non-indexical expressions. To hold that in its use of the indexical expression "I" it refers to an entity that also can be referred to with a non-indexical such as "Descartes", "PB", "TT", or "T" would be to hold that there are such entities as Descartes, PB, TT, or T, and thus to beg the question against the skeptic. This has always been obvious in the case of "Descartes" and "PB", but, as we have seen, it is also true in the case of "TT" and "T". Both to have a subject matter and not to beg the question, subjective epistemology must be satisfied with a subject matter that consists of entities that *could* be referred to only with indexicals like "I". It must allow for the *possibility* that only such entities exist. But would anything be an entity if it could be referred to only with an indexical, if it were in principle unnamable, if it could present itself in only one mode and thus be referred to through only one sense? To suppose that there could be thinkers who are only *Is* borders on incoherence, just as to suppose that there could be times and places that are only *nows* and *heres* borders on incoherence. Even saying this already involves three grammatical monstrosities. Subjective epistemology seems to be, so to speak, an epistemology of solitary pronouns, pronouns without nouns, modes of presentation without presentation, aspects that are aspects of nothing, mere perspectives. This is why it is often described as epistemology from the first-person perspective. The description is suggestive, but incomplete. The first person is *only* a perspective, and subjective epistemology is *only* perspectival. There is no *entity* that is just *the first person*, and so the subject matter of subjective epistemology is not that privileged entity. *The first person* is not a person.

Before his optimistic inferences to God and beyond, Descartes seemed to have only himself, to be left in a state of absolute solitude. But in fact he did not even have himself. The deeper fallacy in his *cogito* argument is not that it is an inference to a thinker from a thinking but that it is an inference to a *thing* from a mere *perspective*. Subjective epistemology began as a search for an answer to the skeptic. We can now see that such an answer is not possible because the very search for it is misguided. Subjective epistemology must presuppose that the indexical terms it uses have reference because to answer the skeptic it must rely on premises that are true. Only from true premises would an adequate answer follow. But it also must not presuppose that the terms have reference, because this would beg the question against the skeptic.

After saying all this, however, we must acknowledge that, though subjective epistemology is only perspectival, the rationale for the perspective is impeccable. The lack of subject matter does not imply unimportance. The perspective is overwhelmingly important, even though it is a mere perspective.

The first-person pronoun is important, indeed indispensable, but not because of what it refers to. It is important because of the role it serves. It is essential to all talk and thought, and thus to all inquiry. Subjective epistemology may be an epistemology of pronouns without nouns, but to get nouns we must, so to speak, begin with pronouns. Of course, it is not the word "I" that is essential, but rather its use, even if other expressions are put to that use. In some languages, first-person reference is achieved with the verb, not a separate word. Sometimes, nouns or words destined to be nouns work. Baby might not yet be able to say "I cry", Baby might just say "Baby cries", but "Baby", then would not function as it does in "Baby cries" when said by Baby about another baby.

In normal contexts, heedfully to assert p one must be willing to assert "p is true". But heedfully to assert "p is true" (rather than the very different "I think that p" or "p is probably true"), one must be willing to assert "I know that p". Even heedfully to assert "He (she, Jack, the expert) knows that p", one must be willing to assert "I know that p". In any inquiry, one must begin with the first-person perspective, with the use, however implicit, of "I", even if only in judgments, implicit or not, such as "I'll look for it in the bush", "I'll ask Jane", or "I'll check the dictionary". This is a proposition neither of physics nor of metaphysics. It's like "Every journey must begin somewhere", not like "Every journey must begin in Iowa City". Yet the proposition enjoys the abstraction characteristic of philosophy, and bequeaths it to subjective epistemology. "I think" must be able to accompany all our representations, Kant held, even though, as Sartre later argued, it seldom actually does. Russell wrote:

When you are considering any sort of theory of knowledge, you are more or less tied to a certain unavoidable subjectivity, because you are not concerned simply with the question what is true of the world, but 'What can I know of the world?' . . . You cannot go outside yourself and consider abstractly whether the things that appear to you to be true are true.[14]

Russell was wrong in thinking that there is an "inside" to be contrasted with an "outside", but otherwise his grasp of the rationale for subjective epistemology was firm.

This is why the allure of the subjective turn that led to Cartesian epistemology is ever present. It would be sad if subjective epistemology were all there

---

[14] Bertrand Russell, *The Philosophy of Logical Atomism* (Chicago and La Salle: Open Court, 1985), 37.

is to epistemology, but outrageous to deny its essential place in thought. It is futile and usually misguided, but as indispensable and unavoidable as being aware that to get anywhere one must start somewhere. The mistake is to suppose that it is about *me*, even if there is such an entity, be it a human, a mere thinking thing, or just a thinking. It is the mistake of supposing that subjective epistemology has a subject matter and thus is a cognitive discipline, a theory of something, presumably knowledge or cognition, when in fact it is only the necessary entry to any subject matter and the prelude to any discipline.

In Section 1, I drew attention to the proposition that how we perceive and understand the world, and thus the world itself as perceived and understood, depend on our faculties of perception and understanding, that they depend on *us*. I also pointed out, however, that this is not a zoological proposition, that it is not about *humans* even though we are humans. We can now see better how it should be understood. Indeed, it is not about humans, but neither is it about non-humans. It is not about entities at all, but rather about the necessary conditions of thought, talk, and inquiry about entities. As such, it is intimately related to subjective epistemology, as intimately as Kant was related to Hume. That Hume's skepticism led to Kant's transcendental idealism was not just an event in Kant's life, however important he thought it was. It manifested a phase in the very logic of the development of epistemological thought, just as the emergence of Descartes's epistemology manifested a no less necessary earlier phase. The subjective epistemologist makes essential use of the first-person *singular*, "I", but it is the first-person *plural*, "we", that is essential to the transcendental idealist. The self-centered focus on the conditions one's own heedful talk, thought, and inquiry must satisfy deepens and broadens into a focus on the conditions all talk, thought, and inquiry must satisfy, somewhat as youth deepens and broadens into adulthood. But adulthood is not a substitute for youth. To heedfully assert '*p*', one must still be willing to assert "I know that *p*." This is so even when *p* is about the conditions of all talk, thought, and inquiry. However, now we can see this requirement as a necessary prelude to cognition, not a barrier to it.

3. Epistemology-as-logic

Subjective epistemology has no subject matter. Naturalistic epistemology does, though one that is human and thus lacking the abstraction and generality needed to be properly philosophical. Epistemology-as-logic also has a subject matter, but it exceeds the bounds of the special science and does belong in philosophy. Like formal logic, it is unambiguously "dehumanized". All three varieties of epistemology, however, are legitimate, given their very different yet not incompatible purposes. Their differences call not for mindless quarrel but for mindful distinctions.

Contrary to what textbooks sometimes say, formal logic is concerned not with inferences as activities, presumably human and thus properly studied by psychology, but with their formal validity, the relation of the truth value of the premises to the truth value of the conclusion, in particular the formal consistency of the conjunction of the former and the negation of the latter. Its general subject matter thus consists of alethic relations. If some propositions, or at least sentences, are neither true nor false, as a consequence of the truth-value of other propositions or sentences, this fact too would belong in its subject matter. Formal logic epitomizes the generality and abstraction characteristic of philosophy. This is why Aristotle assigned "the principles of the syllogism", especially the principle of non-contradiction, to the science of being qua being. And this is why Frege wrote: "Just as 'beautiful' points the way for aesthetics and 'good' for ethics, so do words like 'true' for logic . . . [I]t falls to logic to discern the laws of truth . . . The *Bedeutung* [reference, meaning] of the word 'true' is spelled out in the laws of truth."[15] Elsewhere, he explained: "What is distinctive about my conception of logic is that I begin by giving pride of place to the content of the word 'true' . . . "[16] If metaphysics is the science of being qua being, logic may be said to be the science of being qua truth, ethics of being qua goodness, and aesthetics of being qua beauty. The subject matter of all four is what the medievals called transcendentals.

Epistemology-as-logic differs from formal logic by focusing on the validity—legitimacy, cogency, worth—of non-formal inferences, but its subject matter, too, consists of alethic relations, in particular the relation of the truth value of the premises of the non-formal inference to the truth value of its conclusion. It too enjoys the level of generality and abstraction characteristic of philosophy. Like formal logic, it is concerned with inferences not as human activities but with their cogency, and generally with the alethic relations they exemplify. Unlike subjective epistemology, it does not lack subject matter, it is

---

[15] Gottlob Frege, "Thought", in M. Beaney, *The Frege Reader* (Oxford: Blackwell), 325–6.
[16] Ibid. 362.

not just perspectival. And, unlike naturalistic epistemology, which does have a subject matter, it is not just programmatic. Of course, epistemology-as-logic does apply to human matters, just as formal logic does. But it is not about them. There is nothing puzzling about this. Arithmetic is applicable to humans, bats, and stars, but it is not about humans, bats, or stars. It is about numbers.

In its attempts to answer the skeptic, subjective epistemology sought cogent non-formal inferences from premises known to be true. Epistemology-as-logic, however, does not ask whether the premises of the inference are true, nor does it agonize over the fact that it is not deductive, that the conjunction of the premises and the negation of the conclusion is not a contradiction. It is free from obsession with skepticism, just as naturalistic epistemology enjoys such freedom. In this it follows the lead of its older sibling. In evaluating a deductive argument, formal logic is not concerned with the truth of its premises. And it does not fret that, even if they are true, the formal validity of the argument might not suffice for the truth of its conclusion because God might be deceiving us about logic just as he might be deceiving us about arithmetic.

Epistemology-as-logic may seek a general theory of the alethic relations exemplified in non-formal inferences. But it can begin by examining specific kinds of such inference, just as formal logic began with the examination of specific kinds of formal inference and only later, mainly through Frege's work, offered a general theory of the alethic relations they exemplify. Inferences involving probability, induction, and abduction are standard topics in subjective epistemology. They would be also topics in epistemology-as-logic, though in abstraction from possible use against skepticism. Appeals to probability did not satisfy the skeptic, who either denied that it is enough (would a religious person be satisfied if told that God only probably exists, and would anyone be satisfied if told that other people only probably exist?), or questioned the truth of a premise (do the universe and other humans' behavior really display design?). But the calculus of probability remains an established discipline of some distinction. Appeals to induction and abduction, notoriously, also have failed to satisfy the skeptic. Nevertheless, they remain standard topics in the philosophy of science, which seldom strays into Cartesian discussions. And the tradition has held, independently of epistemological concerns, that there are relations of *non-formal* entailment. A standard example is the entailment of being colored by being red, and anyone who, like Kant, regards mathematical truths to be necessary but "synthetic" would allow for non-formal entailments in mathematics. Such entailments would also be examples of the sort of relations belonging in the subject matter of epistemology-as-logic. The philosophy of mathematics exists not because of worries that God might be deceiving us even about $3 + 2 = 5$.

Here, however, I shall limit myself to the non-formal alethic relation of presupposition. It was the focus on it that marked the development of epistemology beyond its subjective stage. If we call subjective epistemology Cartesian, then epistemology-as-logic, insofar it focuses on that relation, may be called Kantian. Hence the application of Kant's term "transcendental" to recent arguments from presupposition. But epistemology-as-logic need not adopt Kant's essentially mentalistic approach to epistemology, nor any of his specific doctrines. It is not what Kant meant by transcendental logic.

The relation of presupposition became a major topic in the philosophy of language because of Strawson's criticism of Russell's theory of descriptions.[17] He gave as examples the presupposition of "There is a king of France" by "The king of France is wise", and the presupposition of "He is not dead" by "He cares about it".[18] A proposition p presupposes a proposition q, according to Strawson, when *both* "If p then q" and "If not-p then q" are true—when, though neither p formally entails q, nor not-p formally entails q, q is a necessary condition of both the truth and the falsity of p, of its being coherent.[19] In the example of the king of France, the presupposition manifests itself in our dismissing anyone who said that the king of France is wise but denied that France has a king, or said that the king of France is not wise but denied that France has a king, as confused, not as inconsistent. Our judgment of anyone who said, "He cares about it but he is dead", would be similar.

Presupposition is neither entailment, formal or non-formal, nor a probabilistic, inductive, or abductive relation. This is why appeals to it have seemed to provide answers to skepticism entirely different from those dating from the seventeenth century. The latter are almost certainly either formally invalid or contain premises the skeptic finds as questionable as the conclusion. The

---

[17] P. F. Strawson, "On Referring", *Mind* (1950), and *Introduction to Logical Theory* (London: Methuen, 1952), 175—9. In the former, more influential work, Strawson did not use the term "presupposition", and wrote instead of "some sense of 'imply'" that is "not equivalent to 'entails' or 'logically implies'".

[18] "Does he care about it? He neither cares nor doesn't care; he is dead" (*Introduction to Logical Theory*, 18).

[19] Ibid. 175.

anti-skeptic's predicament has been that to answer the skeptic one must assume more than the skeptic would allow, but, if one assumes less, then the answer does not follow. In appeals to presupposition, however, the consequence of denying the presupposed proposition is not the falsity but the incoherence of the proposition presupposing it, whether a trifling incoherence, as in the example of the king of France, or a deep one, as in the examples I shall give shortly.

Some have said that presupposition is merely a feature of language, just "pragmatic", not "logical" or "semantic", as if pervasive features of language are ever merely features of language. Aristotle defended the principle of non-contradiction, not by trying to infer it from "more certain" propositions, but by showing that it is presupposed even by reasoning intended to cast doubt on it. And Russell repeatedly pointed out that all deductive reasoning presupposes the "primitive proposition" that "what follows from a true proposition is true".[20] The complaint that presupposition has no place in logic is not just false; it shows misunderstanding of the very nature of logic. Of course, that the natural sciences are rife with presuppositions has always been evident. Physics presupposes, does not discover, the existence of space and time. Psychiatrists presuppose, do not discover, that mental illness is not caused by evil spirits.

The examples from Strawson I mentioned are of little intrinsic interest. This cannot be said of those in his major metaphysical work, *Individuals*, or his book on Kant, *The Bounds of Sense*. Certainly, it cannot be said of the examples in Kant's own works. Kant defended important but controversial philosophical propositions on the ground that they are presupposed by other propositions that are not controversial. His argument that morality presupposes freedom is familiar. Indeed, freedom seems to be presupposed by all genuine actions, moral, immoral, and non-moral, and thus by any fully human life. It is what seems to distinguish them from mere bodily movements. No less famous but much more difficult is Kant's argument that objective order in time presupposes causal necessity. It is complex and not to be dealt with lightly, whether in agreement or disagreement, but we need not go into its details to get a glimpse. If we ask whether Jack first met Mary before or after she moved to

---

[20] Alfred North Whitehead and Bertrand Russell, *Principia Mathematica* (Cambridge: Cambridge University Press, 1913), 1.1, Bertrand Russell, *The Problems of Philosophy* (Oxford: Oxford University Press, 1953), 71–2.

town, the answer would depend in part on reasoning about when and where he *could* have met her. If it really mattered (as it might in a court of law), we would be foolhardy to rely just on memory impressions, on what Kant called a subjective play of fancy. As this example shows, what is presupposed need not be a single proposition, just as a deductive proof ordinarily does not rest on a single premise. It might even be a *system* of propositions, and what presupposes it might also be a system. This is why the philosophically interesting examples of presupposition seldom have the simple structure of the examples about the present king of France and the man who is dead.

The presupposition especially relevant to traditional epistemology is that of the existence of a material world. It assumes many forms, and is neither simple nor obvious. It can be argued that in doubting the existence of the material world Descartes presupposed the existence of certain parts of it. Therefore, his doubt was incoherent, like doubting that France has a king when asserting that the king of France is wise. In particular, it can be argued, as G. E. Moore noted, that Descartes would have had to doubt the existence of philosophers, past and present, including those he had read, heard, argued with, and whose works and views were the context of his doubt, through agreement or disagreement.[21] Philosophers are human, therefore parts of the material world. The history of philosophy is not a history of philosopher-angels. Descartes could not have taken his doubt seriously as *philosophical* if he had considered these details about what he doubted, what would be the case with respect to his own doubt if there were not a material world. Philosophical skepticism about the material world questions its own existence. Let me explain.

The philosophical context of philosophical thinking, such as Descartes's doubt, is *essential* to it, however original the thinking may be. It is essential to it even more obviously than, as contemporary essentialists have argued, the biological origin of an organism is essential, "metaphysically necessary", to that organism. The "historicity" of a philosophical view is no more a contingent fact than the historicity of a political event. Both bear necessary relations to their past. Neither Cartesian epistemology, nor Democratic or Republican politics in the twenty-first century, would be comprehensible if stripped of those relations. Skepticism questions what makes possible its being

---

[21] G. E. Moore, "A Defense of Common Sense", in *Philosophical Papers* (London: Allen & Unwin, 1959), 32–60. I discuss the argument in *Skepticism about the External World* (New York: Oxford University Press, 1998).

the philosophical view it is: its roots in what other philosophers have held. It would not exist if the material world did not exist. Descartes's methodological doubt would not have occurred had the propositions the truth of which he doubted not been true.

Indeed, the very language in which he developed and explained it would not have existed. Presumably, employment of language is essential to philosophical thought, even if some thoughts are possible without language. Philosophical thought, whether superior or mediocre, involves argumentation, good or bad, with a fairly complex structure, distinct premises and conclusions, each with its own structure, and logical connections rooted directly or indirectly in that structure. The terms employed are chosen from a fairly extensive and often technical lexicon, with deliberation and discretion. But any actual language employed in philosophy, say, Descartes's French or Latin, involves phonemes and inscriptions, and is shaped by a human community. All these are parts of the material world. Therefore, it must be possible for argumentation in a subjective epistemology such as Descartes's, one that takes the skeptic and thus itself seriously, to be developed and explained in a *private* language, at least in the minimal, not necessarily Wittgenstein's, sense that the language was created by the epistemologist alone and without reliance (as in devising a secret code) on a public language. But surely such a private language would be too primitive for epistemology. The reader is invited to try constructing a fragment of one and then translating into it a philosophical fragment from Descartes's *Meditations*. Writing philosophy is not like recording one's sensations. Perhaps a private language for the latter is possible, and sometimes actually concocted by hypochondriacs, but we would be only posturing if we said that the sort of rich and sophisticated language the argument of the philosophical skeptic requires could be one. Might that argument take place just in the skeptic's thought, without use of language? Even if some thought without language is possible—for example, recalling an unusual sensation—to suppose that philosophical thought might be one would be like supposing that we might understand differential equations without using symbols, or even just what it is for a car to travel at 79, rather than 78, miles an hour. The skepticism in Descartes's first meditation was not like a tipsy sailor's declaration: "Maybe I know nothing." It was a professional, serious and informed, philosophical view. This is why we still take it seriously. Of course, that philosophical skepticism about the material world questions its own existence does not entail that it is false. It does not render it self-contradictory. But it does make it deeply incoherent. For, if the material world did not exist, then it too would not exist.

A strikingly original appeal to presupposition was made by Sartre in defense of the existence of other minds. Our acceptance of the "Other" is not discursive, he pointed out. It is presupposed by certain psychological states of oneself. It is essential to them. Sartre gave shame as an example. It is "an immediate shudder that runs through me from head to foot without any discursive preparation". But it is "shame of *oneself before the Other*", even if no one is actually looking.[22] Perhaps what is presupposed is only the possibility of being the object of another's consciousness. But this is what is denied by the interesting sort of skepticism about the existence of other minds, one that is not just a trivial consequence of skepticism about the existence of bodies. It questions the very intelligibility of there being anyone "other than myself". Even skepticism about the existence of bodies is most interesting when it denies, as Berkeley did, that we can conceive of unperceived bodies.

Another kind of presupposition belongs to an even deeper level. We may call it conceptual. What is presupposed is a particular understanding of the concepts employed. For example, all discussions of the existence of bodies, skeptical and anti-skeptical, presuppose some particular understanding of the concept of existence. Even to ask whether bodies exist presupposes an answer to the question of what it is for a body to exist, and ultimately of what it is for anything to exist. Is existence a property? If not, then what is skepticism *about*? Could we intelligibly speak of the truth or falsity of sentences asserting or denying existence, and thus of knowledge or ignorance of it? Would such sentences express genuine propositions, or might they rather be analogous to "I will finish writing this page", when this is said as an expression of determination, not as prediction?

Standard epistemology, whether naturalistic or subjective, provides little guidance. It usually takes for granted Kant's view that existence is not a real predicate, meaning that it is not a property, a "determination", of a thing (*res*), but fails to consider its deep epistemological implications.[23] Kant wrote that the existence of a thing has to do "only with the question whether [the] thing is given to us in such a way that the perception of it could in any case precede

---

[22] Jean-Paul Sartre, *Being and Nothingness*, trans. Hazel E. Barnes (New York: Philosophical Library, 1956), 222, emphasis in original.

[23] Kant states his view succinctly at A598/B626 of *Critique of Pure Reason*.

the concept".[24] This was not Berkeley's "to be is to be perceived". Nor was it Mill's "matter is a permanent possibility of sensations". Kant did hold that to be actual (*wirklich*) a thing must "stand . . . in accordance with the laws of empirical progression",[25] but these laws, like any other laws for Kant, involve application of the pure concepts of the understanding. If so, the actuality or existence of a thing, like its causality, is "transcendentally ideal", even if also "empirically real". The application of a concept of the understanding was for Kant a matter not of *discovery* but of *imposition*. This does not mean that how we apply the concept of existence is mere caprice, any more than that how we apply the concept of causality is one. What is meant is closer to what Goodman meant by the "entrenchment" of the predicate "green", which "grue" lacks, though for Kant it was grounded in the activity of our cognitive faculties, not in our linguistic practices. Clearly, such a view of existence requires that skepticism and subjective epistemology, insofar as they concern the existence of bodies, be drastically rethought—or altogether bypassed.

Might existence be just what the existential quantifier expresses, the satisfaction of a propositional function, as Russell argued and most contemporary epistemologists take for granted?[26] But this is a non-starter. Whether the propositional function "*x* is a horse" is satisfied depends on what we allow as values of the variable *x*. Is "*x* is a horse" satisfied by both Secretariat and Pegasus, or only by Secretariat? If we say the latter, our reason is that Pegasus does not exist, but in a sense of "exist" obviously other than, yet presupposed by, Russell's. It is its ordinary sense, the one we employ in saying, for example, that the Loch Ness monster and Jack, a child's imaginary friend, do not exist. I have suggested that, according to Kant, it expresses not a property we *find* in things, but rather a conception of them that we *contribute*.[27]

Conceptual presupposition differs from the other kinds of presupposition in that the skeptic is not likely to question it. An answer to a question obviously presupposes how the question is understood. The skeptic cannot deny the central place of the concept of existence in any question about what does or does not exist, or what we can or cannot know to exist. But the skeptic might well deny, however implausibly, that philosophical thought presupposes the existence of the material world, that objective order in time presupposes causal

---

[24] *Critique of Pure Reason*, A225/B272.   [25] Ibid., A493–B521.

[26] Bertrand Russell, *Introduction to Mathematical Philosophy* (New York: Simon and Schuster, 1971), 164.

[27] I develop this point in *Skepticism about the External World*.

necessity, or that the phenomenon of shame presupposes the Other. In any plausible case of inference involving presupposition, there is a natural desire to think of it as formal entailment, since that is the relevant alethic relation most familiar and best understood. And, when we see that the conditional corresponding to the inference does not have the form of a tautology, we are tempted to declare the inference invalid. Or, if we find it compelling, we are tempted to change the conditional, so that it becomes a tautology, and we bless the change by calling it an "analysis" or "translation". This is what Russell did in his theory of definite descriptions. He saw that, if the present king of France is wise, then, of course, France has a king. He also saw, however, that this is not a tautology. He proceeded to "translate" it into one. In the philosophically substantive cases, however, such as those from Kant and Sartre, no such analyses or translations seem plausible. The conditional "If there is objective order in time, then there is causal necessity" is not a tautology, and to try to change it into one would hardly be a task worth undertaking. So we are tempted just to deny it.

Would the examples of presupposition I have given count as answers to the skeptic, whom naturalistic epistemology properly ignores and subjective epistemology is incapable of answering? They do not refute skepticism—they are not proofs that we do know what according to it we do not know—but they might silence the skeptic. Whether they do or do not, epistemology-as-logic is concerned with them independently of their relevance to skepticism. Skepticism is a problem for subjective epistemology. A question of the form "But how do I know that p?" as understood by it may be a question for *me*, but it is not a question for *us*. It has no theoretical substance, for subjective epistemology has no subject matter, its essential use of "I" involving reference to nothing. The question that does have theoretical substance is how we human beings know that *p*. But it belongs in naturalistic epistemology, and today calls for answers from the natural sciences specializing in human cognition, not from philosophy. Epistemology-as-logic asks neither question, just as formal logic does not.

NAME INDEX